The Clean Development Mechanism (CDM)

An Early History of Unanticipated Outcomes

World Scientific Series on the Economics of Climate Change

ISSN: 2010-2127

Series Editor: Robert Mendelsohn *(Yale University, USA)*

Published

Vol. 1   The Clean Development Mechanism (CDM): An Early History of Unanticipated Outcomes
by Ariel Dinar (University of California, USA), Donald F. Larson (World Bank, USA) and Shaikh M. Rahman (Texas Tech University, USA)

Forthcoming

Managing the Transition to a Low Carbon Future
by Geoffrey Blanford and Richard G. Richels (Electric Power Research Institute, USA)

Integrated Assessment Models: State of the Art and Horizons for the Future
by John P. Weyant (Stanford University, USA)

World Scientific Series on the Economics of Climate Change

Volume 1

The Clean Development Mechanism (CDM)

An Early History of Unanticipated Outcomes

Ariel Dinar
University of California, Riverside, USA

Donald F Larson
World Bank, USA

Shaikh M Rahman
Texas Tech University, USA

World Scientific

NEW JERSEY · LONDON · SINGAPORE · BEIJING · SHANGHAI · HONG KONG · TAIPEI · CHENNAI

Published by

World Scientific Publishing Co. Pte. Ltd.

5 Toh Tuck Link, Singapore 596224

USA office: 27 Warren Street, Suite 401-402, Hackensack, NJ 07601

UK office: 57 Shelton Street, Covent Garden, London WC2H 9HE

British Library Cataloguing-in-Publication Data
A catalogue record for this book is available from the British Library.

World Scientific Series on the Economics of Climate Change — Vol. 1
THE CLEAN DEVELOPMENT MECHANISM (CDM)
An Early History of Unanticipated Outcomes

ISBN 978-981-4401-09-8

In-house Editors: Divya Srikanth/Sandhya Venkatesh

Typeset by Stallion Press
Email: enquiries@stallionpress.com

Printed in Singapore

CONTENTS

ACKNOWLEDGMENTS

The work leading to this book is based on an extensive research study "Local Actions for Global Impact: Inference of the Role of the Flexible Mechanisms in Reducing Greenhouse Gases" by the Sustainable Rural and Urban Development Team, Development Research Group of the World Bank. The study was supported by funding from the Knowledge for Change Program (KCP) Trust Fund at the World Bank. We would like to thank Gershon Feder for advice during the preparation of the study and Michael Toman and Will Martin for comments during the preparation of the various publications.

ABOUT THE AUTHORS

Ariel Dinar is a Professor of Environmental Economics and Policy and the Director of Water Science and Policy Center at the Department of Environmental Sciences, University of California, Riverside, USA. He teaches, conducts research, and publishes on water economics, economics of climate change, strategic behavior and the environment, and regional cooperation over natural resources.

Don Larson is a Senior Economist with the World Bank's Research Group. His research areas include the study of markets for tradable permits and rural development. Dr. Larson was a member of the team that launched the World Bank's first carbon fund.

Shaikh M Rahman is an Assistant Professor of Agricultural and Applied Economics at Texas Tech University, Lubbock, Texas, USA. His research focuses on various aspects of applied microeconomics, including economics of climate change with special emphasis on the Kyoto Protocol, industrial organization of US agriculture, and the interface between agricultural production and climate change.

1. CLEAN DEVELOPMENT MECHANISM: PAST, PRESENT, AND FUTURE

"The Kyoto Protocol's clean development mechanism (CDM) has registered its 2000th project [on 6 January 2010], a biogas extraction and
utilization project, in Sakaeo Province, Thailand, expected to reduce
carbon dioxide emissions by more than 56,000 tonnes annually. The first
CDM project was registered on 18 November 2004. It took almost three
and a half years for the 1000th project to be registered on 14 April 2008.
The CDM has passed another milestone. It is fascinating to look back
at how it started, and consider how far it has come."
— Lex de Jonge, Chair of the CDM Executive Board (2010).

As the publication deadline for this volume grows near, so does the close
of the first commitment period under the Kyoto Protocol. Without a
clear way forward, we are left to wonder about the future of the local,
regional, national, and international policies and agreements that collectively influence how rapidly greenhouse gases will accumulate in our shared
atmosphere. The future of the Clean Development Mechanism (CDM) is
wrapped in uncertainty as well.

With all of its complexity and history, it is easy to forget that the
"Kyoto Surprise" is an institution that was created to reconcile three fundamental aspects of climate change: the notion of common but differentiated responsibilities: a guiding principle for treaty negotiators, a need
to leverage private investment capital, and the observation that many of
the best opportunities for mitigating climate change resided in poor countries. The principal guiding negotiators formulated a solution in which the
burden of slowing climate change fell on a group of wealthy industrial
countries, where abatement costs are sometimes high. Since mitigation
activities have the same consequences for climate change regardless of
where emissions or sequestrations occur, countries also looked for a way to
bridge the negotiated geography of obligation under the UNFCCC and the

1

natural geography of mitigation opportunities. Moreover, because the level of investment needed to generate a significant level of mitigation was beyond the practical capacity of governments, a market mechanism was sought to motivate profit and competition. These fundamental forces drove the creation of the CDM and other "flexibility" mechanisms. Additional objectives for the CDM, including the goal of promoting development, were incorporated. Moreover, the experimental nature of the CDM design drove specific implementation rules, safeguards, and limits that have further shaped incentives and outcomes.

Ultimately, the CDM was defined using the following language: "[T]he purpose of the clean development mechanism shall be to assist Parties not included in Annex I in achieving sustainable development and in contributing to the ultimate objective of the Convention, and to assist Parties included in Annex I in achieving compliance with their quantified emission limitation and reduction commitments under Article 3" (UNFCCC, 1997: Article 12).

While the CDM was introduced relatively later in the sequence of intervention tools, it has made a significant mark on climate change mitigation efforts (Schroeder, 2010). It also has been in the eye of the storm of public debate regarding its effectiveness and whether or not it achieved its dual goals — generating a significant reduction of greenhouse gases in the atmosphere and fostering development in the poor countries (Paulson, 2009).

ABOUT THIS BOOK

Although extensive analysis is available on CDM, very little comprehensive analysis addressing the various aspects of CDM under a unified analytical framework is available. The chapters of this volume explore how the CDM came into being, how it evolved, and the consequences it has had for climate change. Taken together, the chapters address how well the CDM has performed, given the objectives that shaped its design. The analysis is relevant for future agreements, including those under the UNFCCC. Whether it includes a continuation of the CDM in full or modified form depends, in large measure, on whether the political objectives and the forces that shaped the CDM are carried forward.

This book culminates the results of a research program at the World Bank during 2004–2011. The objective of the study was to provide better assessment of the potential of the project-based mechanisms and economic assessment of their likely future direction. Building on the analysis of the Activities implemented Jointly (AIJ) phase (Chapter 3), we will expand the AIJ dataset on projects including project information from CDM and Joint Implementation (JI). We compare among AIJ, CDM, and other JI projects. We also estimate the diffusion pattern of CDM and extrapolate for its likely expansion. We estimate abatement cost functions, using the CDM mechanism and explain how the CDM is seen as a cooperation mechanism and what determines the level of adoption of the CDM.

BOOK OUTLINE

Following this introduction, Chapter 2 is an in-depth literature review of recent work on the various aspects of carbon markets and institutions, including the CDM. This chapter provides a context for the CDM, based on the current literature. Chapter 3 analyzes the United Nations' AIJ program, a precursor of the CDM, and explores how the program influenced the eventual design of the CDM. Chapter 4 examines the cost structure of emissions abatement in various types of projects and across time. This examination is important to evaluate whether abatement costs drive project investments. Chapter 5 introduces a framework that presents CDM as an innovation that is diffused across time. The analysis describes the global diffusion patterns of CDM and provides estimates of its ability to deliver the expected carbon reduction by various time milestones. Chapter 6 attempts at explaining why the adoption of CDM differs across countries, by providing quantitative measures of parameters that affect its adoption. Chapter 7 develops a framework that allows examining the CDM market from the perspective of cooperation between host and investor countries. Chapter 8 reviews the agricultural projects in the CDM and discusses the problem of a seemingly missed opportunity by having too few agricultural projects in the CDM portfolio and the measures that can be undertaken to address such problems. And finally, Chapter 9 concludes with an elaboration on policy and future options.

BOOK CHAPTERS

We use data on CDM projects to address several questions regarding the nature of the projects, their performance, and the future expansion of the CDM mechanism. The following provides a detailed description of the individual chapters.

An Updated Review of Carbon Markets, Institutions, Policies, and Research

The scale of investment needed to slow greenhouse gas emissions is larger than what governments can manage through transfers. Therefore, climate change policies rely heavily on markets and private capital. This is especially true in the case of the Kyoto Protocol, with its provisions for trade and investment in joint projects. This chapter describes the role of CDM projects in such markets, the institutions and policies affecting its performance, and their origins. Research efforts that explore conceptual aspects of the current carbon policy are surveyed, along with empirical studies that make predictions about how carbon markets will work and perform. This chapter summarizes investment and price outcomes from newly formed markets, of which CDM projects are a part, and points out areas where markets have performed as predicted and where markets remain incomplete. Overall, the scale of the CDM and other carbon market investments planned exceeds earlier expectations, but the geographic dispersion of investment is uneven, and important opportunities for abatement remain untapped in some sectors, indicating a need for additional research on how investment markets work. How best to promote the development and deployment of new technologies is another promising area of study identified in the chapter.

The Activities Implemented Jointly Pilots: A Foundation for Clean Development Mechanism?

Under the Kyoto Protocol, countries can meet treaty obligations by investing in projects that reduce or sequester greenhouse gases elsewhere. Prior to ratification, treaty participants agreed to launch country-based pilot projects, referred to collectively as Activities Implemented Jointly (AIJ), to test novel aspects of the project-related provisions. Relying on a 10-year history of projects, the chapter investigates the determinants of an AIJ investment. The findings suggest that national political objectives and possibly deeper cultural ties influenced project selection. This characterization differs from the market-based assumptions that underlie well-known estimates of cost-savings related to the Protocol's flexibility mechanisms. The authors conclude that if approaches developed under the AIJ programs to approve projects are retained, benefits from Kyoto's flexibility provisions will be less than those widely anticipated.

Cost of Mitigation under the Clean Development Mechanism

This chapter examines the cost structure of emissions abatement delivered through CDM projects worldwide. Because of competition between suppliers and trade in emissions credits, CDM projects might be expected to deliver uniformly low-cost offsets. But using firm-level data, the authors show that production costs vary significantly among projects, even after adjusting for differences in the timing of offset delivery. Some of this has to do with the size and timespan of the projects, as results based on alternative specifications of a cost-function show that CDM project costs remain constant or fall with scale. Mitigation costs are also lower for projects entering the pipeline later, suggesting a learning process as project rules are clarified. Credit production costs also vary by location and project type, even though all credits count equally toward Kyoto commitments. This is consistent with the studies that find large differences in productivity among firms and farms, but the range of differences is notable, since theory and empirical studies indicate that such differences diminish under trade. This may come about because a significant component of CDM project investment is government-led, and governments may care about where and how credits are generated. The average abatement costs are relatively high for transportation and forestry projects, project types associated with large health and environmental benefits, suggesting scope for adjustments to the CDM that take co-benefits into account.

Diffusion of Kyoto's Clean Development Mechanism

To date, developed countries can only tap mitigation opportunities in developing countries by investing in projects under the CDM. Yet CDM investments have so far failed to reach all of the high-potential sectors identified in IPCC reports. This raises doubts about whether the CDM will be able to generate an adequate supply of credits from the limited areas where it has proved successful. This chapter examines the current trajectory of potential mitigation entering the CDM pipeline and projects it forward under the assumption that the diffusion of the CDM will follow a path similar to other kinds of innovations. Projections are then compared to pre-CDM predictions of the mechanism's potential market size used to assess Kyoto's cost, in order to discern whether limits on the types of project entering the pipeline will also limit the eventual supply of certified emission reductions (CERs). The main finding of the chapter is that the mechanism is on track to deliver an average annual flow of roughly 700 million CERs by the close of 2012 and nearly 1,100 million tons by 2020. Parameter tests suggest that currently identified CDM investments will exceed early model predictions of the potential market for CDM projects.

Why Adoption of the Clean Development Mechanism Differs Across Countries?

The CDM is an innovative method that combines greenhouse gas abatement with sustainable development objectives. In this chapter, we examine the determinants of incidence, extent, and rate of cross-country CDM adoption over time. The main results of adoption determinants suggest the following: the rate of CDM adoption increases as the first commitment period of the Kyoto Protocol approaches; CDM adoption is higher for the industrialized countries than for the developing countries; CDM adoption is higher (lower) for the developing countries (industrialized countries) with larger renewable energy resource potentials; and CDM adoption is higher for the developing countries with more AIJ experience.

Clean Development Mechanism as a Cooperation Mechanism

This chapter examines the CDM market from the perspective of cooperation between developing (host) and developed (investor) countries. First, a dichotomous variable is used to indicate the incidence of country involvement in CDM projects. Then, three continuous variables are used to measure the level of cooperation, namely the number of joint CDM projects, volume of CO_2 abatement that can be realized from the CDM projects, and volume of investment in the CDM projects. Empirical results suggest that the economic development, institutional development, energy structures of the economies, country vulnerability to various climate change effects, and international relations between the host and investor countries are good predictors of the level of cooperation in CDM projects. The main policy-relevant conclusions include the importance of simplifying the CDM project regulation/clearance cycle as an essential policy option for further growth of joint CDM projects; improving governance structure in the host and investor countries that would lead to higher political stability and trust between the countries for business, including CDM; and strengthening trade or other long-term economic activities that connect the countries for fostering CDM cooperation.

Why So Few Agricultural Projects in the Clean Development Mechanism?

Many experts believe that low-cost mitigation opportunities in agriculture are abundant and comparable in scale to those found in the energy sector. They are mostly located in developing countries and involve land-user planning. By investing in projects under the CDM, countries can tap these opportunities to meet their own Kyoto Protocol obligations. The CDM has been successful in financing some types of agricultural projects, including projects that capture methane or use agricultural by-products as an energy source. But agricultural land-use projects are scarce under CDM, which represents a missed opportunity to promote sustainable rural development since land-use projects that sequester carbon in soils can help reverse declining soil fertility, a root cause of stagnant agricultural productivity. This chapter reviews the process leading to current CDM implementation rules and describes how the rules, in combination with challenging features of land-use projects, raise transaction costs and lower demand for land-use credits. Procedures by which developed countries assess their own mitigation performance are discussed as a way of redressing current constraints on CDM investments. Nevertheless, even with improvements to the CDM, an under-investment in agricultural land-use projects is likely, since there are hurdles to capturing associated ancillary benefits privately. Alternative approaches outside of the CDM are discussed, including those that build on recent decisions taken by governments in Copenhagen and Cancun.

CONCLUSION AND POLICY IMPLICATIONS

This chapter includes a technical and policy-focused discussion, addressing the main themes discussed in the book — diffusion, adoption, abatement cost, market efficiency, R&D, equity and efficiency of CDM, and international cooperation.

EPILOGUE

At the time of going to print, the Eighteen's Conference of the Parties (COP18) was culminated on December 7, 2012. COP18 yielded the "Doha Climate Gateway," which is a detailed roadmap to a 2015 global agreement and a renewed Kyoto Protocol. The Kyoto Protocol was awarded a second commitment period, which will run from 2013 to 2020, with countries agreeing to revise their emission reduction pledges in 2014.

The CDM-related decisions in COP18 include (UNFCCC, 2012):

1. Whilst the CDM remains open to all developed countries, those that have not committed to the second commitment period are not permitted to trade in CDM credits.
2. There will be an important review of the CDM during 2013. Important issues that could have had impact on the CDM were not addressed at the COP18. They were postponed to be dealt with at the COP19.

REFERENCES

de Jonge, L (2010). Press release. Available at: http://unfccc.int/files/pressre leases/application/pdf/press_release_cdm_passes_2000th_registered_project. pdf. Accessed 1 August 2012.

Paulsson, E (2009). A review of the CDM literature: From fine-tuning to critical scrutiny? *International Environmental Agreements*, **9**, 63–80.

Schroeder, H (2010). The history of international climate change politics: Three decades of progress, process and procrastination. In: Max Boykoff (Ed.), *The Politics of Climate Change: A Survey*, London: Routledge.

UNFCCC (1997). Kyoto Protocol to the United Nations Framework Convention on Climate Change. Available at: http://unfccc.int/cop3/resource/ docs/cop3/07a01.pdf. Accessed 27 June 2012.

United Nations Convention on Climate Change (UNFCCC) (2012). Decisions adopted by COP 18 and CMP 8. Available at: http://unfccc.int/2860. php#decisions. Accessed 22 December 2012.

2. AN UPDATED REVIEW OF CARBON MARKETS, INSTITUTIONS, POLICIES, AND RESEARCH[*]

With Contributions by Philippe Ambrosi and Rebecca Entler

There is a longstanding and continuing debate on how countries should manage their greenhouse gas emissions. For nearly three decades, the issue has been the focus of international institutions established by the World Meteorological Organization (WMO) and the United Nations. During this time, an international treaty has been forged and new national and regional policies promoted. This has had several practical consequences. For one, the broad process of debate has led to a large body of research and a specialized set of institutions that influence how the predictions of physical and social outcomes from climate change are assessed. In addition, there are both public and market-based policy instruments associated with international treaty and domestic policies. This has given rise to a rapidly expanding set of institutions to manage, implement, and evaluate policy.

The influence institutions have on carbon policy and related markets is considerable and cascading. The special characteristics of climate change — that the potential effects of climate change are global and that the greenhouse gas emissions that contribute to climate change matter in the aggregate, irrespective of their source — creates a need for a coordinated international response, and new institutions have evolved to organize debate and establish a common set of objectives. At the same time, because of uncertainty over natural, economic, and social consequences of climate change, a widely shared understanding of the science of climate

---

[*]This chapter is an extension of Larson, Ambrosi, Dinar, Rahman, and Entler (2008). Permission from the *Journal International Review of Environmental and Resource Economics* is acknowledged.

change is needed as a starting point for a coordinated strategy. In response, organizations and procedures have been built up in recent years to develop informed judgments — for example, dedicated research centers, non-government organization, and panels under United Nations sponsorship.

Another key characteristic of the policy framework currently in place is its reliance on markets, which is motivated in part by the scale of investment needed to significantly reduce global emissions. In turn, this has given rise to a set of sophisticated markets for pricing carbon and financing carbon mitigation, and associated market-supporting institutions, including those that certify tradable permits and support trade and private investment flows. This in turn has resulted in the build-up of a large body of practical knowledge about project-based approaches, which were novel in 1995. Separate complementary mechanisms, largely public in nature, have evolved as well for financing activities that help countries adapt to future climate change.

In this chapter, we describe important institutions that shape climate change policies, together with a set of key instruments. We selectively review related research, emphasizing empirical studies that assess the effects of current policies and that evaluate the markets upon which current policies depend. Early on, as key elements of the current policy framework were devised, much of the empirical analyses relating to climate change policies was forward looking and anticipatory. This is changing as evidence about the consequences of the policies emerges.

Following this introduction, the remainder of the chapter is organized as follows. The second section briefly describes the process by which scientific predictions of climate change are incorporated into policy and policy evaluations. The third section delineates key features of the climate change framework and the related debate over the framework's design, with special attention to the amendments and rules related to the Kyoto Protocol's flexibility mechanisms. The fourth section examines alternative evaluations of expected outcomes. The fifth section discusses market-based domestic policies in Australia, the European Union, and the US. The sixth section looks at the current state of carbon markets. Finally, the last section concludes and indicates areas for future research.[1]

---

[1]Language describing the objectives and workings of the Climate Change Treaty is laden with acronyms and we include a glossary in the annex to this chapter to help the readers.

SCIENCE AND POLICY

Motivation for a treaty limiting greenhouse gas emissions stems from evidence that the global climate is warming and the strengthening inference that human activity is a significant contributing factor. In turn, the degree to which interventions are required depends first on an evaluation of both points, and second, on an assessment of the damages caused by global warming and the costs and benefits of altering its mutable components.

The conceptual foundation for the contribution of human activity to global warming is not controversial in itself and relates to the greenhouse effect. Briefly, as the earth constantly receives energy from the sun and radiates energy back into space, water vapor, clouds, and long-lived gases, including carbon dioxide, work to reduce the outflow of radiated light, creating an energy imbalance known as the greenhouse effect. In 1861, John Tyndall speculated that the accumulated release of carbon dioxide from combustible fossil fuels might increase the energy imbalance, resulting in a warming of the earth's surface. Later, the Swedish physicist, Svante Arrhenius (1896), provided a formal model of the phenomenon. Arrhenius predicted a gradual warming of the climate but did not view the consequences as threatening. Later, as global consumption of fossil fuels increased and the earth's cooling and warming mechanisms became better understood, the subject was revived. In 1957, an important paper by Revelle and Suess (1957) suggested that the oceans' capacity to absorb carbon dioxide from the atmosphere was more limited than previously thought. The authors went on to stress the potential risks and uncertainties associated with a continuing buildup of greenhouse gases in the atmosphere. In the ensuing years, measurements of atmospheric carbon dioxide taken at the Mauna Loa Observatory, starting in 1958, revealed increasing concentration of carbon dioxide in the atmosphere. Later on, corroborating evidence from ice-core analysis suggested a trend of building accumulations going back to the 19th century (Siegenthaler and Oeschger, 1987).

Nevertheless, predicting the consequences of increased concentrations of atmospheric carbon dioxide and induced global warming proved a difficult task. Hurdles included inexact historic climatic measures and an incomplete understanding of the complex natural relationships among the mechanisms that heat and cool the earth's oceans and atmosphere.[2] By the close of the 1970s, no consensus had emerged among scientists as to the effects increased

---

[2]See, for example, Lindzen (1990) for a discussion.

concentrations of greenhouse gases might have on climate, and no formal mechanism existed to reach one. By extension, the economic analysis of the consequences of climate change lacked a common starting point.[3]

A series of conferences sponsored by the WMO, the United Nations Environment Program, and the International Council for Science led to the establishment of an Advisory Group on Greenhouse Gases in 1985 and, ultimately, the establishment of the Intergovernmental Panel on Climate Change (IPCC) in 1988, which is the formal mechanism by which studies concerning human-induced climate change are reviewed by experts with the goal of providing an objective evaluation to policy makers.[4] The first panel report was submitted to the UN General Assembly in 1990 and was instrumental in the eventual negotiation of an international treaty, the United Nations Framework Convention on Climate Change (UNFCCC), intended to protect the global climate by limiting greenhouse gas emissions.[5] Significant additions to the treaty, known as the Kyoto Protocol, were negotiated in 1997 and entered into force in February 2005, following IPCC reports in 1995, 1997, and 2001. The most recent IPCC report was issued in 2007, with a fifth set of assessments due in 2014.

Of special interest to this chapter is the structure of the IPCC and the topics it is designed to review, since much of the literature cited here directly addresses questions posed by the IPCC. As a practical matter, the work of the IPCC is carried out by separate groups of experts aligned around three general topics. The first working group is concerned primarily with evaluating the drivers of climate change and evaluating ongoing evidence of global warming. Much of the evaluation of physical models of climate change takes place within this group. The remaining groups deal with the predicted consequences. The second working group assesses current knowledge about and predicted effects of climate change on nature and on human welfare, vulnerability, and adaptability. Much of the economic analysis evaluated by this group concerns an accounting of economic gains and losses due to climate change. The third working group focuses on

---

[3]For an early example of integrated analysis and a related discussion, see Nordhaus (1977).

[4]See IPCC (2004) for a history of the panel.

[5]The first IPCC report was instrumental in the negotiation of three treaties, which formed the basis for the Rio Earth Summit in 1992. In addition to the UNFCCC discussed here, the Rio Conference also resulted in the Convention on Biological Diversity and the United Nations Convention to Combat Desertification.

mitigation. Related economic studies reviewed by the group include both general equilibrium studies and sectoral studies of mitigation costs. The effects of market mechanisms are also reviewed by this group. Experts who draft and review initial reports are chosen by member governments, and the governments participate in the reviews of final drafts. As a general practice, draft summaries intended for policy makers are closely reviewed by national representatives external to the working groups and actively debated before their release. The panel is not the only group engaged in assessing the likely economic impact of climate change, other summary evaluations exist, most notably the *Stern Review on the Economics of Climate Change* issued by the British Government in November 2006.

Before proceeding to the third section, it is useful to draw some parallels between the physical and social sciences as they relate to climate change. In both instances, the expected outcomes lie largely outside current experience. Many of the tools that applied science and social science researchers use are based on repeatable experiments or the analysis of historical data. While these approaches are useful in building up analytic components, numerical models of highly complex relationships are relied upon to provide quantitative judgments and predictions.

FEATURES OF THE CLIMATE CHANGE FRAMEWORK

The broad international legal framework that greatly shapes the international carbon markets and national policies includes the United Nations Framework Convention on Climate Change, additions to the Convention under the Kyoto Protocol, and related decisions taken by Parties to the Convention and the UNFCCC Secretariat. The set of agreements and rules has been built up over time, and the full set of rules pertinent to a given policy instrument is usually spread over sets of decisions. For convenience, we use the term "climate change framework," or simply "the framework," to refer to the full set of components.

As mentioned earlier, the objective to limit greenhouse gas emissions is set out in the UNFCCC, which entered into force in March 1994. In particular, Article 2 of the treaty calls for the "stabilization of greenhouse gas (GHG) concentrations in the atmosphere at a level that would prevent "dangerous anthropogenic interference with the climate system (...) within a time-frame sufficient to allow ecosystems to adapt (...), to ensure that food production is not threatened and to enable economic development to proceed in a sustainable manner." The UNFCCC covers six greenhouse gases: carbon dioxide, methane, nitrous oxide, hydrofluorocarbons, perfluorocarbons, and sulfur hexafluoride. There are standard rates of conversion among the gases, and most of the reporting and rule-making is done in terms of carbon equivalents.[6] Following its adoption, the treaty evolved through a series of decisions taken by treaty participants, known as UNFCCC Conferences of the Parties (COP).

At the third Conference of the Parties held in Kyoto, Japan, additions to the treaty, known as the Kyoto Protocol, were negotiated that delineated an international mechanism for reducing greenhouse gas emissions.[7] The key features of the Kyoto Protocol relate the notion of common but differentiated responsibility. Commonality comes from the physical property that greenhouse gases have a uniform effect on global warming independent of the source of emission; differentiation stems from the historical nature of current levels of accumulated anthropogenic greenhouse gases, which are primarily the consequence of emissions from developed countries. This guiding principle, along with recognition of differentiated abatement costs and impacts, gave rise to the climate change framework's unusual structure.

Obligations Under the Framework

Currently, the framework sets out three levels of obligations among party participants. Over the first commitment period from 2008 to 2012, industrialized countries, generally referred to as Annex I countries in reference to the annexed list in the Kyoto Protocol, obligate themselves to take specific steps to bring their overall carbon emissions below a 1990 baseline.[8] Commitments are listed in Annex B of the Kyoto Protocol and vary among the countries. By way of example, targets for the European Union and many transitional economies are set at 8% below 1990 levels, Russian targets are set at 1990 levels, and Australian emission targets are 8% above 1990 levels. In addition, a wealthier subset of the Annex I countries, known as

---

[6]For example, one ton of nitrous oxide is equivalent to 281 tons of carbon dioxide.

[7]As of July 2012, 191 countries plus the EU had ratified the treaty, including 38 Annex I countries that represent about 64% of 1990 emissions (UNFCCC, 2012).

[8]Not all Annex I countries ratified the Kyoto Protocol, so it is a slightly different group of countries, known as Annex B countries, that are obligated to reduce emissions. Moreover, for some transitional economies, commitments are based on years other than 1990.

Annex II Parties, pledged to provide new and additional financial resources to facilitate and finance technology transfer and cover the costs of compliance incurred by developing countries.[9] Developing country members of the UNFCCC, known as Non–Annex-I Parties, are obliged to develop and periodically update their national inventories of greenhouse gas emissions by sources and removals by sinks but are not committed to reduce emissions during the first commitment period.[10]

To complete some key definitions associated with the framework, the amount to which an Annex I Party must reduce its emissions over the commitment period is known as its "assigned amount." These Parties are allocated "assigned amount units" (AAUs) up to the level of their assigned amount, corresponding to the quantity of greenhouse gases they can release in accordance with the Kyoto Protocol (Article 3), during the first commitment period. One AAU equals one ton of emissions, expressed as a carbon-equivalent (tCO_2e). Parties may offset their emissions by enhancing greenhouse gas sinks in land use, land-use change, and forestry (LULUCF) sector. Greenhouse gases removed from the atmosphere through eligible activities within this sector generate credits known as "removal units" (RMUs).

Flexibility Mechanisms

In addition to domestic actions, the Kyoto Protocol allows for three flexibility mechanisms intended to reduce the overall cost of the treaty. First, countries facing emission limits can purchase AAUs from other Annex B countries under the International Emission Trading provision (Article 17). In addition, countries can contribute to projects that reduce carbon emissions abroad. The Protocol distinguishes between projects hosted in Annex B countries and non–Annex-I countries — that is, between countries that have pledged to limit emissions and those that have not. Though conceptually similar, there are differences in how the programs are administered and implemented. The two programs are authorized under separate articles of the Protocol, Articles 6 and 12, respectively. The

---

[9]Current Annex II countries that have ratified the Protocol are: Australia, Austria, Belgium, Canada, Denmark, Finland, France, Germany, Greece, Iceland, Ireland, Italy, Japan, Luxembourg, Netherlands, New Zealand, Norway, Portugal, Spain, Sweden, Switzerland, and the United Kingdom.

[10]Sinks are natural or manmade systems that absorb and store more greenhouse gases than they emit.

mechanism for projects in Annex B countries is referred to as Joint Implementation (JI) and the mechanism for projects in developing countries is referred to as the Clean Development Mechanisms (CDMs). Offsets (credits) arising under JI are known as Emission Reduction Units (ERUs), while credits generated by CDM are known as Certified Emissions Reductions (CERs). CERs and ERUs can be used to meet treaty obligations. Each CER and ERU represents one tCO_2e of greenhouse gas emission reductions and both can be traded.[11]

Solving pollution problems through international cooperation had several precedents prior to Kyoto, but key aspects of the framework with regard to project credits were unique and have been controversial.[12] To start with, credits emanating from projects are based on a hypothetical baseline of emissions that would have occurred absent the CDM or JI investment. Judging an appropriate counter-factual is difficult at best and entails both economic and engineering challenges. As a practical consequence, the rules and procedures for approving and implementing CDM and JI projects have grown complex. In addition, CDM projects are expected to also advance development objectives. The criterion is loosely defined and judging whether it is met is difficult. Moreover, the twin objectives imply tradeoffs, since setting a high development objective for CDM projects can slow investment transfers and hamper the scope of the flexibility mechanisms to lower implementation costs. And finally, the flexibility mechanisms are expected to be supplemental to domestic action, and this has prompted debates about domestic policies governing the use of offsets. We return to these topics below.

Emission Allocations and the Choice of Policy Instruments

By all accounts, the decision to employ quantitative controls among industrial countries took place early in the process of negotiating the Kyoto Protocol. This was formalized at the first Conference of the Parties in 1995 as part of the "Berlin Mandate," which called for binding emission limits

---

[11]Only sovereign entities can trade AAUs, while both private and public entities can trade and own CERs and ERUs.

[12]Examples of international cooperative action include the 1976 Convention Concerning the Protection of the Rhine River against Pollution by Chlorides and the 1985 Vienna Convention for the Protection of the Ozone Layer (Hanafi, 1998).

while excluding developing countries from new commitments. Subsequent negotiations focused on a proposal for uniform reduction rates favored by the European Union and a proposal for differentiated reductions favored by Australia, Iceland, and Norway, among others countries. The differentiated proposal won out, based on the argument that the burden of limiting greenhouse gas emissions should be equally shared, rather than the reductions themselves (Fisher, Tulpule, and Brown, 1998).[13]

Still, the early consensus among negotiators has not stalled the debate about burden-sharing under future agreements, and a number of approaches have been proposed.[14] In general, the proposed allocations are based on historical responsibility (Pinguelli, Luiz, and Ribeiro, 2001), population (Baer *et al.*, 2000; Bode, 2004), and single or multiple measures of development or economic need (Jacoby, Prinn, and Schmalensee, 1998; Gupta and Bhandari, 1999; Aslam, 2002; Ringius, Torvanger, and Holtsmark, 1998). Moving emission targets based on overall or sector-specific intensity targets have been proposed as well (Lutter, 2000; Kolstad, 2006). How allocations are made have implications for equity because they imply uncertain transfers of wealth. And adaptation associated with ongoing climate change generates an added set of uncertain costs. This makes it hard to judge the overall costs and benefits of the climate change framework. It also makes it difficult for countries or groups of countries to decide which competing targets and design features associated with the framework best match their own interests. Additional discussions of these topics are included in Panayotou, Sachs, and Zwane (2002); Leimbach (2003); Vaillancourt and Waaub (2004); Tol and Verheyen (2004); and Halsnæs *et al.* (2007). We return to this topic later when we discuss model measures of the benefits and costs of competing policies.

In the lead-up to the Kyoto Protocol, another debate emerged that still endures, centering on a choice of a coordinating policy instrument, with carbon taxes and tradable permit systems emerging as the primary candidates. Pearce (1991) provides an early and still relevant discussion of the advantages and problems of using a carbon tax to limit greenhouse gas emissions that reflects the state of the debate at that time. Cooper (1998) and Pizer (1998) provide additional arguments as does Nordhaus (2007) more recently. Tietenberg (2010) provides a good review of the evolution of

---

[13]Bertram (1992) and Rose *et al.* (1998) provide early reviews. See Whalley and Wigle (1991) for an early quantitative assessment of policies under debate.

[14]Gupta *et al.* (2007) provides an extensive and recent review.

economic thought leading to cap-and-trade policies and discusses current examples. Ellerman (2005) also provides a good introduction to the cap-and-trade systems and tradable permits.[15]

Permit systems versus carbon taxes

Depending on how they are implemented, the tradable permit and carbon tax systems share many of the same benefits and suffer many of the same problems. The chief advantage of both approaches is that they result in a price for emitting greenhouse gases, which in turn encourages a switch to low-emission technologies and activities and the development of emission-reducing technologies. In turn, these general equilibrium effects create opportunities for cost-savings over command-and-control approaches.

Both systems can be used to raise revenues. In the case of carbon tax, this comes directly through collections, while raising revenue in a permit system requires that emission allowances be sold or auctioned. Revenue raised under either system can be used to displace economically less-efficient taxes on productive factors, potentially leading to a positive welfare externality. This is known as a "double-dividend," a topic discussed later in the fourth section. Revenue could also be transferred among countries to encourage wider international participation in the climate framework.

To work well, either system should lead to a common price for emissions, which requires a harmonization of policies among countries and also across sectors within economies. Otherwise problems of spillovers and leakages arise through trade. In practice, both systems are open to domestic capture when important sectors vie for tax breaks or for preferential permit allocations. Still, very few governments have pursued mitigation policies based on a carbon tax, and fewer have survived for long (Larson and Parks, 1999; Mathys and de Melo, 2011). And there are political economy elements that may favor permit systems. In the beginning, it may be easier for policy makers to agree on quantitative emission levels based on scientific evaluations of sustainability rather than to establish the price of an externality.

---

[15]Hybrid trading systems have been discussed as well, including cap-and-safety-value systems where the regulatory authority stands ready to issue new permits should permit prices exceed some threshold. In a guide-rail system, regulators also intervene to buy-up permits when prices fall below a threshold. See, among others, McKibbin and Wilcoxen (2002); Pizer (2002); Jacoby and Ellerman (2004); and Aldy, Barrett, and Stavins (2003).

What's more, regulated industries that receive tradable permits under cap-and-trade or similar systems have a vested interest in the regulatory system. Although how permits are allocated has equity implications, initial allocations are not expected to affect the eventual outcomes.[16] Of course, this line of reasoning sets aside issues of equity and cost-burden.[17] We return to this topic later.

Both systems generate administrative and related transaction costs. To a degree, carbon-tax systems can make use of the existing tax collection mechanisms and require less intensive emission monitoring, both of which reduce implementation costs. However, proponents of permit systems will counter that measuring emissions is required in either case in order to judge the environmental efficacy of the policy. Moreover, the costs of financial monitoring can be high. For example, Victor (2001) points to the difficulty in determining net carbon taxes, especially when other taxes are levied.

There are substantive differences between the two instruments that have to do with the effects of different types of uncertainty. Both systems require some prior judgment about the desired level of emission reductions either instrument is expected to accomplish. The optimal level is uncertain, and Nordhaus (2007) points out that this dynamic uncertainty works against permit systems. With economic growth and changes in technologies, base-year emissions of the type often used in permit systems become increasingly irrelevant. Making adjustments to allocations implies welfare transfers, and this introduces equity issues, although the same can be said about changes to tax rates or transfers.

In principle, carbon tax systems effectively fix the price of emissions while permit systems fix emission levels and uncertainty. Consequently, permit systems are expected to result in greater price variability while tax system results in greater emission variability. In turn, this has implications for two other types of uncertainty: uncertainty about the relationship between emissions and changes in climate, and uncertainty about the relationship between tax rates and emission levels. If only the first type of uncertainty

---

[16]This outcome is known as the Coase Theorem, based on an influential article by Ronald Coase (1960). Hahn and Stavins (2011) explore the circumstances leading to this outcome in the context of several implemented cap-and-trade systems, finding mixed results. In addition to Hahn and Stavins, see related discussions by Tietenberg (2010) and Hazlett (2009).

[17]Based on positive and normative arguments, Mathys and de Melo (2011) make a case that, because of lobbying and other political-economy considerations, carbon taxes lead to better outcomes.

was present, a preference for one instrument over the other could be made based on the relative nonlinearities in costs and benefits, with costs that are nonlinear relative to benefits favoring price systems (Weitzman, 1974).

Because both types of uncertainty are present, the choice may be less clear. Pearce (1991) and subsequent authors have argued that a fixed price for carbon has an uncertain effect on the environment, and the safest approach is to directly target the proximate cause of carbon accumulation, emissions, rather than rely on relationships between price and emissions that are imprecisely understood. This is especially important because damages from climate change are potentially large and irreversible. At the same time, Nordhaus (2007) points out that carbon taxes generate stable incentives for investment and development of new technologies, which are key to long-term success.

Evidence from the commodity storage literature suggests another less-discussed difference between carbon taxes and permit systems that has to do with the pricing of uncertainty. In tradable permit systems, forward and futures markets evolve in order to determine a price at which inventories of unused permits are carried forward. These markets can be utilized to provide an implicit market-driven evaluation of evolving risks profiles, information that is not provided under carbon taxes. Moreover, while uncertainty creates incentives to delay irreversible investments that reduce emissions, it also drives up the shadow price of permits held in inventory, thereby reducing current emission levels and partly reducing the negative effects of uncertainty on investment.[18]

Current Instruments

In the lead-up to the Kyoto Protocol, most countries' experiences related to carbon emission abatement focused on command-and-control style regulations. However, a few countries had experimented with carbon taxes, but the efforts were not encouraging, and the inability of European governments to implement a uniform carbon tax across sectors may have influenced the preference for a permit system.[19] In contrast, proponents of permit systems could point to the success of the US cap-and-trade program for

---

[18]See Larson (2007) in the context of commodity markets and Considine and Larson (2006) in the context of the US sulfur dioxide permit markets.

[19]For discussions of the Danish and the Norwegian experiences with carbon taxes, see, respectively, Andersen (2005) and Bruvoll and Fæhna (2006).

sulfur dioxide (SO_2), which led to a rapid decrease in emissions and a transparent pricing market for SO_2 permits (Ellerman *et al.*, 2000). Tradable permit systems had been applied successfully to other problems as well. For example, a related system of individual transferable fishing quotas had been introduced in New Zealand in 1986, and similar approaches had been adopted subsequently in Australia, Canada, Iceland, Italy, the Netherlands, South Africa, and the US (Larson and Parks, 1999; Newell, Sanchirico, and Kerr, 2005). Positive experience with tradable permits also resulted from the phase-out of lead gasoline in the US, limits on emissions from electricity producers in the Netherlands, and a regional air pollution program in the Los Angeles Basin.[20] Taken together, favorable prior experience with tradable permit systems and difficulties with the current carbon tax efforts appeared to sway policy makers, and from the Berlin Mandate forward, negotiations focused on a tradable permit system supplemented with project-based components. Even so, the system that would eventually be codified in the Kyoto Protocol differed from prior experience, in that new permits could be generated through project investment.

The logic behind the project-based flexibility mechanisms rests on the observation that the cost of reducing emissions varies greatly among countries, though the effects of greenhouse gas emissions on climate change are uniform, regardless of where the gases are emitted. Countries where greenhouse gas emissions were already low were particularly interested in finding ways to lower the cost of treaty emission goals. In the course of negotiation, the Government of Norway suggested a mechanism to allow those countries facing emission limits to receive credit for investments made elsewhere that reduce global emissions (Carraro, 1999; Dixon and Mintzer, 1999). The concept came to be known as Joint Implementation (JI) and was subsequently adopted into the treaty negotiating documents (articles 4.2 and 3.3 of the UNFCCC) and eventually, as discussed, into the Protocol.[21]

The notion of supplementing emission constraints through bilateral project-based investments was untried and controversial among negotiators and non-government organizations. To demonstrate that the approach was

---

[20]Lambert (1996) and Hahn and Hester (1989) discuss the leaded gas phase-down. Klaassen (1996) discusses the Dutch covenant; Prager, Lier, and Matton (1996) discuss the Regional Clean Air Incentives Market.

[21]As discussed, the term Joint Implementation refers to a specific set of partnerships in the Kyoto Protocol. This is different from the more general use of joint implementation, which leads to some confusion.

practical, advocates proposed a coordinated group of country pilots under the UNFCCC. The pilots, known as Activities Implemented Jointly (AIJ), were meant to provide practical experience about baselines and other practical design features related to the creation of project-based finances. The agreement to do so, known as Decision 5 of the UNFCCC, provided broad guidelines for establishing a voluntary AIJ program and also established a common reporting system.[22] By design, early crediting was prohibited during the AIJ pilot phase. Nevertheless, Schwarze (2000) notes that many of the AIJ projects had project lives extending well into the CDM and JI crediting periods and surmises that many AIJ investors hoped to receive credits for offsets generated after the close of the pilot phase. Even so, given the contrast in incentives between AIJ projects and the current Kyoto mechanisms, the AIJ experience is most informative about the process of government project approval and transaction costs related to bilateral investments and the practical lessons learned about baselines.[23]

Project Rules

As discussed, the Kyoto Protocol established two mechanisms by which countries facing emission limits meet those obligations by investing in projects that reduce emissions elsewhere. Very broadly, credits generated by CDM and JI projects are calculated by comparing the emissions or reductions from each project against a business-as-usual scenario or baseline. Consequently, a significant portion of the project cycle entails developing arguments about why low-emission outcomes would not occur without investments associated with the project. Because this process is rule-based and because there are arguably incentives for both the investor and host to exaggerate the environmental consequences of the project, the mechanisms were viewed with suspicion. Delegates and observers worried that weak

---

[22] Convention participants assigned an advisory committee, the Subsidiary Body for Scientific and Technological Advice (SBSTA) to establish reporting guidelines and to compile and publish the reports on an on-going basis.

[23] Michaelowa, Dixon, and Abron (1999) look at early AIJ participation and Lile, Powell, and Toman (1998) describe the US programs. Michaelowa, Dixon, and Abron (1999) examine the application and approval process for AIJ projects in 11 investor countries. Heister *et al.* (1999) discuss concurrent World Bank experiences with baselines. Selected projects are reviewed by Schwarze (2000) and Barrera and Schwarze (2004). Larson and Breustedt (2007) discuss how policy preferences and transaction costs affected the location of AIJ projects.

controls and imprecise baselines might allow countries that had pledged reductions to purchase watered-down credits cheaply from developing countries, thereby attenuating the environmental benefits of the treaty and forestalling the development of new technologies. In addition, delegates from developing countries expressed concern that donor countries would meet emission reduction targets by redirecting existing aid flows to JI projects (Ghosh and Puri, 1994; Parikh, 1995).[24] One consequence was an extended period of rule making, and details of the programs were left unfinished until the announcement of the Marrakesh Accords in 2001.[25] The concerns also affected the design of the programs and have given rise to a specific set of national and international institutions that, in turn, shape private markets for carbon projects.

In particular, the final rules called for a centralized project-by-project review process and a conservative approach to validation. Less-specific language in the treaty and the implementation rules calls for projects to promote sustainable development and asks developed countries to ensure that Overseas Development Assistance (ODA) is not diverted to finance CDM projects. Language calling on countries not to depend too heavily on project-derived credits to meet treaty obligations and specific rules limiting the use of credits from sinks reflect the qualified support given to the CDM by the negotiators.

The CDM Project Cycle

In order to generate certified credits, projects located in developing countries must materially reduce or remove atmospheric greenhouse gas emissions and also contribute to sustainable development. In practice, most aspects of the CDM project cycles fall under the supervision of host national regulatory agencies — known as Designated National Agencies in UNFCCC parlance. And, in general, it is up to the host government to determine whether projects meet its sustainable development goals.

---

[24]Lecocq and Ambrosi (2007) provide a good historical account of the CDM. Gulbrandsen and Andresen (2004) discuss the role played by non-governmental organizations in this debate. Grubb, Vrolijk, and Brack (1999) provide a good account of the negotiations. See also criticisms in Cullet and Kameri-Mbote (1998). Chomitz (1999) discusses moral hazard problems relating to baselines.

[25]Werksman (1998) gives an account of the CDM negotiations. den Elzen and de Moor (2002) discuss rules emerging from the Marrakesh Accords.

This determination is part of the CDM project cycle and is signaled by a project-specific letter from the host country to the UNFCCC.[26]

In contrast, the environmental integrity of a CDM project is subject to specific supervision rules and a series of checks along the project cycle by the UNFCCC Secretariat. To start with, methodologies for establishing baselines must be approved on behalf of the UNFCCC by an international supervisory group, known as the CDM Executive Board. Approved methodologies are published and these can be drawn on by project developers. However, projects relying on new methods face the additional task of gaining approval. In either case, regardless of whether new or established methods are employed, developers must also convince the CDM board that their project methodology has been appropriately applied.

The project cycle also contains checks carried out by an independent firm or organization that has been accredited by a CDM Board. This entity, known as a Designated Operational Entity (DOE), initially validates the baseline design and the project's plan to monitor and measure outcomes.[27] This occurs before the project is registered, i.e., officially recognized by the CDM Board. For large CDM projects, a separate independent entity carries out the project's monitoring protocol, the process by which emissions or sequestrations are measured. The DOE is also responsible for certifying all emission reductions, although it is the CDM Board that issues and tracks the ownership all CERs. To boost the contribution of the CDM to sustainable development, a 2% levy on CERs goes toward an Adaptation Fund, designed to cover the CDM's administrative costs and to fund projects that help the poorest countries adapt to climate change.[28]

The JI Project Cycle

Conceptually, JI, the second project-based mechanism established by the Kyoto Protocol, is less controversial since, because of an overall cap on allowed emissions from the JI host, any project that abates greenhouse

---

[26] Of course, additional criteria can be applied. For example, the Gold Standard Foundation requires additional stakeholder consultations for projects to qualify for its voluntary certification. In February 2008, the British government announced plans for a voluntary certification for CDM projects that conform to its Code of Best Practice for Carbon Offsetting. The Code is voluntary and is administered by an Accreditation Board. The Code may be extended to Voluntary Emission Reductions soon (DEFRA, 2008).

[27] The overall design of the project is laid out in a Project Design Document (PDD).

[28] The levy is not assessed against projects hosted by developing countries.

gases potentially leads to tradable units of carbon. Domestically financed projects do so by creating more headroom under the cap of allowed emissions, potentially contributing to a surplus that could be traded to other countries in the form of AAUs. The JI program provides an additional mechanism for foreign investment projects that directly create tradable carbon units in the form of ERUs. At the end of the Convention's accounting period, all types of carbon units are balanced, so the primary distinction between traded AAUs and traded ERUs has to do with how the underlying projects were financed.

Notionally, the practical hurdles of implementing JI projects are also lower. Since the Annex I countries have pledged to cap domestic emissions, national guidelines used to measure emissions from wholly domestic projects can be applied to JI projects as well. Moreover, in contrast to the CDM project cycle, the JI program is designed to place full responsibility for the environmental integrity of the projects in the hands of the hosting countries. In practical terms, Annex I countries that have the necessary national guidelines in place to track, measure, and report emissions and reductions are able to issue and transfer ERUs without recourse to an international body for approval.[29]

As a practical matter however, many Annex I countries do not currently have in place the domestic institutions needed to fully comply with UNFCCC JI eligibility rules.[30] And, rather than preclude projects in countries that have pledged emission ceilings while permitting them in countries that have not, the UNFCCC devised a second Track-Two procedure for JI similar in structure to the CDM project cycles. Track-Two projects are monitored by the Article 6 supervisory committee, also known as the Joint Implementation Supervisory Committee (JISC), which plays a role similar to the CDM Board. ERUs generated by Track-Two projects are measured against a baseline, whose methodology has been approved, as determined by an accredited independent entity (AIE) recognized by the JISC. In practice, several of the firms certified to validate CDM baselines (as DOEs) are also certified as to validate JI baselines (as AIEs).

---

[29]To be eligible for participation in either project-based mechanism, Annex I countries ratify the Kyoto Protocol, calculate their assigned amount, establish a national system for estimating emissions and removals, and put in place a national registry to record and track the creation and movement of related tradable assets.

[30]As of February 2008, only the Czech Republic, Greece, Japan, New Zealand, and Slovakia had met UNFCCC eligibility requirements.

Land Management Projects

Rule-making for sinks and land-use projects proved difficult, and it was not until the Bonn Conference of the Parties in 2003 that guidelines for LULUCF CDM projects emerged. The projects are complex and involve measuring the net change in carbon stocks for particular sites and any related increases in emissions off-site, taking into account above-on-and-below-ground biomass and soil organic carbon. The projects are also long-lived and subject to reversibility because of human activity such as logging or natural events such as forest fires or disease. Because of these characteristics, many feared that the projects would not deliver sound environmental benefits. Added to this was a concern that CDM market economics would favor projects based on fast-growing industrial plantations, crowding out projects that are community-based and that promote biodiversity.[31] Consequently, there was opposition to allowing land-use projects under CDM, and the rules that eventually emerged are cautious and restrict the scope for land-use projects.

In particular, current rules permit afforestation and reforestation projects but exclude projects designed to slow deforestation. Moreover, rules limit the total amount of land-use CERs that can be used to meet Kyoto obligations during the first commitment period.[32] To address reversibility, net removals from the project are certified every five years. Certified reductions from land-use projects are given a different status, and project developers can choose between two types of CERs: Long-term CERs (lCERs), which expire at the end of the project's crediting periods, or temporary CERs (tCERs), that expire at the end of the next commitment period.[33] (For example, tCERs issued during the first commitment period would expire at the end of the second commitment period.) If the project performs as planned, new tCERs are issued to replace expiring ones until the end of the project's crediting period. However, Annex B countries that use tCERs during the first commitment period have to replace them during the next commitment period with so-called permanent credits: AAus, ERUs, RMUs, or CERs from non-LULUCF projects. The same restriction does

---

[31] Hunt (2008) reports that this may be the case for tropical Australia.

[32] An Annex-B party's use of LULUCF CERs cannot exceed 5% of their base-year emissions.

[33] To complicate matters, project developers can choose two types of project crediting periods: one with a set crediting period of 30 years, and a 20-year crediting period eligible for two renewals (for a maximum of 60 years.)

not apply to the use of lCERs; however, if the accumulated stocks of stored carbon from a project for which lCERs have been issued declines during the five-year certifications, Annex-B countries must replace a proportional share of the lCERs that they used. If a project fails to submit a certification report, all lCERs issued to the project must be replaced with other credits.

Even though IPCC reports note the large potential for enhancing or preserving sinks, especially in Latin America, few CDM projects have been proposed to date.[34] And, as a practical matter, the limit on their use during the first commitment period has not been binding; less than 2.5% of the allowed amount has been contracted so far by governments with Kyoto obligations.[35]

Supplementarity, Additionality, Diversion, and Carry Over

Supplementarity

As discussed, there is a long-standing concern that the flexibility mechanisms will weaken the environmental efficacy of the climate change framework. In turn, these have led to safeguards in the project cycles and explicit or implied constraints on how tradable carbon permits can be traded. A principal concern relates to emission trading and a belief that reduction pledged under the Kyoto Protocol are, in the aggregate, not significantly different from the level of emissions that would otherwise occur. This concern stems chiefly from a large supply of excess allowances resulting from a restructuring of transitional economies since 1990. These allowances are referred to as "hot air," and modeling results suggest that the availability of excess allowances will lower the overall price of tradable permits. The issue also relates to credits arising from projects since these can add to the overall supply of tradable permits.

While lower carbon prices would reduce many of the economic costs of the treaty, lower prices would also lead to fewer emission reductions in Annex B countries. Moreover, lower prices would provide lower incentives

---

[34]In their IPCC report, Fisher *et al.* (2007) note studies indicating that 15%–40% of total cumulative abatement of the next century could be provided by land-use mitigation options.

[35]See Pedroni (2005) for a general discussion. Olschewski *et al.* (2005) provides a case study from Patagonia.

to develop and use new technologies. During negotiations, moral and equity arguments were put forward as well against relying on traded permits (Lecocq and Ambrosi, 2007).

As discussed, negotiators reached agreement on emission allocations well before deciding on how the flexibility mechanisms would work. Consequently, as concerns rose over the aggregate supply of first-period allowances, negotiators chose to focus on restricting how the allowances might be used, rather than revisiting the allocation decision. In particular, although the treaty places no explicit restrictions on the combination of instruments that Annex B countries can use to meet their obligations, there is ample language in the climate change framework that implies restrictions on the use of credits overall and on the use of project credits. For example, Article 17 of the Kyoto Protocol states that the use of emissions trading to meet Kyoto commitments shall be "supplemental to domestic actions." Article 6 says that credits from JI projects shall be "supplemental to domestic actions" for the purpose of meeting reduction commitments. And Article 12 says that countries can use credits from the CD to meet "part of their quantified emission limitation and reduction commitments." The uncertain question of how substantially countries can depend on traded credits is referred to as *supplementarity*, based on the language of Article 17, and remains controversial. The role of excess allowances factor into most of the modeling efforts discussed later in the chapter. Studies that focus especially on "hot air" include Ellerman and Wing (2000); Victor, Nakićenović, and Victor (2001); Böhringer and Löschel (2003); Maeda (2003); Klepper and Peterson (2005); and Böhringer, Moslener, and Sturm (2007).

As will be discussed in more detail in the fourth section, there is political resistance in several Annex B countries to rely significantly on emission trading and policies that limit the use of tradable units are in place. As the term "hot air" connotes, there is a view that some AAUs do not contribute materially to emission reductions. From the perspective of countries holding surplus AAUs, this undermines their value. In response, countries like Bulgaria, Latvia, and Ukraine have developed green investment schemes (GISs), where proceeds from the sale of AAUs are invested in other projects with environmental integrity. Blyth and Baron (2003) provide an overview.

Additionality and baselines

A related concern with the flexibility mechanisms has to do with environmental gains arising from project investment. Here the concern is that project outcomes may not be different from business-as-usual outcomes. Language in the Kyoto Protocol (Article 12) states that reductions in emissions from CDM projects should be "additional to any that would occur in the absence of the certified project activity" (Para 5c), and this has given rise to the notion of baseline additionality.

There are several types of additionality discussed in the literature on carbon projects that potentially have a bearing on CDM baselines and approval by the CDM Board. The ones that relate most closely to baselines are environmental additionality, technology additionality, and investment additionality. *Technology additionality* implies using the best available technologies. This relates to the CDM in that the mechanism is expected to facilitate technology transfer. *Environmental additionality* is, at least conceptually, straightforward and implies that project emission outcomes are lower when compared to a business-as-usual baseline. *Investment additionality* is a related baseline concept that means that the project in question would not be profitable without additional funding — presumably obtained in return for offsets. This means that any investment project that meets certain profitability standards falls within the business-as-usual scenario, even if the project displaces emissions. In this sense, investment additionality precludes a re-labeling of existing projects as CDM projects. It also addresses the emergence of new technologies that are, in and of themselves, profitable and emission-reducing. Even so, finding the appropriate measure of profitability is difficult. Moreover, establishing a too-stringent standard would exclude projects that can deliver offsets at low cost, while setting lax standards can undercut the project's environmental additionality.[36]

Another type of additionality, *financial additionality*, has to do with the use of bilateral aid. The term was originally used in connection with the AIJ program and has to do with a fear that Annex B countries would simply divert existing overseas development assistance (ODA) into AIJ projects.[37] More recently, financial additionality is addressed in the Marrakesh Accords, which state that public funding for CDM projects should not "result in the diversion of official development assistance and is to be separate from and not counted towards the financial obligations of Parties included in Annex I." (Preamble of Decision 17/CP.7, UNFCCC,

---

[36]Asuka and Takeuchi (2004) discuss environmental, investment, and financial additionality. Greiner and Michaelowa (2003) provide a good discussion of the debate concerning investment additionality rules.

[37]See discussions in Ghosh and Puri (1994) and Parikh (1995).

2001: p. 20). As Dutschke and Michaelowa (2006) point out, financial additionality would appear to rule out the use of ODA funds for the direct purchase of CERs, and the authors note that the OECD's Development Assistance Committee has proposed rules that would deduct publicly financed CERs from official ODA. However, CDM projects are intended to contain a sustainable development element, and a case can be made that public funds spent to bolster the development impact of CDM projects should count as ODA. Similarly, there may be good reasons for ODA on public goods such as building the institutions that support and monitor CDM markets. Even so, controversy persists on whether such spending is additional or a diversion of existing funds and the practical problem of how to measure financial additionality remains.

As discussed, the decision by delegates to require project-level reviews of project-level baselines was prompted by a desire to safeguard the environmental integrity of the climate change framework. Even so, several authors have advocated setting sectoral or industry-level baselines. For example, Zhang, Heller, and May (2005) discuss how this might be accomplished for electricity producers in China. Largely, the arguments for doing so are based on arguments that project baselines are costly, arbitrary, and unlikely to fully safeguard environmental integrity.[38] Moreover, project-by-project approval precludes the potential for the restructuring of transport systems, which may have substantial positive spillover effects in the long run. In contrast, the environmental safeguards associated with sectoral baselines may be second best but may substantially lower costs and regulatory uncertainty and could potentially play a large role in establishing low-emission development pathways.

Managing tradable units inventories under Kyoto

The Kyoto Protocol and a series of rules issued as part of the Marrakesh Accords govern how countries manage their inventories of measured emissions and tradable permits. For one, in order to participate in emission trading, Annex I countries must create a national registry to keep track of

---

[38] Geres and Michaelowa (2002) and Shrestha and Timilsina (2002) discuss indirect leakages related to project baselines. Transaction costs and barriers that may not be fully accounted when investment additionality is determined are discussed by Renz (1998); Heller (1998); Michaelowa and Fages (1999); Woodward (2000); and Brechet and Lussis (2006).

their tradable units and must file annual reports on emissions. In addition, a series of rules govern how countries must mange their inventories within a reporting period and across reporting periods. How countries manage their inventories within the first commitment period is governed by the *commitment period reserve rule*. This rule is designed to address concerns that incautious sales of excess permits would leave some countries unable to meet their targets. Keeping in mind that the current commitment period spans five years while greenhouse gas inventories are reviewed annually, each Annex I Party must maintain in its national registry a "commitment period reserve," which cannot be below 90% of the Party's assigned amount or five times its most recently review inventory, whichever is lowest.[39]

How inventories can be managed between commitment periods are governed by the banking rule, the suspension rule, and the restoration rule. The *banking rule* is straightforward and set out in Article 3 of the Kyoto Protocol, which states that any difference between emissions and assigned amounts can be carried forward into the next commitment period. Borrowing from future commitment periods is limited by the suspension rule and penalized by the restoration rule. The *suspension rule*, based on Article 17 of the Protocol, states that countries that are in deficit at the end of the first commitment period cannot export additional transfers until the deficit is eliminated. What's more, the *restoration rule* states that each unit deficit during the first commitment period will be matched by a reducing second period allowances by 1.3 units.

Even so, because compliance is voluntary and because the cost of rebalancing inventories is low, the combined rules are not expected to greatly influence the overall cost of the treaty or ultimately affect compliance. For example, Godal and Klaassen (2006) use a numerical model to assess the role of the four rules on costs to treaty participants individually and collectively and also Hovi, Froyn, and Bang (2007) discuss the determinants of treaty compliance.

Compatibility with the Trade Agreements[40]

Generally, Parties to the UNFCCC are also members of the World Trade Organization and language in the climate change framework urges

---

[39]Net holdings of ERUs, CERs, AAUs, and RMUs for the relevant commitment period comprise the commitment period reserve.

[40]Brewer (2003) and the World Bank (2008a) provide good overviews.

compatibility between the two.[41] Even so, the basic principles underlying the treaties differ, and there are potential areas for conflict.[42] As discussed, the Kyoto Protocol is built around a principle of common but differentiated responsibilities. In contrast, the WTO promotes trade based on the principle that national policies will not discriminate against goods based on national origin. Moreover, for the most part, the international trade system characterizes goods based on physical description, while the processes by which goods are produced are central to greenhouse gas accounting. At the same time, Brewer (2003) makes the point that the two are, from a narrow legalistic point of view, compatible because the climate change framework has no enforcement mechanism that would conflict with WTO judgments. Additionally, Werksman (1999) argues that the system of emission trading established under the Kyoto Protocol should be unaffected by the WTO agreement, since emission allowances are licenses or permits rather than goods or services under WTO law. Still, there are potential conflicts.

As discussed, differences in how greenhouse gas emissions are regulated generate terms-of-trade effects because some industries pay to use the atmosphere as a depository for greenhouse gases while others do not, thereby creating advantages for industries that are unregulated.[43] The resulting trade diversion can affect incomes and can also lead to increased emissions elsewhere, an example of a more general problem known as "leakage" in the climate change literature. Modeling results suggest this problem can be significant, a topic we return to later in the chapter.

While the best approach may be to reach a satisfactory policy treatment for climate change separately, Barrett (2011) notes that an absence of progress on climate change may provoke countries to seek alternatives via trade policy. He points to examples where trade agreements have been used effectively to enforce natural resource concerns but argues that the problem of climate change is ill suited to this type of remedy. Still, climate policy instruments based on trade have been discussed. For example,

---

[41] As Brewer (2003) points out, Article 2.3 of the Kyoto Protocol and Articles 3.5 and 4.2 of the UNFCCC urges Parties to implement policies that minimize adverse effects on international trade and refrain from arbitrary restrictions on trade.

[42] For example, Green (2006) argues that the WTO Agreement in its current form precludes some types of beneficial subsidies.

[43] See Considine and Larson (2006) for a related discussion on the use of atmosphere as an input to production.

Biermann and Brohm (2005) argue that there is scope under trade law for border-tax adjustments that would penalize imported goods that embody higher emissions, but concede that the related rules are far from clear. Stiglitz (2006) suggests using the WTO appeals process to force wealthy countries to adequately regulate greenhouse gas emissions since failing to do so creates trade advantages.[44] Zhang and Assunção (2003) point out potential areas of conflict regarding subsidies, energy efficiency standards, eco-labeling, government procurement, and carbon taxes.

Separate from potential conflict, several authors point out that there is ample scope for reducing greenhouse gas emissions by removing trade obstacles. For example, a World Bank study (2008a) concludes that removing trade barriers to clean energy technologies in 18 developing countries would significantly boost related trade, result in technology transfers, and reduce emissions.[45] Reducing restrictions on goods and services related to the CDM project cycle is another example. Brewer (2003) provides additional examples.

EXPECTED OUTCOMES FROM THE CLIMATE CHANGE FRAMEWORK

Negotiators faced the practical tasks of deciding upon the objectives of the climate change framework and devising instruments that achieve those objectives in a fair and efficient way. Both tasks are steeped in uncertainty. Even so, decisions have been taken based on informed expectations about the relationships between greenhouse gas emissions and climate change and on how the provisions of the treaty will work, including the Protocol's innovative flexibility mechanisms. In particular, the flexibility mechanisms are expected to lessen the cost of meeting the environmental objectives of the treaty. Incentives and new markets related to the treaty are expected to mobilize private capital. For developing countries, the treaty is expected

---

[44] Article XX of GATT 1994 allows for trade interventions to protect necessary to protect human, animal, or plant life or health or exhaustible natural resources as long as they are not arbitrarily or inconsistently applied. Whether this provides an endorsement of process- and production-related criteria for trade interventions is subject to debate. See Ahn (1999) and Jackson (2000) and the discussion in Zhang and Assunção (2003).

[45] The studied technologies are clean coal, wind power, solar power, and efficient lighting.

to generate inflows of capital and technology and contribute to sustainable development. Early project investments through JI and CDM are expected to set countries on a lower carbon path, by supplanting commonly used technologies in long-lived and irreversible investments with carbon-saving alternatives. In this section, we briefly discuss the literature related to evaluating the benefits and costs of limits on greenhouse gas emissions and how the flexibility mechanisms might work.

Policy Evaluations and Predictions

Most often in economics, policy evaluations are based on historical assessments. In the case of integrated evaluations of climate change and its economic impact, evaluations are forward looking and rely heavily on models built up from current and historical physical, technical, institutional, and economic relationships. For the most part, the model predictions are against hypothetical alternatives, some of which are unlikely to occur. Still, the models used to evaluate climate change policy contain predictions about the scale of carbon markets and how markets they might work. There is a substantial literature on how to model climate change policies. It is well reviewed elsewhere, and this section draws on that work. Comprehensive surveys are given in Weyant (1999, 2004), Löschel (2002), Springer (2003), Sands (2004), and most recently in the Working Group III contribution to the Fourth IPCC Assessment (IPCC, 2007a).

Model Structures and Technology

Springer (2003) broadly categorizes the reviewed models into five groups. The first is composed of integrated assessment models, where physical and human activities are jointly modeled. As Springer notes, there is some overlap between this group and the remaining, since the economic components of the integrated models employ CGE or energy system models. Examples of integrated models are discussed in Manne and Richels (1999), Nordhaus and Boyer (2000), Nordhaus (2001), and Jacoby *et al.* (2006). Another common approach relies on marginal abatement cost curves to examine the effects of trade. Examples include Jotzo and Michaelowa (2002), Löschel and Zhang (2002), and Stevens and Rose (2002). A less common approach focuses on the macroeconomic tradeoffs between monetary policy and employment [see, for example, McKibbin, Shackelton, and Wilcoxen (1999)]. An alternative approach is to employ technical engineering models of sectors or energy systems. These bottom-up models are sometimes integrated with other sectors via a CGE model. IPCC (2007a) contains a review of several bottom-up sector models.

An important distinction between the models is whether greenhouse gas concentration is exogenous to the model.[46] Optimization models let the economic sectors maximize profits while adjusting the level of emissions endogenously. This can be done either by adjusting levels of production and the mix of sectoral output or by introducing and endogenously selecting production technologies with different greenhouse gas intensities. The other approach is to exogenously impose a greenhouse gas concentration level on the model and find the most cost-effective way to reach it. Both approaches can be either static or dynamic. While endogenous technology adoption can be part of the model, CO_2 concentration can also be addressed via level of production only.

Springer notes a variety of common outcomes from most modeling exercises. For example, most models find that trade in permits substantially lowers the cost of meeting Kyoto objectives, while trade restrictions increase costs and potentially lead to market power concerns. The withdrawal of the US is expected to substantially lower the environmental efficacy of the climate change framework. Dynamically, most modeling exercises reveal what Nordhaus (2007) describes as a climate-policy ramp, whereby policies aimed at slowing climate change tighten over time.

Another important modeling dynamic involves the treatment of technical change.[47] In most modeling efforts, technical change most often enters climate change policy models exogenously. In bottom-up models, technical change consists of optimizing among a fixed set of engineering technical relationships. The same can be said of some of the models that rely on abatement cost curves built up from information on the energy structure of economic regions. In top-down models, technology is reflected in the parameters of the modeled economic relationships, which are expected to change with shifting technologies. The most straightforward way is to think in terms of the parameters of a production function where the parameters imply an underlying technology. For this reason, Löschel (2002) argues that endogenous technical change is more easily modeled within a top-down

---

[46]See Manne and Rutherford (1994) for a discussion.
[47]See Carraro and Galeotti (1997), Löschel (2002), and references therein.

structure. Still, shifts in production function parameters are also consistent with the endogenous adoption of existing technologies (Mundlak, 1993).[48] Moreover, efficiency gains can also come about because of a changing input composition as capital levels change over the longer term (Sands, 2004). Consequently, what distinguishes the endogenous technology change models is a structural link between research expenditures and innovation. Endogenous technical change models that take into account research and development investments include Goulder and Schneider (1999); Buonanno, Carraro, and Galeotti (2003); and Nordhaus (2002).

One primary purpose to which models have been put into action is the development of a schedule of carbon prices that is consistent with different carbon concentration levels and that leads to stable but different long-run climates. Estimates gathered for the Fourth IPCC Assessment suggest a carbon dioxide price from US\$20–80 per ton by 2030 and rising to US\$30–155 by 2050 is consistent with scenarios that stabilize atmospheric carbon concentrations at 550 ppm, a level thought to be consistent with moderate climate change. Importantly, models that allowed for endogenous technical change suggested that the same level of atmospheric concentration levels could be obtained at significantly lower carbon prices (IPCC, 2007b). The modeling results, which suggest a significant role for new technologies, are reflected in a set of policy proposals aimed at funding global research. We take up this topic in the following section. The same models are used to measure any adverse impacts of economic growth resulting from Annex B emission reductions. For purposes of comparison, the costs are often expressed in terms of reduced GDP. Model predictions of 2050 GDP reductions reviewed by the IPCC (2007b) associated with stabilization around 550 ppm range from near zero to 4%.[49]

Numeric models have also been relied upon to provide estimates of the potential benefits of the Kyoto Protocol's flexibility mechanisms. As Springer (2003) notes in his review, a common finding is that the costs of reaching greenhouse reduction goals are greatly reduced by rules that allowed spatial and temporal flexibility. By way of example, early model results by Bernstein, Montgomery, and Rutherford (1999) suggest that flexible trading rules could reduce the price of carbon permits — which can be

---

[48]The diffusion of known technologies is well illustrated by Oda *et al.*'s (2007) bottom-up study of the Japanese steel industry.

[49]Sathaye *et al.* (2007) provide a survey of alternative welfare indicators.

seen as the marginal cost of emission reductions — by a factor of 7 in the European Union and by a factor of 16 in Japan.[50]

Early results, which indicate the importance of trade and project investment, have held up with time; however, recent modeling efforts have illustrated how the stringency of emission reduction targets significantly affects the quantitative estimates of the cost-saving from trade. For example, under scenarios consistent with earlier assumptions, den Elzen and Both (2002) estimate that the Kyoto flexibility mechanisms reduce the overall cost of meeting the first commitment period targets by 40%. However, the authors also show that US withdrawal from the agreement greatly reduces the need for the provisions; the predicted trade under the provisions is cut in half as aggregate abatement levels drop significantly without demand for offsets from the US.

Global averages of the costs of mitigation mask differences in the distributional effects of climate change. As Mendelsohn, Dinar, and Williams (2006) note, early models of climate change suggested that the effects of climate change would be distributed uniformly among the rich and poor. More recent results suggest that this is not the case and that the world's poor will be disproportionately affected. The study suggests this result comes about primarily because of where the poor live. In the abovementioned paper by Mendelsohn, Dinar, and Williams, the authors develop sectoral response functions and country-specific measures of geography, population, and income to develop country-specific measures of climate change. They conclude that the poorest half of the world's nations will suffer most from climate change while the net consequences for wealthy countries are mild. Based on current income, land use, and population distributions, Dasgupta *et al.* (2007) conclude that the countries mostly likely affected by rising sea levels are poor. Bosello, Roson, and Tol (2007) reach a similar conclusion based on modeling results. In a related paper, Bosello, Roson, and Tol (2006) conclude that adverse health consequences from climate change will also fall most heavily on poor countries. Hertel and Rosch (2010) review modeling efforts that quantify the consequences for poverty of climate change via its effects on agriculture. This problem is complex since

---

[50]See Nordhaus and Boyer (2000), Springer (2003), Weyant (2004), Sands (2004), and Working Group III's contribution to the Fourth IPCC Assessment (IPCC, 2007) for additional reviews of modeling approaches and results. Painuly (2001) reviews numerical models that address project-based investments in developing countries; Muller and Mestelman (1998) review related laboratory-based experiments.

farmers and agronomists constantly adapt to changes in biological threats resources prices by through changes in crop selection and farming methods and adoption of new technologies. Still, the authors note that most studies conclude that food prices will rise in the face of climate change, bringing with it hardship for the urban poor.

Market Power

As discussed, the supply of excess AAUs available in the economies that have restructured to become more energy efficient since 1990 has spurred a set of policy discussions around the topic of supplementarity. More recently, authors have argued that the concentration of excess allowances in a handful of countries, especially in Russia and Ukraine, conveys a degree of market power that might encourage countries to withhold AAUs from the market, resulting in a higher price than competitive models might suggest (Barron, 1999). This possibility raises the question of whether or not there is a practical way to exercise this latent market power. As Klepper and Peterson (2005) point out, the climate change framework is not explicit about the relative roles that governments and private firms play in emission trading, so it is possible for governments to restrict trade in a cooperative way that extracts rents and the prices of tradable permits. Hagem and Maestad (2006) analyze optimal strategies for a country that has market power in an international market for emission permits and at the same time is an oil and gas exporter. In applying the analysis to the case of Russia, they show that a country can benefit from coordinating the permit and oil and gas exports, depending on the level of substitution between the types of fuels exported. They conclude that strategic behavior affects decisions that lead to market power and may impose inefficiencies on carbon trading, either directly or indirectly.

Market power can arise from the buyer's side as well. Carlén (2003) uses a laboratory experiment to explore this question, but does not "observe that the dominant buyer country exerts market power by withholding demand from the market as predicted by standard economic theory ... the outcome casts doubt over the validity of assessment of market power effects in international carbon emission trading that indicate substantial efficiency losses" (Carlén, 2003: p. 23).

Several authors have also explored whether issues of market power, raised initially in the context of international trading, arise in the context of domestic market regulations. For example, Kuik and Mulder (2004), in their analysis of alternative regulatory approaches to emissions in the Netherlands, assert that the trading schemes will lead to different market clearing permit prices, the effects of which will differ depending upon the scale of the firm. Firms in sectors such as agriculture will be disadvantaged, because the sector is composed of relatively many small units that face higher transaction costs under trading schemes. Using a static game theory model applied to a regional electricity market, Lise *et al.* (2006) find that a reduction in the market power of large producers may benefit both the consumers and the environment. Taken together, the two studies indicate the importance of domestic structure on policy outcomes and suggest that more work is still needed to better understand the relationship between market power and the efficiency of the carbon market and its impact on global emissions.

Leakages, Ancillary Benefits, and Crowding Out

A practical concern arising from differentiated obligations has to do with the interaction between those who have assumed obligations and those who have not. The set of secondary effects, known as carbon leakage, can come about because economic activities shift due to changing prices and terms of trade. Leakage can occur because of differences in a variety of policy instruments, but the term most often refers to the set of secondary effects that result in increased emissions in countries without emission limits that partly or fully offset the environmental gains from limiting emission in Annex B countries. As discussed, this has to do in part with trade rules and their compatibility with climate change obligations.

General equilibrium models are well suited for analyzing carbon leakages, and this literature is reviewed in Burniaux and Martin (2000) and Barker *et al.* (2007). These studies find evidence of leakages of varying degrees. For example Paltsev (2001) reports a leakage rate of around 10%, while Babiker (2005), observing energy-intensive activities, reports scenario outcomes ranging in global leakage rates between 25% and 130% — i.e., under some scenarios, emission limits increased net emissions. At the same time, studies suggest that leakages are likely to vary greatly among subsectors. For example, in a detailed study of the cement industry, Szabó *et al.* (2006) suggest leakage rates of 29% in the EU. More recently, Di Maria and van der Werf (2008) develop a conceptual model that suggests that the terms-of-trade effects captured by most CGE models ignore the offsetting effect of induced technological change and consequently overestimate leakages.

Other secondary effects, often referred to as ancillary effects in the climate change literature, have to do with positive welfare gains that accrue from greenhouse gas mitigation. One example is associated with the double-dividend welfare gain arrived at by taxing a negative externality instead of economic goods and services (Terkla, 1984; Lee and Misiolek, 1986). The "double dividend" stems from the recovery of deadweight welfare losses related to taxing productive economic activity. In the case of climate change policy, a positive effect on economic growth is accomplished by using revenue raised by a carbon tax or by auctioned permits to displace distortionary factor taxes, such as payroll taxes or taxes on capital assets, thereby generating both environmental and economic benefits. A series of numerical studies showing that factor market distortions swamped the positive effects of marginal tax cuts and cast doubt on the potential for a double dividend (Bovenberg and de Mooij, 1994; Parry, 1995; Bovenberg and Goulder, 1996; Koskela, Schon, and Sinn, 1998). Later, Williams (1999, 2002) and Parry and Bento (2000) described special situations that might lead to a double dividend. Most recently, Bento and Jacobsen (2007) use a conceptual and numeric model to show that, when rents related to the use exhaustible resources are not fully taxed, net welfare gains constituting a double dividend can be generated when environmental taxes are used to cut pre-existing labor taxes. Country studies include McKitrick (1997), Canada; Garbaccio, Mun, and Jorgenson (1999), China; Edwards and Hutton (2001), UK; Ibarraran, Viniegra, and Boyd (2001), Mexico; Roson (2003), Italy; and Takeda (2007), Japan.

In their review of country studies, Barker *et al.* (2007) conclude that the benefits associated with revenue recycling (replacing current taxes with revenues raised through climate policy) can be significant. Taken in combination with other ancillary benefits, this greatly expands the scope for low-cost and no-regrets outcomes. We return to this topic later in this section.

Another set of positive externalities, referred to collectively as co-benefits, include collateral health benefits that are realized when other types of pollutants are reduced together with greenhouse gases. Both top-down and bottom-up models have been employed to measure such effects. For example, Li (2002, 2006) looks at health benefits associated with greenhouse gas emissions in Thailand, and Burtraw *et al.* (2003) examine the potential for positive health gains associated with the limits on US greenhouse gas emissions. Dudek, Golub, and Strukova (2003); Dessus and O'Connor (2003); and Aunan *et al.* (2003) examine the same issue in Russia,

Chile, and China, respectively. A series of papers, including Gundimeda (2004), Plantinga and Wu (2003), Feng and Kling (2005), and Yemshanov *et al.* (2005), look at forestry and carbon sequestration co-benefits. These benefits are tied to both the environmental services generated by sustained forests and incomes associated with payments for environmental services. Pendell *et al.* (2007) provide an example related to soil fertility.

In their synthesis, Barker *et al.* (2007) note that conservative studies of the ancillary health benefits associated with climate change policy can equal 30%–50% of estimated mitigation costs, while some studies, especially of developing countries, indicate that health benefits can exceed mitigation costs. They also note that several studies suggest that a large share of business-as-usual emissions that can be reduced without welfare loss: 13%–23% in India (Bussolo and O'Connor, 2001); 15%–20% for China (O'Connor, 2003); and 20% for Chile (Dessus and O'Connor, 2003). Other studies suggest savings could be done on other types of air pollution controls as well. For example, Burtraw *et al.* (2003) estimate that a 31% reduction in CO_2 emissions in the US would drive the price of SO_2 permits to zero.

Agriculture relies heavily on land use, and there are substantive low-cost mitigation opportunities from storing carbon in soils and by protecting existing carbon pools (Barker *et al.*, 2007; Lal, 2009). Land restoration efforts, cropland and pasture management, and improved management of animal and crop wastes can boost on-farm productivity while contributing to adaptation and mitigation efforts. Often, changing agricultural land-use leads to greater co-benefits than mitigation benefits (Larson, Dinar, and Frisbie, 2011; Larson, Dinar, and Blankespoor, 2012).

A potential negative externality recently identified by Nordhaus (2007) has to do with the consequences of large inflows of carbon financing into small economies. Potentially, large inflows of investment tied to one sector can lead to a currency appreciation, changing domestic relative prices to the disadvantage of parts of the economy and crowding out economic activity in those sectors. This phenomenon is known as the Dutch Disease and is most often explained in terms of commodity booms (Corden, 1984; van Wijnbergen, 1986).[51] There is also a body of research that suggests that economic growth in resource-rich developing countries has been slow because of related rent-seeking, corruption, violence, fiscal mismanagement, and a

---

[51] There is a related literature having to do with aid flows as well. See Agénor, Bayraktar, and Aynaaoui (2008) for a recent discussion.

crowding-out of other economic activities.[52] While crowding-out stems from a general equilibrium trade effect, the remaining problems relate to weak institutions. To date, the most significant investment flows under CDM have gone to large economies, and few studies have considered the possible consequences of project-based investment flows. In one innovative study focusing on two large economies, Böhringer, Conrad, and Loshel (2003) look at a joint model of Germany and the Indian electricity sector and find large welfare gains for both countries.[53]

Uncertainty, Discounting, and Intergenerational Tradeoffs

How best to model the uncertainties associated with climate change remains an unresolved challenge. The recent IPCC assessment reviews the potential for abrupt climate change with catastrophic results, including raising sea levels, droughts, and an increased intensity of tropical typhoons (Meehl *et al.* 2007). Moreover, because greenhouse gases are long-lived, policy decisions have cumulative and irreversible effects. Wirl (2006, 2007) provides a conceptual approach to model types of environmental irreversibility under uncertainty in a stochastic setting and provides a brief review of the related literature. Still, little is known about the point at which a particular extreme climate event would occur or, for that matter, about the associated probabilities. Even so, decisions are taken sequentially, and this provides some scope for developing and incorporating new information through time (Valverde, Jacoby, and Kaufman, 1999). As Pindyck (2007) points out, the practical consequence of limited information on probabilities is that uncertainty is handled in the context of specific models.

In terms of numeric modeling efforts to assess policy outcomes, the consequences of uncertainty come into play largely through discounting rates used to value future events. Since the consequences of near-term policies persist in accumulations of greenhouse gases in the atmosphere and in accumulations of capital and technologies, advantages or disadvantages gained by one set of policies over another are difficult to reverse as time goes by.

---

[52]For an early discussion of the "resource curse," see Gelb *et al.* (1988). See also Mehlum, Moene, and Torvik (2006); Auty (2007); and references therein.

[53]Advocates also argue that administrative and other transaction costs would be lower under a carbon tax. See Hahn and Hester (1989) and Stavin (1995) for early general discussions of tradable permits and transaction costs.

For this reason, the rate of comparing early costs to future benefits is crucial to modeling efforts. Halsnaes *et al.* (2007) review the risk and uncertainty literature as it relates to climate change and describe how the issue affects IPCC assessments.

Arguments about appropriate rates of social discounting relate to positive conceptual and empirical studies as well as more controversial normative approaches. Studies of past returns to capital (financial and human) suggest positive rates of return, which imply positive discount rates for future benefits arrived from present investments. This finding is not controversial in itself and is discussed in Arrow *et al.* (1996) as the background to the second IPCC assessment. In contrast, normative arguments over whether market-based rates are indicative and an appropriate measure for discounting future welfare are controversial and pivotal for policy assessments.

Generally, assessments of climate change policy are based on positive and often constant discount rates. In some instances, these are based on observed market rates on the notion that policy tradeoffs reflected in climate change scenarios should use the same metric as other policy tradeoffs related to trade or debt. Critics argue that, because of market imperfections, such rates are biased upward and that lower rates should be employed. Even so, separate from arguments concerning appropriate levels, an important consequence of positive discount rates is that the welfare of future generations has little present value. Some writers find this objectionable based on moral grounds and argue that the approach for valuing intergenerational transfers should differ from the approach taken for capital. To take this into account, studies sometimes distinguish between the rate used to reflect the time-value of capital and the rate used to discount future welfare, sometimes referred to as the pure rate of social time preference. While rates measuring returns to capital have an empirical basis, arguments concerning an appropriate way to discount the interests of future generations are philosophical and subject to stark dissonance. Yet the assumption matters critically for numerical models of the cost and benefits of climate change policies. For example, Nordhaus (2007b) maintains that the use of a near-zero social time-preference rate explains why the *Stern Review* (Stern, 2007) calls for stronger early mitigation interventions than does the general literature.

Most studies use positive and constant rates to discount future welfare, but several authors propose that discount rates should fall with time. For example, based on uncertain returns to capital, Weitzman (2001) argues for a declining discount rate as do Gollier (2002) and Newell and Pizer (2004).

Weitzman (1998) argues in favor of using a zero discount rate for half-century time horizons and, as mentioned, the *Stern Review* relies on a near-zero discount rate. Portney and Weyant (1999) provide a good review of the related literature. Dasgupta (2005, 2007) looks at the discounting issue. The ethical and conceptual bases for the discount assumptions of the Stern report are discussed by Beckerman and Hepburn (2007), Dasgupta (2007), and Nordhaus (2007a).

Uncertainties over the consequences of climate change and over climate change policies have microeconomic effects on the decisions taken by firms to invest and scientists to invent. When uncertainties are likely to diminish with time, procrastination on both types of decisions carries a "real options" value, an evaluation that researchers have applied to climate change problems. See for example, Heydari, Ovenden, and Siddiqui (2012); Kikuchi (2011); and Kettunen, Bunn, and Blyth (2011).

Technology Development and Transfer as a Policy Instrument

As discussed, modeling outcomes point to the importance of new technologies in affecting the cost of meeting emission reduction goals. However, several studies indicate that past investments in related research and development have been insufficient, suggesting that markets for new technologies will need non-market support. For example, Margolis and Kammen (1999) show, using data from the US, that there has been a long-term pattern of underinvestment in R&D in the energy sector, compared to other sectors. They conclude that a deployment effort for increased research in the energy sector is needed. Subsequent authors conclude that, while additional research in energy technologies is necessary to improve energy efficiency, a broader approach is needed. For example, Sagar (2000) argues that development and deployment efforts should focus on additional sectors as well as energy. Sagar and van der Zwaan (2006), using data from OECD countries, demonstrate a lack of correlation between the energy efficiency level and energy R&D. They conclude that energy R&D is a sufficient but not a necessary condition for improved energy efficiency. They identify roles for institutions, deployment, and learning as necessary conditions for transfer of energy R&D innovations to the market.

Modeling results indicating a strong role for technology and that carbon prices will be lower than expected, following the US decision not to ratify the Kyoto Protocol, have also worked to focus attention on policy instruments that support technology development and technology transfer. This interest is reflected in the climate change literature and in actions taken by the UNFCCC delegates. Institutionally, a framework was developed during the Marrakesh Conference of the Parties to enhance the implementation of Article 4.5 of the Convention, which recognizes the importance of technology development and transfer in battling climate change and allowing steady growth in developing countries. The framework includes five activities/requirements, namely technology needs and needs assessments; available technology information; enabling environments in developed and developing countries; capacity building in developing countries; and mechanisms for technology transfer. To date, there are three special funding mechanisms under the UNFCCC: the Least Developed Countries Fund, the Special Climate Change Fund, and the already-mentioned Adaptation Fund.[54] To a degree, the three funds offer ways to promote technology transfer, although the emphasis of the funds is on adaptations and also on specific areas, including agriculture, health, water resources, and disaster protection, that are expected to promote development objectives. Additionally, as discussed, CDM and JI are expected to promote technology transfer. Still, policy makers and researchers have suggested that current incentives and funding is unlikely to generate significant new technologies and have proposed additional funds emphasizing research and development.[55] Worth noting as well is a Clean Technology Fund, managed by the World Bank and backed by donor pledges of US$ 5 billion (World Bank, 2008b). The Fund, viewed as an interim measure until a future financing architecture can be established under the UNFCCC, is aimed at finding policy instruments that can accelerate the deployment, diffusion, and transfer of low-carbon technologies.

Buchner and Carraro (2005) review proposals for an international agreement for the development and diffusions of new technologies.[56] Such an agreement can be supplemental to emission controls; however, using a conceptual model, Barrett (2006) argues that agreements to limit emissions

---

[54] In addition, funding for mitigation and adaptation efforts is available under the Global Environment Facility.

[55] Within the UNFCCC framework, discussion at the Bali COP focused on new funding mechanisms for adaptation and mitigation research and the Expert Group on Technology Transfers was asked to make recommendations to develop a strategic plan to scale up investment in technology transfer (FCCC/CP/2007/L.2).

[56] Examples include Benedick (2001) and Barrett (2003).

are likely to be ineffective, leaving an agreement to promote technologies as the most practical approach to climate change. At the same time, numerical models provide evidence that the secondary effects of induced technology are small relative to the direct effects of a carbon tax and generate lower welfare gains than an equivalent control on emissions (Nordhaus, 1998; Goulder and Mathai, 2000; Parry, Pizer, and Fischer, 2003). The previously mentioned study by Buchner and Carraro concludes that a self-enforcing agreement to cooperate on technological innovation and diffusion is more likely than a cooperative agreement on emissions, but also concludes that technological cooperation by itself will be insufficient to meet reasonable abatement goals.

Technology transfer and project financing

Various approaches have been used in the literature to incorporate technology transfer in models that deal with country policies and carbon offset markets. Approaches used include country and regional case studies, optimization approaches such as growth models and CGE models, and negotiation and strategic approaches such as Game Theory. Some of the papers are process oriented and some provide estimates of economic savings.

Irrespective of the approach used, the repeated messages from the literature are similar, namely, a need for enabling local and global institutions and other arrangements that are directly and indirectly related to technology development, adjustment, and transfer. Both the case studies (Forsyth, 1999; Duic *et al.*, 2003; Forsyth, 2005), the partial equilibrium (Kemfert, 2003), the general equilibrium (Sahlén and Aronsson, 2006), and the strategic approaches (Matsuhashi, Chang, and Ishitani, 1999; Millock, 2002) suggest that there is no one policy that similarly addresses the issues countries face, but rather, each country or partnership that collaborates in the CDM setting needs a specific solution to allow technology development and its transfer. Finally, an econometric study of the reported technology transfer by project types and countries also suggests a more microscopic analysis and understanding of the differences between determinants of technology transfer (Haites, Duan, and Seres, 2006).

Present policies to technology transfer are criticized for not taking advantage of private sector capacities and international trade. Distinction is made between long-term technology sharing policies, used at present, that ignore the potential benefits of the globalization of technology investment and ownership (Forsyth, 1999). The present policy is claimed to be heavily subsidized and to the deterrence of private investors. Rather than having the state focus on the direct innovation development process, states could better impact development and transfer of technologies by improving fair trade policies, protecting intellectual property rights, and increasing public access to information about technologies (Forsyth, 2005; Millock, 2002).

Early on, researchers noted that abatement costs and the shape of the marginal abatement curves play a crucial role in rates of technology transfer. For example, based on a comparison of input–output tables, Matsuhashi, Chang, and Ishitani (1999) conclude that the potential for technology transfer between Japan and China is large under CDM; however, using game-theory and sensitivity analysis, they also show that small changes in underlying assumptions about the structure of abatement costs have significant consequences for predicted rates of transfer. They point to expected lower price of the technology and the potential for lower financial cost for the technology transfer and its positive impact on the economy as key factors affecting the economic viability of CDM technologies. Similarly, Duic *et al.* (2003) show that small changes in cost can dramatically change incentives to switch to new renewable energy technologies, even in a small economy of island nations such as Santiago and Cape Verde, where carbon intensity is low but fossil fuel prices are high.

The global (both partial and general equilibrium) models demonstrate the importance of indirect effects of trade on the transfer of clean energy technologies and hence, on economic growth. Using a partial equilibrium model, Kemfert (2003) shows that trade barriers would not only damage the economy but could also deter investments in climate-friendly technologies. Using a general equilibrium model, Sahlén and Aronsson (2006) also add labor barriers into the market of factors of production to account for north economies (capital intensive) and south economies (labor intensive). The effects of trade barriers (including labor) imply that, for a CDM setting with allowed flows of factors of production sans borders, a technology transfer from the North to the South is clearly desirable from the perspective of a "global social planner," since the welfare gain for the South outweighs the welfare loss for the North. However, if the regions impose trade barriers, then the incentives to introduce the technology transfer appear to be relatively weak from the perspective of the North. Finally, by imposing the Kyoto emission reductions on the otherwise uncontrolled market economy, the technology transfer leads to higher welfare in both regions.

The literature reviewed above employs models and normative assumptions to predict the rate of clean technology transfer between investor and host countries in the CDM-JI operations. However, looking at specific projects provides additional insights. Haites, Duan, and Seres (2006) examine claims of technology transfer in the project proposal documents of 854 early CDM projects. As the authors point out, the CDM does not have an explicit technology-transfer mandate, even though several provisions of the overall Climate Change Convention commit developed-country Parties to promote and finance such transfers. Even so, the authors find that about one-third of the CDM projects they examined made claims of technology transfer, where technology transfer takes the form of use of equipment or knowledge, not previously available in the host country. On average, more large projects claimed to transfer technology, so that two-thirds of the emission reductions from the studied projects were associated with transfer claims. Technology transfer claims also varied by technology type. In general, few projects in hydro- and energy-efficiency claimed to transfer technology (less than 15%) while most projects in agriculture, wind, and biomass claimed to promote technology transfer (81%, 41%, and 21% of the projects in each class). About half of the projects studied do not have foreign partners. Only about a quarter of these "unilateral" projects made technology transfer claims; within this group, transfer claims were higher among larger projects. This leads the authors to conclude that the probability of technology transfer increases with project size and with foreign participation.

DOMESTIC POLICIES IN THE EUROPEAN UNION, THE US, AND AUSTRALIA

As discussed, while Kyoto Protocol obligations ultimately fall to governments, the architecture of the agreement relies on markets to mobilize capital, technology, and foreign direct investment. Doing so is expected to reduce the cost of meeting the framework's environmental objectives. Still, while project cycle rules for CDM and Track-Two JI projects are explicit and apply to all Parties, domestic rules and policies are relevant. Because tradable permits have value to private firms primarily because they can be used to meet regulatory rules, differences in domestic rules can also lead to price differences for otherwise equivalent offsets. In the case of the US, which has not ratified the Protocol, and Australia, which only recently ratified the Protocol, separate voluntary and regional markets have evolved that are not entirely distinct from Kyoto markets. We discuss policies related to carbon markets for these three countries in anticipation of the market discussion in the next section.

EU Emissions Trading Scheme

The European Union's Emissions Trading Scheme (EU ETS) is one of the principal instruments that the EU relies on to meet its GHG emissions reduction requirements under the Protocol — an 8% reduction compared to 1990 levels by the first commitment period. Presently, the plan covers carbon dioxide emissions from more than 10,000 installations in the EU's 27 Member States plus, as of 2008, Norway, Iceland, and Liechtenstein, members of the European Economic Area.[57] Together, the installations account for about 40% of the EUs greenhouse gas emissions. Legislation that eventual launched the EU ETS in 2005 was approved by the European Council and the European Parliament in 2003.[58]

To date, the policy has covered two periods. Phase 1 (2005–2007) of the cap-and-trade program was intended as a trial prior to the first commitment period of the Kyoto Protocol, which coincides with Phase 2 (2008–2012). Emission allowances, called EU allowances (EUAs), are permits equivalent to one ton of emitted carbon dioxide. During the first two phases, Member States allocated allowances to their regulated installation in accordance with a National Allocation Plan (NAP). At the end of each year, regulated installations must surrender allowances equivalent to their emissions. Surplus and shortfalls can be matched through sales and purchases.

Under current rules, NAPs are subject to European Commission oversight, and the Commission has the authority to reduce (as it has done before) the number of overall EUAs under national plans if the plans appear inconsistent with business-as-usual scenarios and climate change framework obligations. The back and forth between national planners and the Commission has generated delays and regulatory uncertainties.[59] Moreover, differences and inconsistencies in the process by which national governments allocated allowances created distortions and inefficiencies, which are discussed

---

[57]Currently, the sectors covered include energy activities (e.g., electric-power generation greater than 20 MW), ferrous metals industries (iron and steel), mineral industries (cement, glass, ceramics, oil refineries, etc.), and pulp and paper industries.

[58]For background information on the EU ETS see Watanabe and Robinson (2005), Convery and Redmond (2007), and Europa (2007).

[59]For example, the Commission's review of Member NAPs required for the start of Phase II in January 2008, did not conclude until the fourth quarter of 2007.

later in this section. Under a current proposal, national plans would be abolished and replaced with an EU-wide cap based on harmonized rules. The proposal would also extend the system beyond 2012 and cover additional industries and two additional greenhouse gases, nitrous oxide and perflurocarbons. Proposed rules would also allow Phase II EUAs to be carried forward into future periods.

Although the second phase of the EU ETS has only recently begun, a growing literature assesses the early effects of the policy. The research focuses primarily on the two-stage process by which overall levels of national allowances were set and distributed to regulated installations. One area of study focuses on the bureaucratic process itself and the motivations for decisions. For example, the volume edited by Ellerman, Buchner, and Carraro (2007) looks at the process of setting Phase I allowances and decisions taken by the EC. The volume also contains country-wise case studies.

During the first phase of the EU ETS, exchanges emerged to trade contracts derived from Phase I and Phase II. As the first phase ended, contracts based on Phase I allowances drifted down to near-zero values after a dramatic price collapse in April 2006. The low ending price for Phase I contracts is taken as an indication of an overallocation; the structural break in the contract pricing has been attributed to a poorly developed system for measuring emissions and uncertain policy (Ellerman and Buchner, 2007). As discussed in Alberola, Chevallier, and Chèze (2008), allocations were based on emission projections rather than verified emission data, and when initial results on verified emissions became public, demand expectations for Phase I EUAs were revised downward. Moreover, an initial decision by France and Poland to allow firms to carry over (bank) Phase I allowances for use in Phase II was reversed during the planning of Phase II NAPs, further reducing the value of Phase I EUAs.

The sequential nature of EU policy making creates moral hazard problems when firm behavior can affect future permit allocations. This topic is discussed in the case of power generation by Neuhoff, Keats, and Sato (2006). Along a similar line, Demailly and Quirion (2006) contrast the affects of allowance allocation rules based on historic emissions (grandfathering) with the effects of output-based rules for the cement industry. Not all industries fall within the EU ETS, and differences in regulatory rules between firms inside and outside the EU ETS creates distortions, as discussed in the context of German regulations by Böhringer, Hoffmann, and Manrique-de-Lara-Peñate (2006). The free allocation of permits creates wealth transfers and these are measured in the context of power generators by Keats and Neuhoff (2005). They argue in favor of increased permit auctions, a topic also discussed by Hepburn *et al.* (2006).

Integration with the Climate Change Framework

The EU ETS is intentionally designed to work well with rules established under the Kyoto Protocol and the Marrakesh Accords.[60] In general, CERs or ERUs generated by Kyoto projects can be exchanged one-to-one with EUAs, although offsets generated from nuclear energy projects and, importantly, land-use projects are excluded. However, as discussed, most greenhouse gas emissions in the EU are regulated outside of the trading scheme, and these rules work to limit the extent to which firms can rely on Kyoto project offsets under Phase II. For one, under EC rules on supplementarity, Member States must meet at least 50% of their emission reductions domestically. In practice, Member States have placed additional (and varying) limits on the share of total emission reductions that can be met by purchasing tradable units, ranging from 8% (i.e., the Netherlands) to 50% (i.e., Spain and Ireland). Moreover, recall that countries must keep inventories of offsets in line with the commitment period reserve rule. This creates complications for managing Kyoto projects offsets since these national supplementarity targets could be exceeded if firms regulated under the EU ETS were allowed to purchase CERs and ERUs without limit. As a way of managing supplementarity, Phase II NAPs under the EU ETS place explicit caps within the national plans. In the aggregate, the national plans allow member states to supplement their allowed emissions under the EU ETS by no more than 13.36%. The limits vary among countries, ranging from zero (Estonia) to 20% (Lithuania, Norway, and Spain). In addition, in order to avoid direct and indirect "double counting," ERUs allowed into the EU ETS must originate in sectors not covered by the EU ETS.[61] These limitations potentially affect price arbitrage opportunities among the tradable permits, a topic we return to later in the chapter.

---

[60] Legislation known as the "Linking Directive" lays out the relationship between EUAs and the Kyoto-system tradable units.

[61] Direct double counting can occur when ERUs are issued after a firm reduces emissions relative to a baseline and also receives EUAs based on historical emissions. Indirect double counting can occur when a JI project earning ERUs displaces a firm that still receives EUAs. Both concepts are distinct from actual double counting when two firms surrender identically coded EUAs against their emissions — a problem that occurred repeatedly during Phase I of the EU ETS.

Regional Initiatives and Voluntary Markets

In the absence of federal regulation, alternative state, municipal, and corporate initiatives to manage greenhouse gas emission in the US have emerged. The programs encompass a range of standards for environmental and investment additionality. In general, comprehensive and binding regulations of the type found among countries that have ratified the Kyoto Protocol are absent. Nevertheless, large regional schemes are under discussion, and some innovative programs predate the EU ETS. Even so, in contrast to the European trading system, studies of US systems are not well represented in peer-reviewed economic journals.

Oregon

One example is the Oregon Carbon Dioxide Emissions Standard for New Energy Facilities, enacted in 1997 by Oregon, the first State to regulate GHG emissions. The statute requires all new power plants (and large energy facilities) to meet a carbon dioxide emissions target that is 17% better than the most efficient base-load gas plant currently operating in the US. Any emissions exceeding that standard must be matched by financed or purchased project offsets or by a fee of US$0.85 per short ton of CO_2 paid into The Climate Trust, a non-profit group established to manage offset projects on behalf of its members. There are no limitations on the geographic location or type of project providing the offsets. So far, the Climate trust manages a portfolio of 15 projects that will offset 2.7 $MtCO_2e$ (of which 1.5 $MtCO_2e$ are linked to the compliance with the Oregon Standard). In addition to common offset classes such as energy efficiency (supply side), renewable energy, and sequestration, the Climate Trust has sponsored more innovative projects, especially in the transportation sector. Some of its portfolio has besides been sold to the voluntary market.

California[62]

In 2006, the California legislature passed Assembly Bill 32 (AB 32), also called the Global Warming Solutions Act of 2006 (Global Warming Solutions Act, 2006), which legally requires California to reduce greenhouse gas emissions to 1990 levels of 427 million $MtCO_2e$ by the year 2020.

---

[62]This section draws on Dinar, Larson, and Frisbie (2011).

This amounts to a 15% reduction in 2008 GHG emissions levels, or a 30% reduction in forecasted "business as usual" GHG emissions in 2020. AB 32 directs the California Air Resources Board (CARB) to develop a plan for reducing greenhouse gas (GHG) emissions, which the agency has completed and made available for public comment (CARB, 2008, 2011). The plan has identified various emission reduction (ER) strategies targeting California subsectors and production processes, nine of which are for the agricultural sector (Climate Action Team, 2006). While ERs are mandatory for some California sectors such as industry and electricity, ERs in agriculture are voluntary under AB 32.

The implementation plan proposed by the ARB includes a combination of direct regulations, performance-based standards, and market-based mechanisms. However, the centerpiece of the proposed plan is a cap-and-trade program that would initially target selected production or distribution processes, including cement production, oil refining, and significant users of fossil fuels. The program is designed so that, potentially, it can be linked with similar programs, in particular, an envisioned regional program that includes New Mexico, British Columbia, Quebec, and Ontario. Under the proposed cap-and-trade scheme, allowances would be issued that regulated firms must match with GHG emissions. The number of allowances would decline over time to match emission reduction targets. Firms with surplus allowances could sell their allowances or save (bank) them for future use. Those firms unable to reduce their emissions or looking to increase emissions could enter the allowance market to purchase surplus allowances (CARB, 2011). An innovative feature of the program, patterned on the CDM and JI mechanisms of the Kyoto Protocol, is that the system would be open to additional private or public mitigation activities that reduce emissions or sequester greenhouse gases. See Dinar, Larson and Frisbie (forthcoming) for a related discussion.

Northeastern US

The Regional Greenhouse Gas Initiative (RGGI) is another cap-and-trade program that targets power-sector sources in 10 US states: Connecticut, Delaware, Maine, Maryland, Massachusetts, New Hampshire, New Jersey, New York, Rhode Island, and Vermont. In addition, the District of Columbia, Pennsylvania, the Eastern Canadian Provinces, and New Brunswick are observers in the process and could opt-in at some point. The goal of the program is to reduce to 2008 levels by 2014 and then reduce the cap by 2.5% annually through 2019 (Hahn and Stavins, 2010). It targets carbon dioxide emissions from electric power generators (25 MW or more and which burns 50% or more of fossil fuel). Burtraw, Kahn, and Palmer (2006) describe the regional program and analyze its potential effect on electricity prices.

Chicago Climate Exchange

The Chicago Climate Exchange (CCX) was an early voluntary cap-and-trade scheme, where members made voluntary but contractually binding commitment to reduce GHG emissions. Trading on the exchange began in 2003. At one point, there were more than one hundred members in the exchange, from all sectors of the economy (including entities such as universities or municipalities), based mostly in the US. The CCX traded the same six gases covered by the Kyoto Protocol, converted to a standard unit, the Chicago Financial Instrument (CFI), which represents 100 tCO_2e. CFIs were based on allowances issued to members according to their baseline and emissions reduction commitment, or offset credits from third-party-verified projects. Offset categories included agricultural methane, landfill methane, coal mine methane, agricultural soil carbon, rangeland soil carbon management, forestry, renewable energy and energy efficiency, and fuel switching. Trading and interest in the exchange declined as prospects for a US regulatory framework diminished and trading on the exchange stopped in 2010. Sabbaghi and Sabbaghi (2011) discuss the consequences of declining volume on CFI price volatility.

Australia

Before Australia's ratification of the Kyoto Protocol, a number of initiatives to reduce GHG emissions emerged at the state level, mostly based on the mandated use of renewable energy. However, there have been trade-based programs as well. For example, between 2003 and 2012, Australia's New South Wales (NSW) operated a program based on tradable permits, called the NSW Greenhouse Gas Abatement Scheme (GGAS), which is intended to reduce greenhouse gas emissions from the power sector. Under the program, retailers and large electricity customers in NSW (and since 2005 in the Australian Capital Territory) were required to meet mandatory intensity targets to reduce (or offset) the emissions of GHG arising from the production of electricity they supplied or used. They could meet their targets by purchasing certificates (NSW Greenhouse Abatement Certificates or NGACs). NGACs were generated through the following activities: low-emission generation of electricity and improved generator efficiency, activities that result in reduced consumption of electricity or on-site generation of electricity and carbon sequestration into biomass. Renewable Energy Certificates were also eligible.[63] No other form of credit (e.g., JI or CDM) was eligible. A buy-out penalty applied, set at AU$11.50 (about US$9 at the time) for the compliance year 2006. After the EU ETS, the NSW GGAS was the second largest greenhouse gas abatement market. At the end of February 2007, 201 projects were accredited, for the most part under the "generation" and "demand-side abatement" rules. Credits issued from carbon sequestration also entered the scheme in 2005. Over 40 million NGACs had been created by the end of March 2007, with "generation" certificates dominating at 70% of volumes followed by "demand-side abatement" certificates at 25%.

CARBON MARKETS[64]

As discussed, the flexibility mechanisms of the Kyoto Protocol are designed to bring about the same type of market efficiencies that are generally associated with trade. Moreover, they are expected to mobilize private capital on a scale that public transfers cannot. Through price discovery, private markets associated with the flexibility mechanisms are expected to reveal whether current regulations place a value on greenhouse gases emissions that is consistent with what modeling efforts suggest are needed to curb global warming.

In this section, we discuss what can be broadly termed carbon financial markets. These are the markets that are motivated directly by greenhouse gas policies. As the discussion of national policies in the preceding section suggests, the markets operate across a heterogeneous set of public and private institutions. Regulatory uncertainty associated with some markets is high, and basic information can be scarce. Even so, the scale, sophistication, and pace of growth in these markets and derived risk markets are remarkable. Project investment levels supported by these markets are likely to be larger than that anticipated by model studies.

---

[63]Their share in the total number of certificates surrendered for compliance decreased from 29% in 2003 to 11% in 2006.

[64]This and the following two sections draw heavily on Capoor and Abrosi (2007).

Table 2.1: Study estimates of the demand for emission reductions and the size of the CDM market.

Study	Annex I countries' demand for emission reductions under the Kyoto Protocol	Potential size of the CDM market
	MtCO₂e per year	
Blanchard, Criqui, and Kitous (2002)[a]	688–862	0–174
Eyckmans, Van Regemorter, and van Steenberghe (2001)[a]	1,414–1,713	261–499
Grütter (2001)[a]	1,000–1,500	0–500
Haites (2004)[b]	600–1,150	50–500
Halsnaes (2000)[b]	600–1,300	400–520
Holtsmark (2003)[b]	1,246–1,404	0–379
Jotzo and Michaelowa (2002)[a]	1,040	0–465
Vrolijk (2000)[b]	640–1,484	300–500
Zhang (2000)[b]	621	132–358
Range	600–1,713	0–520

[a]Model assumes that only the US does not ratify the Kyoto Protocol.
[b]Model assumes that both Australia and the US do not ratify the Kyoto Protocol.
Source: Haites (2004) and Zhang (2000).

Model Studies of Potential Size of the Market for the Flexibility Mechanisms

Several estimates of the potential demand for emissions reductions as well as the size of the CDM market are listed in Table 2.1. The estimates of the potential demand for GHG offsets ranges from 600 to 1,713 MtCO₂e (million tons of CO_2 equivalent) per year over the first commitment period, 2008–2012. The estimates differ substantially, mainly due to uncertainties involved with the projection of emissions growth in Annex I countries and alternative macroeconomic model specifications (Springer, 2003). The estimates of the size of the CDM market ranges from 0 to 520 MtCO₂e per year.

The wide range is due primarily to alternative assumptions about the supply of Kyoto allowances (AAUs) from Russia and Ukraine, which can serve as an alternative for project credits. In many of the modeling exercises, the combination of US withdrawal from Kyoto markets and the unconstrained sales of allowances from Russia and former Soviet countries drives CER prices to zero and supplies of project credits to zero. Nevertheless, as discussed, market incentives may encourage Russia and Ukraine to withhold some of their allowances, and this creates opportunities for project credits in several model scenarios. By way of example, Haites (2004) suggests that if Russia and Ukraine restrict the supply of their surplus Kyoto units to about 40%, the market demand for CERs would be about 1,250 MtCO$_2$e over the first commitment period. However, most modeling exercises suggest that emission trading and project credits are likely to meet only a small portion of the demand for the emission reduction units (Zhang, 2000).

In actuality, the investment flows under the CDM have exceeded all expectations. Rahman, Dinar, and Larson (2010) examine the trajectory of expected CERs from projects entering the CDM pipeline and project it forward based on the assumption that the diffusion of the CDM will follow a path similar to other kinds of innovation. They find that the mechanism will likely exceed the upper bound of *ex ante* modeling forecasts, even when relatively high delivery failures are taken into account.

The Evolution of Carbon Project Financing

In a broad sense, carbon markets began in the late 1990s, when corporations, non-government organizations, and governments began experimental programs in market-based regulations — including pilots under the already discussed AIJ program.[65] Moreover, because of a provision allowing for early action, the CDM market emerged before the rules governing the CDM were finalized. In fact, when Russia agreed to ratify the Protocol in October 2004, thereby making it certain that the Kyoto Protocol would enter into force, more than 120 CDM transactions had already been recorded.

The participants in the Prototype Carbon Fund (PCF), 6 governments and 15 private companies, were the first investors in the CDM. The PCF is a closed $180 million mutual fund managed by the World Bank to purchase emission reduction credits under JI and CDM. The PCF was established in 1999, became operational in April 2000, and signed its first emission reduction purchase agreement for a CDM project in Chile in 2002.

Another key player in the early market was the Netherlands government, which decided early on to purchase emission reductions through flexibility mechanisms as part of a comprehensive strategy to meet its Kyoto target. In addition to participating in the PCF, the Netherlands government also developed the first carbon tenders for CDM and JI in 2001. In

---

[65]For a discussion of early greenhouse gas market-based programs, see Sonneborn (1999) and Sandor, Bettelheim, and Swingland (2002).

2004, the two original players in the CDM market — the Netherlands government and the World Bank (whose carbon finance activity had by then grown to include new funds besides the PCF) — still represented about a third of the total volume of project-based transactions. The adoption of the Marrakesh Accords in December 2001 led more players to move in. Private firms from Japan started to enter the market in 2002 and 2003, despite the absence of a domestic climate policy in Japan; the Japanese climate policy was approved only at the end of 2005. European firms followed about a year later, when it became clear that the EU Emissions Trading Scheme would become operational and that CERs would become eligible at least in part, under the EU-ETS. Around 2005, other Annex B governments came into the market as the Kyoto Protocol entered into force. By 2007, a number of secondary market participants had entered the market, including banks and investor funds that do not need CERs or ERUs for compliance.

The first CDM transaction was struck in early 2002 followed by more than one hundred transactions during the next two years. Still, three years elapsed between the adoption of the Marrakesh Accords and the registration of the first CDM project by the Executive Board in 2004.[66] Moreover, by the close of 2005, only 63 projects were registered by the Board, despite a growing number of projects entering the pipeline. Still, as the number of CDM projects entering the pipeline grew steadily, lag times increased along the project cycle. The average time spent between a request for registration and registration went from around 80–100 days in 2006 to around 250 days in early 2008 and again in early 2010, before falling dramatically to less than 50 days in 2011 (UNEP RISOE, 2012).

The slow start and high initial transaction costs for early projects are consistent with experience in other tradable schemes.[67] This generally comes about because of the time and costs associated with building public and private institutions. In the particular case of CDM, a project enters the CDM pipeline at the start of the 30-day public comment period, which is the first step of the validation phase of the project cycle. During this phase, a third-party DOE reviews and validates the project's baseline and monitoring plans. As discussed, new baseline technologies must be

---

[66]The first project registered was the Brazil NovaGerar Landfill Gas to Energy Project.
[67]Hahn and Hester (1989) and Gangadharan (2000) provide examples from US air pollution markets. Michaelowa *et al.* (2003) discuss transaction costs from early AIJ and Prototype Carbon Fund projects. Chadwick (2006) provides an example from Ghana.

approved by the CDM Board. Early on, capacity constraints among the small number of designated third-party validators (DOEs), drawn-out rule making by the CDM Board, and a low stock of approved methodologies all worked against speedy registration. Conversely, start-up costs declined as the stock of approved baseline and monitoring methodologies accumulated and as project managers, third-party entities, and regulators gained experience.

In 2006, developing countries supplied nearly 450 $MtCO_2e$ of primary CDM credits for a total market value of US$4.8 billion. The carbon market and associated emerging markets for clean technology and commodities have attracted a significant response from the capital markets and from experienced investors, including those in the US. Analysts estimated that US$11.8 billion had been invested in 58 carbon funds as of March 2007, compared to US$4.6 billion in 40 funds as of May 2006, half of which is managed in the UK (New Carbon Finance, 2007). By August 2007, the CDM Board had registered 760 projects expected to deliver about 1 billion CERs by 2012. In addition, 1,500 projects were at the validation stage or ready for registration. Together, these 2,260 projects could deliver close to 2.2 billion CERs by 2012.

JI shares the same origins as CDM, since early treaty negotiations concerning project credits made no distinction between projects located in transitional or developing countries. Consequently, some exploratory project investments hosted in Annex I countries were made in 2001 — before the first CDM transaction — by public buyers. Nevertheless, as separate mechanisms evolved, JI project development stalled — due in large part to a decision to allow early crediting only under CDM. Delays among Annex I countries to meet JI eligibility requirements, along with uncertainty and delays associated with establishing Track-Two project-cycle rules, further dampened investment. Nevertheless, as UNFCCC and host country domestic rules evolved, projects began to enter the JI pipeline, beginning in late 2006, and by February 2008, pipeline projects represented a potential of 188 $MtCO_2e$ by 2012 (UNEP RISOE, 2008).

Evaluations of mitigation potential and project investment

As discussed earlier, bottom-up and top-down methods have been employed to provide an understanding of how emission trading might affect abatement activities. To start, the viability of a given offset project has to do with basic physical and economic characteristics. Bottom-up studies, in particular, take stock of the potential for different types (asset classes) of investment over a range of potential market prices for carbon. For example, reducing emissions by switching fuels might be economically viable at lower prices for carbon, while investing in alternative sources of energy may be viable at higher prices. In the aggregate, the distribution of viable technologies also has implications for the geographic distribution of investments. Both the geographic and asset class distribution of potential projects are important for policy makers. For one, different types of abatement activities are associated with different costs, and the relative potential supply of low- or high-cost mitigation opportunities will affect the costs of meeting the policy emission goals. Different types of abatement activities also have different implications for additional spillover benefits such as health or biodiversity co-benefits and technology transfer. The location of the project is important as well, since it determines who benefits from any economic, developmental, or spillover effects associated with the project.

A number of studies have looked at the composition of project location under alternative policy settings; Haites (2004) provides a review, as do recent IPCC evaluations.[68] These studies roughly indicate the country or regional potential for Kyoto project offsets since they are driven by abatement costs. In general, most models suggest that Asia has the largest potential for CERs. For example, Jakeman et al. (2000) place about 62% of the predicted CDM market in Asia; Sijm et al. (2000) suggest 71%–78%; and Jotzo and Michaelowa (2002) estimate 72%. For studies that provide country detail, China is usually the largest source of potential offsets.[69] Asia's dominance is partly due to its large population but also because of the composition of the region's industrial base and its reliance on coal and oil.

There is less agreement as to differences in sectoral potential. In their synthesis of sector studies, Barker et al. (2007) suggest large potential savings in all regions based on improving energy efficiencies in residential and commercial buildings, accomplished through, for example, improved lighting and insulation, gains in small appliance efficiency, and the use of alternative coolants. Sijm et al. (2000) suggest that potential gains in energy efficiency account for most potential emission reductions. In developing

---

[68]See especially Barker et al. (2007).

[69]For example, Chen (2003) estimates that roughly 55% of the potential for CDM projects is in China alone, with another 10% in India.

countries, agriculture and forestry projects are significant when carbon prices remain under \$20 per tCO_2e.[70] This includes the use of better soil management techniques to improve soil sequestration and adding to sinks through afforestation and reforestation projects. At higher prices, the composition of potential projects expands to include more industry-based (the use of more efficient equipment, the control of non–carbon dioxide emissions, etc.) and energy-supply projects (renewables, fuel-switching, etc.)

The Geographic Distribution of Kyoto-Project Credits

As of March 2008, the supply of issued and potential CERs remained firmly centered in Asia. Nearly 75% of the pipeline projects accounting for about 79% of potential first-period CERs were hosted in Asia.[71] This was largely due to the relative population size and also the relatively high levels of oil and coal consumption levels based on older technologies in Asia. Latin America accounted for 21% of the projects and 15% of pipeline CERs and, on a per capita basis, hosted a larger share of the first-period pipeline than Asia. Sub-Saharan Africa accounted for about 2.6% of the pipeline potential. Across all regions, the least-developed countries hosted few projects and accounted for about 1% of potential first-period CERs. A relatively small set of countries accounted for most of the CDM pipeline credits; most of the potential CER supply originated in from (53.2 %); India ranked second (15%), Brazil third (6%), and South Korea (4.1%) fourth. Similarly, the JI first-period pipeline was centered in Russia (61%) and Ukraine (26%).

Capoor and Ambrosi (2006) provide estimates of market activity based on interviews with a range of market participants and voluntary reporting of emission reduction purchase agreements. They estimate that, in 2006, developing countries supplied nearly 450 $MtCO_2e$ of primary project credits for a total market value of US\$4.8 billion, up from \$2.4 billion in 2005. China accounted for 61% of transacted volumes, down slightly from 73% in 2005. Next was India at 12%, increasing from 3% in 2005. Asia as a whole led with an 80% market share. Latin America — an early pioneer in the market — accounted for 10% of CDM transactions overall, with Brazil alone contributing 4%. The share for Africa remained constant, at about 3%; however, African volumes transacted increased proportionally to the

---

[70] See a related study by Makundi and Sathaye (2003).
[71] UNEP/RISOE, March 2008.

increase of overall volumes transacted. The smaller market for credits from JI projects also grew in 2006, with 16.3 MtCO$_2$e transacted, up 45% over the 2005 levels. Russia, Ukraine, and Bulgaria provided more than 60% of transacted volumes — for a value of US$141 million.

Ukraine, Russia, and Bulgaria accounted for 20% each of the ERUs supply traded through 2003–2006 (44 M tCO$_2$e transacted, or about 10% of the primary CDM market in 2006). Other countries — and not only in Eastern and Central Europe, but also New Zealand for instance — have also taken part in the market, although to a lesser extent. Transactions in the second half of 2006 and the first quarter of 2007 already exhibit a trend, with fewer emission reduction purchase agreements (ERPAs) signed in Europe (as was historically the case) and more in Russia and Ukraine. This is no surprise as the biggest potential is expected to lie in these two countries associated with large projects in the oil and gas as well as the power sector (refurbishment and energy efficiency improvements as well as methane capture). In addition, the EU decision on double counting discussed earlier means that the JI potential can only be realized from projects outside the sectors covered by the EU ETS, particularly restricting opportunities in the newer members of the EU.[72] However, it remains to be seen what portion of the JI potential in Russia and Ukraine may materialize, given remaining uncertainties with regard to issuance procedures and a limited five-year crediting period that may not be sufficient to get many projects up and running.

Balance across asset classes

By project count, most projects involved renewable energy sources. For example, in February 2008, hydro (26%), biomass (16%), and wind projects (12%) accounted for 54% of the CDM pipeline. However, the largest source of CERs (31%) originated from a small number of industrial gas projects, considered the low-hanging fruit of greenhouse gas projects. The projects involve reducing the emissions of very concentrated greenhouse gases, or converting them to less harmful gases. The projects are straightforward from an engineering and baseline point of view and deliver CERs at low risk for a limited upfront investment with a short lead-time. In 2005, HFC23-destruction projects account for two-thirds of CERs entering the CDM pipeline and in 2006 projects for the destruction of N$_2$O captured a

---

[72]In addition, several of these opportunities in the EU newer Member States countries may already have been secured by early public procurement programs.

13% market share of volumes transacted. These projects have been heavily criticized as delivering few additional development benefits and may work to slow the phase-out of ozone-reducing gases (Pearson, 2007).[73] In the case of China, concerns prompted interventions, and the government chose to funnel most proceeds from related CER sales into a Clean Development fund that finances mitigation projects in priority sectors (World Bank, 2006). Moreover, proposals have been advanced under the UNFCCC to limit credits from new facilities.

Separately, there are indications that new opportunities for these types of projects may be tapering off. For example, by February 2008, the supply of pipeline CERs for renewables had grown considerably, representing about 30% of first-period CERs. Moreover, Capoor and Ambrosi (2006) conclude that CDM projects have been successful in jump-starting clean energy projects in developing countries. They estimate that financial flows to developing and transition countries through Kyoto projects grew to about US$7.8 billion in 2006 (signed contract value). By some estimates, carbon finance — in 2006 alone — leveraged approximately US$10 billion in clean technology investments in developing countries, about 48% of their total investments in clean technologies.

The share of transactions from energy efficiency projects and fuel switching projects increased dramatically from 1% in 2005 to 9% in 2006. Together, these types of projects now comprise over 19% of the CDM pipeline and are mostly energy efficiency projects at industrial facilities. Despite their overall potential demand-side management, energy-efficiency projects were held back by methodological challenges (additionality requirements for activities that are considered economically rational or because of issues with monitoring) and, as of February 2008, made up about 1% of the pipeline.

Similarly, carbon assets from land use (LULCF) projects are rare in the CDM market; their cumulative market share, in terms of volumes transacted, hardly reaches 0.2%.[74] This is largely due to their exclusion from Europe's ETS.[75] Even so, this is striking and is viewed by many as a failure of current policies since emissions from deforestation and land

---

[73]In the case of projects involving the destruction of HFC-23, a bi-product of producing HCFC-22, used in coolants and the production of Teflon, there are also concerns that income generated from the projects create incentives to delay the phase-out of HCFC-22 coolants under the Montreal Protocol (Schwank, 2004).

[74]See Neeff *et al.* (2007) for an exhaustive review of the market for forestry offsets.

[75]See a related discussion by Schlamadinger *et al.* (2005).

degradation account for an estimated 18% to 25% of all global greenhouse gas emissions.[76]

To a degree, obstacles for including forestry projects under the Kyoto mechanisms have given rise to projects in the voluntary markets that emphasize additional biodiversity benefits and other positive spillovers. Examples include the World Bank's Forest Carbon Partnership Facility, the Australia Global Forest Fund, and Carbon Neutral Norway, among others. They have also prompted new investment vehicles under the UN-REDD (2012) program, launched in 2008.

Carbon credits from clean energy projects comprised the greatest share of the JI market, with slightly less than two-thirds of volumes transacted over 2003–2006. ERUs from energy efficiency improvement and fuel switching projects were first at 28%, followed by biomass, wind, and hydro with, respectively, 13%, 12%, and 10% of the market. N_2O projects from industrial installations accounted for 8%. Expected credits by 2012 from reducing fugitive emissions are expected to make up 44 % of the total, emission reductions from energy efficiency improvement and fuel switching 32%, and coal mine methane reductions 12%.[77] Unlike projects in developing countries, where green-field projects have long lead times, many opportunities in JI countries are associated with existing facilities and sites and have relatively shorter lead times. Many such projects are likely to be implemented within the 2012 timeframe, provided financing is available before the window of opportunity starts to close.

Who is buying project credits?

European buyers dominated the primary CDM and JI market with 86% market share (versus 50% in 2005), with Japanese purchases sharply down at only 7% of the primary market in 2006 (versus 46% in 2005). Within Europe, the United Kingdom had a 50% market share of volumes transacted (up from 15% in 2005), consolidating its leadership position as the carbon finance hub for the world. Many companies, including project developers and players with an eye on the secondary market, have opened accounts on the UK national registry. Private sector players were the main buyers of CDM assets

---

[76]As of end of January 2008, the UN reported 15 land-use projects in the CDM pipeline.
[77]The term "fugitive emissions" refers to pollutants released to the air other than those from stacks or vents. They can occur due to equipment leaks, evaporative processes, and windblown disturbances.

in 2006, with about 90% of purchases coming from the European private sector in 2006. In contrast, the JI market has long been dominated by public buyers (mainly the Netherlands, Denmark, and Austria), representing 92% of those transactions in 2006 (up from 80% in 2004 and 2005).

By the end of first quarter 2007, EU governments had purchased 143 $MtCO_2e$, about 30% of the assets identified for purchase from the flexible mechanisms (CDM, JI, and AAUs).[78] A total of 506 $MtCO_2e$ credits, about 45% of the expected demand for CDM and JI credits from EU ETS installations in Phase II, have already been contracted by European entities, either directly, by natural compliance buyers and the funds in which they are participants, or indirectly, by entities planning to sell back these credits on the secondary market.[79] As far as Japan is concerned, the 266 $MtCO_2e$ credits purchased by Japanese entities so far account for around half of the expected shortfall for Japan.[80] Together, these sources of demand could add up to at least one billion tCO_2e in the next year or so. Even without factoring in any potential demand from Australia, Canada, and the US, there is still significant potential demand for CDM and JI from Japan and the EU before 2012.

The carbon market and associated emerging markets for clean technology and commodities have attracted a significant response from the capital markets and from experienced investors, including those in the US. Analysts estimated that US$11.8 billion had been invested in 58 carbon funds as of March 2007, compared to US$4.6 billion in 40 funds as of May 2006, half of which is managed in the UK (New Carbon Finance, 2007).

Markets and the pricing of project credits

Though nascent, formal market for pricing emission reduction units are quickly forming for Kyoto project-based offsets, CERs, and ERUs. Exchange-traded futures and options contracts for CERs were launched

---

[78]Based on Fourth National Communications from EU Members States, the 2006 European Environment Agency report on GHG emissions trends and projections and updates from the NAPs, one may estimate a 450 $MtCO_2e$ demand for CDM and JI over 2008–2012.

[79]Using a 1.25 billion tCO_2e estimate for CDM and JI demand over 2008–2012 by EU ETS installations, an average across assessments by Fortis, Merrill Lynch, New Carbon Finance, Point Carbon, Société Générale, and UBS.

[80]This is based on estimates from the 4th National Communication in the "with existing measures" scenario.

in late 2007 on the Chicago Climate Futures Exchange and the Norwegian exchange Nord Pool and in March 2008 on the European Climate Exchange (ECX) and the European Energy Exchange (EEX). Similar contracts are in place for allowance under the EU ETS. When traded volumes are sufficiently large, exchange-based contracts offer the most transparent form of pricing. The contracts are of standard quality and the exchange stands behind delivery. For example, the exchange guarantees that buyers will receive CERs if they decide to take future delivery. Behind the exchange markets are a range of related markets, differentiated by quality or risks associated impediments to their delivery.

Prices for project-based offsets have increased regularly through 2008 before falling as the global economy slowed. The pricing process has become more transparent and market-driven, largely because the rules governing how credits can be used in Annex B countries have become clearer and because of the development of formal markets for European allowances. The largest class of CDM transactions involves the direct purchase of CERs from registered projects. According to Capoor and Ambrosi (2007), weighted average prices for these primary CERs reached about US$10.90 in 2006, representing a 52% increase over 2005 levels.[81] Still, these average prices mask a range (US$6.80–US$24.75) related to the heterogeneity of the underlying projects and contracts.

Transactions on the primary market involve forward streams of credits and therefore the buyer faces a number of risks, linked to project performance and to the eligibility of the generated credits for its compliance purposes. Some risks are project specific — for example, risks related to the variability of rainfall feeding a small scale hydro-power project — while others may be country specific — for example, risks related to the performance of the Designated National Authority. And, since most projects are related to an underlying business — for example, the production of electricity — vagaries associated with that side of the project can affect emission performance as well. In addition, uncertainties about policy can affect how useful the credit is for meeting regulatory or even contractual obligations. By way of example, credits from land-use CDM projects are ineligible for delivery against CER future contracts sold on the EEX and the ECX.

CERs that have already been issued sell at a significant premium, since they are without project performance risk. By June 2008, more than 150 million CERs had been issued by the CDM board, but many of these were

---

[81] All prices in US$ per tCO_2e, unless otherwise indicated.

sold under existing contracts, so pricing information is scarce. Still, Capoor and Ambrosi note that issued CERs can trade at nearly double the prevailing price for primary CERs. However, even issued CERs were not without risks through much of the first reporting period, in part because the International Transaction Log — a system for tracking and affecting the transfer of tradable Kyoto units — including CERs — was not yet fully implemented. The ITL went live in 2007 and faced security concerns soon thereafter.

Another strategy for managing performance risk relates to a secondary market, which grew to 25 $MtCO_2e$ in 2006. The market draws on portfolios of guaranteed-delivery CERs, with most if not all delivery risk assigned to the seller. Players in this market are primarily financial institutions, large energy players, and investors' funds. Buying on the secondary market certainly has some advantages: the buyer is purchasing a near compliance-grade asset with firm volumes and guarantees, and the buyer also does not have to create an infrastructure or team to source and structure carbon transactions. There is increased standardization of contracts in the secondary market, and this standardization considerably facilitates the trade of CERs for compliance purposes, for hedging purposes and for arbitrage purposes.

As discussed earlier, exchange-based instruments for managing risk are developing to round out the range of markets developing around the Kyoto flexibility mechanisms. In addition to futures and options contracts, which open the door to a range of traditional hedging techniques, some insurance products have emerged as well. An example is a recent MIGA guarantee against certain sovereign and non-commercial risks related to a CDM project involving Luxembourg and El Salvador.

To date, many of the developments in the CDM market are motivated in part by the EU ETS and a clarification of rules concerning the use of CERs and ERUs within the significantly large European system (1,100 $MtCO_2e$ in 2006 transacted volume). Still, the same set of supporting markets is not yet as developed for JI markets. The prices at which ERUs transacted in 2006 increased to an average of US\$8.70, representing a 45% year-on-year rise, but ERUs remained cheaper than CERs on average. JI assets traded in a range from US\$6.60 up to US\$12.40, which is lower than the range at which primary CERs (US\$6.80–US\$24.75) were transacted. In many cases, host country rules and laws are unclear, and this sovereign risk may translate into a discount compared to the CDM price. Market players report that the key to closing JI deals is the ability to bring upfront financing (up to 50% of ERPA value). The price of ERUs is often discounted in transactions to reflect the cost of providing upfront finance.

CONCLUSIONS AND AREAS FOR FUTURE STUDY

During the last two decades, there has been a remarkable build-up of institutions related to climate change. The institutions are broadly organized around: the assessments and synthesis of findings from climate scientist; reaching political agreement and formalizing the agreements as treaties; establishing rules of implementation; support to markets for offsets and investments; and providing public financing for a range of activities outside of mitigation. The links between the components are unusual, especially the extent to which the fact-finding function of the IPCC is formally linked to policy debate. Unusual as well is the extent to which the political agreements formalized in the Kyoto Protocol resulted in large capital flows into mitigation activities and the development of private secondary markets. Still, as the first commitment period nears an end, there is concern that the set of climate change policies currently in place are insufficient to slow anticipated climate change. This is because the growth rate in current emissions appears inconsistent with trajectories that scientists predict would stabilize the global climate, even though most governments have expressed their intent to slow or reverse emission rates. Moreover, failure by the Parties to reach a binding agreement at the 2009 meetings in Copenhagen raises questions how future emission reductions will be achieved.

Beneath the overarching unease about future policies is an ongoing debate about whether current market-based policies deliver expected environmental benefits. This is a continuing concern that was present when the flexibility instruments were first debated. In the specific case of voluntary and Kyoto project-based emission reductions, there are a variety of issues. For one, policy makers worry that safeguards built into the respective project cycles are not sufficient to guarantee delivery of the combination of environmental and developmental benefits the projects promise. One consequence is that EU member states have placed limits on how related tradable permits can be used. In addition, a variety of supplemental private and public quality certifications have emerged in order to further distinguish among UNFCCC-approved offsets. Stalled efforts to solve project design obstacles in forestry projects that would allow project-based investments to go forward are another area of concern. At present, investments in reforestation and afforestation are meager. More substantive progress has been made with regard to deforestation; however, the related question of how to protect carbon sequestered in soils remains unresolved. In addition, problems about how to accurately gauge emission reductions from sector-wide projects and current implementation rules for CDM and JI appear to leave identified sources of mitigation untapped in transport and energy systems and inefficient buildings. Even so, the ability of private markets to mobilize capital in other areas has proved much greater than originally anticipated. Moreover, in the case of Australia and possibly the US, domestic tradable permit programs will become better integrated with Kyoto's international system. These points are encouraging, because they suggest a strengthening of the markets needed for effective policy, but they also raise questions about how voluntary and regional systems in those countries will transform under new rules and how those systems will influence present markets for framework-based credits and projects.

All of this can be expected to influence the future direction of policy research. As has been discussed, much of the economic literature to date has been predictive and focused on evaluating alternative policy proposals this is reflected in the large portion of the associated economics literature devoted to numeric models and methods. Looking forward, this type of research will certainly remain important for several reasons. First, an ongoing analysis of related proposals will be needed within and outside the IPCC process. For this, policy makers will want to focus increasingly on explaining the relationships among carbon-market policy, research and technology diffusion, and capital formation. In addition, the most recent research on vulnerability suggests large differences in the geographic distribution of climate change effects. For this reason, countries will want to develop greater detail on the differences that specific policies have on their own vulnerability. These areas of research will require further advances in modeling approaches and a greater level of specificity than the current models can manage. An increase in the use of country-specific modeling is also anticipated, as countries will want to evaluate the adaptation policies and the effects of tradable instruments.

REFERENCES

Agénora, P-R, N Bayraktarc and K El Aynaoui (2008). Roads out of poverty? Assessing the links between aid, public investment, growth, and poverty reduction. *Journal of Development Economics*, **86**(2), 277–295.

Ahn, D (1999). Environmental disputes in the GATT/WTO: Before and after US — Shrimp case. *Michigan Journal of International Law*, **20**(4), 819–870.

Alberola, E, J Chevallier and B Chèze (2008). Price drivers and structural breaks in European carbon prices 2005–2007. Energy Policy, 36(2), 787–797.

Aldy, JE, S Barrett and RN Stavins (2003). Thirteen plus one: A comparison of global climate policy architectures. Climate Policy, 3(4), 373–397.

Andersen, MS (2005). Do green taxes work? Decoupling environmental pressures and economic growth. Public Policy Research, 12(2), 79–84.

Arrhenius, S (1896). The influence of the carbonic acid in the air upon the temperature of the ground. Philosophical Magazine Series, 5(41), 237–276.

Arrow, KJ, W Cline, KG Maler, M Munasinghe, R Squitieri and J Stiglitz (1996). Intertemporal equity, discounting, and economic efficiency. In JP Bruce, H Lee and EF Haites (eds.), Climate Change 1995: Economic and Social Dimensions of Climate Change, pp. 125–144. Cambridge; New York and Melbourne: Cambridge University Press, for the Intergovernmental Panel on Climate Change.

Aslam, MA (2002). Equal per capita entitlements. In KA Baumart, O Blanchard, S Llosa and JF Perkaus (eds.), Building a Climate of Trust: Kyoto Protocol and Beyond. Washington: World Resources Institute.

Asuka, J and K Takeuchi (2004). Additionality reconsidered: Lax criteria may not benefit developing countries. Climate Policy, 4(2), 177–192.

Aunan, K, HE Mestl, HM Seip, J Fang, D O'Connor, H Vennemo and F Zhai (2003). Co-benefits of CO_2-reducing policies in China — A matter of scale? International Journal of Global Environmental Issues, 3(3), 287–304.

Auty, RM (2007). Natural resources, capital accumulation and the resource curse. Ecological Economics, 61(4), 627–634.

Babiker, MH (2005). Climate change policy, market structure, and carbon leakage. Journal of International Economics, 65(2), 421–445.

Baer, P, J Harte, B Haya, AV Herzog, J Holdren, NE Hultman, DM Kammen, RB Norgaard and L Raymond (2000). Climate change: Equity and greenhouse gas responsibility. Science, 289(5488), 2287.

Barker, T, I Bashmakov, A Alharthi, M Amann, L Cifuentes, J Drexhage, M Duan, O Edenhofer, B Flannery, M Grubb, M Hoogwijk, FI Ibitoye, CJ Jepma, WA Pizer, K Yamaji (2007). Mitigation from a cross-sectoral perspective. In B Metz, OR Davidson, PR Bosch, R Dave and LA Meyer (eds.), Climate Change 2007: Mitigation. Contribution of Working Group III to the Fourth Assessment Report of the Intergovernmental Ponel on Climated Chagne. Cambridge and New York: Cambridge University Press.

Barrera, J and R Schwarze (2004). Does the CDM contribute to sustainable development? Evidence from the AIJ pilot phase. International Journal of Sustainable Development, 7(4), 353–368.

Barrett, S (2003). Environment and Statecraft: The Strategy of Environmental Treaty-Making. Oxford and New York: Oxford University Press.

Barrett, S (2006). Climate treaties and breakthrough technologies. *American Economic Review*, **96**(2), 22–25.

Barrett, S (2011). Rethinking climate change governance and its relationship to the World Trading System. *The World Economy*, **34**(11), 1863–1882.

Barron, R (1999). Market power and market access in international GHG emission trading. IEA Information Paper. Paris, International Energy Agency and Organization for Economic Cooperation and Development.

Beckerman, W and C Hepburn (2007). Ethics of the discount rate in the Stern Review on the economics of climate change. *World Economics*, **8**(1), 187–210.

Benedick, RE (2001). Striking a new deal on climate change. *Issues in Science and Technology*, **18**(1), 71–76.

Bento, AM and M Jacobsen (2007). Ricardian rents, environmental policy and the double-dividend hypothesis. *Journal of Environmental Economics and Management*, **53**(1), 17–31.

Bernstein, PMW, D Montgomery and TF Rutherford (19990). Global impacts of the Kyoto agreement, results from the MS-MRT model. *Resource and Energy Economics*, **21**(3), 375–413.

Bertram, G (1992). Tradeable emission permits and the control of greenhouse gases. *Journal of Development Studies*, **28**(3), 423–446.

Biermann, F and R Brohm (2005). Implementing the Kyoto Protocol without the USA: The strategic role of energy tax adjustments at the border. *Climate Policy*, **4**(3), 289–302.

Blanchard, O, P Criqui and A Kitous (2002). After The Hague, Bonn and Marrakech: The future international market for emissions permits and the issue of hot air. Cahier de Recherche No. 27 bis. Grenoble: Institut d'Economie et de Politique de l'Energie.

Blyth, W and R Baron (2003). *Green Investment Schemes: Options and Issues*. Paris: IEA/OECD.

Bode, S (2004): Equal emissions per capita over time–A proposal to combine responsibility and equity of rights for post-2012 GHG emission entitlement allocation. *European Environment*, **14**(5), 300–316.

Böhringer, C and A Löschel (2003). Market power and hot air in international emissions trading: The impacts of US withdrawal from the Kyoto Protocol. *Applied Economics*, **35**(6), 651–663.

Böhringer, C, K Conrad and A Loschel (2003). Carbon taxes and joint implementation: An applied general equilibrium analysis for Germany and India. *Environmental and Resource Economics*, **24**(1), 49–76.

Böhringer, C, T Hoffmann and CM de Lara-Peñatec (2006). *Energy Economics*, **28**(1), 44–61.

Böhringer, C, U Moslener and B Sturm (2007). Hot air for sale: A quantitative assessment of Russia's near-term climate policy options. *Environmental and Resource Economics*, **38**(4), 545–572.

Bosello, F, R Roson and RSJ Tol (2006). Economy-wide estimates of the implications of climate change: Human health. *Ecological Economics*, **58**(3), 579–591.

Bosello, F, R Roson and RSJ Tol (2007). Economy-wide estimates of the implications of climate change: Sea level rise. *Environmental and Resource Economics*, **37**(3), 549–571.

Bovenberg, AL and LH Goulder (1997). Costs of environmentally motivated taxes in the presence of other taxes: General equilibrium analyses. *National Tax Journal*, **50**(1), 59–87.

Bovenberg, AL and RA de Mooij (1994). Environmental levies and distortionary taxation. *American Economic Review*, **84**(4), 1085–1089.

Brechet, T and B Lussis (2006). The contribution of the clean development mechanism to national climate policies. *Journal of Policy Modeling*, **28**(9), 981–994.

Brewer, TL (2003). The trade regime and the climate regime: Institutional evolution and adaptation. *Climate Policy*, **3**(4), 329–341.

Bruvoll, A and T Faehn (2006). Transboundary effects of environmental policy: Markets and emission leakages. *Ecological Economics*, **59**(4), 499–510.

Buchner, B and C Carraro (2005). Economic and environmental effectiveness of a technology-based climate protocol. *Climate Policy*, **4**(3), 229–248.

Buonanno, P, C Carraro and M Galeotti (2003). Endogenous induced technical change and the costs of Kyoto. *Resource and Energy Economics*, **25**(1), 11–24.

Burniaux, J-M and JO Martins (2000). Carbon emission leakages: A general equilibrium view. OECD Economics Department Working Paper 242. Paris: OECD.

Burtraw, D, A Krupnick, K Palmer, A Paul, M Toman and C Bloyd (2003). Ancillary benefits of reduced air pollution in the US from moderate greenhouse gas mitigation policies in the electricity sector. *Journal of Environmental Economics and Management*, **45**(3), 650–673.

Burtraw, D, D Kahn and K Palmer (2006). CO_2 allowance allocation in the regional greenhouse gas initiative and the effect on electricity investors. *The Electricity Journal*, **19**(2), 79–90.

Bussolo, M and D O'Connor (2001). Clearing the air in India: The economics of climate policy with ancillary benefits. OECD Development Centre Working Papers 182. Paris: OECD.

Capoor, K and P Ambrosi (2007). State and Trends of the Carbon Market 2006. Washington: World Bank and International Emissions Trading Association.

CARB (2011). Final Supplement to the AB32 Scoping Plan Functional Equivalent Document Prepared California Air Resources Board. Available at: http://www.arb.ca.gov/cc/scopingplan/document/final_supplement_to_sp_fed.pdf (accessed on 3 August 2012).

CARB (2008). Climate Change Scoping Plan: A Framework for Change. California Air Resources Board. Available at: http://www.arb.ca.gov/cc/scoping-plan/document/psp.pdf (accessed on 3 August 2012).

Carlén, B (2003). Market power in international carbon emissions trading: A laboratory test. *The Energy Journal*, **24**(3), 1–26.

Carraro, C (1999). Introduction. In C Carraro (ed.), *International Environmental Agreements on Climate Change*. Boston: Kluwer Academic Publishers.

Carraro, C and M Galeotti (1996). WARM: A European model for energy and environmental analysis. *Journal Environmental Modeling and Assessment*, **1**(3), 171–189.

Carraro, C and M Galeotti (1997). Economic growth, international competitiveness and environmental protection: R & D and innovation strategies with the WARM model. *Energy Economics*, **19**(1), 2–28.

Chadwick, BP (2006). Transaction costs and the clean development mechanism. *Natural Resources Forum*, **30**(4), 256–271.

Chen, W (2003). Carbon quota price and CDM potentials after Marrakesh. *Energy Policy*, **31**(8), 709–719.

Chomitz, KM (1999). Evaluating carbon offsets from forestry and energy projects: How do they compare? Policy Research Working Paper Series 2357. Washington, DC: World Bank.

Climate Action Team (2006). CAT Subgroup Report Supporting AB 32 Scoping Plan: Documentation of Inputs to Macroeconomic Assessment of the Climate Action Team Report to the Governor and Legislature. Available at: http://www.climatechange.ca.gov/climate_action_team/reports/2006report/2006-03-24_INPUTS_MACROECONOMICS.PDF (accessed on 26 July 2011).

Coase, RH (1960). The problem of social cost. *Journal of Law and Economics*, **3**(Oct.), 1–44

Considine, TJ and DF Larson (2006). The environment as a factor of production. *Journal of Environmental Economics and Management*, **52**(3), 645–662.

Convery, FJ and L Redmond (2007). Market and price developments in the European union emissions trading scheme. *Review of Environmental Economics and Policy*, **1**(1), 88–111.

Cooper, R (1998). Toward a real treaty on global warming. *Foreign Affairs*, **77**(2), 66–79.

Corden, WM (1984). Booming sector and Dutch disease economics: Survey and consolidation. *Oxford Economic Papers*, **36**(3), 259–280.

Cullet, P and AP Kameri-Mbote (1998). Joint implementation and forestry projects: Conceptual and operational fallacies. *International Affairs*, **74**(2), 393–408.

Dasgupta, P (2005). Three donceptions of intergenerational justice. In H Lillehammer and DH Mellor (eds.), *Ramsey's Legacy*. Oxford, UK: Clarendon Press.

Dasgupta, P (2007). Commentary: The stern review's economics of climate change. *National Institute Economic Review*, **199**(4), 4–7.

Dasgupta, S, B Laplante, C Meisner, D Wheeler and J Yan (2007). The impact of sea level rise on developing countries: A comparative analysis. Research Working Paper Series 4136. Washington DC: World Bank.

DEFRA (2008). Draft Code of Best Practice for Carbon Offset Providers Accreditation Requirements and Procedures. London: Department for Environment, Food and Rural Affairs.

Demailly, D and P Quirion (2006). CO_2 abatement, competitiveness and leakage in the European cement industry under the EU ETS: Grandfathering versus output-based allocation. *Climate Policy*, **6**(1), 93–113.

den Elzen, MGJ and APG de Moor (2002). Analyzing the Kyoto protocol under the Marrakesh accords: Economic efficiency and environmental effectiveness. *Ecological Economics*, **43**(2/3), 141–158.

den Elzen, MGJ and S Both (2001). Modeling emissions trading and abatement costs in FAIR 1.1 case study: The Kyoto protocol under the Bonn-Marrakesh agreement. RIVM Report 728001021/2002. Bilthoven, Netherlands: National Institute of Public Health and the Environment.

Dessus, S and D O'Connor (2003). Policy without tears: CGE-based ancillary benefits estimates for Chile. *Environmental and Resource Economics*, **25**(3), 287–317.

Di Maria, C and E van der Werf (2008). Carbon leakage revisited: Unilateral climate policy with directed technical change. *Environmental and Resource Economics*, **39**(2), 55–74.

Dinar, A, DF Larson and JA Frisbie (2011). How California can take advantage of the Clean Development Mechanism to achieve its AB 32 goals by 2020. *California Agriculture*, **66**(4), 137–143.

Dinar, A, SM Rahman, and DF Larson (2011). Local actions, global impacts: International Cooperation and the CDM. *Global Environmental Politics*, **11**(4), 108–133.

Dixon, RK and I Mintzer (1999). Introduction to the FCCC activities implemented jointly pilot. In Dixon, RK (ed.), *The U.N. Framework Convention on Climate Change Activities Implemented Jointly (AIJ) Pilot: Experiences and Lessons Learned*. Dordrecht: Kluwer Academic Publishers.

Dudek, D, A Golub and E Strukova (2003). Ancillary benefits of reducing greenhouse gas emissions in transitional economies. *World Development*, **31**(10), 1759–1769.

Duic, N, LM Alves, F Chen and M da Gracia Carvalho (2003). Potential of Kyoto protocol clean development mechanism in transfer of clean energy technologies to small island developing states: Case study of Cape Verde. *Renewable and Sustainable Energy Reviews*, **7**(1), 83–98.

Dutschke, M and A Michaelowa (2006). Development assistance and the CDM–How to interpret financial additionality. *Environment and Development Economics*, **11**(2), 235–246.

Edwards, TH and JP Hutton (2001). Allocation of carbon permits within a country: A general equilibrium analysis of the United Kingdom. *Energy Economics*, **23**(4), 371–386.

Ellerman, AD and BK Buchner (2007). The European union emissions trading scheme: origins, allocation, and early results. *Review of Environmental Economics and Policy*, **1**(1), 66–87.

Ellerman, AD and IS Wing (2000). Supplementarity: An invitation to monopsony? *Energy Journal*, **21**(4), 29–59.

Ellerman, AD, BK Buchner and C Carraro (eds.) (2007). *Allocation in the European Emissions Trading Scheme: Rights, Rents and Fairness*. Cambridge, United Kingdom: Cambridge University Press.

Ellerman, AD, PL Joskow, R Schmalensee and J-P Montero (2000). *Markets for Clean Air: The U.S. Acid Rain Program*. Cambridge; New York and Melbourne: Cambridge University Press.

Ellerman, AD (2005). A note on tradeable permits. *Environmental and Resource Economics*, **31**(2), 123–131.

Europa (2007). Emission Trading Scheme (EU ETS). Available at: http:\ec.europa.eu.

Eyckmans, J, D van Regemorter and V van Steenberghe (2001). Is Kyoto fatally flawed? Center for Economic Studies Working Paper 2001-18. Leuven: Katholieke Universiteit Leuven.

Feng, H and CL Kling (2005). The consequences of cobenefits for the efficient design of carbon sequestration programs. *Canadian Journal of Agricultural Economics*, **53**(4), 461–476.

Fisher, BS, N Nakicenovic, K Alfsen, JC Morlot, F de la Chesnaye, J-C Hourcade, K Jiang, M Kainuma, E la Rovere, A Matysek, A Rana, K Riahi, R Richels, S Rose, D van Vuuren, R Warren (2007). Issues related to mitigation in the long term context. In B Metz, OR Davidson, PR Bosch, R Dave and LA Meyer (eds.), *Climate Change 2007: Mitigation. Contribution of Working Group III to the Fourth Assessment Report of the Intergovernmental Ponel on Climated Chagne*. Cambridge and New York: Cambridge University Press.

Fisher, BS, V Tulpule and S Brown (1998). The climate change negotiations: The case for differentiation. *Australian Journal of Agricultural and Resource Economics*, **42**(1), 83–97.

Forsyth, T (1999). Flexible mechanisms of climate technology transfer. *Journal of Environment and Development*, **8**(3), 238–257.

Forsyth, T (2005). Partnerships for Technology Transfer–How Can Investors and Communities Build Renewable Energy in Asia? Sustainable Development Programme SDP BP 05/01. Available at: http://personal.lse.ac.uk/FORSYTHT/RIIA_partnership_paper05.pdf.

Gangadharan, L (2000). Transaction costs in pollution markets: An empirical study. *Land Economics*, **76**(4), 601–614.

Garbaccio, RF, MS Ho and DW Jorgenson (1999). Controlling carbon emissions in China. *Environment and Development Economics*, **4**(4), 493–518.

Gelb, A *et al.* (1988). *Oil Windfalls: Blessing or Curse?* New York, London, Toronto and Tokyo: Oxford University Press for the World Bank.

Geres, R and A Michaelowa (2002). A qualitative method to consider leakage effects from CDM and JI projects. *Energy Policy*, **30**(6), 461–463.

Ghosh, P and J Puri (eds.) (1994). *Joint Implementation of Climate Change Commitments: Opportunities and Apprehensions*. New Delhi: Tata Energy Research Institute.

Godal, O and G Klaassen (2006). Carbon trading across sources and periods constrained by the Marrakesh accords. *Journal of Environmental Economics and Management*, **51**(3), 308–322.

Gollier, C (2002). Discounting an uncertain future. *Journal of Public Economics*, **85**(2), 149–166.

Goulder, LH and K Mathai (2000). Optimal CO_2 abatement in the presence of induced technical change. *Journal of Environmental Economics and Management*, **39**(1), 1–38.

Goulder, LH and SH Schneider (1999). Induced technological change and the attractiveness of CO_2 abatement policies. *Resource and Energy Economics*, **21**(3/4), 211–253.

Green, A (2006). Trade rules and climate change subsidies. *World Trade Review*, **5**(3), 377–414.

Greiner, S and A Michaelowa (2003). Defining investment additionality for CDM projects-practical approaches. *Energy Policy*, **31**(10), 1007–1015.

Grubb, M, C Vrolijk and D Brack (1999). *The Kyoto Protocol: A Guide and Assessment*. London: Royal Institute of International Affairs.

Grütter, J (2001). The GHG market after Bonn. *Joint Implementation Quarterly*, **7**(3), 9.

Gulbrandsen, LH and S Andresen (2004). NGO influence in the implementation of the Kyoto protocol: Compliance, flexibility mechanisms, and sinks. *Global Environmental Politics*, **4**(4), 54–75.

Gundimeda, H (2004). How sustainable is the sustainable development objective of CDM in developing countries like India? *Forest Policy and Economics*, **6**(3/4), 329–343.

Gupta, S, DA Tirpak, N Burger, J Gupta, N Höhne, AI Boncheva, GM Kanoan, C Kolstad, JA Kruger, A Michaelowa, S Murase, J Pershing, T Saijo, A Sari

(2007). Policies, insturments and co-operative arrangements. In B Metz, OR Davidson, PR Bosch, R Dave and LA Meyer (eds.), *Climate Change 2007: Mitigation. Contribution of Working Group III to the Fourth Assessment Report of the Intergovernmental Ponel on Climated Change.* Cambridge, United Kingdom and New York, NY, USA: Cambridge University Press.

Gupta, S and PM Bhandari (1999). An effective allocation criterion for CO_2 emissions. *Energy Policy*, **27**(12), 727–736.

Hagem, C and O Maestad (2006). Russian exports of emission permits under the Kyoto Protocol: The interplay with non-competitive fuel markets. *Resource and Energy Economics*, **28**(1), 54–73.

Hahn, RW and GL Hester (1989). Where did all the markets go? An analysis of EPA's emissions trading program. *Yale Journal on Regulation*, **6**(1), 109–153.

Hahn, RW and RN Stavins (2010). The effect of allowance allocations on cap-and-trade system performance. Nota di Lavoro 80.2010. Fondazione Eni Enrico Mattei, Milan.

Haites, E, D Maosheng, S Seres (2006). Technology transfer by CDM projects. *Climate Policy*, **6**(3), 327–344.

Haites, E (2004). Estimating the market potential for the clean development mechanism: Review of models and lessons learned. PCFplus Report 19. Washington DC: The World Bank Carbon Finance Business PCFplus Research Program.

Halsnæs, K (2000). Estimation of the global market potential for cooperative implementation mechanisms under the Kyoto protocol. In: P Ghosh (ed.), *Implementation of the Kyoto Protocol: Opportunities and Pitfalls for Developing Countries.* Manila: Asian Development Bank.

Halsnæs, K, P Shukla, D Ahuja, G Akumu, R Beale, J Edmonds, C Gollier, A Grübler, M Ha Duong, A Markandya, M McFarland, E Nikitina, T Sugiyama, A Villavicencio and J Zou (2007). Framing issues. In B Metz, OR Davidson, PR Bosch, R Dave and LA Meyer (eds.), *Climate Change 2007: Mitigation. Contribution of Working Group III to the Fourth Assessment Report of the Intergovernmental Ponel on Climated Change.* Cambridge and New York: Cambridge University Press.

Hanafi, AG (1998). Joint implementation: Legal and institutional issues for an effective international program to combat climate change. *The Harvard Environmental Law Review*, **22**(2), 441–508.

Hazlett, TW and RH Coase (2009). In LR Cohen and JD Wright (eds.), *Pioneers of Law and Economics.* Cheltenham, UK and Northampton, MA: Elgar.

Heister, J, P Karani, K Poore, CS Sinha and R Selrod (1999). The World Bank's experience with the activities implemented jointly pilot phase. In RK Dixon (ed.), *The U.N. Framework Convention on Climate Change Activities Implemented Jointly (AIJ) Pilot: Experiences and Lessons Learned.* Dordrecht: Kluwer Academic Publishers.

Heller, TC (1998). Additionality, transaction barriers and political economy of climate change, economics energy environment. Working Paper. Milano, Italy: Fondazione Eni Enroco Matei.

Hepburn, C, M Grubb, K Neuhoff, F Matthes and M Tse (2006). Auctioning of EU ETS phase II allowances: How and why? *Climate Policy*, **6**(1), 137–160.

Hertel, TW and SD Rosch (2010). Climate change, agriculture and poverty. *Applied Economic Perspectives and Policy*, **32**(3), 355–385.

Heydari S, N Ovenden and A Siddiqui (2012). Real options analysis of investment in carbon capture and sequestration technology. *Computational Management Science*, **9**(1), 109–138.

Holtsmark, B (2003). Russian behaviour in the market for permits under the Kyoto Protocol. *Climate Policy*, **3**(4), 399–415.

Hovi, J, CB Froyn and G Bang (2007). Enforcing the Kyoto Protocol: Can punitive consequences restore compliance? *Review of International Studies*, **33**(3), 435–450.

Hunt, C (2008). Economy and ecology of emerging markets and credits for bio-sequestered carbon on private land in tropical Australia. *Ecological Economics*, **66**(203), 309–318.

Ibarraran, V, M Eugenia and RA Boyd (2001). Computable general equilibrium analysis of taxes and double dividend: An application to the Mexican carbon tax. *Economic and Financial Modeling*, **8**(1), 3–27.

IPCC (2004). 16 years of scientific assessment in support of the Climate Convention. Geneva: Intergovernmental Panel on Climate Change.

IPCC (2007a). *Climate Change 2007: Mitigation. Contribution of Working Group III to the Fourth Assessment Report of the Intergovernmental Panel on Climate Change*, B Metz, OR Davidson, PR Bosch, R Dave, LA Meyer (eds.). Cambridge, United Kingdom and New York, NY, USA: Cambridge University Press.

IPCC (2007b). Summary for policy makers. In B Metz, OR Davidson, PR Bosch, R Dave and LA Meyer (eds.), *Climate Change 2007: Mitigation. Contribution of Working Group III to the Fourth Assessment Report of the Intergovernmental Ponel on Climate Change*. Cambridge, United Kingdom and New York, NY, USA: Cambridge University Press.

Jackson, JH (2000). Comments on Shrimp/Turtle and the product/process distinction. *European Journal of International Law*, **11**(2), 303–307.

Jacoby, HD and AD Ellerman (2004). The safety valve and climate policy. *Energy Policy*, **32**(4), 481–491.

Jacoby, H, R Prinn and R Schmalensee (1998). Kyoto's unfinished business. *Foreign Affairs*, **77**, 54–66.

Jacoby, HD, JM Reilly, JR McFarland and S Paltsev (2006). Technology and technical change in the MIT EPPA model. *Energy Economics*, **28**(5/6), 610–631.

Jakeman, G, E Heyhoe, H Pant, K Woffenden and BS Fisher (2001). The Kyoto protocol, economic impacts under the terms of the Bonn agreement. ABARE Conference Paper 2001.28. Canberra: The Australian Bureau of Agricultural and Resource Economics.

Jotzo, F and A Michaelowa (2002). Estimating the CDM market under the Marrakech accords. *Climate Policy*, **2**(1), 179–196.

Keats, KM and K Neuhoff (2005). Allocation of carbon emission certificates in the power sector: How generators profit from grandfathered rights. *Climate Policy*, **5**(1), 61–78.

Kemfert, C (2003). International trade and climate policy–A win-win strategy? Working Paper. University of Oldenburg and FEEM.

Kettunen, J, D Bunn and WW Blyth (2011). Investment propensities under carbon policy uncertainty. *Energy Journal*, **32**(1), 77–117.

Kikuchi, R (2011). Environmental and socio-economic factors in carbon offsets: An approach to sustainable management and planning in climate change strategy. *Journal of Environmental Planning and Management*, **54**(3), 355–367.

Klaassen, G (1996). *Acid Rain and Environmental Degradation: The Economics of Emission Trading*, New Horizons in Environmental Economics Series. Cheltenham, UK, Lyme, NH and Williston, Vt: Elgar in Association with the International Institute for Applied Systems Analysis; distributed by American International Distribution Corporation.

Klepper, G and S Peterson (2005). Trading hot-air: The influence of permit allocation rules, market power and the US withdrawal from the Kyoto protocol. *Environmental and Resource Economics*, **32**(2), 205–227.

Kolstad, CD (2006). The simple analytics of greenhouse gas emission intensity reduction targets. *Energy Policy*, **33**(17), 2231–2236.

Koskela, E, R Schöb and H-W Sinn (1998). Pollution, factor taxation and unemployment. *International Tax and Public Finance*, **5**(3), 379–396.

Kuik, O and M Mulder (2004). Emission trading and competitiveness: Pros and cons of relative and absolute schemes. *Energy Policy*, **32**, 737–745.

Lal, R (2009). Challenges and opportunities in soil organic matter research. *European Journal of Soil Science*, **60**, 158–169.

Lambert, N (1996). Was the Use of Economic Incentives Successful in the Phaseout of Leaded Gasoline in the United States? Available at: http://www.colby.ed/upersonallthtieten/air-lead.html. Accessed 8 December 2012.

Larson, DF (2007). On inverse carrying charges and spatial arbitrage. *Journal of Futures Markets*, **7**(4), 305–336.

Larson, DF and G Breustedt (2009). Will markets direct investments under the Kyoto protocol? Lessons from the activities implemented jointly pilots. *Environmental and Resource Economics*, **43**(3), 433–456.

Larson, DF and P Parks (1999). Risks, lessons learned, and secondary markets for greenhouse gas reductions. Policy Research Working Paper Series 2090. Washington DC: World Bank.

Larson, DF, A Dinar and F Frisbie (2011) The present and future role for agricultural projects under the clean development mechanism. In A Dinar and R Mendelsohn (eds.), *Handbook on Climate Change and Agriculture*. Chelteham UK: Edward Elgar.

Larson, DF, A Dinar and B Blankespoor (2012). Aligning climate change mitigation and agricultural policies in Eastern Europe and Central Asia. Policy Research Working Paper 6080. Washington, DC: World Bank.

Larson, DF, P Ambrosi, A Dinar, SM Rahman and R Entler (2008). A review of carbon market policies and research. *International Review of Environmental and Resource Economics*, **2**(3), 177–236.

Lecocq, F and P Ambrosi (2007). The clean development mechanism: History, status, and prospects. *Review of Environmental Economics and Policy*, **1**(1), 134–151.

Lee, DR and WS Misiolek (1986). Substituting pollution taxation for general taxation: Some implications for efficiency in pollution taxation. *Journal of Environmental Economics and Management*, **13**(4), 338–347.

Leimbach, M (2003). Equity and carbon emissions trading: A model analysis. *Energy Policy*, **31**(10), 1033–1044.

Li, JC (2002). Including the feedback of local health improvement in assessing costs and benefits of GHG reduction. *Review of Urban and Regional Development Studies*, **14**(3), 282–304.

Li, JC (2006). A multi-period analysis of a carbon tax including local health feedback: An application to Thailand. *Environment and Development Economics*, **11**(3), 317–342.

Lile, R, M Powell and M Toman (1998). Implementing the clean development mechanism: Lessons from U.S. private-sector participation in activities implemented jointly. Discussion Paper No. 99-08. Washington, DC: Resources for the Future.

Lindzen, RS (1990). Some coolness concerning global warming. *Bulletin of the American Meteorological Society*, **71**(3), 288–299.

Lise, W, V Linderhof, O Kuik, C Kemfert, R Ostling, and T Heinzow (2006). A game theoretic model of the Northwestern European electricity market — market power and the environment. *Energy Policy*, **34**(15), 2123–2136.

Löschel, A and Z Zhang (2002). The economic and environmental implications of the US repudiation of the Kyoto protocol and the subsequent deals in Bonn and Marrakech. *Review of World Economics* (Weltwirtschaftliches Archiv) **138**(4), 711–746.

Löschel, A (2002). Technological change in economic models of environmental policy: A survey. *Ecological Economics*, **43**(2/3), 105–126.

Lutter, R (2000). Developing countries' greenhouse emissions: Uncertainty and implications for participation in the Kyoto protocol. *Energy Journal*, **21**(4), 93–120.

Maeda, A (2003). The emergence of market power in emission rights markets: The role of initial permit distribution. *Journal of Regulatory Economics*, **24**(3), 293–314.

Makundi, WR and JA Sathaye (2003). GHG mitigation potential and cost in tropical forestry–Relative role for agroforestry. *Journal Environment, Development and Sustainability*, **6**(1/2), 235–260.

Manne, AS and RG Richels (1999). The Kyoto protocol: A cost-effective strategy for meeting environmental objectives? In J Weyant (ed.), *The Cost of the Kyoto Protocol: A Multi-Model Evaluation, Energy Journal*, (Special Issue), pp. 1–23.

Manne, AS and TF Rutherford (1994). International trade in oil, gas and carbon emission rights: An intertemporal general equilibrium model. *Energy Journal*, **15**(1), 57–76.

Margolis, RM and DM Kammen (1999). Evidence of under investment in energy R&D in the United States and the impact of federal policy. *Energy Policy*, **27**(10), 575–584.

Mathys, NA and J de Melo (2011). Political economy aspects of climate change mitigation efforts. *The World Economy*, **34**(110), 1938–1954.

Matsuhashi, R, W Chang and H Ishitani (1999). A study on systems for a clean development mechanism to reduce CO_2 emission. *Environmental Economics and Policy Studies*, **2**(4), 289–303.

McKibbin, WJ and PJ Wilcoxen (2002). The role of economics in climate change policy. *Journal of Economic Perspectives*, **16**(2), 107–129.

McKibbin, WJ, R Shackleton and PJ Wilcoxen (1999). What to expect from an international system of tradable permits for carbon emissions. *Resource and Energy Economics*, **21**(304), 319–346.

McKitrick, R (1997). Double dividend environmental taxation and Canadian carbon emissions control. *Canadian Public Policy*, **23**(4), 417–434.

Meehl, GA, TF Stocker, WD Collins, P Friedlingstein, AT Gaye, JM Gregory, A Kitoh, R Knutti, JM Murphy, A Noda, SCB Raper, IG Watterson, AJ Weaver and Z-C Zhao (2007). Global climate projections. In S Solomon, D Qin, M Manning, Z Chen, M Marquis, KB Averyt, M Tignor and HL Miller (eds.), *Climate Change 2007: The Physical Science Basis. Contribution of Working Group I to the Fourth Assessment Report of the Intergovernmental Panel on Climate Change.* Cambridge University Press, Cambridge, United Kingdom and New York, NY, USA.

Mehlum, H, K Moene and R Torvik (2006). Institutions and the resource curse. *Economic Journal*, **116**(508), 1–20.

Mendelsohn, R, A Dinar and L Williams (2006). The distributional impact of climate change on rich and poor countries. *Environment and Development Economics*, **11**(2), 159–178.

Michaelowa, A and E Fages (1999). Options for baselines of the clean development mechanism. *Mitigation and Adaptation Strategies for Global Change*, **4**(2), 167–185.

Michaelowa, A, K Begg, S Parkinson and RK Dixon (1999). Interpretation and application of FCCC AIJ pilot project development criteria. In RK Dixon (ed.), *The U.N. Framework Convention on Climate Change Activities Implemented Jointly (AIJ) Pilot: Experiences and Lessons Learned*. Dordrecht: Kluwer Academic Publishers.

Michaelowa, A, M Stronzik, F Eckermann and A Hunt (2003). Transaction costs of the Kyoto Mechanisms. *Climate Policy*, **3**(3), 261–278.

Michaelowa, A, RK Dixon and L Abron (1999). The AIJ project development community. In RK Dixon (ed.), *The U.N. Framework Convention on Climate Change Activities Implemented Jointly (AIJ) Pilot: Experiences and Lessons Learned*. Dordrecht: Kluwer Academic Publishers.

Millock, K (2002). Technology transfers in the clean development mechanism: An incentives issue. *Environment and Development Economics*, **7**(3), 449–466.

Muller, RA and S Mestelman (1998). What have we learned from emissions trading experiments? *Managerial and Decision Economics*, **19**(4/5), 225–238.

Mundlak, Y (1993). On the empirical aspects of economic growth theory. *American Economic Review*, **83**(2), 415–420.

Neeff, T, L Eichler, I Deecke and J Fehse (2007). Update on markets for forestry offsets. CATIE (Costa Rica).

Neuhoff, K, KM Keats, M Sato (2006). Allocation, incentives and distortions: The impact of EU ETS emissions allowance allocations to the electricity sector. *Climate Policy*, **6**(1), 73–91.

New Carbon Finance (2007). UK in Pole Position as Carbon Funds Surge — But More Funds Required. Press Release 4 April 2007. Available at: www.newcarbonfinance.com. Accessed 8 December 2012.

Newell, RG and WA Pizer (2004). Uncertain discount rates in climate policy analysis. *Energy Policy*, **32**(4), 519–529.

Newell, RG, JN Sanchirico and S Kerr (2005). Fishing quota markets. *Journal of Environmental Economics and Management*, **49**(3), 437–462.

Nordhaus, WD (1977). Economic growth and climate: The carbon dioxide problem. *American Economic Review*, **67**(1), 341–46.

Nordhaus, WD (2001). Global warming economics. *Science*, **294**(5545), 1283–1284.

Nordhaus, WD (2002). Modeling induced innovation in climate-change policy. In A Grübler, N Nakićenović and WD Nordhaus (eds.), *Technological Change and the Environment*. Washington, DC, Luxemburg: Resources for the Future, International Institute for Applied Systems Analysis.

Nordhaus, WD (2007). To tax or not to tax: Alternative approaches to slowing global warming. *Review of Environmental Economics and Policy*, **1**(1), 26–44.

Nordhaus, WD (2007b). A review of the stern review on the economics of climate change. *Journal of Economic Literature*, **45**(3), 686–702.

Nordhaus, WD and JG Boyer (2000). *Warming the World: Economic Models of Global Warming*. Cambridge, MA: MIT Press.

O'Connor, D, F Zhai, K Aunan, T Berntsen and H Vennemo (2003). Agricultural and human health impacts of climate policy in China: A general-equilibrium analyses with special reference to Guangdong. Technical Paper 206. Paris: OECD.

Oda, J, K Akimoto, F Sano and T Tomoda (2007). Diffusion of energy efficient technologies and CO_2 emission reductions in iron and steel sector. *Energy Economics*, **29**(4), 868–888.

Olschewski, R, PC Benitez, GHJ de Koning and T Schlichter (2005). How attractive are forest carbon sinks? Economic insights into supply and demand of certified emission reductions. *Journal of Forest Economics*, **11**(2), 77–94.

Painuly, JP (2001). The Kyoto protocol, emissions trading and the CDM: An analysis from developing countries perspective. *Energy Journal*, **22**(3), 147–169.

Paltsev, SV (2001). The Kyoto protocol: Regional and sector contributions to the carbon leakage. *Energy Journal*, **22**(4), 53–79.

Panayotou, T, JD Sachs and AP Zwane (2002). Compensation for meaningful participation in climate change control: A modest proposal and empirical analysis. *Journal of Environmental Economics and Management*, **43**(3), 437–454.

Parikh, J (1995). North-South cooperation in climate change through joint implementation. *International Environmental Affairs*, **7**(1), 22–43.

Parry, IWH (1995). Pollution taxes and revenue recycling. *Journal of Environmental Economics and Management*, **29**(3), S64–77.

Parry, IWH and AM Bento (2000). Tax deductions, environmental policy, and the Double Dividend hypothesis. *Journal of Environmental Economics and Management*, **39**(1), 67–96.

Parry, IWH, WA Pizer and C Fischer (2003). How large are the welfare gains from technological innovation induced by environmental policies? *Journal of Regulatory Economics*, **23**(3), 237–255.

Pearce, DW (1991). The role of carbon taxes in adjusting to global warming. *Economic Journal*, **101**(407), 938–948.

Pearson, B (2007). Market failure: Why the clean development mechanism won't promote clean development. *Journal of Cleaner Production*, **15**(2), 247–252.

Pedroni, L (2005). Carbon accounting for sinks in the CDM after COP-9. *Climate Policy*, **5**(4), 407–418.

Pendell, DL, JR Williams, SB Boyles, CW Rice and RG Nelson (2007). Soil carbon sequestration strategies with alternative tillage and nitrogen sources under risk. *Review of Agricultural Economics*, **29**(2), 247–268.

Pindyck, RS (2007). Uncertainty in environmental economics. *Review of Environmental Economics and Policy*, **1**(1), 45–65.

Rosa, LP and SK Ribeiro (2001). The present, past, and future contributions to global warming of CO_2 emissions from fuels. *Climatic Change*, **48**(2/3), 289–307.

Pizer, WA (1998). Prices vs. quantities revisited: The case of climate change. Resources for the Future Discussion Paper 98-02. Washington.

Pizer, WA (2002). Combining price and quantity controls to mitigate global climate change. *Journal of Public Economics*, **85**(3), 409–434.

Plantinga, AJ and JunJie Wu (2003). Co-benefits from carbon sequestration in forests: Evaluating reductions in agricultural externalities from an afforestation policy in Wisconsin. *Land Economics*, **79**(1), 74–85.

Portney, P and J Weyant (1999). *Discounting and Intergenerational Equity*. Washington: Resources for the Future.

Prager, M, T Klier and R Mattoon (1996). A mixed bag: assessment of market performance and firm trading behavior in the NO_x RECLAIM program. Federal Reserve Bank Chicago Working Paper Series WP-1996-12. Chicago: Chicago Federal Reserve.

Rahman, SM, A Dinar and DF Larson (2010). Diffusion of Kyoto's clean development mechanism. *Technological Forecasting and Social Change*, **77**(8), 1391–1400.

Renz, H (1998). Joint implementation and the question of additionality–A proposal for a pragmatic approach to identify possible joint implementation projects. *Energy Policy*, **26**(4), 275–279.

Revelle, Roger and Hans Suess (1957). Carbon dioxide exchange between atmosphere and ocean and the question of an increase of atmospheric CO_2 during the past decades. *Tellus* **9**, 18–27.

Ringius, L, A Torvanger and B Holtsmark (1998). Can multi-criteria rules fairly distribute climate burdens? OECD results from three burden sharing rules. *Energy Policy*, **26**(10), 777–793.

Rose, A, B Stevens, J Edmonds and M Wise (1998). International equity and differentiation in global warming policy: An application to tradeable emission permits. *Environmental and Resource Economics*, **12**(1), 25–51.

Roson, R (2003). Climate change policies and tax recycling schemes: Simulations with a dynamic general equilibrium model of the Italian economy. *Review of Urban and Regional Development Studies*, **15**(1), 26–44.

Sabbaghi, O and N Sabbaghi (2011). Carbon financial instruments, thin trading, and volatility: Evidence from the Chicago climate exchange. *The Quarterly Review of Economics and Finance*, **51**(4), 399–407.

Sagar, AD (2000). Evidence of under investment in energy R&D in the United States and the impact of federal policy: A comment on Margolis and Kammen. *Energy Policy*, **28**(9), 651–654.

Sagar, AD and B van der Zwaan (2006). Technological innovation in energy sector: R&D, deployment, and learning-by-doing. *Energy Policy*, **34**(17), 2601–2608.

Sahlén, L and T Aronsson (2006). Technology transfers and the clean development mechanism in a North-South general equilibrium model. FEEM Working Paper 145, Venice, Italy.

Sandor RL, EC Bettelheim and IR Swingland (2002). An overview of a free-market approach to climate change and conservation. *Philosophical Transactions A*, **360**(1797), 1607–1620.

Sands, RD (2004). Dynamics of carbon abatement in the second generation model. *Energy Economics*, **26**(4), 721–738.

Sathaye, J, A Najam, C Cocklin, T Heller, F Lecocq, J Llanes-Regueiro, J Pan, G Petschel-Held , S Rayner, J Robinson, R Schaeffer, Y Sokona, R Swart, H Winkler (2007). Sustainable development and mitigation. In B Metz, OR Davidson, PR Bosch, R Dave and LA Meyer (eds.), *Climate Change 2007: Mitigation. Contribution of Working Group III to the Fourth Assessment Report of the Intergovernmental Panel on Climate Change*. Cambridge, United Kingdom and New York, NY, USA: Cambridge University Press.

Schlamadinger, B, B Bosquet. C Streck, I Noble, M Dutschke and N Bird (2005). Can the EU emission trading scheme support CDM forestry? *Climate Policy*, **5**(2), 199–208.

Schwank, O (2006). Concerns about CDM Projects Based on Decomposition of HFC-23 Emission from 22 HCFC Production Sites. Public Comment Provided to the CDM Board. Available at: cdm.unfccc.int. Accessed 8 December 2012.

Schwarze, R (2000). Activities implemented jointly: Another look at the facts. *Ecological Economics*, **32**(2), 255–267.

Shrestha, RM and GR Timilsina (2002). The additionality criterion for identifying clean development mechanism projects under the Kyoto protocol. *Energy Policy*, **30**(1), 73–79.

Siegenthaler, U and H Oeschger (1987). Biospheric CO_2 emissions during the past 200 years reconstructed by deconvolution of ice core data. *Tellus*, **39B**, 140–154.

Sijm, JPM, FT Ormel, J-W Martens, SNM van Rooijen, MH Voogt, MT van Wees and C de Zoeten-Dartenset (2000). Kyoto mechanisms: The role of joint implementation, the clean development mechanism and emissions trading in reducing greenhouse gas Emissions. ECN Report C-00-026. Petten, The Netherlands.

Sonneborn, CL (1999). An overview of greenhouse gas emissions trading pilot schemes and activities. *Ecological Economics*, **31**(1), 1–10.

Springer, U (2003). The market for tradable GHG permits under the Kyoto protocol: A survey of model studies. *Energy Economics*, **25**(5), 527–551.

Stavin, RN (1995). Transaction costs and tradable permits. *Journal of Environmental Economics and Management*, **29**(2), 133–148.

Stern, N (2007). *The Economics of Climate Change: The Stern Review*. Cambridge and New York: Cambridge University Press.

Stevens, B and A Rose (2002). A dynamic analysis of the marketable permits approach to global warming policy: A comparison of spatial and temporal flexibility. *Journal of Environmental Economics and Management*, **44**(1), 45–69.

Stiglitz, JE (2006). A new agenda for global warming. *The Economists' Voice*, **3**(7). Available at: http://www.bepress.com/ev/vol3/iss7/art3. Accessed 8 December 2012.

Szabó, L, I Hidalgo, JC Ciscar and A Soria (2006). CO_2 emission trading within the European Union and Annex B countries: The cement industry case. *Energy Policy*, **34**(1), 72–87.

Takeda, S (2007). The double dividend from carbon regulations in Japan. *Journal of the Japanese and International Economies*, **21**(3), 336–364.

Terkla, D (1984). The efficiency value of effluent tax revenues. *Journal of Environmental Economics and Management*, **11**(2), 107–123.

Tietenberg, T (2010). Cap-and-trade: The evolution of an economic idea. *Agricutltural and Resource Economics Review*, **39**(3), 359–367.

Tol, RSJ and R Verheyen (2004). State responsibility and compensation for climate change damages — A legal and economic assessment. *Energy Policy*, **32**(9), 1109–1130.

UNEP RISOE (2008). CDM/JI Pipeline Analysis and Database, 1 March 2008. RISCOE, Roskilde Denmark.

UNFCCC (2001). Report of the Conference of the Parties on its seventh session, held at Marrakech 29 October–10 November, Part two: Action taken by the Conference of the Parties, Vol. II. FCCC/CP/2001/13/Add.2, Marrakech.

UNFCCC (2012). Status of Ratification of the Kyoto Protocol. Available at: http://unfccc.int/kyoto_protocol/status_of_ratification/items/2613.php (accessed on 1 August 2012).

UN-REDD (2012). United Nations Collaborative Programme on Reducing Emissions from Deforestation and Forst Degradation in Developing Countries. Available at: www.un-redd.org (accessed 3 August 2012).

Vaillancourt, K and JP Waaub (2004). Equity in international greenhouse gas abatement scenarios: A multicriteria approach. *European Journal of Operational Research*, **253**(3), 489–505.

Valverde, LAJ, HD Jacoby and GM Kaufman (1999). Sequential climate decisions under uncertainty: An integrated framework. *Environmental Modeling and Assessment* **4**(2/3), 87–101.

van Wijnbergen, S (1986). Aid, export promotion and the real exchange rate: An African dilemma. Working Paper Series 199. Washington, DC: World Bank.

Victor, DG, N Nakićenović and N Victor (2001) The Kyoto protocol emission allocations: Windfall surpluses for Russia and Ukraine. *Climatic Change*, **49**(3), 263–277.

Victor, D (2001). *The Collapse of the Kyoto Protocol and the Struggle to Slow Global Warming*. Princeton, NJ: Princeton University Press.

Vrolijk, C (2000). Quantifying the Kyoto commitments. *Review of European Community and International Environmental Law*, **9**(3), 285–295.

Watanabe, R and G Robinson (2005). The European Union emissions trading scheme (EU ETS). *Climate Policy*, **5**(1), 10–14.

Weitzman, ML (1974). Prices versus quantities. *Review of Economic Studies*, **41**(4), 477–491.

Weitzman, ML (1998). Why the far-distant future should be discounted at its lowest possible rate. *Journal of Environmental Economics and Management*, **36**(3), 201–208.

Weitzman, ML (2001). Gamma discounting. *American Economic Review*, **91**(1), 260–271.

Werksman, J (1998). The clean development mechanism: Unwrapping the Kyoto surprise. *Review of European Community and International Environment Law*, **7**(2), 147–158.

Werksman, J (1999). Greenhouse gas emissions trading and the WTO. *Review of European Community and International Environmental Law*, **8**(3), 251–264.

Weyant, JP (ed.) (1999). The cost of the Kyoto protocol: A multi-model evaluation. *Energy Journal* (special edition) May, 1–24.

Weyant, JP (2004). Introduction and overview. *Energy Economics*, **26**(4), 501–515.

Whalley, J and RM Wigle (1991). Cutting CO_2 emissions: The effects of alternative policy approaches. *Energy Journal*, **12**(1), 109–124.

Williams, RC III (1999). Revisiting the cost of protectionism: The role of tax distortions in the labor market. *Journal of International Economics*, **47**(2), 429–447.

Williams, RC III (2002). Environmental tax interactions when pollution affects health or productivity. *Journal of Environmental Economics and Management*, **44**(2), 261–270.

Wirl, F (2006). Consequences of irreversibilities on optimal intertemporal CO_2 emission policies under uncertainty. *Resource and Energy Economics*, **28**(2), 105–123.

Wirl, F (2007). Corrigendum to consequences of irreversibilities on optimal intertemporal CO_2 emission policies under uncertainty. *Resource and Energy Economics*, **29**(4), 325–326.

Woodward, RT (2000). Market-based solutions to environmental problems: Discussion. *Journal of Agricultural and Applied Economics*, **32**(2), 259–266.

World Bank (2006). Big Chinese step in carbon emissions trading. News Release No. 2006/224/ESSD. Washington, DC: World Bank.

World Bank (2008). *International Trade and Climate Change: Economic, Legal and Institutional Perspectives*. Washington, DC: World Bank.

World Bank (2008b). News Press Release No. 2009/092/SDN. Washington, DC: World Bank.

Yemshanov, D, DW McKenney, T Hatton and G Fox (2005). Investment attractiveness of afforestation in Canada inclusive of carbon sequestration benefits. *Canadian Journal of Agricultural Economics*, **53**(4), 307–323.

Zhang, C, TC Heller and MM May (2005). Carbon intensity of electricity generation and CDM baseline: Case studies of three Chinese provinces. *Energy Policy*, **33**(4), 451–465.

Zhang, Z and L Assução (2004). Domestic climate policies and the WTO. *World Economy*, **27**(3), 359–386.

Zhang, Z (2000). Estimating the size of the potential market for the Kyoto flexibility mechanisms. *Journal Review of World Economics*, **136**(3), 491–521.

ANNEX 2.1: Glossary of Acronyms.

Acronym	Meaning
AAU	Assigned Amount Unit
AIJ	Activities Implemented Jointly
AIE	Accredited Independent Entity
CCX	Chicago Climate Exchange
CDM	Clean Development Mechanism
CER	Certified Emission Reduction
CFI	Chicago Financial Instrument
CGE	Computable General Equilibrium
COP	UNFCCC Conference of the Parties
DOE	Designated Operational Entity
ERPA	Emissions Reduction Purchase Agreement
ERU	Emission Reduction Unit
EU ETS	The European Union Emission Trading Scheme
GGAS	Greenhouse Gas Abatement Scheme
GHG	Greenhouse Gas
IPCC	Intergovernmental Panel on Climate Change
JI	Joint Implementation
JISC	Joint Implementation Supervisory Committee
lCER	Long-term CER under LULUCF
LULUCF	Land Use, Land-Use Change, and Forestry
NAP	National Allocation Plan
NETS	National Greenhouse Gas Emissions Trading Scheme
NGAC	New South Wales Greenhouse Gas Abatement Certificate
ODA	Overseas Development Assistance
OECD	The Organization for Economic Co-operation and Development
$MtCO_2e$	Million tons of CO_2 equivalent
PCF	Prototype Carbon Fund
PDD	Project Design Document, for CDM
RGGI	Regional Greenhouse Gas Initiative
RMU	Removal Unit, for GHG removal from the atmosphere through LULUCF
SBSTA	Subsidiary Body for Scientific and Technological Advice
tCER	Temporary CER under LULUCF
tCO_2e	Ton of CO_2 equivalent
UNFCCC	United Nations Framework Convention on Climate Change

3. THE ACTIVITIES IMPLEMENTED JOINTLY PILOTS: A FOUNDATION FOR CLEAN DEVELOPMENT MECHANISM?*

With Contribution by Gunnar Breustedt

As we have already described in the earlier chapters, the Flexibility Mechanisms in the Kyoto Protocol include Joint Implementation (JI), the Clean Development Mechanism (CDM), and emissions trading. JI allows emission reductions or sink enhancement to be undertaken where they are cheapest within the group of Annex I countries, including economies in transition, through the implementation of projects (Schroeder, 2010).

In addition, to gain experience in using CDM, participants of the United Nations Framework Convention on Climate Change (UNFCCC) agreed to set up national pilot programs and report results from the pilots in a standard format. The national pilots, collectively referred to as Activities Implemented Jointly (AIJ), provide the most significant source of available experience on projects intended to offset greenhouse gas emissions prior to the implementation of CDM. We make use of outcomes from the AIJ pilots to draw inferences about how project investments might be determined under the investment provisions of the ratified Kyoto Protocol. Of particular interest are the rules and procedures for reviewing, approving, and monitoring projects that were developed under the national pilots.

An important feature of the AIJ program that continues under the CDM of the Kyoto Protocol is that investor and host government approval is required for private bilateral project investments to move forward. Descriptive studies of the AIJ program suggest that these approval processes provided opportunities for additional, sometimes unrelated, national political

*This chapter is based on Larson and Breustedt (2009). Permission from the *Journal Environmental and Resource Economics* is acknowledged.

objectives to influence project selection. This differs from the conceptual depiction of Kyoto-related institutions as impartial regulators of project quality and suggests that the institutional arrangements that gave rise to AIJ investments outcomes are not fully consistent with the competitive market outcomes that are anticipated from the flexibility provisions of the Kyoto agreement. In this chapter, we test this characterization of the AIJ program. We find evidence that project investments under the national AIJ programs were not independent of the types of political and cultural considerations that motivate traditional models of development assistance and that this limited the number of implemented projects.

Although the AIJ program and the current Kyoto project mechanisms differ in significant ways, we argue that the AIJ experience is relevant to current climate change policies for two reasons. First, because the national pilots were undertaken to build experience relevant for treaty implementation, countries may be inclined to retain institutions built up during the pilots. If so, and if these institutions continue to work to constrain investment choice, efficiency gains from the proposed flexibility mechanisms will be reduced. Therefore, a better understanding of the determinants of investments under early pilots can potentially identify key policies that could minimize or mitigate investment hurdles under current programs. The participation in the AIJ program is used in the analysis we present in the coming chapters as a positive determinant of participation in the CDM. Second, the characterization of an investment process limited by an additional layering of bilateral selection is also at odds with the cost assumptions that underlie most quantitative estimates of benefits related to the Protocol's flexibility mechanisms. Potentially, most efforts to value the economic effects of the Protocol are based on a flawed view of how the implemented treaty might work. Our findings suggest the need to find alternative modeling approaches that take into account bilateral relationships.

ORIGINS OF THE AIJ PROGRAM

A series of debates in the scientific community over the potential risks and uncertainties associated with a continuing buildup of greenhouse gases led to political concerns and, in 1989, the UN initiated the process of negotiating an international treaty to protect the global climate by limiting greenhouse gas emissions. The framework for this treaty was eventually established in the Kyoto Protocol to the United Nations Framework Convention on Climate Change (UNFCCC) in December 1997. The Protocol entered into force in February 2005.[1]

The cost of reducing emissions varies greatly among countries, though the effects of greenhouse gas emissions on climate change are uniform, regardless of where the gases are emitted. Early drafts of the treaty soon settled on restricting the richest countries to historical emission levels as the primary mechanisms for limiting emissions, but debate continued on how to control abatement costs.[2] In the course of negotiation, the Government of Norway suggested that a mechanism be introduced to allow partnerships between countries that would achieve emission reductions at a lower cost (Carraro, 1999; Dixon and Mintzer, 1999). Broadly, the approach allowed those countries facing emission limits to receive credit for investments made elsewhere that reduce global emissions. The concept came to be known as Joint Implementation (JI) and was subsequently adopted into the treaty negotiating documents (Articles 4.2 and 3.3 of the UNFCCC) that are now part of the Protocol.[3]

The notion of solving pollution problems through international cooperation had precedent, but key aspects of the climate proposal related to JI were unique.[4] The proposed measures included caps (assigned amounts) on emissions for the richest countries that could be supplemented when JI projects resulted in certified reductions. Both assigned amounts and newly created offset credits could be traded. The supplemental credits, measured in tons of carbon, were to be calculated by comparing actual project emissions against a hypothetical counterfactual known as a baseline.[5] This framework, based on trade and the opportunity to supplement

---

[1] As of May 2008, 181 countries had ratified the treaty, including 39 Annex I countries that represent about 64% of 1990 emissions.

[2] Early policy discussions centered on whether permitted emission levels should be based on history or whether common ownership rights applied (Bertram, 1992). Proposed approaches included carbon taxes, national quantitative restrictions, and tradable quotas. See Whalley and Wigle (1991) for an early quantitative assessment of policies under debate.

[3] Under current usage, JI refers to projects hosted in the developed countries and transitional economies listed in Annex I of the Kyoto Protocol. Projects hosted in non–Annex-I countries fall under CDM.

[4] Examples of international cooperative action include the 1976 Convention Concerning the Protection of the Rhine River against Pollution by Chlorides and the 1985 Vienna Convention for the Protection of the Ozone Layer (Hanafi, 1998).

[5] See Heister *et al.* (1999) on early World Bank experiences with baselines.

fixed emission allocations with project-based offsets, evolved into the "flexibility mechanisms" of the current Kyoto Protocol.

At subsequent negotiations in Berlin, delegates agreed that pilot projects could help inform the debate on practical issues surrounding JI.[6] The agreement, known as Decision 5 of the UNFCCC, provided broad guidelines for establishing a voluntary AIJ program that reflected then-current deliberations. It declared that all AIJ projects should benefit the climate in real and measurable ways, that each AIJ project should be agreed upon by host and investor governments, and that any financing from investor-governments must be additional to planned aid flows — a condition termed "financial additionality." Moreover, to prevent the stockpiling of projects under lax baselines, the decision explicitly precluded the accrual of credits under AIJ projects during the pilot phase.

The rules set out in Decision 5 influenced the expectations and motivations for AIJ projects in standard ways for all participating countries. In addition, participants forged a common reporting standard to record key characteristics of projects implemented under national AIJ programs.[7] Both features help make comparisons among AIJ projects feasible. Even so, as discussed below, differences among the national programs emerged, giving rise to differing incentives and procedures.

RELATED STUDIES

In the next sections, we develop an applied model of how project investments came about under the AIJ program. In order to provide context for the models, we briefly review results from numeric studies that measure the expected benefits of the Kyoto flexibility mechanisms. We also discuss the theoretical and practical motivations for carbon project investments and the country-specific processes by which the AIJ project were approved

---

[6]A key concern was that imprecise baselines would allow countries that had pledged reductions to purchase watered-down credits cheaply from developing countries, attenuating the environmental benefits of the treaty. Delegates from developing countries worried that donor countries would redirect aid flows to JI projects (Grubb, Vrolijk, and Brack, 1999). See also criticisms in Ghosh and Puri (1994), Parikh (1995), and Cullet and Kameri-Mbote (1998). Gulbrandsen and Andresen (2004) discuss non-governmental organizations.

[7]Convention participants assigned an advisory committee, the Subsidiary Body for Scientific and Technological Advice (SBSTA) to establish reporting guidelines and to compile and publish the reports on an ongoing basis.

and touch on the potential role transaction costs might play in influencing investment outcomes.

Numeric Studies

Among related studies, the largest group comprises studies that estimate the potential benefits of the Kyoto Protocol's flexibility mechanisms. As Springer (2003) notes in his review, a common finding is that the costs of reaching greenhouse reduction goals are greatly reduced by rules that allowed spatial and temporal flexibility. By way of example, early model results by Bernstein, Montgomery, and Rutherford (1999) suggest that flexible trading rules could reduce the price of carbon permits — which can be seen as the marginal cost of emission reductions — by a factor of 7 in the European Union and by a factor of 16 in Japan.[8]

Generally, numeric studies focus on incentives created by differences in the marginal abatement costs among regions and model the resulting demand for permits arising from project investments.[9] Benefits related to Kyoto's flexibility mechanisms are calculated by comparing market-clearing outcomes under alternative policy scenarios that permit varying levels of trade. Model structure varies considerably, and Springer (2003) categorizes reviewed models into five broad groups. The first is composed of integrated assessment models, where physical and human activities are jointly modeled. As Springer notes, there is overlap between this group and the remaining, since the economic components of the integrated models employ CGE or energy system models. Examples of integrated models are discussed in Manne and Richels (1999), Nordhaus (2001), and Jacoby *et al.* (2006). Another common approach relies on marginal abatement cost curves to examine the effects of trade. Examples include Jotzo and Michaelowa (2002), Löschel and Zhang (2002), and Stevens and Rose (2002). A less-common approach focuses on macroeconomic tradeoffs between monetary policy and employment (see, for example, McKibbin, Shackelton, and Wilcoxen, 1999). An alternative approach is to employ technical engineering

---

[8]See Nordhaus and Boyer (2000), Springer (2003), Weyant (2004), Sands (2004), and Working Group III's contribution to the Fourth IPCC Assessment (IPCC, 2007) for additional reviews of modeling approaches and results. Painuly (2001) reviews numerical models that address project-based investments in developing countries; Muller and Mestelman (1998) review related laboratory-based experiments.

[9]Haites (2004) reviews model predictions of the potential size of CDM markets.

models of sectors or energy systems. These bottom-up models are sometimes integrated with other sectors via a CGE model. IPCC (2007) contains a review of several bottom-up sector models.

Despite differences in their structure, the models generally employ solution mechanisms that seek out market-clearing carbon prices or carbon tax rates. In most cases, price differences only prevail under scenarios in which trade in carbon is restricted by policy. In some cases, the solutions are dynamic and include the endogenous effects of carbon prices on capital stocks and available technologies (Löschel, 2002; Sands, 2004). However, model solutions generally do not take into account differences in profit or cost related to differences in bilateral transaction costs.

This is somewhat surprising since, at a conceptual level, considerable attention has been focused on how transaction costs related to carbon markets might differ among countries and traded instruments.[10] And some researchers have explored ways of incorporating differences in transaction costs into numeric models.[11] However, to date, transaction costs that are incorporated into modeling efforts are tied to specific characteristics of the host, such as sovereign risk, or characteristics of the projects, such as scale or technology, and have no direct effect on bilateral investment outcomes in the model. Consequently, the models implicitly predict that all investors are equally likely to invest in any given host country. We return to this topic below.

Investment and Agency Approval

There is a separate and smaller literature that discusses early experiences from pilots. One area of study concerns the question of what motivated private sector investment in pilot projects and a small group of case-based studies examined the self-declared motivations of early project participants. This includes a discussion of private sector participation in the US AIJ program by Lile, Powell, and Toman (1998); a study by Michaelowa, Dixon, and Abron (1999) that looks at early AIJ participation; a study by Larson and Parks (1999) that surveys a broad group of early pilot participants

---

[10]See, for example, Woerdman (2001).

[11]Bréchet and Lussis (2006) employ transaction costs when modeling the effects of CDM markets on reducing greenhouse gas emissions in Belgium. Michaelowa and Jotzo (2005) use measures of transaction costs taken from AIJ and early World Bank projects to modify marginal abatement cost curves in a numerical model of Kyoto Protocol permit markets to assess the effects of transaction costs on market size.

about investment rationales; a review of selected AIJ projects by Schwarze (2000); and a broader review by Barrera and Schwarze (2004).

The studies identify a variety of factors motivating early participants. Some factors, most notably a desire to influence policy, are indirectly linked to market incentives. Nevertheless, the studies also find that many participants anticipated future regulations on greenhouse gas emissions and hoped to position themselves in ways that would prove useful as policies became clear. For some, this meant finding ways to reduce future regulatory costs, while others looked toward opportunities that might arise from new markets for carbon offsets. Moreover, although early crediting was prohibited during the pilot phase, Schwarze (2000) notes that many of the AIJ projects have project lives extending well into the CDM and JI crediting periods and surmises that many AIJ investors expected to receive credits for offsets generated after the close of the pilot phase.[12] Haites (2004) identifies 54 AIJ projects that are potentially eligible for CDM registration and estimates that the projects could generate reductions equivalent to 20 metric tons of carbon dioxide annually for the 2008–2012 commitment period.

Separate from the issue of what motivated firms to participate in pilot projects are examinations of the national processes by which proposed investments were approved. Michaelowa *et al.* (1999) investigate the application and approval process for AIJ projects in 11 investor countries.[13] They report that most countries established panels drawing on staff from three to eight ministries with sometimes competing objectives. In addition, 6 of the 11 study countries explicitly imposed additional criteria to reflect domestic policy goals. They conclude that these design features of the approval process encouraged the incorporation of broad policy considerations into the project selection process. Similarly, Lile, Powell, and Toman (1998) report that the evaluation process for projects submitted to the United States Initiative on Joint Implementation Evaluation Panel allowed seven departments and agencies to influence the project approval.

To summarize, the descriptive literature suggests that private sector participants were influenced in part by economic incentives motives derived directly from the potential for late-stage credits or indirectly as initial investments in the development of future markets. In addition, the research suggests that the design of the process by which projects were approved played a significant role in investment outcomes.

---

[12]Schwarze examines 96 AIJ projects and finds that all projects lasted well beyond 1999, the scheduled close of the program, and that the average duration of the projects is 31 years.
[13]The countries are Australia, Belgium, Canada, France, Germany, Japan, the Netherlands, Norway, Sweden, Switzerland, and the US.

Multilateral and Bilateral Transaction Costs

As discussed, transaction costs have been a subject of recent interest for numeric modelers, and both administrative costs related to agency approval and transaction costs related to investment generally play a role in the applied model developed in Sec. 4.

In general, transaction costs are associated with all types of economic exchange and are most often related to the costs of acquiring information, addressing risks, enforcing contracts, and protecting rights and property. Public institutions are expected to play an important role in reducing private transaction costs (North, 1987). Practical experience suggests transaction costs are important for tradable emission programs, especially when related markets are nascent (Hahn and Hester, 1989). Hahn (1990), Stavins (1995), Gangadharan (2000), and Cason and Gangadharan (2003) provide additional examples. The same is true for foreign direct investment (FDI) markets (Chakrabarti, 2001; Bénassy-Quéré, Coupet, and Mayer, 2007). And this has relevance to AIJ investments, which can be seen as a special type of FDI.

Later, as part of the discussion of data used for the applied model, we return to the specifics of what might determine transaction costs for AIJ projects. However, it is useful to note that even in the case of bilateral transactions, many of the determinants of transaction costs are not themselves bilateral in nature. Country-specific institutions and characteristics are expected to influence bilateral incentives and costs in general ways, while bilateral characteristics are expected to influence transactions among particular country pairings.

Of particular relevance for the bilateral component of bilateral investment is the role cultural ties might have on transaction costs.[14] Strong cultural ties might be expected to lower search costs and other costs related to information as well as costs associated with counter-party risks. For example, common cultures can give rise to similar legal systems that lower the costs and risks of entering into long-term contractual agreements. Contemporaneously, strong cultural ties can provide popular and reciprocal political support for the strong bilateral political ties and bilateral aid flows.

---

[14]See reviews by Kogut and Singh (1988); Choi (1999); Shenkar (2001); and Siegel, Licht, and Schwartz (2007) on the link between culture and investment.

In this regard, one striking feature of the AIJ pilots is the degree to which investments took place along lines where bilateral relationships were already strong (Barrera and Schwarze 2004). To some extent, this can be attributed to the project selection process and the preferences of policy makers to see investments flow to favored countries. Even so, as with other forms of direct foreign investment, the same dynamics that give rise to strong bilateral ties between governments may also work to hold down private transaction costs. Such ties may be especially important for reducing transaction costs when alternative formal institutions are weak.[15] We take up the implications of this for the conceptual and applied models in the next section.

A MODEL OF PROJECT INVESTMENT

In this section, we develop a conceptual model of the AIJ investment process, motivated by the descriptive literature from the third section. The key feature of the conceptual model is that it distinguishes between investment choices that are exclusively motivated by uncertain profits and those that are additionally constrained by an approving agency's preferences and related transaction costs. We also develop two related statistical models.

In the base model, we explain the number of joint projects using a set of variables thought to determine private investment in combination with a model intended to explain bilateral aid flows. The result is a mixed-regime count model that allows us to test whether bilateral relationships tied to bilateral aid limited the number of observed project investments.

We also consider an alternative dichotomous probit-with-selection model that focuses on whether bilateral investment relationships occurred. Information about the number of projects between a given investor–host combination is retained in this model to explain heterogeneity in the error terms, but it is not taken to indicate the strength of the bilateral partnership. The related point of interest is whether the agency-approval hurdle is cleared for any given potential partnership, rather than how frequently it is cleared. As we discuss later, another motivation for the alternative model has to do with differences in the scale and structure of AIJ projects in instances when project counts are high. The dichotomous model serves as

---

[15]Michaelowa and Jotzo (2005) argue that weak institutions currently limit the overall market for project-investments under the Kyoto mechanisms.

a check that this feature of the data does not unduly influence conclusions drawn from the base model.

Conceptual Model

As a starting point, consider an irreversible investment in a JI project where the profit flow, $\pi(t)$, associated with an investment I follows the stochastic process:

$$dz = \phi(s)\pi_0 dt + \sigma(s)\pi_0 dz \tag{1}$$

where dz is an increment in a Wiener process and where the growth parameter, ϕ, and the dispersion parameter, σ, depend on exogenous state variables, s. It is assumed that the investment is sufficiently long-lived to be represented by the infinite-horizon value function:

$$v(s_t) = E \int_t^\infty \pi_m e^{-\delta(m-t)} dm \tag{2}$$

where E is the expectations operator, δ is a discount rate, and Eq. (2) is conditional on the restriction given in Eq. (1). Dixit and Pindyck (1994: pp. 144–145) show that associated with this investment evaluation problem is a critical level, $v^*(s)$, that exceeds the combined present value of the investment and any option value associated with postponing an irreversible investment. In passing, it is important to point out that factors that reduce uncertainty decrease the option value associated with delay and results in a larger number of desired investment projects.

Now suppose that an interested firm considers a fixed number of investment opportunities. By repeating for each project, the valuation in (2), the firm can match an evaluation, v^i, with each project, I^i. After ranking the projects, the firm will consider that set of projects, $\Omega(s_t)$, where $v(s_t) \geq v^*(s_t)$. The firm may consider additional restrictions, given by vector c.[16] With this in mind, the firm choice problem can then be written as:

$$Max_I \ P(I; c) \ s.t. \ I \in \Omega(s_t) \tag{3}$$

where P represents the firm's decision process for evaluating risk and profit. Changes in the values of s that lower $v^*(s_t)$ will result in a larger number of desired investment projects.

---

[16]For example, the firm may want to limit total investments by country because of portfolio risk considerations.

Next, suppose the firm must also seek approval from an agency that has its own objective function, derived from a set of broad policy objectives, characterized by the vector $z(t)$. Further, assume that, through a ranking process analogous to the firm's ranking process, the agency derives its own set of desired investments, $\Psi(z_t)$. If the agency only approves investments from its desired set, the choice problem now becomes:

$$Max_I \ P(I;c) \ s.t. \ I \in \{\Omega(s_t) \cap \Psi(z_t)\} \tag{4}$$

That is, the set of feasible investments is reduced to the subset of investments that the firm desires and the agency will approve. Designating the solution to (3) as P^* and the solution to (4) as P', it follows that $P^*(s) \geq P'(s,z)$, since the reduction in feasible projects cannot improve the solution to the maximization problem. Said differently, the approval process can be non-binding, in which case the two outcomes are identical; however, when the approval process constitutes a binding constraint, the number of observed projects will decline for a given value of s. Finally, in anticipation of the discussion below, it should be noted that s and z may contain common elements and that information about $\Psi(z)$ may be available to the firm and reflected in s.

Applied Model

Given the foregoing discussion, we represent the firm-ranking outcomes with the index η^* and represent the unobserved ranking process as a linear function of the state variables that determine the set $\Omega(s)$. In our base model, the index is a count of desired projects between investor–host partners, where i represents the country in which the investing firm resides and h represents the country hosting the project. For each investor–host dyad, we model an investment equation giving the desired number of projects as a function of the state variables:

$$\eta^*_{ih} = n_0 + \sum_j n_j s_j \geq 0 \tag{5}$$

where n are parameters associated with the j state variables. It should be kept in mind that while the projects are pairwise outcome, the relevant state variables may be specific to the investor, to the host, or to a relationship between the host and investor.

In practice, observed AIJ projects are rare relative to the number of potential investor–host partnerships, and when relationships are observed,

the number of investment projects is generally low. Both characteristics
are suggestive of the Poisson and negative binomial distributions, which
are associated with many forms of count data. Consequently, count-model
methods are well suited to estimating Eq. (5). However, when the investment decision is additionally constrained, a modification is required that
results in a mixed regime model.

As a starting point for developing the agency constraint, we assume that
the approving agency's preferences relate to broad national policy objectives and that the same objectives that influence the project-ranking process
permeate other aspects of the bilateral relationships. One tangible indication of national preferences is the expenditure of public funds for bilateral
aid. Fortunately, because the UNFCCC and the OECD use the same set of
income classifications, the possible pairwise combinations of OECD donors
and aid recipients correspond to the potential flow of investment (from
investor to host) anticipated under the AIJ program. Consequently, the use
of bilateral aid as a proxy for unobservable agency preferences is attractive
conceptually and practically, and we utilize this in the applied model.

In particular, we assume that governments' ordering of preferences, as
revealed in the provision of bilateral aid, correspond to the ranking that
finding agencies apply to the proposed projects as they consider which
projects to approve. Therefore, in a way analogous to the firm's preference
function, we model the intensity of an agency's ranking of projects, α,
proxied by bilateral aid, as a linear function of the k state variables that
determine the preference set, $\Psi(z)$ and a vector of fixed parameters, a, so
that:

$$\alpha_{ih} = a_0 + \sum_k a_k z_k \qquad (6)$$

To combine the investment and agency preference components into a single
model, let A represent a binary variable set to one when agency approval
is granted. The number of observed projects can then be written as: $\eta_{ih} = \eta_{ih}^* A_{ih}$, where $\Pr ob[A = 0]$ can be modeled as a function of aid levels α_{ih}
or the corresponding aid determinants z_{ih}. In the parlance of count models,
the agency preference component is considered an "inflation" equation that
accounts for an observed excess of zeroes, implying that fewer projects are
observed than predicted by the investment function alone.

Several variations of this class of models based on alternative assumptions about the underlying probability distributions have been used in earlier studies. In our application, we model the underlying desired number

of projects using a negative binomial distribution and the probability of agency approval using the normal distribution. We also test our choice against commonly used alternatives. This type of mixed count-and-probit model is discussed by Greene (1994) and Long (1997).

An Alternative Dichotomous Model

With modification, the model can be adjusted to focus on whether or not an investor–host partnership occurred. In the dichotomous case, the binary variable $N_{ih} = 1$ if $\eta_{ih}^* > 0$; otherwise $N_{ih} = 0$ is introduced, which gives the alternative specification:

$$N_{ih} = \begin{cases} 1 & \text{if } n_0 + \sum_j n_j s_j + \varepsilon_\eta > 0 \\ 0 & \text{otherwise} \end{cases}$$

subject to

$$A_{ih} = \begin{cases} 1 & \text{if } a_0 + \sum_k a_k z_k + \varepsilon_\alpha > 0 \\ 0 & \text{otherwise} \end{cases} \tag{7}$$

By assumption, the error-terms, $\varepsilon_{n(i,h)}$ and $\varepsilon_{\alpha(i,h)}$, are distributed normally and potentially correlated. Written in this way, the alternative model takes the form of a probit-with-selection model as developed by van de Ven and van Pragg (1981).

Internalized Agency Preferences and Transaction Costs

To this point in the discussion, information concerning bilateral aid has been treated as separate from the information upon which firms base their investment decisions. However, there are a couple of reasons to believe this is not the case.

For one, firms and NGOs investing in projects under the pilots had an incentive to seek out information about agency preferences in order to avoid the cost of submitting projects that had little chance of approval. In practice, gaining insight to agency preferences may not have been difficult. The case studies suggest that the experimental nature and small scale of the AIJ programs encouraged a dialogue between investors and administrators. And in some instances, administrating agencies signaled their preferences by actively seeking out participants.[17] Consequently, firms may have internalized the agency preferences signaled by bilateral aid.

While anticipating agency preferences would have helped firms avoid some of the administrative and regulatory costs associated with the pilot, other types of transaction costs may have played a role as well. As discussed, deep-seated cultural ties are expected to reduce transaction costs related to gaining information and enforcing contracts and have been shown to influence other types of direct foreign investment. Strong bilateral ties are expected to influence aid flows as well, suggesting that information on bilateral aid carries information about otherwise unobservable bilateral effects on investment costs and risks. For both reasons, we expect bilateral aid to carry information relevant for the project investment equation.

Additional Estimation Concerns

The expectation that agency preferences are endogenous to the investment decision raises a potential estimation problem due to simultaneity bias, where bilateral aid is directly included as both a determinant of investment and a proxy for agency preferences. In the context of the base count model, the problem is easily avoided, since the proposed vector of bilateral aid determinants can be used as an alternative proxy for agency preferences.

In the case of the dichotomous model, another strategy is needed. This is because, in contrast to the count model where the two components of the mixed regime are estimated in combination, the probit-with-selection model requires the specification of a system of two equations with separate error terms. To address potential simultaneity bias in this form, we use a two-stage process in which instruments generate predicted values of bilateral aid that are subsequently used in the project investment function in lieu of observed values. Standard errors are found by using a bootstrapping method in which both stages are estimated from repeated draws on the original sample.[18]

---

[17]See, for example, Lile, Powell, and Toman (1998).

[18]In particular, a regression of bilateral aid on all exogenous variables and their cross products was used to generate predictions that were subsequently used in the investment equation. The two-stage estimation process was repeated 500 times with random draws from the original sample to generate the standard errors reported in Table 3.

DATA DESCRIPTION

AIJ Investments

A count of AIJ projects, which serves as our dependent measure of AIJ investment, is calculated from data on AIJ projects reported to the UNFCCC and compiled by the SBSTA. As of February 2002, the UNFCCC reported 156 projects. Among these, 147 projects reached the point at which a letter of intent was signed with the host country. For this study, two projects, both investments in the Solomon Islands, were dropped because some of the corresponding data on institutions were unavailable. Consequently, the study is based on 145 projects begun between 1993 and 2000 among 12 investor countries and 41 host countries.

A list of investor countries and their host partners is given in Table 3.1. The 145 projects are spread among 64 investor–host partnerships. The total number of implemented projects and partnerships is small relative to the potential for investment. To see why this is so, consider that when the AIJ program was established, 193 countries participated in the UNFCCC.[19] Implicit in Decision 5 is the expectation that investments would originate from the 24 wealthier Annex II countries.[20] Excluding the Holy See, this makes for 4,032 potential pairwise combinations. We are constrained by data to consider a subset of countries, although the subset is large. We include 22 investor countries and 134 potential host countries in our study and therefore 2,948 dyads in our sample.[21] Consequently, there are 2,884 investor–host combinations for which no AIJ project is observed between 1993 and 2000. Defined in this way, actual partnerships comprise about 2% of potential partnerships.

Generally, each partnership consists of one or two projects. The notable exceptions are the 50 Swedish AIJ projects spread among Estonia, Latvia, and Lithuania. Many of the projects are replications of a common approach

---

[19]The 194 parties to the Convention during the study period include all member countries of the United Nations plus the Cook Islands, the Holy See, and Niue, a former territory of New Zealand and one non-country member, the European Union.

[20]The name Annex II arises from the country-list annexes of the Framework Convention. Annex I contains the list of 36 countries, mostly OECD countries and transitional economies, that initially pledged to limit emissions. Annex II is the subset of wealthier Annex I countries. Prior to ratification, the list of countries capping emission changed and that eventual list of 39 countries is listed in Annex B of the Protocol.

[21]A list of countries included in this study is available on request.

Table 3.1: AIJ projects included in the sample, 1992–2001 by host and investor countries.

Investor countries	Projects	Host countries
Australia	10	Chile, Fiji, Indonesia (3), Mauritius (2), Solomon Islands (2), Vietnam
Belgium	1	Croatia
Canada	2	Jordan, Zimbabwe
France	5	Czech Republic, Hungary, Jordan, Mauritania, Zimbabwe
Germany	6	Czech Republic, Jordan, Latvia, Russia (2), Zimbabwe
Italy	2	Jordan, Morocco
Japan	5	China (3), Thailand, Vietnam
Netherlands	16	Bhutan, Bulgaria, Costa Rica, Czech Republic, Hungary (2), Latvia (2), Poland (2), Romania, Russia (2), Slovak Republic (2), South Africa
Norway	6	Burkina Faso, China, India, Mexico, Poland, Slovak Republic
Sweden	51	Estonia (21), Latvia (21), Lithuania (9)
Switzerland	2	Romania, Slovak Republic
United States	41	Argentina (2), Belize (2), Bolivia (3), Chile (4), Costa Rica (7), Czech Republic, Ecuador, Equatorial Guinea, El Salvador, Guatemala (3), Honduras (2), Indonesia, Mali, Mexico (4), Nicaragua, Panama, Russia (4), Sri Lanka, Uganda

and distinguished primarily by differences among second-tier counter-parts.[22] These projects motivate the alternative dichotomous model.

Variables Affecting Investment Choice

As discussed, abatement costs are expected to vary among countries, and this variation is expected to influence which countries host carbon projects. To proxy unobserved abatement costs, we use a measure of the greenhouse gas intensity of a host country's economy with the notion that low-cost reductions can be more easily found where the emission intensity is high.

---

[22]For example, many of the projects between Sweden and Estonia involved upgrading public heating systems. The projects were organized under a common national frame-work, with projects differentiated when local government counterparts differed.

Also important is the emission intensity for the investor country. Demand for emission reductions overall may be high when the domestic emission intensity is high, but the cost of domestic abatement relative to host-country abatement costs will be high when the domestic emission intensity is low. To capture these relationships, we include measures of host-country and investor-country emission intensity as well as an interactive term. The greenhouse gas intensity measure is calculated by the World Bank (2006) and is the ratio of greenhouse gas emissions measured in kilograms per dollar constant GDP, where the national GDPs have been deflated using the 2000 purchasing power parity conversion factor.[23]

Credits generated by carbon-market projects have value because they can be used to meet treaty or related regulatory obligations. Consequently, firms investing in carbon projects will take into consideration the specific host-country and investor-country institutions that govern their creation and use. At the same time, because carbon-market projects involve fixed upfront investments, they also face the more conventional types of risks faced by other forms of direct foreign investment. We therefore consider two classes of state variables related to transaction costs.

The first includes general factors that influence the level of profit and the associated risk for all types of investments flowing into host countries. As discussed, these variables describe a general investment climate and include variables related to policies, expected profitability, and a variety of risks. Factors that make up the general investment climate — that is, those factors that are not specific to bilateral pairings or the offset-project market — are summarized by the ability of countries to attract international investors, and we use total foreign direct investment (FDI) as our indicator of the general investment climate. Our measure is calculated by averaging the net inflows of foreign direct investment as a share of GDP reported by the World Bank (2006) over the study period 1992–2001. Because this measure is an aggregate, it can be observed independently of bilateral investment flows. As discussed, general investment incentives may also have a bilateral component related to strong bilateral ties. In the model, a continuous measure of real bilateral aid is included to capture this phenomena.

---

[23]The measure is imprecise, but information on the potential cost of abatement was not well developed during the pilots. Since then, coming up with better estimates of abatement costs has been a key objective of recent assessment reports by the Intergovernmental Panel on Climate Change.

The second class of state variables relates to institutions that are more specific to emission trading. All things equal, it is likely that AIJ investing firms preferred to gain experience in host countries where local institutions could lower costs, reduce risk, or otherwise provide additional value to carbon credit streams flowing from JI projects. Likewise, because investor-country regulations were expected to influence how earned credits could be used, it is also likely that domestic investor-country institutions were important to observed investment outcomes. At the same time, because the AIJ pilots preceded the eventual treaty, investors had to anticipate how future institutions might evolve. In the applied model, we assume that related commitments by governments, extant during the study period, provide an indication of the capacity of host and investor countries to put the implementing institutions in place; we use these to proxy investor judgments. We construct commitment indicator variables for investor and host countries based on their participation in five international agreements: the Convention on Biological Diversity, the Montreal Protocol on Substances That Deplete the Ozone Layer, the United Nations Convention on Climate Change, and the United Nations Convention on the Law of the Sea. To measure whether environmental issues are a policy priority, we also consider whether a country had an environmental strategy and a biodiversity action plan in place during the study period (World Bank, 2002). To identify countries with relatively strong institutions, we count the cumulative number of years between 1992 and 2001 that the environmental commitments were in place. Host and investor countries were separately ranked according to this cumulative measure and countries falling into the top of three respective quantiles were designated as highly committed to policies consistent with Kyoto objectives.

As discussed in the fourth section, uncertainty over investment outcomes generates incentive to delay otherwise desirable investment. This is especially true of long-lived carbon investment projects that depend especially on government institutions. Consequently, we include in the investment equation measures related to the capacity of host governments to sustain and carry-out processes leading to eventual carbon offset certification. In particular, we include a measure of government efficiency that relates to the quality of services provided by host governments and the political independence of their bureaucracies. We also include a measure of political stability that relates (inversely) to the likelihood that the government will be destabilized or toppled by external or internal violence.

The measures used in the study are described in Kaufmann, Kraay, and Mastruzzi (2005).[24] Finally, we also include a dummy variable set to one for Norway, the Netherlands, Sweden, and Switzerland, where subsidies are provided to domestic project participants (Michaelowa, Dixon, and Abron, 1999) and zero otherwise. All things equal, the subsidies are expected to have lowered the investment threshold criteria for firms in the four countries.

And finally, we also include a continuous measure of bilateral aid to capture endogenous policy effects and the effects of bilateral ties on transaction costs. The measure is an average value of real bilateral aid for the period 1992–2001 for each investor–host dyad, based on pairwise data on Net Official Development Assistance (ODA) to recipient countries from OECD country members, as reported to the Development Assistance Committee (OECD, 2006).

Variables Affecting Agency Preferences

The applied model considers whether the same factors that determine bilateral aid flows also determine agency rankings of AIJ projects in the applied model — that is, both aid and agency approval are a function of a set of common state variables, z. However, despite much research, finding a parsimonious set of determinants for bilateral aid is challenging.[25] For our purposes, we use a selective but representative set of variables meant to capture the following host-country characteristics: need, size, hegemony, democratic institutions, civil order, and bureaucratic integrity. Other studies using these or similar variables include Frey and Schneider (1986), Wall (1995), Alesina and Weder (2002), and Collier and Dollar (2002). In particular, we use the following statistical measures.

We take as our indicator of need, average per capita income for the period, measured in 1995 US$. Because large countries are expected to have strategic importance, the average host-country population is included. Motivated by the presumption that donor countries want to influence the policies of neighbors and important trade partners, we include two fixed

---

[24]Because indicators were not available for all study years, averages for 1996, 1998, 2000, and 2002 were used.

[25]Following Dudley and Montmarquette (1976), most studies suggest that aid flows are best explained by donor-country demand for specific outcomes that foreign aid helps to achieve, and by recipient country characteristics that determine aid effectiveness. In practice, applied studies ascribe a wide range of benign and predatory objectives to donor countries. See, for example, Pronk (2001) and Petras and Veltmeyer (2002).

effects: one based on proximity and a second to indicate that the host and investor countries have entered into bilateral or regional trade agreements.[26] Because most donors have voiced support for democratic principles, we include an indicator of the openness and accountability of host governments to their citizens, referred to in the tables as "voice and accountability." Poorly performing bureaucracies and corruption are expected to diminish the efficacy of aid and discourage donor support. To capture this, we include measures to indicate host countries with bureaucracies of above-average quality (government effectiveness) where public and private sectors levels of corruption are below average (control of corruption). Political instability due to external or internal violence and armed conflict is expected to diminish the effectiveness of aid, and we include this measure in our selection equation. At the same time, donors may also take a lack of civil order as an additional measure of need, so the relationship between aid and civil order is ambiguous. The measures on income and population are averages for 1992–2001 (World Bank, 2006). The trade agreement and proximity variables are constructed. The institutional measures are described in Kaufmann, Kraay, and Mastruzzi (2005).

As discussed earlier, the specification of the alternative model includes a dichotomous measure of bilateral aid not required in the count model. The measure is based on our continuous measure of bilateral aid and indicates whether aid was given during the study period.

EMPIRICAL RESULTS

A simple prediction of the conceptual model is that, because donor-country agencies prefer projects that reinforce the national policy objectives that are also pursued through bilateral aid, AIJ projects will be observed together with bilateral aid flows. At the same time, because firms invest for separate reasons, not all countries receiving aid are expected to host projects. Among the 2,948 potential investor–host relationships in our sample, this simple prediction holds over study period averages (Table 3.2). And, in all but four of the 147 AIJ projects, bilateral aid was given during the year that the project was launched.[27] So, in general, the pattern of investment observed

---

[26]A dummy variable was set to one for investor–host dyads when both countries were members of the Commonwealth, ASEAN, or NAFTA and for dyads containing an EU investor-country and a host country participating in the Phare program.

[27]The exceptions are given in the supplemental annex.

Table 3.2: Bilateral aid and AIJ
partnerships.

AIJ projects	Bilateral aid, investor to host	
	No	Yes
No	337	2,546
Yes	0	65

under the AIJ program is consistent with the conceptual model in that investment is not observed separately from bilateral aid. In passing, it is also worth noting that Table 3.2 is based on dichotomous measures of whether or not bilateral aid and bilateral investment occur, which corresponds to the dependent variables in the probit-with-selection model.

As discussed, the applied models provide a framework that allows exploration of the underlying determinants of project investment and to evaluate whether bilateral relationships tied to bilateral aid limited the number of observed project investments. Because AIJ investment and bilateral aid are observed contemporaneously, the first round of estimates takes into account potential simultaneity problems. In a second round of estimates, we examine the issue of contemporaneous correlations more closely and show that key outcomes from the baseline analysis do not depend on our simultaneity treatment.

Baseline Model Specification

Baseline estimation results for the count model and the dichotomous alternative of the model are given in Table 3.3. Overall, the models perform well. Statistical tests are consistent with the chosen specification and the parameters that are statistically significant take on expected signs.

Project investment

Turning first to the AIJ investment equation in the count model, the three investor attributes are significant and take on reasonable signs. The results suggest that investment was more likely if host-country environmental policies were strong and when the investor-government offered subsidies to investors. The parameter on carbon intensity is significant and positive.

Clean Development Mechanism

Table 3.3: Estimation results.

	Count model		Dichotomous model	
	Coefficient	Std. Err.	Coefficient	Std. Err.
Investment equation				
Investor attributes				
Carbon intensity	6.049[a]	1.354	1.634[a]	0.415
Environmental policies	0.845[a]	0.328	0.351[a]	0.113
Subsidies offered	2.964[a]	0.581	0.539[a]	0.148
Host attributes				
Carbon intensity	0.456	0.328	0.139[a]	0.053
General investment climate	0.065[a]	0.027	0.020	0.030
Environmental policies	0.373	0.425	0.140	0.118
Government effectiveness	1.176[b]	0.521	0.032	0.112
Political stability	0.572[c]	0.339	0.408[a]	0.116
Bilateral characteristics				
Carbon cross-product	−1.466[b]	0.619	−0.330[b]	0.150
Bilateral aid	0.011[a]	0.003	0.014[b]	0.006
Constant	−6.111[a]	1.237	−3.003[a]	0.366
Agency preferences				
Bilateral characteristics				
Proximity	−1.918[a]	0.424	0.560[a]	0.131
Trade agreements	0.350	0.416	0.415[a]	0.134
Host attributes				
Income	0.052	0.148	−0.112[a]	0.036
Population	−0.212[b]	0.097	0.219[a]	0.028
Government effectiveness	0.360	0.595	0.126	0.130
Political stability	−0.190	0.358	−0.146[b]	0.072
Voice and accountability	0.088	0.196	0.129[a]	0.053
Corruption controls	0.027	0.487	−0.192	0.120
Constant	4.080[b]	2.027	−1.448[a]	0.512
Over-dispersion parameter (log)	1.677[a]	0.513		
Correlation between equations			−0.692[a]	0.162
Tests				
Investment independent of bilateral aid	$\chi^2(1) = 16.86$[a]		$\chi^2(1) = 5.69$[b]	
Poisson versus negative binominal	$\chi^2(1) = 115.24$[a]			
Investment unaffected by agency preferences	Vuong $z = 3.29$[a]			
Investment and agency preference equations independent			$\chi^2(1) = 7.52$[a]	

Note: Results for the count model are based on a robust variance estimator. Standard errors for the two-stage dichotomous model are based on a bootstrapping procedure using 500 replications. [a,b] and [c] indicate significance at the 1%, 5%, and 10% levels, respectively.

Observing host-country characteristics, the carbon intensity parameter is also positive. It is not significant by itself, but is significant in combination with the cross-product of host and investor carbon intensity. The imprecision of the estimate may be due to the crudeness of our measure, as already discussed. In addition, as a reviewer of an earlier draft pointed out, early projects may have been intra-marginal, that is, some investors may have been attracted to "low-hanging fruit," even if abatement costs in the country were expected to be high on average.

Among the remaining host-country characteristics, the investment climate indicator, which is based on the ability of the host country to attract direct foreign investment, is positive and significant. The parameter associated with host-country environmental policies is positive but small, relative to its standard error. The parameters on government effectiveness and political stability were positive and statistically significant at reasonable confidence levels.

Turning to the bilateral characteristics, the cross-product measure of carbon intensity is negative (indicating declining marginal effects) and significant. Importantly, the bilateral aid parameter is positive and significant, which we take as evidence that bilateral relationships, working either through agency preferences or transaction costs, positively affect investment decisions. We return to this topic later in this section.

Results from the alternative dichotomous form of the investment equation are given in the upper right-hand panel of Table 3.3. Because the range of outcomes is limited to zero and one, the parameters are scaled differently from the count model. Setting this aside, the results are largely consistent with results from the count model, although there are some differences in the statistical significance of some of the parameters associated with host characteristics. The parameter on carbon intensity, which was not statistically significant in the count model, is significant in the dichotomous model, and the parameters on the investment climate and government effectiveness, which were significant in the count model, are not so significant in the dichotomous model.

Agency preferences

Parameters associated with the agency preference component of the count model are reported in the lower left-hand-side panel of Table 3.3. When interpreting the signs of the parameters, it should be kept in mind that agency preferences represent the "inflation" component of the mixed count model. The inflation component explains an excess of zeroes relative to the associated negative binomial component. An increase in a variable expected to positively influence agency preferences reduces the constraint on investment outcomes, generating fewer zeros and thus increases the probability of investment between the investor–host pair. For this reason, the signs on the parameters are somewhat counter-intuitive.

Turning first to bilateral characteristics, the geographic proximity parameter is negative and statistically significant. The trade agreement parameter is positive in contrast to expectations but is not statistically distinguishable from zero. Among the host-country characteristics, only size emerges as a significant parameter. Together with the earlier result, the count model suggests that approving agencies promote projects in neighboring countries and countries that are populous.

Results from the agency preference component of the dichotomous model are reported in the lower right-hand panel of Table 3.3. Recall that, in this form, a probit-equation indicating the probability of a bilateral aid flow is used as the selection component of a dichotomous indicator of investment. This has the practical consequence of reducing the importance given to the Swedish AIJ experience. It also results in a functional form for the agency preference that more closely resembles the regressions reported in other studies of bilateral aid.

Turning to the selection equation and the determinants of bilateral aid, the parameters are statistically significant for the most part and in line with findings from previous studies.[28] The two bilateral indicators — geographic proximity and participation in bilateral or regional trade agreements — are both statistically significant determinants. The estimated coefficient on income suggests that need plays a role in determining bilateral aid, with the probability of aid increasing as per capita income falls. The size of a country's population seems to matter as well, with larger countries more likely to receive bilateral aid. Among the institutional measures, institutions that tend to expand political participation are positively and significantly related to expanded aid flows. The parameter associated with government efficacy is positive, but not significantly so. While political stability contributed positively to the likelihood of bilateral investment, the results suggest that less-stable governments were more likely to receive aid,

---

[28] In this form of the model, a positive coefficient indicates a higher preference and is associated with a greater probability of bilateral aid and a higher probability of observing an investment relationship between the investor and host.

which may indicate that donors sometimes use aid to promote stability in aid recipients. The results also suggest that failure to control corruption was not an impediment to receiving bilateral aid.[29]

Model specification tests

The lower part of Table 3.3 contains results from tests about the chosen model specifications. The first is an alternative form of the significance test for the bilateral aid parameter. In both versions of the model, outcomes are consistent with the earlier result, implying that investors in the AIJ program took into account information on bilateral aid when making investment decisions.

The next test applies only to the count model and has to do with whether or not the Poisson distribution is preferred to the negative binomial distribution used to specify the investment function. The test is based on the over-dispersion parameter recovered from the underlying likelihood function and reported in Table 3.3. A restriction setting this parameter to zero (as would be the case for a Poisson distribution) is rejected, providing evidence in favor of the negative binomial specification used in the base model.

The last test linked to the count model addresses the central hypothesis of the chapter. The test compares the fit of the mixed regime model to an unconstrained investment model that depends on the investment determinants alone. The test is due to Vuong (1989) and is described in Greene (1994). For our sample, the unconstrained investment model is rejected with a high level of confidence in favor of the base model in which investment decisions are constrained by agency preference. Said differently, the test provides evidence that the agency selection determinants explain why fewer investments occurred under the AIJ program than that predicted by the negative binomial investment function alone.

In contrast to the count model, it is not possible to directly test whether agency preferences are binding in the dichotomous model. This is because the selection structure is used to construct the likelihood function associated with the statistical model. However, within the context of the selection model, it is possible to test whether the investment and the agency preference equation are independent. Results reported in Table 3.3 suggest that they are not, which is consistent with the conceptual model.

---

[29]This is consistent with other studies. See, especially, Alesina and Weder (2002).

The estimated correlation parameter is high at -0.692 and statistically significant. A related Wald test, also reported in the table, implies the same.

Revisiting the Contemporaneous Correlation Assumption

Results presented in the previous section depend on statistical models constructed under the assumption that bilateral aid and project investment decisions under the AIJ pilots are contemporaneously correlated, and the assumption is tested in this section. There are two reasons to do so. The first is technical: in the absence of simultaneity, more parsimonious specifications of both models can be estimated that might produce different outcomes for the parametric tests reported in Table 3.3. A second reason is that evidence for or against the contemporaneous correlation assumption influences how we should interpret the policy implication of the results.

As discussed, there are two motivations for including bilateral aid as a determinant of project investment: an endogenous-policy hypothesis and a transaction-cost hypothesis. The first is that investors may have learned about agency country preferences, which are in turn related to bilateral aid. From a policy perspective, changing agency preferences is straightforward — at least conceptually — since the approving agencies can be issued new guidelines. The second reason for including bilateral aid as a determinant is that the strong bilateral ties that motivate bilateral aid flows also help reduce private transaction costs. The transaction-cost hypothesis suggests that information or contract enforcement hurdles exists that strong bilateral ties mitigate. From a policy perspective, changing agency guidelines will not resolve these types of investment hurdles. Instead, policy makers will want to focus on building up institutions that facilitate information flows and contract enforcement.

To a degree, tests for contemporaneous errors (simultaneity) can help distinguish between the two hypotheses. The transaction-cost hypothesis implies contemporaneous errors since unobserved bilateral effects (related to culture and history) are expected to be present in both the investment and aid equations. Consequently, test results that rule out a contemporaneous error problem are inconsistent with the transaction-cost hypothesis. In contrast, the endogenous policy assumption that investors anticipate agency behavior does not necessarily imply simultaneity, since the effects can be one-way since agency preferences are arguably unaffected by investor preferences. That is, while agency preferences influence investor outcomes, the reverse is not necessarily true. In turn, this implies a recursive system and an absence of noncontemporaneous errors. Of course, this need not be the case and, in fact, feedback from investors to approving agencies may have influenced investment outcomes. In this form, the endogenous-policy hypothesis also implies contemporaneous errors. To summarize, evidence in favor of contemporaneous errors, together with evidence that bilateral aid is a determinant of private investment, is consistent with both hypotheses, while evidence ruling out a contemporaneous error problem is consistent only with the endogenous-policy hypothesis.

The procedure used to test for contemporaneous correlation is a variation of Hausman's test. In the case of the count model, bilateral aid, rather than its determinants, are used in the agency preference (inflation) component of the model, while residuals from a regression of bilateral aid on the vector of aid-determinants and their cross-products is added to the investment component of the model. For the dichotomous model, the predicted values of bilateral aid used in the investment equation are replaced by actual values and their associated residuals.[30] In the absence of contemporaneous correlations, the residuals are expected to contribute no additional information and the parameter associated with the residuals should be indistinguishable from zero.

As with many parametric tests, results from the simultaneity tests depend crucially on how the standard errors of parameters are calculated. As shown in the first row of Table 3.4, Wald tests, based on robust standard errors from the full sample, suggest that contemporaneous correlation is present, which would appear to rule out the recursive model. However,

Table 3.4: Results from Hausman tests for contemporaneous correlation.

	Count model	Dichotomous model
Standard errors used in test		
Sample (Robust)	5.17[b]	12.50[a]
Bootstrap (500 replications)	2.29[d]	2.55[c]

Note: Wald test has a χ^2 distribution with one degree of freedom. [a,b,c] and [d] indicate significance at the 1%, 5%, 11%, and 13% levels, respectively.

---

[30] The full set of estimates parameters are included in Tables 3 and 4 of the supplemental annex.

Table 3.5: Tests of key hypotheses under "recursive policy" assumption.

	Count model	Dichotomous model
Investment independent of bilateral aid	$\chi^2(1) = 9.75^a$	$\chi^2(1) = 12.50^a$
Poisson versus negative binominal	$\chi^2(1) = 133.96^a$	
Investment unaffected by agency preferences	Vuong $z = 2.08^b$	
Investment and agency preference equations independent		$\chi^2(1) = 32.58^a$

Note: Results for the count model are based on a robust variance estimator. In the dichotomous model, potential heterogeneity in the investment error term is accounted for by including information on the project count for each investor–host dyad. [a] and [b] indicate significance at the 1% and 5% levels, respectively.

when the tests are repeated based on bootstrap standard errors, which Wong (1996) suggests as a more reliable approach, the results are less robust, and levels of significance fall slightly below 10%, providing weak evidence in favor of the recursive model. (See the second row of Table 3.4.)

Even so, key conclusions from the previous estimation results remain under the alternative assumption that contemporaneous correlations are absent in the data. Tests conducted under the assumption of contemporaneous correlation and reported in the lower section of Table 3.3 are repeated using recursive versions of both models. Test outcomes, reported in Table 3.5, are unchanged. Results from both models suggest that agency preferences — as proxied by bilateral aid — influenced project investment in a positive and statistically significant way. In the recursive version of the count model, an alternative specification based on the Poisson distribution is rejected in favor of the negative binomial specification, and the Vuong test indicates that agency preference limited investment outcomes. In the recursive dichotomous model, test results suggest that the investment equation and the agency preference (selection) equations are correlated.

Epilogue

Experience has begun to accumulate recently about project investment under CDM. One surprising feature is that many of the early projects are "unilateral" in the sense that the projects appear to be financed domestically (Michaelowa, 2007). However, for projects involving direct foreign investment, a pattern similar to the AIJ experience has emerged. By May 2007, 316 projects involving bilateral or multilateral direct foreign investment had been registered under CDM. As with the AIJ experience, bilateral investment relationships were rare and associated with established bilateral ties. In no case did an investment occur between investor–host pairings in which bilateral aid relationships had not already been established during the AIJ period.[31]

CONCLUSION

Case studies of national AIJ pilot programs describe approval processes that allowed general national policy objectives to influence project investment outcomes. Our findings are consistent with this characterization and suggest more specifically that AIJ investments were partly determined by the same factors that determine bilateral aid. Quantitative evidence supporting this conclusion is robust and holds up under a series of alternative specifications.

One implication is that CDM and JI investments might be similarly constrained if the institutional arrangements built up to approve projects under the national pilots are maintained as the Kyoto Protocol is implemented. As discussed, this depiction of how investments were determined under the AIJ programs is inconsistent with often-used descriptions of how markets might work under an implemented Kyoto Protocol. Nevertheless, if policy preferences and the agency approval process alone constrain project investment, then the question of whether broader policy objectives should play a role in determining project location is a normative one, and policy makers can set agency approval rules accordingly.

Alternatively, a more nuanced interpretation of the conceptual link between aid and investment suggests that deep-seated bilateral ties are relied upon to reduce otherwise insurmountable private transaction costs. Tests results are not fully consistent with this interpretation, but do not rule it out in a convincing way. For policy, distinction matters since private bilateral transaction costs can remain even if regulatory transaction costs are fully reduced. Moreover, in contrast to the case of regulatory transaction costs, policy instruments to address private transaction costs are less direct and require build-up institutions that address underlying problems related to the cost of information and contract enforcement. Experience suggests that private agents such as brokers or rating agencies emerge to fill gaps related to risk and asymmetric information. However, public agencies may find additional scope for enhancing information flows and reducing performance risk.

---

[31] See Table 5 of the supplemental annex.

In either case, a key finding of the study is that the cost-reducing benefits of the project-based components of Kyoto's flexibility mechanisms may be less than what empirical studies predict. This is because the numeric models that provide the best guidance on how alternative policies might affect the implementation costs do not take into account either regulatory or private bilateral transaction costs that were important during the AIJ pilots and that may be important at present. From a methodological point of view, the results suggest that taking bilateral relationships into account might allow numeric models to better predict cost savings and the geographic distribution of project investment under the Kyoto Protocol investment mechanisms.

Even so, findings suggest that national investor-country policy goals did not exclusively drive the AIJ investment process, leaving room for host countries to influence outcomes by taking up specific policies. By implication, countries that take policies that support investment generally and build the specific institutions needed to facilitate Kyoto-related markets will likely see greater investment flows under the Protocol's JI and CDM provisions.

REFERENCES

Alesina, A and B Weder (2002). Do corrupt governments receive less foreign aid? *American Economic Review*, **92**, 1126–1137.

Barrera, J and R Schwarze (2004). Does the CDM contribute to sustainable development? Evidence from the AIJ pilot phase. *International Journal of Sustainable Development*, **7**(4), 353–368.

Bénassy-Quéré, A, M Coupet and T Mayer (2007). Institutional determinants of foreign direct investment. *World Economy*, **30**(5), 764–782.

Bernstein, PMW, D Montgomery and TF Rutherford (1999). Global impacts of the Kyoto agreement, results from the MS-MRT model. *Resource and Energy Economics*, **21**, 375–413.

Bertram, G (1992). Tradeable emission permits and the control of greenhouse gases. *Journal of Development Studies*, **28**, 423–446.

Bréchet, T and B Lussis (2006). The contribution of the clean development mechanism to national climate policies. *Journal of Policy Modeling*, **28**(9), 981–994.

Carraro, C (1999). Introduction. In C Carraro (ed.), *International Environmental Agreements on Climate Change*. Boston: Kluwer Academic Publishers.

Cason, TN and L Gangadharan (2003). Transactions costs in tradable permit markets: An experimental study of pollution market designs. *Journal of Regulatory Economics*, **23**(2), 145–165.

Chakrabarti, A (2001). The determinants of foreign direct investment: Sensitivity analyses of cross-country regressions. *Kyklos*, **54**(1), 89–114.

Choi, CJ (1999). Global competitiveness and national attractiveness. *International Studies of Management & Organization*, **29**(1), 3–13.

Collier, P and D Dollar (2002). Aid allocation and poverty reduction. *European Economic Review*, **46**,1475–1500.

Cullet, P and KP Kameri-Mbote (1998). Joint implementation and forestry projects: Conceptual and operational fallacies. *International Affairs*, **74**(2), 393–408.

Dixit, AK and RS Pindyck (1994). *Investment Under Uncertainty*. Princeton: Princeton University Press.

Dixon, RK and I Mintzer (1999). Introduction to the FCCC activities implemented jointly pilot. In RK Dixon (ed.), *The U.N. Framework Convention on Climate Change Activities Implemented Jointly (AIJ) Pilot: Experiences and Lessons Learned*. Dordrecht: Kluwer Academic Publishers.

Dudley, L and C Montmarquette (1976). A model of the supply of bilateral foreign aid. *American Economic Review*, **66**, 132–142.

Frey, BS and F Schneider (1986). Competing models of international lending activity. *Journal of Development Economics*, **20**, 225–245.

Gangadharan, L (2000). Transaction costs in pollution markets: An empirical study. *Land Economics*, **76**(4), 601–614.

Ghosh, P and J Puri (1994). Joint Implementation of Climate Change Commitments: Opportunities and Apprehensions. New Delhi: Tata Energy Research Institute.

Greene, WH (1994). Accounting for excess zeros and sample selection in Poisson and negative binomial regression models. Working Paper No. EC-94-10. New York: New York University, Department of Economics, Stern School of Business.

Grubb, M, C Vrolijk and D Brack (1999). *The Kyoto Protocol: A Guide and Assessment*. London: Royal Institute of International Affairs.

Gulbrandsen, LH and S Andresen (2004). NGO influence in the implementation of the Kyoto Protocol: Compliance, flexibility mechanisms, and sinks. *Global Environmental Politics*, **4**(4), 54–75.

Hahn, RW (1990). Regulatory constraints on environmental markets. *Journal of Public Economics*, **42**(2), 149–175.

Hahn, RW and GL Hester (1989). Where did all the markets go? An analysis of EPA's emissions trading program. *Yale Journal on Regulation*, **6**(1), 109–153.

Haites, E (2004). Estimating the market potential for the clean development mechanism: Review of models and lessons learned. PCFplus Report 19. Washington, DC: The World Bank Carbon Finance Business PCFplus Research Program.

Hanafi, AG (1998). Joint implementation: Legal and institutional issues for an effective international program to combat climate change. *The Harvard Environmental Law Review*, **22**(2), 441–508.

Heister, J, P Karani, K Poore, CS Sinha and R Selrod (1999). The World Bank's experience with the activities implemented jointly pilot phase. In RK Dixon (ed.), *The U.N. Framework Convention on Climate Change Activities Implemented Jointly (AIJ) Pilot: Experiences and Lessons Learned.* Dordrecht: Kluwer Academic Publishers.

IPCC (2007). *Climate Change 2007: Mitigation. Contribution of Working Group III to the Fourth Assessment Report of the Intergovernmental Panel on Climate Change*, B Metz, OR Davidson, PR Bosch, R Dave and LA Meyer (eds.). Cambridge, United Kingdom and New York, NY, USA: Cambridge University Press.

Jacoby, HD, JM Reilly, JR McFarland and S Paltsev (2006). Technology and technical change in the MIT EPPA model. *Energy Economics*, **28**(5/6), 610–631.

Jotzo, F and A Michaelowa (2002). Estimating the CDM market under the Marrakech accords. *Climate Policy*, **2**(1), 179–196.

Kaufmann, D, A Kraay and M Mastruzzi (2005). Governance matters IV: Governance indicators for 1996–2004. World Bank Policy Research Working Paper Series No. 3630. Washington, DC: World Bank.

Kogut, B and H Singh (1988). The effect of national culture on the choice of entry mode. *Journal of International Business Studies*, **19**(3), 411–432.

Larson, DF and P Parks (1999). Risks, lessons learned and secondary markets for greenhouse gas reductions. Policy Research Working Paper 2090. Washington, DC: World Bank.

Larson, DF, Gunnar Breustedt (2009). Will markets direct investments under the Kyoto protocol? Lessons from the activities implemented jointly pilots. *Environmental & Resource Economics*, **43**(3), 433–456.

Lile, R, M Powell and M Toman (1998). Implementing the clean development mechanism: Lessons from U.S. private-sector participation in activities implemented jointly. Discussion Paper No. 99-08. Resources for the Future, Washington.

Long, JS (1997). *Regression Models for Categorical and Limited Dependent Variables*. Thousand Oaks, CA: Sage Publications.

Löschel, A (2002). Technological change in economic models of environmental policy: A survey. *Ecological Economics*, **43**(2/3), 105–126.

Löschel, A and ZX Zhang (2002). The economic and environmental implications of the US repudiation of the Kyoto Protocol and the subsequent deals in Bonn and Marrakech. *Review of World Economics* (Weltwirtschaftliches Archiv) **138**(4), 711–746.

Manne, AS and RG Richels (1999). The Kyoto Protocol: A cost-effective strategy for meeting environmental objectives? In J Weyant (ed.), *The Cost of the*

Kyoto Protocol: A Multi-Model Evaluation. Energy Journal, (Special Issue) 1–23.

McKibbin, WJ, R Shackleton and PJ Wilcoxen (1999). What to expect from an international system of tradable permits for carbon emissions. *Resource and Energy Economics*, **21**(3/4), 319–346.

Michaelowa, A (2007). Unilateral CDM — Can developing countries finance generation of greenhouse gas emission credits on their own? *Journal International Environmental Agreements: Politics, Law and Economics*, **7**(1), 17–34.

Michaelowa, A, K Begg, S Parkinson and RK Dixon (1999). Interpretation and application of FCCC AIJ pilot project development criteria. In RK Dixon (ed.), *The U.N. Framework Convention on Climate Change Activities Implemented Jointly (AIJ) Pilot: Experiences and Lessons Learned*. Dordrecht: Kluwer Academic Publishers.

Michaelowa, A, RK Dixon and L Abron (1999). The AIJ project development community. In RK Dixon (ed.), *The U.N. Framework Convention on Climate Change Activities Implemented Jointly (AIJ) Pilot: Experiences and Lessons Learned*. Dordrecht: Kluwer Academic Publishers.

Michaelowa, A and F Jotzo (2005). Transaction costs, institutional rigidities and the size of the clean development mechanism. *Energy Policy*, **33**(4), 511–523.

Muller, RA and S Mestelman (1998). What have we learned from emissions trading experiments? *Managerial and Decision Economics*, **19**, 225–238.

Nordhaus, WD (2001). Global warming economics. *Science*, **294**(5545), 1283–1284.

Nordhaus, WD and JG Boyer (2000). *Warming the World: Economic Models of Global Warming*. Cambridge, MA: MIT Press.

North, DC (1987). Institutions, transaction costs and economic growth. *Economic Inquiry*, **25**(3), 419–428.

OECD (2006). The International Development Statistics (electronic). Paris: OECD.

Painuly, JP (2001). The Kyoto protocol, emissions trading and the CDM: An analysis from developing countries perspective. *Energy Journal*, **22**(3), 147–169.

Parikh, J (1995). North-South cooperation in climate change through joint implementation. *International Environmental Affairs*, **7**, 22–43.

Petras, J and H Veltmeyer (2002). Reverse aid: Neo-liberalism as catalyst of regression. *Development and Change*, **33**, 281–293.

Pronk, JP (2001). Aid as a catalyst. *Development and Change*, **32**, 611–629.

Sands, RD (2004). Dynamics of carbon abatement in the second generation model. *Energy Economics*, **26**(4), 721–738.

Schwarze, R (2000). Activities implemented jointly: Another look at the facts. *Ecological Economics*, **32**(2), 255–267.

Shenkar, O (2001). Cultural distance revisited: Towards a more rigorous conceptualization and measurement of cultural differences. *Journal of International Business Studies*, **32**(3), 519–535.

Schroeder, H (2010). The history of international climate change politics: Three decades of progress, process and procrastination. In M Boykoff (ed.), *The Politics of Climate Change: A Survey*. London: Routledge.

Siegel, JI, AN Licht and SH Schwartz (2007). Egalitarianism, Cultural Distance, and FDI: A New Approach. Available at: SSRN.com. Accessed 7 December 2012.

Springer, U (2003). The market for tradable GHG permits under the Kyoto protocol: A survey of model studies. *Energy Economics*, **25**(5), 527–551.

Stavins, RN (1995). Transaction costs and tradeable permits. *Journal of Environmental Economics and Management*, **29**, 133–148.

Stevens, B and A Rose (2002). A dynamic analysis of the marketable permits approach to global warming policy, a comparison of spatial and temporal flexibility. *Journal of Environmental Economics and Management*, **44**, 45–69.

van de Ven WPMM and BMS van Praag (1981). The demand for deductibles in private health insurance: A Probit model with sample selection. *Journal of Econometrics*, **17**, 229–252.

Vuong, QH (1989). Likelihood ratio tests for model selection and non-nested hypotheses. *Econometrica*, **57**(2), 307–333.

Wall, HJ (1995). The allocation of official development assistance. *Journal of Policy Modeling*, **17**, 307–314.

Weyant, JP (2004). Introduction and overview. *Energy Economics*, **26**, 501–515.

Whalley, J and RM Wigle (1991). Cutting CO_2 emissions: The effects of alternative policy approaches. *Energy Journal*, **12**(1), 109–124.

Woerdman, E (2001). Emissions trading and transaction costs: Analyzing the flaws in the discussion. *Ecological Economics*, **38**, 293–304.

Wong, K (1996). Bootstrapping Hausman's exogeneity test. *Economics Letters*, **53**(2), 139–43.

World Bank (2002). Statistical Information Management and Analysis Database (electronic). Washington, DC: World Bank.

World Bank (2006). Development Data Platform (electronic). Washington, DC: World Bank.

4. THE COST OF MITIGATION UNDER THE CLEAN DEVELOPMENT MECHANISM

In response to the Clean Development Mechanism (CDM) provision, a large number of emission-reduction projects have been initiated in different developing countries, which vary widely both in the type of abatement technology and the size of operations. This chapter examines the abatement cost structure of the CDM projects in the pipeline with the objective of assessing the prospect of GHG reductions through CDM and providing policy relevant perspectives for improving the existing incentive structure of the mechanism.

Potentially, the CDM allows Annex B countries to meet their targets at lower costs. For measurable and verifiable emissions reductions that are in addition to what would have occurred without the CDM project, investors earn certified emission reduction (CER) credits, each equivalent to one ton of CO_2 equivalent (tCO_2e hereafter) abatement. Annex B participants can subsequently use the earned CERs to meet obligations under the Protocol or sell the credits to other parties. Under the terms of the Protocol, all CERs count equally toward treaty obligations.[1] In turn, the CDM is expected to benefit developing countries that host projects by stimulating sustainable development through technology transfer and foreign direct investments.

Both industrialized and developing countries have responded to incentives under the mechanism. As of December 2009, there were 5,760 projects at different stages in the CDM project cycle. If all projects were validated by the Executive Board (EB) and implemented to their full potential, they would generate emissions reductions totaling 2.79 billion tCO_2e and generate an equal number of CERs during 2008–2012, the first commitment period of the Kyoto Protocol (Risoe, 2010).

---

[1]While this is generally true, sequestration projects based on land-use have their own special rules that affect the value of the credits. See Larson *et al.* (2008) for a discussion of CDM implementation rules and the CDM project cycle.

The rapid increase in the number of CDM projects (see Chapter 5) indicates that the mechanism aligns the incentives of the Annex B and non–Annex-B parties; however, the role of abatement cost as a motive for investment is less well understood. Improving on this understanding is crucial for policy, since most numerical analyses on how CDM affects the cost of meeting the Kyoto Treaty objectives are based on specified abatement cost curves and the assumption that investors will seek out least-cost projects. The same approach also leads to prediction of the sectors and regions likely to benefit from project investment flows. However, project costs are not synonymous with abatement costs since there are additional characteristics that influence project investment decisions. Our results suggest these factors are consequential and explain why the current pool of project investments differs from *ex ante* predictions.

While previous studies provide useful estimates of abatement costs of various pollutants, most are based on secondary data or approximated coefficients in the abatement functions. In this chapter, we take advantage of project-level data that distinguishes among the types of projects, the countries hosting the projects, and the sequence of new project investments for the period 2003–2009. Thus, our dataset allows distinction among projects across types (technologies), locations, and time. In turn, this allows us to address questions about how firms respond to incentives that are important for CDM policy reform or the introduction of new mechanisms of this type. Specifically, these features of the data allow us to explain the relative role of project costs in explaining the pool of observed investments. It also allows us to test to hypotheses important for policy: (1) whether CDM projects exhibit economies of scale in emission abatement, and (2) whether the marginal cost (as well as the average cost) of abatement of CDM projects has decreased over time, presumably due to accumulated experience. The lessons from this mechanism are potentially important not just for the long-standing CDM but for similar measures under discussion to combat deforestation (REDD and REDD+).

ESTIMATING EMISSIONS ABATEMENT COST OF THE CDM

Background

In their early studies on pollution abatement cost, Rossi, Young, and Epp (1979) specify a production function associated with water pollution abatement activity. In their model, the volume and quality of an effluent stream is a function of the volume and quality of the influent stream and other factors of production such as land, labor, capital, and materials. They derive an associated cost function in which abatement cost is a function of the volume and quality of both effluent and influent streams and factor prices (i.e., prices of land, labor, capital, and materials). Fraas and Munley (1984) also estimate water pollution abatement costs based on the framework proposed by Rossi, Young, and Epp.

Goldar, Misra, and Mukherji (2001) identify problems associated with the cost function proposed by Rossi, Young, and Epp, and argue that output of abatement activity should be defined as the reduction in the pollution load. They define output of water pollution abatement as a function of the volume of waste water treated, the difference in the pollution levels of influent and effluent water, and inputs used to purify the water. The authors specify a water pollution abatement cost function in which the cost of abatement is an explicit function of the quantum of abatement (i.e., the difference between water quality before and after the treatment) and factor prices. There are some similar studies that do not include factor prices in the abatement cost function (e.g., Mehta, Mundle, and Sankar, 1993).

Another set of studies consider pollution abatement as an inseparable multi-output process that jointly models production and abatement costs (Pizer and Kopp, 2005; Maradan and Vassiliev, 2005; Boyd, Molburg, and Prince, 1996). Gollup and Roberts (1985) use observed data on utility pollution abatement and production costs to estimate a cost function that includes emission control rates as a predictor of production costs. Nordhaus (1994) compares a number of published models in terms of percentage difference of carbon emissions from a baseline path and proposes an aggregate formula relating cost to output and reduction of greenhouse gases. In a similar manner, Newell and Stavins (2003) explore the pollution abatement cost heterogeneity (i.e., the relative cost of uniform performance measured in terms of emissions per unit of product output) using a second-order approximation of the costs around the baseline emissions. The approach is based on variation in baseline emission rates, thus estimation of the underlying cost function requires data on baseline and project emissions. In contrast, Newell, Pizer, and Shih (2003) develop a quadratic abatement cost function in which the cost of pollution abatement per unit of output depends on abatement rather than emissions. Using project-level census data on compliance costs and emissions abatement in four industries, they estimate the parameters of the cost function and compute gains from emission trading.

In their study of power generation and the US SO_2 program, Considine and Larson (2006) consider the use of the atmosphere for the disposal of emissions as a factor of production that is priced by tradable emission permits and derive related input demand schedules in a cost-function framework. They apply a similar approach in their paper on the European Union's program for greenhouse gases (Considine and Larson, 2009).

Several studies estimate the abatement cost function by separating cost of abatement from the cost of production. Using data from the US Census Bureau, Hartman, Wheeler, and Singh (1994) estimate air pollution abatement costs by industry sectors. Assuming that the abatement cost function is separable from the firm's production cost function, they estimate abatement costs as a quadratic function of emissions abatement. Hamaide and Boland (2000) define abatement costs as a second-order polynomial function of abatement alone (which is forced to pass through the origin, i.e., without an intercept).

While estimating the cost of abating agricultural nitrogen pollution in wetlands, Bystrom (1998) tests linear, quadratic, and log-log specifications of the cost function. Since emissions abatement through CDM can be a single- or multiple-output process, we first conceptually define the costs of abatement and then adopt Bystrom's approach to specify the emissions abatement cost function and estimate the model using CDM project-level data.

The Conceptual Model

We start with the basic emissions abatement cost function $C_{it}^n(w_t, A_t)$, where w is a vector of exogenous input prices, A is the given level of mitigation, and C_{it}^n is the cost of the mitigation project i at time period t while the project lasts for n years.

With the exception of the input price vector, the components necessary to estimate the cost function can be derived from the Risoe data. For A, we use the reported number of CERs expected from the project, which are derived by subtracting the net emissions of the project from a baseline business-as-usual counterfactual (i.e., emissions in the absence of the project). The methods for establishing baselines are reviewed by a panel of experts and reported into the public domain by the CDM Executive Board. For our purposes, this introduces consistency in how abatement is measured across a diverse set of projects.

Two further adjustments are required. First, abatement occurs as flow over time. There is variation in the lifespan of the projects, and some projects are more prompt in the delivery of CERs than others. Consequently, we discount the flow of CERs to compensate for these differences. A second adjustment is required since a number of project investments lead to an increase in power generation. Consequently, the value of the two output streams, electricity and abatement, must be untangled prior to discounting.

In order to make these adjustments, we follow Timilsina and Lefevre (1999) and characterize the value of an investment in a CDM project as the discounted flow of profits over the life of the project. To illustrate how this is done, suppose that a CDM project is initiated in year 0 by making an initial investment I_0. The project lasts n years and generates two streams of output every year, CERs and electricity output, starting from year 1. Thus, the CDM project generates two streams of revenue, one from the sale of CERs and another from the sale of electricity. From an investor's perspective, the present value of the project is the discounted flow of profits from the sales of CERs and additional electricity (i.e., the amount of electricity generated in addition to the amount generated by the baseline project). Denoting the amount of CERs by A_t and additional electricity output by E_t, and the two streams of profits by π_t^A and π_t^E, respectively, and setting the project investment equal to the present value of the sum of the profit streams gives:

$$I_0 = \sum_1^n \pi_t^A e^{-rt} + \sum_1^n \pi_t^E e^{-rt} = VA + VE; \quad t = 1, 2, \ldots, n \qquad (1)$$

For a given time period, the return to capital is equal to the revenue minus operating costs. Suppose that the generated CERs can be sold in the carbon market at the ongoing price ρ_t. Denoting operating costs attributable to mitigation alone by O_t^A, the present value of the profits from CER sales is given by

$$VA = \sum_1^n \rho_t A_t e^{-rt} - \sum_s^n O_t^A e^{-rt}; \quad t = 1, 2, \ldots, n \qquad (2)$$

Also, suppose that generated electricity can be sold in local grids at a wholesale price l_t. Denoting operating costs attributable to additional electricity generation by O_t^E, the present value of the profits from the sales of additional electricity is given by

$$VE = \sum_1^n l_t E_t e^{-rt} - \sum_s^n O_t^E e^{-rt}; \quad t = 1, 2, \dots, n \qquad (3)$$

Equations (1)–(3) imply that the present value of the total cost of abatement is

$$C_0^n = \sum_1^n \rho_t A_t e^{-rt} = I_0 - \sum_1^n l_t E_t e^{-rt} + \sum_s^n O_t^A e^{-rt} + \sum_s^n O_t^E e^{-rt}$$

$$(4)$$

As an aside, it should be noted that not all CDM projects lead to additional power generation. When this is the case, the stream of revenue from the sales of byproduct can be ignored.

A key component missing for the cost function is the set of relevant vector of input prices for each project. The underlying input quantities should be roughly the same per project type, since the methodologies for producing CERs are standardized. However, the associated prices themselves for any given set of inputs will likely vary by time and potentially by place. While information about inputs used in the projects is not available, inputs used in the same type of CDM projects are likely to be the same. Moreover, for a given time period, the prices of such inputs can be assumed to be the same for CDM projects in a specific location. To the extent that there are no additional sources of price variability, the set of relevant prices are constant for a triad defined by time, host country, and project type. Because we use a panel of projects, we are able to introduce a corresponding triad of a set of dummy variables to compensate for missing information on input prices.

The Applied Emissions Abatement Cost Function

With the above in mind, the basic expressions for the alternative functional forms of the abatement cost for project i can be given by

$$\ln(C_{it}) = \alpha + \beta \ln(A_{it}) + \theta q_{it} \qquad (5)$$

where C is the net present value of total abatement costs, A is total emissions abatement, and q is a vector of control variables (e.g., project duration, project types, and location). In contrast to Newell, Pizer, and Shih (2003), we do not scale costs and abatement by output in order to take account of the CDM projects that generate only CERs.

Apart from the level of mitigation, abatement costs are likely to vary with the type and location of the project and also over time. Three different sets of dummy variables are used to capture the effects of project type, location, and start year. These dummy variables also serve as proxies for unverifiable input prices. Further, the "economies of time" principle implies that projects with longer duration are likely to be associated with lower cost per unit of CER (Booth, 1991). On the other hand, CDM projects with longer duration are likely to be riskier than the projects of the same size and type with shorter duration. In order to take account of such time relationships, project duration (in years) is also used as a continuous explanatory variable.

Given the parameter estimates, the marginal (as well as the average) cost of abatement can be computed for different types of CDM projects, and the marginal cost of abatement corresponding to Eq. (5) is given by: $\partial C/\partial A = \beta C/A$.

DATA DESCRIPTION

Project Abatement Capacity

The available information about all CDM projects that have been sent to UNFCCC for eventual certification until December 2009 is obtained from the CDM/JI Pipeline Analysis and Database of the United Nations Environment Programme (UNEP) Risoe Center. The dataset includes information about each individual CDM project such as project name, type, and registration or validation status; baseline and monitoring methodologies; involved host countries and credit buyers; expected CERs to be generated in each year during the life of the project; potential power generation capacity, etc. Scrutiny of the dataset shows that the CDM portfolio has been growing very rapidly since its inception in 2003. By December 2009, 5,687 CDM projects have been sent to UNFCCC for validation. 1,066 of these projects have been registered, 339 are in the process of registration, 4,053 are in the process of validation, while the rest were either withdrawn or rejected by the CDM Executive Board (EB) or terminated by independent Designated Operational Entities (DOE) upon audit (Risoe, 2010). In addition, there are 49 observations with missing abatement data and 2 observations

with zero abatement. The remaining 5,407 CDM projects in the pipeline
are expected to reduce approximately 711.75 Million tCO_2e each year and
2.99 billion tCO_2e by 2012.

Following the UNEP Risoe Center, the CDM projects in the pipeline
can be categorized into eight major types: (1) renewable resource based,
(2) methane avoidance, coal bed/mine and cement, (3) supply-side energy
efficiency, (4) demand-side energy efficiency, (5) hydrofluoro-carbon (HFC),
perfluoro-carbon (PFC), and nitrous oxide (N_2O) reduction, (6) fossil fuel
switch, (7) forestation, and (8) transport. Except for fossil fuel switch and
transport projects, each major category can be divided into several specific
types. Table 4.1 reports the number and percentage of the CDM projects
in the pipeline by major types. Annual and total CERs to be generated
during the first commitment period from each major type of CDM projects
are also reported in Table 4.1.

As can be seen from Table 4.1, about 61.9% of the projects in the CDM
pipeline are renewable-resource–based, power-generating projects accounting for 40.9% and 35.9% of the annual and total abatement during the
first commitment period, respectively. Hydro, biomass, and wind energy
projects account for about 57.4% of total number of projects, generating
39.1% of the annual and 33.8% of the total abatement. Methane avoidance, coal bed/mine, and cement is the second largest category in terms

Table 4.1: Major types of CDM projects in the pipeline — number and emissions
abatement.

Project type	No. of projects		Annual abatement		Abatement by 2012	
	Number	Percent total	$KtCO_2e$/yr	Percent total	$KtCO_2e$	Percent total
Renewable resource	3,347	61.90	291,684	40.98	1,077,381	35.91
CH4, coal mine, etc.	934	17.27	131,539	18.48	589,239	19.64
Supply-side energy eff.	582	10.76	94,279	13.25	350,628	11.69
Demand-side energy eff.	225	4.16	6,961	0.98	30,771	1.03
Fossil fuel switch	142	2.63	44,863	6.30	187,170	6.24
HFCs, PFCs, & N_2O	106	1.96	135,692	19.06	742,209	24.74
Forest	53	0.98	4,886	0.69	16,056	0.54
Transport	18	0.33	1,846	0.26	6,377	0.21
Total	5,407	100.00	711,749	100.00	2,999,831	100.00

Source: UNEP Risoe CDM/JI Pipeline Analysis and Database. Available at: http://
cdmpipeline.org/.

of number (17.3%), which accounts for 18.5% of the annual and 19.6% of the total abatement. However, a small number (1.96%) of HFCs, PFCs, and N_2O reduction projects account for about 19.1% and 24.7% of the annual and total abatement during the first commitment period, respectively. Thus, in terms of CO_2e (CO_2 equivalent) abatement, HFCs, PFCs, and N_2O reduction is the second largest category. Supply- and demand-side energy efficiency projects (14.9%) account for 14.2% of the annual and 12.7% of the total abatement. Only 2.6% are fossil fuel switch projects, accounting for about 6.3% of the annual and 6.2% of the total abatement. Forestation and transport projects together account for only 1.3% of the CDM projects in the pipeline and 0.7% of the total CO_2e abatement during the first commitment period.

In terms of both annual and total CO_2 abatement, the size of individual CDM projects varies widely. The smallest project in the CDM pipeline is expected to reduce only 524 tCO_2e per year, while the largest project is expected to abate more than 10.4 million tCO_2e (MtCO_2e) per year. The mean and median of annual abatement by the projects are 131.63 kiloton CO_2 equivalent (KtCO_2e hereafter) and 46.45 KtCO_2e, respectively. Figure 4.1 shows the number and percentage of CDM projects within different size intervals (uneven) specified in terms of KtCO_2e abatement per year. More than 52% of the projects are designed to reduce emissions by less than 50 KtCO_2e annually, while only 4% are designed to reduce emissions by more than 500 KtCO_2e per year. Figure 4.2 shows

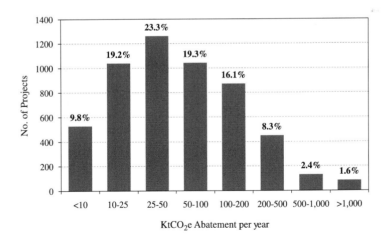

Fig. 4.1: Number and percent of CDM projects in different size intervals.

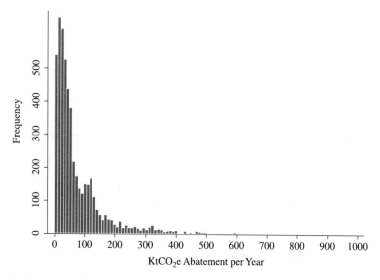

Fig. 4.2: Frequency distribution of the CDM projects by size ($KtCO_2e$ abatement per year).

the frequency distribution of the CDM projects within each capacity interval of 10 $KtCO_2e$ abatement per year.

The scale of the projects, in terms of planned abatement, varies significantly by project type. In addition, projects that result in added power generation are also larger scaled. Table 4.2 shows the range and mean of annual abatement and electricity generation by various types of CDM projects in the pipeline. While the average annual abatement by the CDM projects in the pipeline is 131.6 $KtCO_2e$, project sizes range from 0.52 $KtCO_2e$ to 10.4 $MtCO_2e$ abatement per year. In terms of average annual abatement, HFCs, PFCs, and N_2O reduction projects are the largest, and demand-size energy efficiency projects are the smallest among the major categories. While some HFCs, PFCs, and N_2O reduction projects have the capacity of reducing more than 10 $MtCO_2e$ emissions every year, the smallest project in this category has the capacity of reducing only 7.62 $KtCO_2e$ emissions per year. The size of methane avoidance, coal bed/mine, landfill gas, and cement projects ranges from 1.25 $KtCO_2e$ to 8.36 $MtCO_2e$ emissions abatement per year. Annual emissions abatement by renewable resource projects ranges from 0.52 $KtCO_2e$ to 4.33 $MtCO_2e$. The fossil fuel switch projects range in size from 1.06 $KtCO_2e$ to 3.19 $MtCO_2e$ emissions abatement per year. In terms of annual emissions abatement, the minimum and maximum

Table 4.2: Annual abatement and electricity generation by different types of CDM projects.

Project type	Annual abatement (KtCO$_2$e)				Annual electricity generation (MWh)			
	Projs.	Mean	Min	Max	Projs.	Mean	Min	Max
Renewable resource	3,347	87	0.52	4,334	2,612	118,236	0	5,183,004
CH4, coal mine, etc.	934	141	1.25	8,362	223	53,041	0	1,139,500
Supply-side energy eff.	582	162	0.87	3,026	420	427,543	5,899	29,800,000
Demand-side energy eff.	225	31	0.66	439	16	76,276	7,912	189,214
Fossil fuel switch	142	316	1.06	3,190	53	2,163,691	39,068	9,068,004
HFCs, PFCs, & N$_2$O	106	1,280	7.62	1,0437	—	—	—	—
Forest	53	92	1.12	2,036	—	—	—	—
Transport	18	103	2.78	610	—	—	—	—
Total	5,407	132	0.52	1,0437	3,324	185,357	0	29,800,000

Source: UNEP Risoe CDM/JI Pipeline Analysis and Database. Available at: http://cdmpipeline.org/.

sizes of the supply-side energy efficiency projects are 0.87 KtCO$_2$e and 3.03 MtCO$_2$e. Forestation projects also widely vary in size, with a minimum and maximum annual abatement of 1.12 KtCO$_2$e and 2.04 MtCO$_2$e by a single project, respectively. The size of demand-side energy efficiency and transport projects ranges from 0.66 to 439.25 KtCO$_2$e and 2.78 to 609.53 KtCO$_2$e emissions abatement per year, respectively.

One can distinguish between two types of projects. The first type of project, which include HFCs, PFCs, and N$_2$O reduction, forest, and transport projects, has the sole purpose of emissions reduction. Electricity generation is a joint purpose for about 64% of the CDM projects in other categories. While the average additional electricity generation capacity (megawatt hour, MWh hereafter) of these projects is 185,360 MWh per year, the capacity ranges from 0 to 29.8 million MWh. In terms of the average annual additional electricity generation capacity, fossil fuel switch and supply-side energy efficiency projects are the largest and second largest categories, respectively, followed by the renewable-resource–based category. More than 72% of the renewable-resource–based and supply-side energy efficiency CDM projects are capable of generating electricity. The largest electricity-generating project falls into the category of supply-side energy efficiency projects. Geothermal and hydroelectricity projects are the largest and second largest among the renewable-resource–based electricity generation projects. In particular, electricity generation projects that have the capacity of reducing more than 1,000 ktCO$_2$e per year are in hydro, biogas, landfill gas, coal bed/mine methane capture, cement, fugitive, and energy efficiency, supply-side, and own generation sub-categories.

Initial Investment, Income from Power Sales, and Maintenance Costs

The UNEP Risoe Center reports initial capital investments in 3,531 of the projects in the pipeline. Annual operation and maintenance cost data for 122 projects are obtained from the PDDs with the help of Climate Solutions (2008). Using the available data, initial investment and operation and maintenance costs per unit of KtCO$_2$ abatement are calculated. The average per unit capital costs and operation and maintenance cost of abatement across the CDM projects categorized by project types are calculated and then used as proxies for the projects for which such data were not available.

The net present value of emissions abatement costs for each project are calculated as described in Eq. (4). See Annex 4.1 for details on how abatement costs are calculated. For the electricity-generating CDM projects in particular, the annualized emissions abatement costs are calculated by subtracting the estimated revenue from electricity sales from the annualized fixed and variable (operation and maintenance) costs of the project. Wholesale electricity tariffs in different host countries are obtained from the PDDs. The net present values of the investments are calculated using real interest rates for the year of fixed capital investment (i.e., the prior year of credit start period). Real interest rates in the host countries are used for unilateral projects, while the rates in the partner countries are used for bi- and multi-lateral projects. The real interest rates for the host and partner countries are obtained from the World Bank (WDI, 2010).

For some CDM projects, information on electricity generation was not available. For the purpose of this study, 3,945 projects in the pipeline with complete information are considered. Table 4.3 presents a summary statistics of the total amount of emissions abatement and net present value of total abatement costs of the projects with complete information.

Table 4.3: Estimated total abatement and corresponding net present cost of abatement.

Project type	Number of obs.	Abatement (KtCO₂e)		NP cost (1,000 US$)	
		Mean	Std. dev.	Mean	Std. dev.
Renewable resource	2,493	705	1,299	116,619	195,441
CH4, coal mine, etc.	661	1,033	1,737	60,016	103,345
Supply-side energy eff.	425	1,391	2,346	141,669	265,144
Demand-side energy eff.	168	296	430	50,781	87,697
Fossil fuel switch	73	2,725	4,416	81,415	113,563
HFCs, PFCs, & N₂O	85	7,207	13,489	88,332	172,491
Forest	24	1,658	2,297	522,970	815,867
Transport	16	728	1,082	277,634	433,973
Total	3,945	1,000	2,724	108,894	202,860

Source: UNEP Risoe CDM/JI Pipeline Analysis and Database. Available at: http:// cdmpipeline.org/.

MODEL SPECIFICATION AND ESTIMATION RESULTS

The net present values of the total cost of mitigation by each individual CDM project are plotted against the corresponding total abatement, and presented in Fig. 4.3. Figure 4.4 presents the graphical plots of log-transformed mitigation costs against total abatement by each corresponding project. The data appear to better fit the logarithmic functional form.[2] Therefore, to estimate the mitigation cost, we employ the log-log model in Eq. (5).

We start with ordinary least squares estimation of the log-log model with three alternative specifications. First, the logarithm of abatement cost is regressed on the logarithm of emissions abatement, logarithm of project duration, and dummy variables for major project types and emission reduction credit start years. In particular, eight project-type dummies are used for major project types as described earlier, and eight credit start year dummies are used for each year during 2005–2012. Since the Kyoto protocol was ratified in 2005, projects for which credit starts prior to 2005 are grouped together. In the same fashion, projects for which credit starts after

---

[2]Similar plots for specific project types show a similar pattern.

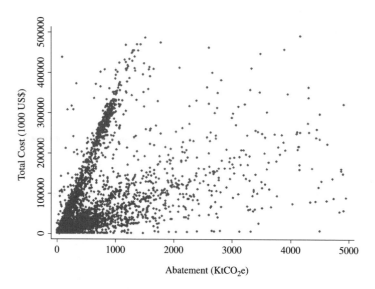

Fig. 4.3: Total cost of abatement.

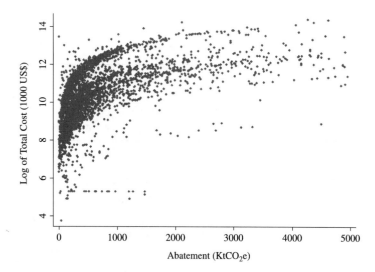

Fig. 4.4: Log-transformed total cost of abatement.

the first commitment period (i.e., after 2012) are categorized in a separate group. Note that for a small number of projects, credit starts prior to 2005 and after 2012. Second, a set of location dummy variables is added to the first model. Four regional dummies are used for the projects located in Africa, Asia, Latin America, and North America. Third, dummy variables for major CDM host countries (Brazil, China, India, Malaysia, and Mexico) are used instead of regional dummies. Robust estimation results for these specifications are presented in Table 4.4. For analytical convenience, we report the results of regressions without the intercept terms.

As can be seen from Table 4.4, the coefficient estimates of abatement and project duration are positive and highly significant in each of the three specifications of the log-log model, suggesting that the cost of abatement increases with the volume of abatement and project duration. These coefficient estimates provide corresponding elasticities. From the first and second models, the mitigation cost appears to be inelastic to the volume of abatement (for a 1% increase in total volume of abatement, net present cost of mitigation increases by 0.95%), while from the third model, mitigation cost appears to be unitary elastic (for a 1% increase in total volume of abatement, net present cost of mitigation increases by 1.005%).[3] From all three models, mitigation costs appear to increase with project duration, although not in proportion (Table 4.4).

The coefficient estimates of the project-type dummy variables are positive and highly significant for all three models (Table 4.4). Considering forestry projects to be the benchmark, we can say that 3.65 (i.e., the coefficient estimate of the dummy variable for forestry projects) is the unconditional expected mean of log of net present value of mitigation cost. In the log scale, the difference between the coefficient estimates of forestry and any other type of projects is equal to the difference in the expected geometric means of the log of mitigation costs for the forestry and other project types. In the original scale, the difference is the ratio of the expected geometric means of mitigation costs for the forestry and other project types. The exponential of the difference between the two coefficients provides the percentage change in mitigation cost for switching from forestry to any

---

[3]Results of F-tests of the null hypothesis that the coefficient estimate of log of abatement is equal to 1.00 indicate that the coefficients in the first and second models are significantly different from 1.00 while the difference is not statistically significant for the coefficient in the third model.

Table 4.4: Estimation results of the alternative specifications of the log-log model.

	I	II	III
Log of abatement (KtCO$_2$e)	0.959[a]	0.951[a]	1.005[a]
Log of project duration (years)	0.792[a]	0.805[a]	0.277[b]
Project-type dummies			
Renewable energy	3.430[a]	3.484[a]	4.259[a]
HFCs, PFCs, N$_2$O	1.048[a]	1.119[a]	1.791[a]
Methane avoidance	2.600[a]	2.749[a]	3.437[a]
Supply-side energy efficiency	3.153[a]	3.197[a]	4.094[a]
Demand-side energy efficiency	3.640[a]	3.684[a]	4.403[a]
Fossil fuel switch	2.566[a]	2.630[a]	3.370[a]
Transportation	4.582[a]	4.629[a]	5.265[a]
Forest	3.646[a]	3.721[a]	4.876[a]
Credit start year dummies			
Prior to 2005 (dropped)			
2005	−0.614[b]	−0.543[b]	−0.515[c]
2006	−0.288[c]	−0.167	−0.119
2007	0.024	0.026	0.091
2008	−0.212[b]	−0.238[b]	−0.115
2009	−0.173[c]	−0.206[b]	−0.069
2010	−0.034	−0.065	0.101
2011	−0.465[a]	−0.455[a]	−0.350[b]
2012	−1.103[a]	−1.047[a]	−1.105[a]
Post 2012	−0.487	−0.346	−0.429
Region dummies			
Asia (dropped)			
Latin America		−0.153[b]	
North America		−0.694[a]	
Africa		0.080	
Country dummies			
China			−0.337[a]
Brazil			−0.074
India			0.138[b]
Mexico			−0.624[a]
Malaysia			0.252[a]

Note: Each of the models employs 3,945 observations. Corresponding F-statistics (not shown) show that all models are highly significant. Adjusted R-squared values are around 0.99 for each of the models. [a], [b], and [c] indicate significance at 1%, 5%, and 10% levels, respectively.

other type of CDM projects. Similar interpretations are applicable to other sets of dummy variable coefficients.

For all three models, only the coefficient estimates of transportation projects are larger than those of the forestry projects, while other project-type coefficients are smaller. Thus, mitigation cost increases for switching from forestry to transportation project and decreases for switching to any other type of projects. According to the first model, the geometric mean of mitigation cost increases by nearly 155% ($=100 \times [\exp(4.582 - 3.646) - 1]$) for switching from forestry to transportation projects and decreases by 19.4% ($=100 \times [\exp(3.484 - 3.646) - 1]$) for switching from forestry- to renewable-resource–based projects. The expected geometric mean of mitigation cost appears to be the lowest for the HFCs, PFCs, and N_2O reduction projects. Switching from the forestry to HFCs, PFCs, and N_2O reduction projects lowers the expected mean of mitigation costs by 92.6% ($=100 \times [\exp(1.048 - 3.646) - 1]$).

The expected mitigation costs for the projects for which credit starts during 2005–2012 appear to be lower than the costs for the project for which credit starts prior to 2005 or after 2012, reflecting the uncertainties about the future of the protocol as it was ratified in 2005 and the first commitment period ends in 2012. However, a continuous change in mitigation cost is not observed for the period of 2005–2012, while for a majority of the projects in the pipeline, credit starts during 2008–2012, the first commitment period.

The coefficient estimates of regional dummy variables for Latin and North America appear to be negative and highly significant. In general, the expected mean of mitigation cost for the projects in Latin and North American developing countries is lower than that of the projects in Asian countries (the benchmark) and African countries (the coefficient is positive but not significant). However, a majority of the CDM projects are located in Asia.

The marginal cost of abatement for different types of CDM projects at different levels of abatement are calculated according to the results of the second model as reported in Table 4.4. Figure 4.5 depicts the marginal cost curves for the seven-year duration of forest, renewable energy, fossil fuel switch, and HFCs, PFCs, and N_2O reduction projects in Asia which start generating CERs in 2008, the first year of the first commitment period. As can be seen from Fig. 4.5, the marginal cost decreases at a decreasing rate with the volume of abatement, indicating slight economies of scale. However, the intercept of the curve varies by the type of project.

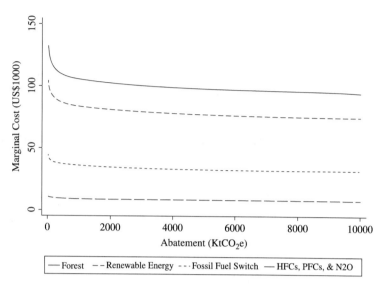

Fig. 4.5: Estimated marginal cost curves for various types of CDM projects.

The marginal cost curves for other types of projects in different regions with alternative duration and credit start years can also be depicted in a similar way.

Estimates of the coefficients for major CDM host countries indicate that, compared to countries that host fewer projects, the expected means of mitigation costs are lower in China and Mexico but higher in India and Malaysia (Table 4.4). Substantially lower cost of mitigation provides a justification for hosting 48.5% of the CDM projects in China. However, another 28.3% of the CDM projects are located in India and Malaysia, where the overall costs of mitigation are higher.

More than 80% of the CDM projects are located in three CDM host countries: Brazil, China, and India. In order to further examine the effects of location on mitigation cost, we estimate the log-log model for the projects located in these countries together as well as separately. The coefficient estimates are presented in Table 4.5. For the pooled model, the mitigation cost seems to be unitary elastic with respect to the volume of abatement and elastic with respect to project duration.[4] When estimated separately,

---

[4]Results of F-tests of the null hypothesis that the coefficient estimate of log of abatement is equal to 1.00 indicate that the coefficient from the pulled model is not statistically significantly different from 1.00.

Table 4.5: Estimation results for selected CDM host countries: Brazil, China, and India.

	Brazil	China	India	Together
Log of abatement (KtCO$_2$e)	0.878***	1.212***	0.944***	1.020***
Log of project duration (years)	−0.019	−0.671***	0.485*	1.147***
Project-type dummies				
Renewable energy	5.700***	5.228***	4.423***	2.458***
HFCs, PFCs, N$_2$O	2.351***	3.416***	1.805**	0.387
Methane avoidance	4.536***	4.910***	3.373***	1.662***
Supply-side energy eff.	5.400***	5.605***	3.631***	2.146***
Demand-side energy eff.	5.293***	5.868***	4.330***	2.611***
Fossil fuel switch	4.765***	3.605***	3.392***	1.380***
Transportation	0	6.057***	5.378***	3.579***
Forest	6.343***	7.621***	4.482***	2.047***
Credit start year dummies				
Prior to 2005 (dropped)				
2005	0.425*	−0.248	0.035	−0.002
2006	0.188	−0.348	0.031	0.008
2007	−0.143	−0.767*	0.046	−0.125
2008	−0.189	−1.122***	−0.076	−0.432***
2009	−0.209	−0.972**	−0.099	−0.387***
2010	0.02	−0.700*	−0.118	−0.193**
2011	0.354	−1.034**	−0.867	−0.520***
2012	0	−2.591**	−1.880***	−1.985***
Post 2012	0	−1.902***	−3.599***	−2.520***
Observations	265	1,915	1,000	3,180
Adj. R-squared	0.990	0.993	0.991	0.991

Note: Corresponding F-statistics show that all models are highly significant. ***, **, and * indicate significance at 1%, 5%, and 10% levels, respectively.

mitigation costs appear to be elastic to the volume of abatement for China while it is inelastic for Brazil and India.[5] The marginal costs of abatement for the seven-year-long renewable energy projects for which credit starts in 2008 are calculated and depicted in Fig. 4.6. The estimated marginal cost curves show economies of scale in Brazil and India but diseconomies of scale in China. However, marginal costs of renewable projects in China are lower than that in India (Brazil) as long as the total volume of mitigation is

[5]Results of F-tests of the null hypothesis that the coefficient estimate of log of abatement is equal to 1.00 indicate that the coefficients from the models for Brazil, China, and India are statistically significantly different from 1.00.

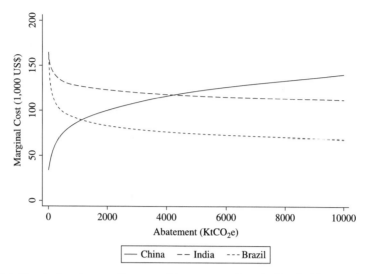

Fig. 4.6: Marginal cost curves for renewable energy projects in Brazil, China, and India.

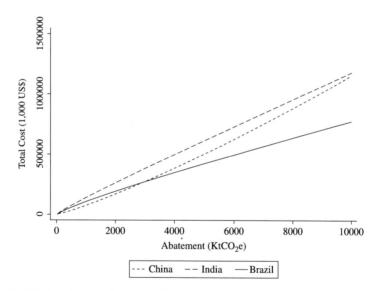

Fig. 4.7: Total cost curves for renewable energy projects in Brazil, China, and India.

lower than 4,200 $KtCO_2e$ (1,700 $KtCO_2e$). Corresponding total cost curves in Fig. 4.7 show that, irrespective of project size, mitigation cost in China is lower than that in India, while mitigation cost in China is lower than that in Brazil for smaller-scale projects (less than 3,000 $KtCO_2e$).

Table 4.6: Average size and duration of CDM projects in China and India.

Year of 30-day public comment	China			India		
	No. of projects	Avg. size (KtCO$_2$e)	Duration (years)	No. of projects	Avg. size (KtCO$_2$e)	Duration (years)
2003	—	—	—	1	23,751.0	7.0
2004	2	635.0	10.0	10	248.3	8.5
2005	25	10,541.8	7.4	199	710.8	9.4
2006	226	2,851.5	7.8	289	760.9	9.8
2007	696	1,252.3	7.5	305	512.1	9.6
2008	596	1,037.1	7.7	315	1,044.3	9.7
2009	493	1,072.4	7.8	317	970.9	9.6
Total	2,038	1,436.5	7.7	1,436	822.1	9.6

The coefficient estimates of log of project duration further suggest that mitigation cost decreases with duration of projects in China, while it increases with duration of projects in India. Note that seven-year projects can be renewed, although renewal requires a review of the project's baseline. Thus, China enjoys a comparative advantage in smaller, longer fixed-term CDM projects. Table 4.6 lists the number, average size, and duration of the CDM projects adopted by China and India during 2003–2009. Nevertheless, it appears that the average size (duration) of the CDM projects in China is larger (shorter) than that of India. The average size of the projects in China is 1,436.5 KtCO$_2$e, while the average size of the projects in India is 822.1 KtCO$_2$e. About 76% of the projects in China are 7 years long while only 19% are 10 years long. On the other hand, only 12% of the projects in India are 7 years long while more than 60% are 10 years long. However, an increasing number of smaller-scale but longer-duration projects in China and larger-scale but shorter-duration projects in India indicates a shifting of strategies over time.

Forestry and transportation projects appear to be the most expensive in all three largest CDM host countries, and HFCs, PFCs, and N$_2$O reduction and fossil fuel switch projects are the least expensive projects. However, more than 67% of the CDM projects in these countries are renewable resource based, while only 4% are HFCs, PFCs, and N$_2$O reduction and fossil fuel switch projects. Coefficient estimates for credit start year further show that mitigation costs are lower for the projects in the countries for which credit starts later during the first commitment period.

CONCLUSIONS AND POLICY IMPLICATIONS

This chapter examines the cost structure of emissions abatement through the various types of CDM projects located in different developing countries. Employing log-log functional form on alternative empirical specifications, we estimate the cost function of CO_2 abatement using CDM plant-specific data. The main results can be listed as follows. First, CDM projects are characterized by constant to increasing economies of scale, except in China. Second, for a given level of CERs, projects of a longer duration are more costly, although not proportionately so. Third, costs of mitigation through HFCs, PFCs, and N_2O reduction, fossil fuel switch, and methane avoidance projects are much lower than those of afforestation and reforestation, transportation, and demand- and supply-side energy efficiency, and renewable-resource–based projects. Fourth, mitigation costs appear to fall sharply after 2005, possibly because of learning and a clarification of rules. Fifth, costs of mitigation through CDM projects in Latin and North American developing countries are lower compared to Asian developing countries. Finally, the largest CDM host country, China, has a comparative advantage in smaller-scale but longer-duration CDM projects relative to the second and third largest hosts, India and Brazil, respectively.

In accordance with the results, continuous increases are observed in the average size and duration of the CDM projects, excluding those in China. While the CDM projects in China are characterized by substantial diseconomies of scale and economies of time, the average size of the projects in this country has decreased over time, with the average duration remaining the same. In general, projects with a 7-year duration are eligible for renewal while 10-year projects are not; however, the renewal comes with a review of the projects' baselines. Increased number of relatively longer-duration (10-year as opposed to 7-year) projects in China in recent years may indicate uncertainty about new baseline rules; about 90% of the projects in China are multilateral (with foreign investors) while more than 82% of the projects in India are unilateral (with domestic investors only).

While CDM projects with relatively lower average costs are more attractive, the distribution of various types of CDM projects does not fully correspond to the relative average costs (see Tables 4.1 and 4.4). The HFCs, PFCs, and N_2O reduction projects are the least expensive. However, only 2.0% of the projects in the CDM pipeline are in this category. Fossil fuel switch projects are next in terms of least cost. Yet only 2.6% of the projects in the CDM pipeline are in this category. On the other hand, despite having relatively much higher average and marginal costs of abatement, about 61.9% of the projects in the pipeline are renewable resource based while another 14.9% are demand- or supply-side energy efficiency projects.

Thus far, there are only 18 transportation projects and 53 forestry projects in the pipeline. Transportation and forestry projects are the most expensive. At the same time, projects in these categories often generate considerable co-benefits associated with health, biodiversity, and the provisioning of environmental services. This may explain why public institutions and development organizations like the World Bank play a proportionately larger role in projects in these categories. Methane avoidance projects are the third least expensive in terms of the marginal cost of mitigation. About 20% of the projects in the pipeline are in this category.

The average and marginal costs of abatement are substantially higher for the CDM projects that began receiving emission reduction credits after the first commitment period. This is consistent with the learning-by-doing approach and also the effects of rule clarifications. Further, despite higher average and marginal costs of abatement than that of the Latin and North American developing countries, about 65% of the projects in the pipeline are located in Asian developing countries. More than 83% of the CDM projects in Asian countries are energy related and located in emerging economies. Energy-related projects comprise about 57% and 23% of the CDM projects in Latin and North America, respectively.

Looking beyond the first commitment period, there is also a need to better understand components other than cost, that drive CDM investment. An underlying principle of most studies about the consequences of Kyoto's flexibility mechanisms is that investors will seek out low-cost abatement opportunities and thereby lower the cost of meeting the mitigation objectives of the Protocol. Finding differences in abatement costs among CDM projects is consistent with other studies showing large productivity differences in firms and farms.[6] However, theory supported by empirical evidence suggests that such differences fade among firms engaging in trade (Melitz, 2003.) Since CDM projects are initiated with the express purpose of generating permits that are destined for "export" to Annex B countries, the large differences among abatement costs are surprising. Does the result have to do with the fact that a significant component of project

---

[6]See Wagner (2007) for a review of firm-level studies. See Larson and Leon (2006) for an example of differences in farm productivity based on census data.

investment is government-led, since governments may have preferences for project characteristics other than cost? Or is it the transaction costs, some of which are not fully captured in our measure of project cost, that affect the results?

And finally, it is worth considering whether additional incentives are needed to take advantage of projects that generate significant co-benefits. Our results suggest that, with all other parameters being equal, transport projects and land-use sequestration projects in forestry or agriculture are expensive when compared to projects in other sectors. In general, these projects are also associated with significant co-benefits not directly related to climate change.[7] Consequently, policies motivated by carbon prices alone will lead to an under-investment in these projects since only the carbon-abatement components of the projects generate revenue.

REFERENCES

Booth, WJ (1991). Economies of time: On the idea of time in Marx's political economy. *Political Theory*, **19**(1), 7–27.

Boyd, G, J Molburg and R Prince (1996). Alternative methods of marginal abatement cost estimation: Non-parametric distance function. United States Department of Energy.

Bystrom, O (1998). The nitrogen abatement cost in wetlands. *Ecological Economics*, **26**(3), 321–331.

Considine, TJ and DF Larson (2006). The environment as a factor of production. *Journal of Environmental Economics and Management*, **52**(3), 645–662.

Considine, TJ and DF Larson (2009). Substitution and technological change under carbon cap and trade: Lessons from Europe. Policy Research Working Paper Series 4957. Washington, DC: World Bank.

Climate Solutions (2008). Available at: http://www.climatesolutions.org. Accessed on 6 October, 2012.

Fraas, AG and VG Munley (1984). Municipal wastewater treatment cost. *Journal of Environmental Economics and Management*, **11**(1), 28–38.

Goldar, BSM, S Misra and B Mukherji (2001). Water pollution abatement cost function: Methodological issues and application to small-scale factories in an industrial estate in India. *Environment and Development Economics*, **6**(1), 103–122.

---

[7]See Younger *et al.* (2008) for a discussion of health co-benefits from transportation and land-use planning. See Larson, Dinar, and Frisbie (2011) for a discussion of co-benefits associated with agriculture and forestry project.

Gollup, FM and MJ Roberts (1985). Cost-minimizing regulation of sulfur emissions: Regional gains in electric power. *Review of Economics and Statistics*, **67**(1), 81–90.

Hamaide, B and JJ Boland (2000). Benefits, costs, and cooperation in greenhouse gas abatement. *Climatic Change*, **47**(3), 239–258.

Hartman, RS, D Wheeler and M Singh (1994). The cost of air pollution abatement. Policy Research Working Paper No. 1398. Washington, DC: The World Bank.

International Energy Agency (2005). *Projected Cost of Generating Electricity–2005 Update*. Paris: Nuclear Energy Agency, IEA.

Larson, DF, P Ambrosi, A Dinar, SM Rahman and R Entler (2008). A review of carbon market policies and research. *International Review of Environmental and Resource Economics*, **2**(3), 177–236.

Larson, DF, A Dinar and JA Frisbie (2011). Agriculture and the Clean Development Mechanism. In A Dinar and R Mendelsohn (eds.), Handbook on Climate Change and Agriculture. Cheltenham: Edward Elgar.

Larson, DF and M Leon (2006). How endowments, accumulations and choice determine the geography of agricultural productivity in Ecuador. *World Bank Economic Review*, **3**(20), 449–471.

Maradan, D and A Vassiliev (2005). Marginal costs of carbon dioxide abatement: Empirical Evidence from cross-country analysis. *Swiss Journal of Economics and Statistics* (SJES), *Swiss Society of Economics and Statistics*, **141**(III), 377–410.

Mehta, S, S Mundle and U Sankar (1993). Incentive and regulation for pollution abatement with an application to waste water treatment. Report. New Delhi: National Institute of Public Finance and Policy.

Melitz, M (2003). The impact of trade on intra-industry reallocations and aggregate industry productivity. *Econometrica*, **71**(6), 1695–1725.

Newell, RG and RN Stavins (2003). Cost heterogeneity and potential savings from market-based policies. *Journal of Regulatory Economics*, **23**(1), 43–59.

Newell, RG, W Pizer and J-S Shih (2003). Estimating the gains from emission trading. Working Paper. Washington, DC: Resources for The Future.

Nordhaus, W (1994). *Managing the Global Commons: The Economics of Climate Change*. Cambridge, MA: MIT Press.

Pizer, W and R Kopp (2005). Calculating the cost of environmental regulation. In K-G Mäler and JR Vincent (eds.), *Handbook of Environmental Economics*. Chap. 20. Amsterdam: Elsevier.

Risoe (2010). UNEP Risoe CDM/JI Pipeline Analysis and Database. Available at: http://cdmpipeline.org/. Accessed on January 1, 2010. [I would also add a note that this is a dynamic web site that is updated on a regular basis. We accessed it for the purpose of downloading the data that was available by December 2009].

Rossi, D, CE Young and DJ Epp (1979). The cost impact of joint treatment of domestic and poultry processing wastewaters. *Land Economics*, **55**(4), 444–459.

Timilsina, GR and T Lefevre (1999). Reducing GHG emissions from the power sector in developing asian countries: An AIJ perspective. *World Resource Review*, **11**(1), 115–131.

Wagner, J (2007). Exports and productivity: A survey of the evidence from firm-level data. *The World Economy*, **30**(10), 60–82.

Younger, M, HR Morrow-Almeida, SM Vindigni and AL Dannenberg (2008). The build environment, climate change and health opportunities fo co-benefits. *American Journal of Preventative Medicine*, **35**(5), 517–526.

ANNEX 4.1. The methodology for calculating (separating) the cost of emissions abatement for the CDM projects that produce tradable outputs

Following Timilsina and Lefevre (1999), the average cost of emissions abatement for the CDM projects that produce tradable output can be calculated according to the equations given below:

$$AC = \frac{C_a - C_b}{E_b - E_a}$$

$$C_i = FC_i + \sum_y \frac{VC_{iy} - R_y}{(1 + r)^y}; \quad \text{for } i = a, b$$

where,

AC = Average cost of emissions abatement

C_a = Net present value of the project costs with the abatement technology

C_b = Net present value of the project costs with the baseline technology

E_a = Emissions (CO_2e) with the abatement technology

E_b = Emissions (CO_2e) with the baseline technology

FC_a = Fixed cost (capital cost or investments) of the project with the abatement technology

FC_b = Fixed cost (capital cost or investments) of the project with the baseline technology

VC_{ay} = Variable cost (operating cost) of the project with the abatement technology in year y

VC_{by} = Variable cost (operating cost) of the project with the baseline Technology in year y

R_y = revenue generated by the project (i.e., revenue from selling the tradable output) in year y

r = Risk-free interest rate

Annual and total (life-time) costs of abatement for a CDM project can be calculated by multiplying AC by the annual and total emissions reduction amounts, respectively.

5. DIFFUSION OF KYOTO'S CLEAN DEVELOPMENT MECHANISM*

The Kyoto Protocol, the convention that regulates the climate change combating activities agreed upon by the international community, has two project-based investment mechanisms that are designed to encourage low-carbon growth and help industrialized countries reduce the cost of meeting their emission reduction targets in the first commitment period, which runs from 2008 to 2012. The first program, Joint Implementation (JI), allows these countries to claim credit for emission reductions that arise from new low-carbon investments in other industrialized countries. The second program, the Clean Development Mechanism (CDM), allows emission-reduction projects in developing countries that generate "certified emission reductions" (CERs) for use by the investor country and foster sustainable development in the host country. Under both programs, participants include both the public and private sector. However, in terms of the scale of current investments under the program and its mitigation potential, the CDM is by far the larger of the two.[1]

Under the Kyoto Protocol, the CDM is the only formal way for the industrialized Annex B countries that have pledged to reduce greenhouse gas emissions to tap potential sources of mitigation in countries that have not pledged reductions.[2] For the most part, developing countries comprise

*This chapter is based on Rahman, Dinar and Larson (2010). Permission from the journal *Technological Forecasting and Social Change* is acknowledged.
[1] Offsets from JI projects are called Emission Reduction Units (ERUs). Both ERUs and CERs are tradable. Another source of flexibility in the Protocol is a provision that allows Annex B countries (named for the UNFCCC annex that lists them) to trade assigned amount units (AAUs), national units that correspond to emission levels permitted under pledged caps.
[2] Annex B countries are named for the section of the Kyoto Protocol in which they are listed. Currently 38 countries, including the European Community, are listed in Annex B.

the second group and are known, in Protocol parlance, as non–Annex-B countries.

In most instances, a CDM project is a direct investment by an Annex-B government or firm hosted by a non–Annex-B country.[3] Projects are designed with the objective of reducing greenhouse gas emissions or speeding the removal of greenhouse gases from the atmosphere relative to a business-as-usual baseline, and must be approved by the governments of both investor and host.[4] In addition, they are reviewed individually by a CDM Board prior to implementation and are subject to continuous monitoring and a verification process. If successful, the projects generate offsets (CERs) that Annex B countries can use to meet their Kyoto obligations. Overall, the CDM is expected to lower the cost of meeting the environmental goals of the Kyoto Protocol by encouraging investments in low-cost abatement efforts wherever they can be found. Another stated objective of the CDM is to assist host developing countries achieve sustainable development through the mobilization of direct private foreign investment and technology transfer.[5]

With its dual objectives, the CDM attracts both Annex B and non–Annex-B parties to the convention. Since its inception in 2003, Greenhouse Gases (GHG) abatement activity under the CDM has increased rapidly. By August 2009, a total of 5,316 CDM projects have been submitted to the United Nations Framework Convention on Climate Change (UNFCCC), the institution created by the initial 1994 international treaty to handle global climate change affairs, for validation UNEP Risoe Center (2009). Of the submitted projects, 1,792 were already validated and registered by the CDM board, 234 were in the process of registration, 2,605 were in the process of validation, and 685 projects were either withdrawn or rejected UNEP Risoe Center (2009). The 4,631 projects in the pipeline are expected to generate approximately 2.79 billion CERs during 2008–2012, the first commitment period of the Kyoto Protocol UNEP Risoe Center (2009). Moreover, many investors expect the CDM or some similar mechanism to continue beyond the first commitment period, and many CDM projects currently underway will generate emission reductions well beyond 2012.

---

[3] In some "unilateral" projects, the eventual credit buyer is determined late in the project cycle.

[4] For a discussion of pilot programs preceding the CDM, see Larson and Breustedt (2009).

[5] A detailed description of the CDM and analysis of the issues related to this provision can be found in Larson *et al.* (2008) and Lecocq ande Ambrosi (2007).

Nevertheless, the scope for additional CDM projects is limited by the fundamental components of demand and supply, which are in turn determined by the rate and composition of global economic growth, current Kyoto targets, expectations about future regulations, as well as domestic and JI mitigation efforts in Annex B countries.

Another line of analysis could be to examine the determinants (including time- and country-specific attributes) that explain differences in the probability and level of CDM adoption over time and across countries, with distinction between developing (host) and developed (investor) countries. The adoption and diffusion functions complement each other in that individual-level explanation is provided in the adoption analysis and an economy-wide explanation is provided in the diffusion analysis, which further help to analyze policy interventions that may affect the trend of CDM adoption.

As is discussed later, there are a variety of predictions about the size of the eventual CDM market that take these fundamentals into account. In this chapter, we look at CDM as a new technology that diffuses over time across adopters. We verify whether or not our predictions of CDM diffusion are consistent with the historic pattern of growth in CDM projects and behave according to conceptual models of technology diffusion. We fit a sigmoid expansion path model to historic CDM expansion data and test whether the predicted size of the CDM market will be exceeded during the first commitment period of the Kyoto Protocol and beyond. Estimates of the future size of the CDM market are of paramount importance to investors and policy makers as both groups are concerned with the attractiveness of the CDM mechanism. One of the questions discussed in the UNFCCC Conference of the Parties (COP) in Copenhagen in December 2009 is whether or not CDM should remain one of the major mechanisms to allow countries reduce the cost of meeting their emission reduction targets. The answer to such question may rely heavily on the trends of the CDM market, as predicted in our analysis.

TECHNOLOGY DIFFUSION LITERATURE

Various models of diffusion have been developed to explain changing populations, technology diffusion, and adoption of new consumer products. All of those models are founded on theories concerning the spread of information either through interactions between adopters and non-adopters or through exogenous sources (Feder and Umali, 1993). Aggregate models on technology diffusion are founded upon the epidemic or the logistic model. The logistic model views the diffusion process to be similar to the spread of an infectious disease, with the analogy that contact with other adopters (i.e., learning from the experience of others) and exposure to information on the innovation (i.e., demonstration effect) leads to adoption. The model is based on the assumption that members of a homogeneous population have an equal probability of coming into contact with each other and that the flow of new adopters of the technology in a given point in time is a function of the stock of existing adopters. When the stock of existing adopters is small, there is little risk of "contagion." The risk of "contagion" increases as the stock of existing adopters increases (potential adopters decreases), and the flow of new adopters rises exponentially. However, as the stock comes closer to the total number of potential adopters, the flow of new adopters gradually decreases and eventually becomes zero. The diffusion of the innovation thus follows a symmetric S-shaped function over time. Since adoption is a cyclical process, new technologies would replace existing ones and thus a process of technology abandonment would take place as well.

The symmetry of the logistic model, however, does not always fit observed patterns. To account for asymmetric growth patterns, a family of exponential growth models has been developed and used (Gregg, Hassell and Richardson, 1964). The exponential growth models include the Gompertz, the flexible logistic, the log-normal, and the cumulative log-normal models. The Gompertz model imposes an asymmetric S-shape on the growth curve and attains its point of inflection when diffusion has reached approximately 37% of the upper bound (Dixon, 1980: pp. 14, 15). While the logistic and Gompertz models have fixed inflection points, the point of inflection and degree of symmetry of the flexible logistic model are also determined by the data (Bewley and Fiebig, 2008). The log-normal distribution may be more appropriate in some economic applications since many economic variables cannot have negative values and do not have symmetric distributions as the normal distribution has (Maddala, 1977). The inflection point is variable in the cumulative log-normal model. Thus, the model can generate a whole family of asymmetric S-shaped curves. However, instead of a single diffusion curve, there may exist an envelope of successive diffusion curves, each associated with a given set of innovations and environmental characteristics, adoption ceiling, and rate of adoption (Metcalf, 1981).

Not only internal sources of information (i.e., learning from the adopters) but also external sources of information (e.g., the mass media) may shape the diffusion process (Lekvall and Wahlbin, 1973). Moreover, heterogeneity of the population may also affect the diffusion process (Coleman, 1964; Davies, 1979). Taking account of dual (endogenous and exogenous) sources of information and population heterogeneity, a new product growth model is developed (Bass, 1969; Mahajan and Schoeman, 1977). The model categorizes the population in two groups: the innovators, who adopt the new technology or product based on exogenous information, and the imitators, who adopt based on endogenous information (learning from the adopters).

While empirical studies show that different diffusion models fit different situations effectively, this chapter employs both logistic and Gompertz models to examine the aggregate diffusion of the CDM. In the case of CDM, the analogy to the epidemic model is that exposure to the opportunity and learning from the experience of the countries that have already adopted the mechanism lead new countries to adopt the mechanism. Also, the ability of investor countries to invest in several host countries leads to increased learning and adoption.

MITIGATION POTENTIAL, MODEL PREDICTIONS, AND THE CDM PIPELINE

Drawing on a combination of top-down and bottom-up studies, the IPCC (2007) concluded that most of the economic potential for emission reduction is in developing countries (Table 5.1). Studies reviewed by the Panel suggest that upwards to 3.3 gigatons of that potential represents possible win-win improvements in efficiency that would pay for themselves in the long run. However, even at a low carbon price of less than US\$ 20 per ton of CO_2 equivalent (tCO_2e), a consensus view is that roughly half of the global mitigation potential of 7.4 $gtCO_2e$ can only be brought into the Kyoto trading system via the CDM. Moreover, as prices increase, developing countries' share of global mitigation potential increases.

At the same time, recent experience suggests that the CDM project cycle is better suited to some types of mitigation projects than others. Because developing countries have not pledged emission reductions, CDM projects rely on counter-factual business-as-usual scenarios, or baselines, to calculate the number of offsets that enter the Kyoto trading system. The

Table 5.1: Estimated economic potential for mitigation in 2030 under alternative price scenarios, Gigatons of carbon dioxide equivalent (GtCO$_2$e).

Mitigation sources	Low prices	High prices
Global	15.80	31.10
OECD countries	4.90	7.40
Transition economies	1.80	2.80
Developing countries	8.30	16.80
Developing country sector		
Energy supply	1.30	2.70
Transport	0.15	0.15
Buildings	2.70	3.30
Industry	1.60	3.80
Agriculture	1.60	4.50
Forestry	0.75	3.00
Waste	0.20	0.70

Source: Table 11.3 in Chapter 11 of IPCC Working Group III, IPCC (2007).

methodology for determining the project baseline and the plan for monitoring project outcomes is reviewed by the CDM Executive Board on a case-by-case basis, and each project must be approved before it can go forward. Outcomes from the project are reviewed as well prior to the issuance of CERs. The approach is intentionally conservative and came about because of conceptual uncertainties about how to construct baselines and a deep suspicion by some treaty negotiators that project monitoring would be weak unless closely watched, which would in turn result in watered-down credits with limited environmental benefits (Larson and Breustedt, 2009; Lecocq and Ambrosi, 2009).

Table 5.2 lists the number and mitigation potential of projects in the CDM pipeline — i.e., projects that are at some stage in the formal CDM project cycle. A quick comparison with the previous table reveals that the distribution of pipeline projects differs from the distribution of project types that the potential-mitigation studies predict. The data in the table is from September 1, 2009, and to that point in time, most of the mitigation potential in identified projects stemmed from hydroelectric power generation, from improvements in manufacturing processes that lowered emissions of heavy greenhouse gas emissions like those associated with

Table 5.2: CDM pipeline inventory of projects, by project type.

	Number of projects	Annual CERs 2008–2012	Annual CERs 2008–2020
	4,631	2,786,791	7,416,430
Project type		Share of Total (%)	
Afforestation	0.11	0.01	0.18
Agriculture	0.02	0.01	0.01
Biomass energy	14.29	7.02	6.49
Cement	0.63	1.13	0.79
CO_2 capture	0.06	0.01	0.01
Coal bed/mine methane	1.45	4.62	4.71
EE households	0.45	0.14	0.14
EE industry	3.13	0.78	0.61
EE own generation	9.78	9.27	8.68
EE service	0.37	0.03	0.03
EE supply side	1.32	1.39	2.70
Energy distribution	0.19	0.35	0.34
Fossil fuel switch	2.33	6.37	6.13
Fugitive gas	0.50	1.92	1.66
Geothermal	0.32	0.60	0.58
HFCs	0.48	17.10	14.83
Hydro	26.97	17.23	20.75
Landfill gas	5.94	7.58	6.78
Methane avoidance	11.34	4.25	3.73
N_2O	1.45	8.95	8.44
PFCs and SF6	0.30	0.46	0.54
Reforestation	0.95	0.49	0.81
Solar	0.78	0.08	0.10
Tidal	0.02	0.04	0.05
Transport	0.26	0.18	0.18
Wind	16.56	10.00	10.75

Source: Based on UNEP Risoe CDM/JI Pipeline Analysis and Database, September 1, 2009.

hydrofluorocarbons, from land-fills and from improvements in "own generation" energy projects in which electricity is recovered or produced from waste gas.[6] In contrast, despite large potential, few projects having to do with forests or soils are in the pipeline. This is because procedures for

---

[6]This last class of projects is most often associated with iron, steel, and cement production.

constructing baselines and monitoring outcomes for land projects are especially complex under the current CDM rules and because the projects face additional restriction on how the CERs that they produced are used (Larson *et al.*, 2008; Williams *et al.*, 2007; Schlamadinger *et al.*, 2005). Similarly, few projects that have to do with improving the efficiency of new or existing buildings are in the pipeline, in part because of issues of scale and prohibitions on sector-wide baselines.

All of this suggests that project developers have drawn on a subset of identified economically viable mitigation sources, presumably because of constraints and incentives provided by current CDM rules. In contrast, predictions of the eventual flow of CERs by well-known models are not similarly constrained and are built up from the type of abatement cost curves that underlie the IPCC reports. An important implication then is that the volume of CERs produced during the Kyoto Protocol's first accounting period may fall short of the volumes anticipated by economic models. This, in turn, implies that developed countries would find it more difficult to meet reduction targets pledged in Kyoto and that the cost of the treaty would be greater than anticipated.

With this as background, Table 5.3 summarizes early model predictions of the Annex B countries' potential demand for total emission reductions and the potential size of the CDM markets.[7] These estimates, which were known and discussed as the CDM program began, range from 0 to 520 million tCO_2e per year by 2010. When looking at the range of values, it is important to keep in mind that the low-end predictions were based on scenarios in which large volumes of "hot air" AAUs, mostly from Russia and Ukraine, entered carbon markets, crowding out offset projects. To date, this scenario has not played out, and current outcomes are more consistent with scenarios associated with the high-end estimates (Larson *et al.*, 2008).

IS CDM ON TRACK?

In this section, we look at the expansion path taken so far by the spreading network of CDM projects and markets in order to judge whether the CDM is on track to meet early expectations, based on the diffusion trajectory

---

[7] Article 6.1.d of the Kyoto Protocol prevent industrialized countries from making unlimited use of CDM by the provision that use of CDM be "supplemental" to domestic actions to reduce emissions. Thus, the estimates of potential demand for CERs are less than the estimates of potential demand for all Kyoto units.

Table 5.3: Estimates of the potential demand for emissions reductions and size of
the CDM market by 2010.

Study	Annex B countries' demand for Kyoto units under the Protocol mtCO$_2$e/year	Potential size of the CDM market mtCO$_2$e/year
Blanchard *et al.* (2002)[a]	688–862	0–174
Eyckmans *et al.* (2001)[a]	1,414–1,713	261–499
Grütter (2001)[a]	1,000–1,500	0–500
Haites (2004)[b]	600–1,150	50–500
Halsnæs (2002)[b]	600–1,300	400–520
Holtsmark (2003)[b]	1,246–1,404	0–379
Jotzo and Michaelowa (2002)[a]	1,040	0–465
Van der Mensbrugghe (1998)	1,298	397
Vrolijk (2000)[b]	640–1,484	300–500
Zhang (1999)[b]	621	132–358
Range	600–1,713	0–520

[a]The forecasts assume that only the US does not ratify the Kyoto Protocol.
[b]The forecasts assume that Australia and the US do not ratify the Kyoto Protocol.
Source: Haites (2004) and Zhang (1999).

taken by new methods and technologies in the past. As prelude, we briefly
discuss the construction of the data and the specification of the applied
models used to fit the data.

Data Description

As discussed, projects that potentially generate Certified Emission Reduction credits must be approved by the CDM Executive Board (EB) in
advance. Project sponsors must show that their method for calculating baselines is consistent with a methodology that has been previously
approved or seek approval for the method that they propose. They must
also lay out a monitoring and verification procedure and identify a third-
party accredited by the CDM Board to implement that process. All of this
is described in a standard format known as the Project Design Document
(PDD). A project visibly enters the CDM project cycle when the PDD is
put up for public comments. The PDD also contains an estimated volume
of CERs that the project is expected to produce over its life as well as
a time-schedule of when project managers expect to ask the EB to issue

Table 5.4: Selected sample summary statistics.

Project start	Number of projects	New CERS mtCO$_2$e		Stock of CERs mtCO$_2$e		Withdrawn CERs
		2008–2012	2008–2020	2008–2012	2008–2020	Share of 2012 stock
2003 (1 month)	4	9.08	8.92	9.08	8.92	—
2004	48	7.91	7.14	16.98	16.05	0.028
2005	441	120.70	120.86	137.68	136.92	0.025
2006	664	131.93	159.62	269.61	296.55	0.067
2007	1165	124.50	171.34	394.11	467.88	0.132
2008	1464	111.55	174.55	505.66	642.43	0.139
2009 (9 months)	845	51.70	99.22	557.36	741.64	0.122

Source: UNEP Risoe CDM/JI Pipeline Analysis and Database, September 1, 2009, and authors' calculations.

offsets from the project. UNEP/Risoe begins tracking a project when it is put up for public comment and also records the CERs that are expected to be produced by 2012, the end of the first Kyoto accounting period, and also by 2020, and we use these variable in our analysis.

Summary statistics for the sample are given in Table 5.4. The first projects entered the pipeline in December 2003, and the sample period ends in our analysis in August 2009, so the first and last rows of the table represent results from partial years. Table 5.4 gives the number of projects entering the pipeline each year, the additional CERs the new projects are expected to provide annually by 2012 and by 2020, and the accumulated stock of annual project CERs for both periods.[8] A quick examination of the table reveals that the expected flow of CERs from the pipeline corresponds to the high end of early predictions of market size reported in Table 5.3. The table also shows that the number of projects has grown each year, although the rate of growth stalled slightly in 2008. Not all projects that enter the pipeline are successful; some projects are withdrawn by the project developer or rejected by the Board. The last column of the table indicates that about 3%–14% of the 2012 CERs entering the pipeline are

---

[8]The UNEP/Risoe data reports total CERs by 2012 and 2020. Annual values are simply the total divided by 5 and 10, respectively. This is done to correspond to model projects, which, by convention, are stated as CERs produced annually.

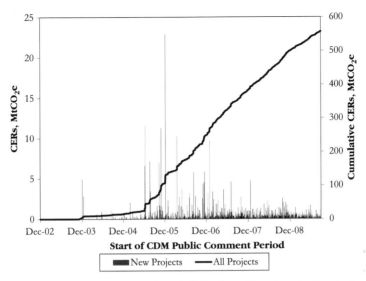

Fig. 5.1: CERS from new projects and total CERs from all projects in the pipeline from December 2003 to August 2009.

withdrawn or rejected. Averaging masks some of the variation in the scale and frequency with which CERs entered the pipeline. Figure 5.1 shows the build-up of the introduction of new projects and the stock of CERs against a daily scale.

Applied Diffusions Models

As discussed, the purpose of this chapter is to estimate the CDM diffusion patterns and compare *ex ante* estimates of CDM market size with predictions from the diffusion models. In particular, we use information about projects entering the CDM pipeline and combine it with an assumption that the adoption of CDM project methodologies follows a path typical of new technologies. We consider two types of models, one is symmetric and the other asymmetric.

Following Feder and Umali (1993), the general form of the logistic model for CDM adoption is

$$\frac{dc_t}{dt} = \beta \frac{c_t}{c^*}(c^* - c_t) \tag{1}$$

where, in our case, c_t denotes the accumulated expected flow of amount of CO_2 to be abated through existing CDM pipeline projects at time t; c^*

denotes the overall saturation point; and β is a parameter measuring the rate of adoption. With time, the spread of CDM markets is expected to slow and reach steady-state equilibrium. This results in a sigmoid cumulative density function over time. The logistic model thus imposes a symmetric S-shaped adoption trend.

Solving the logistic differential equation (1) for c_t yields the standard logistic growth function

$$c_t = \frac{m}{(1 + \exp[(-b_0 - b_1(t - t_0))])} \tag{2}$$

where c_t is the annual flow of CERs implied by the projects that have accumulated in the CDM pipeline from the first project in t_0 to time t. There are three parameters that determine the shape of the function: b_0 is the coefficient of integration, which shifts the location (intercept) of the function without affecting its shape; b_1 is a coefficient representing the rate of adoption over time; and m is an estimate of the saturation point, c^*. Conveniently, these parameters can be directly estimated from a time-series of accumulated CERs implied by the pipeline projects using a nonlinear estimator. Moreover, tests of the reasonableness of previous forecasts about the eventual size of the CDM market can be performed by imposing those values on the saturation parameter, m.

While the parameters of the functional form given in Eq. (2) are easy to interpret and the form itself is convenient for estimation, a defining feature of the specification is that the underlying cumulative distribution is symmetric and implies that the maximum adoption rate occurs at a point half-way between zero and the saturation level. This imposes an arbitrary inflection point on the trajectory, which, in turn, has encouraged researchers to use more flexible forms.[9] Among these, one of the more flexible specifications is the four-parameter Gompertz function, which we estimate as an alternative. The form traces out an asymmetric sigmoid shape and is written out as:

$$c_t = b_0 + me^{-b_1 e^{-b_2(t - t_0)}} \tag{3}$$

where, as before, b_0 shifts the location of the function without affecting its shape, m is an estimate of the saturation point and where b_1 and b_2 together determine the adoption rate.

---

[9]See Michalakelis *et al.* (2008) for a detailed discussion of alternative applied diffusion models.

Table 5.5: Estimation results.

	2008–2012		2008–2020	
	Estimate	Std. error	Estimate	Std. error
Symmetric 3-parameter model				
m	575.414[a]	7.002	799.071[a]	14.280
b_0	−3.638[a]	0.089	−3.852[a]	0.090
b_1	0.003[a]	0.0001	0.003[a]	0.0001
Asymmetric 4-parameter model				
m	694.776[a]	21.338	1,078.38[a]	48.620
b_0	−20.705[b]	9.178	−29.608[b]	12.334
b_1	0.002[a]	0.00007	0.001[a]	0.00007
b_2	17,104.28[a]	5.430	17,330.63	11.856

[a]Indicates significance at the 1% level.
[b]Indicates significance at the 5% level.
Note: The standard errors were adjusted to take into account monthly variations in the number of projects entering the CDM baseline.

Estimation Results

Both models were fitted using nonlinear least squares procedures, and the results are given in Table 5.5. The standard errors were adjusted by taking into account the number of projects associated with the flow of new CERs.[10] Both forms fit the data well and the R^2 statistic exceeded 0.98 in all cases. The estimated parameters are significant at standard levels. As a check, we also estimated a three-parameter version of the Gompertz function in which the intercept term, b_0, is suppressed; however, the hypothesis that the simpler model explained the data as well as the four-parameter model was rejected.[11]

Keeping in mind that the predictions given in Table 5.3 for the CDM markedly ranged from zero to 575 by 2010, while the size of the market for all traded Kyoto instruments ranged from 600 to about 1,734 million CERs annually for 2010, the estimation results suggest that CDM is likely to exceed *ex ante* expectations, even if the flow of new projects into the

---

[10]The practical consequence of this adjustment is to inflate the standard errors, which works against our conclusion that the estimated parameters are statistically significant.
[11]The associated LR test-statistic is distributed $\chi^2(1) = 19.21$ and is significant at a 1% confidence level.

Table 5.6: Related inference tests.

Dependent variable	CERs to 2012	CERs to 2020
Model	Steady-state flows ($mtCO_2e$)	
Symmetric	575	799
Asymmetric	694	1,078
Tests of symmetric and asymmetric models		
Upper bounds are equivalent	$F(1,23) = 31.29^a$	$F(1,23) = 33.00^a$
Models are equivalent	$\chi^2(1) = 1,296^a$	$\chi^2(1) = 1,323^a$
Dependent variable	CERs to 2012	
Model	Symmetric	Asymmetric
Probability that cumulative CERs in August		
2009 exceed 520 $mtCO_2e$	$>90\%$	$>99\%$
Upper bound $= 520\,mtCO_2e$	$F(1,23) = 62.64^a$	$F(1,23) = 67.09^a$

[a]Indicates statistical significance at the 1% level.

CDM pipeline slows as the diffusion model would predict. As summarized in Table 5.6, the saturation parameter, m, from the symmetric model suggests a steady-state flow of about 575 million CERs annually by the close of the first period in 2012 and 799 million CERs by 2020 — the end-date of the projection period for current CDM projects. The related parameter from the more flexible, asymmetric model suggests slightly higher steady-state levels of 695 and 1,078 annual million CERs for 2012 and 2020, respectively. The calculated and projected annual flows are given in Figs. 5.2 and 5.3. In both cases, the predicted net gains in the annual production of CERs begin to ebb by 2012.

As might be expected, the more flexible four-parameter asymmetric model provides a better fit. Two tests that compare the two functional forms are presented in the middle section of Table 5.6. The first is a Wald test inferring that the lower-valued saturation parameter of the symmetric model is statistically indistinguishable from the saturation parameter of the asymmetric model. The second is a likelihood ratio test, inferring that the three-parameter model is not nested in the four-parameter model. In both instances, the results favor the four-parameter asymmetric functional form.[12]

---

[12]Note that the Wald tests reported in Table 5.6 are based on standard errors that are adjusted for the number of projects passed by the CDM Board on a given date. This results in 24 clusters and, consequently, reduces the degrees of freedom in the F-statistic to 24, even though the underlying model is based on 1,131 observations.

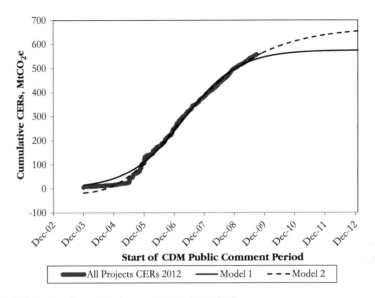

Fig. 5.2: Actual and predicted annual 2008–2012 CERs.

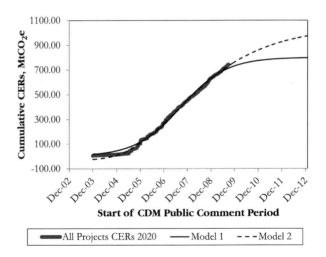

Fig. 5.3: Actual and predicted annual 2008–2020 CERs.

As discussed, recent pipeline data already indicate that the expected CER flows from pipeline projects exceed *ex ante* model predictions. From the model parameters, it is possible to construct confidence intervals around each observation. Using this approach, we calculated the probability that the cumulative number of CERs identified in August 2009 already exceed the upper limit of 520 million tons of carbon dioxide equivalent ($mtCO_2e$) predicted by the *ex ante* model. Based on parameters from the symmetric model, there is a 90% probability that the cumulative level of CERs in the August pipeline top the upper range of the model predictions for 2010. Using the better-fitting asymmetric model parameters, the probability exceeds 99%. Similarly, a test that the upper bound is really 520 $mtCO_2e$ is rejected in both models.[13]

It is likely that not all projects in the pipeline will succeed in producing the full complement of credits predicted in documents submitted to the CDM Board, and some of the credits may arrive after the close of the first commitment period. Moreover, there remains some skepticism in the environmental community about whether leakage and inexactness in project baselines dilute the environmental integrity of the mitigation effects measured by the CDM. Even so, barring a significant departure from current trajectories, the CDM appears on track to match or exceed early expectations when the program was begun.

SUMMARY AND CONCLUSION

There is a consensus view that, at reasonable prices for carbon, most of the global opportunities for mitigation reside in developing countries. And, to date, CDM is the only formal way developed countries can access mitigation opportunities in developing countries to meet their commitments under the Kyoto Protocol. Additionally, recent estimates by the IPCC suggest that a significant portion of the mitigation opportunities in developing countries are in agriculture, forestry, and improving building efficiency. Yet, so far, project investments under the CDM are narrowly focused on the energy and industrial sectors, leaving these broad areas of potential untouched. This differs from earlier assumptions of how the program would work and raises the question of whether mitigation opportunities that the CDM currently taps will be sufficient to meet global demand. It also raises the related question of whether constraints stemming from the design of the CDM will drive up the cost of meeting Kyoto's environmental goals.

With this as motivation, we look at the current trajectory of potential mitigation entering the CDM pipeline and project it forward under the

---

[13]The test is based on setting m in (2) and (3) equal to 520.

assumption that the diffusion of CDM markets will follow a path similar to other kinds of innovation. We then compare those projections to pre-CDM predictions of the mechanism's potential market size used to assess Kyoto's cost, in order to discern whether limits on the types of project entering the CDM project cycle will also limit the eventual supply of CERs. Somewhat surprisingly, we find that it does not. Instead, we find that the current size of the CDM market exceeds the *ex ante* model predictions and that the mechanism is on track to deliver an average annual flow of roughly 700 million CERs by 2012. Uncertainties abound concerning how well the existing projects will perform; however, it is important to note that the projected scale of the CDM market exceeds the most optimistic early model predictions by roughly 30%.

From a policy perspective, the results suggest that the CDM has been, in one sense, extremely successful in achieving significant levels of mitigation by motivating private capital flows. However, the skewed sector composition of CDM projects also suggests that the CDM alone may not be up to the task of fully exploiting known and economically viable sources of mitigation. This suggests great scope for finding additional ways of investing in the mitigation potential of developing countries.

Looking ahead, while the aggregate diffusion functions that we estimate provide an important tool to evaluate global CDM trends, it is important that additional research identifies the determinants of differences in cross-country CDM adoption over time and also differences among sectors. Because incentives may differ among participants, there is a need to better understand the underlying determinants for both host and investor countries as well as the reasons why some countries pursue unilateral investment strategies.

REFERENCES

Bass, FM (1969). A new product growth model for consumer durables. *Management Science*, **15**, 215–17.

Bewley, R and DG Fiebig (1988). A flexible logistic growth model with application in telecommunications. *International Journal of Forecasting*, **4**, 177–192.

Blanchard, O, P Criqui and A Kitous (2002). After the Hague, Bonn and Marrakech: The future international market for emissions permits and the issue of hot air. Cahier de Recherche no. 27 bis. Grenoble: Institut d'Economie et de Politique de l'Energie.

Coleman, KS (1964). *Introduction to Mathematical Sociology*. London: Collier Macmillan.

Davies, S (1979). *The Diffusion of Innovations*. Cambridge: Cambridge University Press.

Dixon, R (1980). Hybrid Corn Revisited. *Econometrica*, **48**, 1451–1461.

Eyckmans, J, D van Regemorter and V and van Steenberghe (2001). Is Kyoto fatally flawed? Working Paper 2001-18. Leuven: Center for Economic Studies, Katholieke Universiteit Leuven.

Feder, G and DL Umali (1993). The adoption of agricultural innovations: A review. *Technological Forecasting and Social Change*, **43**, 215–239.

Gregg, JV, CH Hassell and JT Richardson (1964). *Mathematical Trend Curves: An Aid to Forecasting*. Edinburgh: Oliver and Boyd.

Grütter, J (2001). The GHG market after Bonn. *Grütter Consulting and Joint Implementation Quarterly*, **7**(3), 9.

Haites, E (2004). Estimating the market potential for the clean development mechanism: Review of models and lessons learned. PCFplus Report 19. Washington, DC: The World Bank Carbon Finance Business PCFplus Research Program.

Halsnæs, K (2002). Market potential for Kyoto mechanisms: Estimation of global market potential for co-operative greenhouse gas emission reduction policies. *Energy Policy*, **30**, 3–32.

Holtsmark, B (2003). Russian behaviour in the market for permits under the Kyoto protocol. *Climate Policy*, **3**(4), 399–415.

IPCC (2007) *Contribution of Working Group III to the Fourth Assessment Report of the Intergovernmental Panel on Climate Change, 2007*, B Metz, OR Davidson, PR Bosch, R Dave, LA Meyer (eds.). Cambridge, United Kingdom and New York, NY, USA: Cambridge University Press.

Jotzo, F and A Michaelowa (2002). Estimating the CDM market under the Marrakech accords. *Climate Policy*, **2**(1), 179–196.

Larson, DF and G Breustedt (2009). Will markets direct investments under the kyoto protocol? Lessons from the activities implemented jointly pilots. *Environmental and Resource Economics*, **43**(3), 433–456.

Larson, DF, P Ambrosi, A Dinar, SM Rahman and R Entler (2008). A review of carbon market policies and research. *International Review of Environmental and Resource Economics*, **2**(3), 177–236.

Lecocq, F and P Ambrosi (2007). The clean development mechanism: History, status and prospects. *Review of Environmental Economics and Policy*, **1**(1), 134–151.

Lekvall, P and C Wahlbin (1973). A study of some assumptions underlying innovation diffusion function. *Swedish Journal of Economics*, **75**, 362–377.

Maddala, GS (1977). *Econometrics*. New York: McGraw-Hill.

Mahajan, V and MEF Schoeman (1977). Generalized model for the time pattern of the diffusion process. *IEEE Transactions of Engineering Management*, **24**, 12–18.

Metcalfe, JS (1981). Impulse and diffusion in the study of technical change. *Futures*, **13**, 347–359.

Michalakelis, C, D Varoutas and T Sphicopoulos (2008). Diffusion models of mobile telephony in Greece. *Telecommunications Policy*, **32**(3/4), 234–245.

Rahman, SM, A Dinar and DF Larson (2010). Diffusion of Kyoto's clean development mechanism. *Technological Forecasting and Social Change*, **77**, 1391–1400.

Schlamadinger, B, B Bosquet, C Streck, I Noble, M Dutschke and N Bird (2005). Can the EU emission trading scheme support CDM forestry? *Climate Policy*, **5**, 199–208.

United Nations Environment Programme (UNEP) Risoe Center (2009). CDM/JI Pipeline Analysis and Dataset. Available at: http://cdmpipeline.org.

van der Mensbrugghe, DA (1998). Preliminary analysis of the Kyoto protocol: Using the OECD GREEN model. Presented at the OECD Workshop on the Economic Modeling of Climate Change, 18 September, Paris.

Vrolijk, C (2000). Quantifying the Kyoto commitments. *Review of European Community and International Environmental Law*, **9**(3), 285–295.

Williams, C, N Hanan, J Neff, R Scholes, J Berry, A Denning and D Baker (2007). Africa and the global carbon cycle. *Carbon Balance and Management*, **2**, 1–13.

Zhang, Z (1999). Estimating the size of the potential market for the Kyoto flexibility mechanisms. FEEM Working Paper No. 8.2000. Milan: Fondazione Eni Enrico Mattei.

6. WHY ADOPTION OF THE CLEAN DEVELOPMENT MECHANISM DIFFERS ACROSS COUNTRIES?

The stated objectives of the CDM are to facilitate reductions in global emissions at a lower cost and to promote sustainable development through the mobilization of direct private foreign investment and technology transfer.[1] Critiques blame CDM for not achieving its development objectives (Olsen, 2007). However, with its dual objectives, the CDM has successfully attracted both industrialized (Annex B) and developing (non–Annex-B) countries to the convention. Estimating the overall growth pattern of the CDM activity, the analysis in Chapter 5 suggests that the mechanism could deliver an average annual flow of approximately 700 million CERs by the close of the first commitment period in 2012. However, the incidence, extent, and growth of CDM adoption vary widely across countries and over time. As of 2010, only 50% of Annex B countries and about 50% of non–Annex-B countries have engaged in varying levels of CDM activity.[2]

Previous works on diffusion and adoption of CDM (Rahman *et al.*, 2010; Winkelman and Moore, 2010; Dinar *et al.*, 2011) provide information on variables that affect the participation of host and investor countries in the CDM program. Rahman *et al.* (2010) estimate the diffusion process of CDM over time and Dinar *et al.* (2011) estimate the determinants of cooperation among the host and investor countries. Winkelman and Moore (2010) attempt a similar explanation of adoption decision to the one undertaken in this chapter. However, some differences exist, which are important enough to be highlighted. Winkelman and Moore (2010) estimate adoption only for the host countries, while in this chapter, we estimate adoption also

---

[1]A detailed description of the CDM can be found in Lecocq and Ambrosi (2007), Chapter 2, and in the literature cited there.

[2]In the following we use host, developing, and non–Annex-B interchangeably, and industrialized, investor, developed, and Annex B interchangeably.

by host as well investor countries. Winkelman and Moore (2010) did not take into account the regional nature of CDM adoption, while in this chapter, we identify different regional adoption patterns of CDM. Winkelman and Moore (2010) assume similar adoption patterns over time, while in this chapter we find increased adoption over time. Finally, Winkelman and Moore (2010) use a small dataset of 1,835 projects (between 2003 and October 1, 2009), while in this chapter, we use a much larger dataset of 6,921 projects (between 2003 and December 31, 2010). Only registered projects were included in the analysis in Winkelman and Moore (2010). In our analysis (as will be explained later) all projects (submitted, rejected registered, and under review), except withdrawn projects, were included.

The main purpose of this chapter is to examine the factors that influence developing (host) and developed (investor) countries' decision to engage in CDM activity as well as the extent and rate of CDM adoption over time. The chapter also makes policy suggestions for improving participation in the program. The first question we address is what motivates some countries (either host or investor ones) to participate in the CDM while others do not? The second question we address is what are the factors that affect the *level* of CDM adoption by host and investor countries? In the technology adoption literature (e.g., Rogers, 2003), adoption is measured not only by the extent of adoption but also by the speed of adoption. We can identify early adopters and late adopters of CDM projects, as well as adopters who accumulated relatively small or large shares of CDM activity at a slower or faster rate. Understanding why countries participate in the program and distinguishing between the rate and extent of their participation is important for policy, as it provides insights into the types of instruments necessary to broaden and deepen the reach of the program.

By characterizing the CDM as a new innovation that combines greenhouse gas abatement with sustainable development objectives, we analyze the adoption process in the light of existing theoretical models of technology diffusion and then evaluate the theoretical predictions using project- and country-level data. Based on the history of other innovations, we expect that CDM adoption follows a logistic growth pattern resulting in an S-shaped (symmetric or asymmetric) cumulative adoption curve. We examine whether this holds true and whether the country-specific attributes explain differences in the likelihood and level of CDM adoption over time and across countries. Based on the empirical results, we suggest policy interventions that may affect the trend of CDM adoption.

THEORETICAL FRAMEWORK AND EMPIRICAL MODELS

Various models were developed to explain the adoption of new technologies and consumer products. All of those models are based on theories concerning the spread of information either through interactions between adopters and nonadopters or through exogenous sources (Feder and Umali, 1993). Aggregate models on technology diffusion are founded upon the epidemic or logistic model (e.g., Griliches, 1957, 1980; Mansfield, 1961; Doessel and Strong, 1991; Knudson, 1991; Dinar and Yaron, 1992). The logistic model views the diffusion process to be similar to the spread of an infectious disease, with the analogy that contact with other adopters (i.e., learning from the experience of others) and exposure to information on the innovation (i.e., demonstration effect) leads to adoption. The model is based on the assumption that members of a homogeneous population have an equal probability of coming into contact with each other and that the flow of new adopters of the technology in a given point in time is a function of the stock of existing adopters. When the stock of existing adopters is small, there is little risk of "contagion." The risk of "contagion" increases as the stock of existing adopters increases (potential adopters decreases), and the flow of new adopters rises exponentially. However, as the stock comes closer to the total number of potential adopters, the flow of new adopters gradually decreases and eventually becomes zero. The diffusion of the innovation thus follows a symmetric S-shaped function over time.

The symmetry of the logistic model, however, does not always fit observed patterns. To account for asymmetric growth patterns, a family of exponential growth models has been developed and used (Gregg, Hassell, and Richardson, 1964). The exponential growth models include the Gompertz, the flexible logistic, the log-normal, and the cumulative log-normal models. The Gompertz model imposes an asymmetric S-shape on the growth curve and attains its point of inflection when diffusion has reached approximately 37% of the upper bound (Dixon, 1980; Michalakelis, Varoutas, and Sphicopoulos, 2008). While the logistic and Gompertz models have fixed inflection points, the point of inflection and degree of symmetry of the flexible logistic model are determined by the data (Bewley and Fiebig, 1988). The log-normal distribution may be more appropriate in some economic applications since many economic variables cannot have negative values and do not have symmetric distributions as does the normal distribution (Maddala, 1977). The inflection point is variable in the cumulative log-normal model. Thus, the model can generate a family of asymmetric S-shaped curves. However, instead of a single diffusion curve, there may exist an envelope of successive diffusion curves, each associated with a given set of innovations and environmental characteristics, adoption ceiling, and rate of adoption (Metcalfe, 1991).

Not only internal sources of information (i.e., learning from the adopters) but also external sources of information (e.g., the mass media) may shape the diffusion process (Lekvall and Wahlbin, 1973). Moreover, the heterogeneity of the population may also affect the diffusion process (Coleman, 1964; Davis, 1979). Taking account of dual (endogenous and exogenous) sources of information and population heterogeneity, Bass (1969) developed a model for the growth of market share of a new product. The model categorizes the population in two groups: the innovators, who adopt the product based on exogenous information, and the imitators, who adopt based on endogenous information (learning from the adopters). Mahajan and Schoeman (1977) proposed a similar model for technology diffusion.

In the case of CDM, the analogy to the epidemic model is that exposure to the opportunity and learning from the experience of the countries that have already adopted the mechanism lead new countries to adopt the mechanism. The process is particularly open, since the project proposal documents are posted on the Internet and subject to comment prior to project commencement. The same is true with the methodologies for establishing project baselines. Also, the ability of investor countries to invest in several host countries leads to increased learning and adoption.

The Empirical Models

We start our empirical investigation with a binary response model to examine the factors that influence the incidence of CDM in the host and investor countries. Then we use two empirical versions of the epidemic model to provide a detailed account of the determinants that affect the incidence, extent, and rate of CDM adoption by both host and investor countries.

First, following the adoption literature (e.g., Rogers, 2003; Payne, Fernandez-Cornejo, and Daberkow, 2003; Teklewold *et al.*, 2006), the incidence of CDM adoption can be represented by a dichotomous variable indicating whether a particular country is engaged in CDM activity (i.e., in at least one CDM project by the end of 2010). Using this indicator as a dependent variable in the following equation, we examine whether variations in country attributes sufficiently explain the binary choice.

$$I_i = \alpha + X_i\beta + \varepsilon_i \qquad (1)$$

where I_i indicates CDM incidence in country i which is set equal to 1 if it is involved (as a host or investor) in at least one CDM project, and zero otherwise; X_i is a vector of country-specific variables that determine CDM incidence; ε_i is an independently and identically distributed random disturbance that varies across countries.

Second, a reasonable measure of the extent (level) of CDM adoption by a country at a particular point in time can be given by the cumulative expected CERs per year (i.e., CO_2e abatement per year) through its projects. The Annex B countries' 2012 Kyoto obligation (i.e., the total amount of emissions reductions by Annex B countries in the final year of the first commitment period as set by the Kyoto Protocol) can be used as a proxy for the population in the logistic adoption function. Using the natural log of the ratio of the cumulative expected CERs to the Annex B countries' aggregate emissions reduction target as the dependent variable, the determinants of differences in the levels of CDM adoption across countries can be examined using the equation

$$\ln(y_i/T) = \theta + X_i\gamma + \xi_i \qquad (2)$$

where the entity (y_i/T) is the ratio of cumulative expected CERs per year from the projects of country i to Annex B countries' 2012 emissions reduction target, and ξ_i is an independently and identically distributed random disturbance that varies across countries.

Finally, following Comin and Hobijn (2004) and Casselli and Coleman (2001), the determinants of differences in the levels of CDM adoption across countries and over time can be examined using the equation

$$\ln(y_{it}/T) = \delta + X_{it}\phi + D_t\lambda + \eta_i + \mu_{it} \qquad (3)$$

where y_{it} is the ratio of expected CERs in year t from the projects of country i to Annex B countries' 2012 emissions reduction target, X_{it} is a set of potential determinants of CDM adoption for country i in year t, D_t is a set of year dummies, η_i is a random country effect (unobserved heterogeneity) that differ across countries but not over time, and μ_{it} is independently and identically distributed random disturbance that varies across countries and years. The set of year dummies in Eq. (3) demean the CDM adoption measure in each year. Thus, the deviation $\ln(y_{it}) - D_t$ reflects the CDM adoption disparity of a country from the average adoption rate across countries. The coefficients of year dummies are likely to be positive and increasing as the end of the first commitment period of the Kyoto Protocol approaches.

Since the aggregate Kyoto target, T, is the same across countries and constant over time, the denominators in Eqs. (2) and (3) can be normalized to 1 in order to avoid unnecessary complexity. With this simplification, we use the log of cumulative expected CERs as the dependent variable in Eqs. (2) and (3). We also examine the cumulative number of projects of country i at a specific point in time as a measure of CDM adoption in Eqs. (2) and (3).

The existing theoretical and empirical literature on technology adoption identifies several groups of factors that determine technology adoption: vintage physical capital (Johansen, 1959; Solow, 1960; Gilchrist and Williams, 2001; Laitner and Stolyarov, 2002); vintage human capital (Chari and Hopenhayn, 1991; Brezis, Krugman, and Tsiddon, 1993; Jovanovic and Nyarko, 1996); imitation costs (Barro and Sala-i-Martin, 1997; Eeckhout and Jovanovic, 2002); costs of complementary inventions (Helpman and Traijtenberg, 1998); factor endowments (Basu and Weil, 1998; Jovanovic, 1998; Acemoglu, 2001; Hobijn, 2001); Trade (Grossman and Helpman, 1991; Coe and Helpman, 1995; Holmes and Schmitz); and vested interests and political institutions (Snell, 1974; Comin and Beunza, 2003; Fleck and Hansen, 2003; Lizzeri and Persico, 2003).[3] Several additional variables and their relationship with adoption of CDM are based on Dinar *et al.* (2010).

Variables and Hypotheses

Based on the studies cited in the previous section, the potential determinants of CDM adoption are broadly categorized into five groups: standard macroeconomic variables, energy resources and sequestration potentials, trade openness, human capital, and sociopolitical and business environment.

For the host countries, macroeconomic variables such as per capita real GDP, agricultural value added, manufacturing value added, value of total imports, and net FDI inflow represent the strength of the country economy and its likelihood to be involved in CDM projects. For both host

---

[3]See Comin and Hobijn (2004) for a detailed description of the relevant theories/ hypotheses.

and investor countries, higher levels of the macro-economic variables mean higher likelihood to higher benefit from hosting (adopting) or investing in a CDM project (Dinar *et al.*, 2010).

For the energy resources and sequestration potentials cluster of variables, it is reasonable to hypothesize that, when all other variables are held constant, the level of adoption of CDM by investor countries will increase with higher levels of energy use, and thus emission intensities, of the economy. For an investor country, the level of adoption will decrease and for host country, it will increase with more renewable energy resources available in that country. The more (less) vulnerable to climate change the economies are, the higher (lower) adoption will be observed. Countries with high impact vulnerability and low source vulnerability should be most inclined to support greenhouse gas emissions limits, thus welcoming (investing in) CDM projects. Conversely, countries with high source vulnerability and low impact vulnerability should be most resistant to such limits, thus being reluctant to adopt (invest in) CDM projects.

Trade openness was found to be of great importance in engagement in international cooperation projects (Dinar *et al.*, 2010). We expect that the adoption of CDM projects by both host and investor countries will increase as trade widens.

Regarding the human capital variables, using the traditional adoption literature (Feder and Umali, 1993), it is safe to hypothesize that the adoption of CDM projects by host countries will increase as they are more experienced with AIJ projects, which was the purpose of initiating the AIJ program on the first place.

Sociopolitical and business environment are measured by several variables, such as the Level of Governance and Ease of Doing Business in the country. Following Dinar *et al.* (2010) and the literature they cite, we hypothesize that the level of adoption will decrease as transaction costs of doing business (notice that the higher the value of Ease of Doing Business the higher the transaction cost) increase; will decrease as level of political constraints increases; and will increase as governance level in the country improves.

Because the specific objectives of the host and investor countries are different, the set of potential determinants of CDM adoption and their effects are likely to be different. Two major motivations for the industrialized countries to adopt CDM are the Kyoto obligation to offset carbon emission and lower cost of carbon abatement in developing countries. Therefore, emissions reduction target and average costs of carbon abatement are considered as potential determinants of CDM adoption by investor countries, which is expected to increase with the target and decrease with the cost. The variable representing emission reduction target is irrelevant for the developing countries as they do not face the Kyoto obligation.

It is reasonable to expect that the incidence and extent of CDM will be higher for the developing countries with higher renewable energy resources, sequestration potential, and AIJ experience, but lower for the countries with higher cost of business start-up procedures. Buys *et al.* (2007) suggest that CDM adoption is likely to be higher (lower) for the countries ranked higher (lower) in the impact (source) vulnerability index. Winkelman and Moore (2010) found that economies with higher carbon intensity (carbon emissions per unit of GDP) had greater CER production. While these hypotheses are empirically tested using the data and employing appropriate econometric techniques, effects of other potential determinants are also examined.

In particular, per capita real GDP, agricultural and manufacturing shares of GDP, value of imports and FDI as percentages of GDP, and nonrenewable energy resources are also included in the models. These variables are both analytically and statistically relevant. The per capita real GDP of the developing countries is found to be negatively correlated with the total number of CDM projects and annual CERs to be generated from those projects. This is consistent with developmental objective of the CDM and may reflect the objectives of government-sponsored projects. The manufacturing share of GDP and available nonrenewable energy resources are positively correlated with the total number of CDM projects and annual CERs. Both reflect opportunities; a significant manufacturing sector offers opportunities for projects that improve energy efficiency or the handling of dense greenhouse gases that are byproducts of manufacturing processes. While the agricultural share of GDP and value of imports and net inflow of FDI as percentages of GDP are not found to be significantly correlated with CDM adoption, sectoral composition, trade openness, and environment for FDI are likely to influence the decision and level of adoption. This means that agriculture in developing countries is undervalued as a source for cost-effective CDM investment (see also Larson *et al.*, 2011).

It is also reasonable to expect that the likelihood and extent of CDM will be higher for the investor countries with larger emissions reduction targets, more AIJ experience, and higher source vulnerability, but will be lower for the investor countries with lower costs of abatement (at home). The investor-country–level average costs of abatement through the CDM can be considered as the opportunity costs of abatement abroad. Thus, higher average costs of abatement through the CDM reflect the host countries' domestic abatement costs. Emissions reduction targets for the industrialized countries with higher overall emissions are likely to be larger. In addition, per capita real GDP and value of total imports (as a percentage of GDP) are also included in the empirical model examining CDM adoption by developed countries. Per capita real GDP of the industrialized countries is found to be positively correlated with the measures of CDM adoption, as well as with intensities of energy use and emissions. Imports share of GDP is negatively correlated with the number of CDM projects and annual expected CERs.

The next section describes the how each variable in our dataset was measured and constructed.

DATA AND MEASUREMENTS

The CDM/JI Pipeline Analysis and Database of the United Nations Environment Programme (UNEP) Risoe Center constructs and maintains an up-to-date dataset consisting of all CDM projects that have been sent to the CDM Board for validation. The dataset includes information about each CDM project, such as project name, type, and registration/validation status; baseline and monitoring methodologies; involved host country and credit buyers; expected annual and total CERs to be generated in each year during the life of the project; and potential power generation capacity. In order to analyze the CDM adoption process, information about all CDM projects that have been sent for validation until December 2010 are extracted from that dataset.

Data required to construct the dependent and explanatory variables and estimate the empirical model specified above are derived from several different sources. Data on individual CDM project-level data are obtained from the CDM/JI Pipeline Analysis and Database of the United Nations Environment Programme Risoe Center (UNEP Risoe CDM/JI Pipeline Analysis and Database, January 1, 2011). Observations for the projects that have been submitted up until December 2010 are used. From the project-level data, cumulative number of projects, expected annual and total abatement (KtCO$_2$e), expected annual electricity generation (megawatt-hour), and capital investments are calculated for each host and investor country in each year during 2003–2010.

The UNEP Risoe Center reports initial capital investments in 3,531 of the projects in the pipeline. Annual operation and maintenance cost data for 122 projects are obtained from the PDDs with the help of Climate Solutions (2008). Using the available data, initial investment and operation and maintenance costs per unit of $KtCO_2e$ abatement are calculated. Average per unit capital costs and operation and maintenance cost of abatement across the CDM projects categorized by project types are calculated and then used as proxies for the projects for which such data were not available, by type and size of project. For the electricity-generating CDM projects in particular, annualized emissions abatement costs are calculated by subtracting the estimated revenue from electricity sales from the annualized fixed and variable (operation and maintenance) costs of the project. Wholesale electricity tariffs in different host countries are obtained from the PDDs. Net present value of the investments is calculated using real interest rates for the year of fixed capital investment (i.e., the prior year of credit start period). Real interest rates in the host countries are used for unilateral projects, while the rates in the partner investor countries are used for bi- and multi-lateral projects. Real interest rates for the host and investor partner countries are obtained from the World Bank (World Bank, 2010).

The expected abatement and corresponding costs of a country in a particular year is calculated by adding up the expected $KtCO_2e$ abatement from all of its projects and costs in that year. Although several parties (e.g., host and investors) may be involved in a particular project, the PDDs do not clarify each party's share of the CERs and costs. Assuming that in bilateral and multilateral projects investors bear the costs, capital investments are designated to the accounts of the investors with equal shares in the cases of more than one investor. Expected CERs are also assumed to be equally shared by the investors. For unilateral projects, expected CERs and capital investments are designated to the accounts of the host countries.

Historical macroeconomic data such as total and per capita annual GDP (constant 2000 US$), GDP deflators; energy and electricity production, import, and consumption, and CO_2 emissions (kiloton of oil equivalent); CO_2 per dollar of 2000 PPP GDP; agricultural and manufacturing value added; volume exports; imports, total trade, net inflows, and outflows of foreign direct investments (FDI); and costs of business starting procedures for all countries of the world are obtained from the World Bank (World Bank, 2010). Two-year lagged values for these variables are used. The annual growth rates of these variables are also obtained from the same source or calculated using the flows.

Using the historical CO_2 emissions and GDP data and employing a variance error correction (VEC) procedure, the expected CO_2 emissions by each investor country in each year of the first commitment period and beyond are projected. Emission targets for each of the investor countries are obtained from the Kyoto Protocol Reference Manual (UNFCCC, 2007). Each investor country's initial Assigned Amount Units (AAUs) for the Protocol's five-year first commitment period (2008–2012) is calculated by multiplying the country's CO_2 emission in 1990 by the emission target. The investor countries' emission reduction targets are then calculated by subtracting Assigned Amount Units (AAUs) from the projected CO_2 emissions in each year during the first commitment period.[4]

Estimates of each country's renewable and nonrenewable energy resources, total sequestration potentials, and measures of the country's vulnerability to the impacts of climate change are obtained from Buys *et al.* (2007). In order to provide measures for countries' vulnerability to climate change and emissions reduction mandates, Buys *et al.* (2007) first construct individual indices for alternative sources of vulnerability and then calculate composite index values by categorizing the sources of vulnerability into two major groups: impact and source vulnerabilities. Impact vulnerability refers to the countries' ability to sustain climate change impacts such as weather damage and sea level rise, while source vulnerability refers to the countries' renewable energy resource and sequestration potential along with the countries' willingness and ability to accept restrictions on access to nonrenewable energy resources and employment structure.

Estimates of six dimensions of governance of the host and investor countries are obtained from Kaufmann, Kraay, and Mastruzzi (2007). The six dimensions of governance are: Voice and Accountability, Political Stability and Absence of Violence, Government Effectiveness, Regulatory Quality, Rule of Law, and Control of Corruption. Combining these governance measures, a country-level composite governance variable is constructed employing a Principal Component Analysis (PCA).

Moreover, a composite index namely the ease of doing business (EDB) index that ranks economies according to the state of business regulations and protection of property rights, was constructed. The cost of business

---

[4]The US is yet to ratify the Kyoto Protocol. The Russian Federation and Ukraine have surplus Kyoto units that are not allowed to trade, and calculated emissions reductions for some Annex B countries are negative. The emission reduction targets for all these countries are assumed to be zero.

start-up procedures in terms of percent of GNI per capita, which is a component of the rank of the ease of doing business, is also considered separately. The cost of business start-up procedures includes all official and legal fees for professional and legal services, and purchasing and legalizing company books, if such services are required by law.

Finally, individual country's AIJ experience measured in years are derived from the data used in Larson and Breustedt (2007). Many of the countries having CDM projects previously participated in Activities Implemented Jointly (AIJ).

ESTIMATION PROCEDURES

In order to investigate the differences in CDM adoption across countries, the empirical model specified by Eqs. (1)–(3) is estimated by employing standard econometric techniques, as is described below. First, the incidence of CDM adoption as specified by Eq. (1) is estimated by a *probit* regression, using a dichotomous variable indicating participation in CDM activity as the dependent variable. Second, using the number of CDM projects adopted by each country as the dependent variable in Eq. (2), cross-country CDM adoption is estimated by count data models such as *Poisson, negative binomial, zero-inflated Poisson* (ZIP hereafter), and *zero-inflated negative binomial* (ZINB hereafter). Third, the difference in the extent of CDM adoption across countries as specified in Eq. (2) is estimated using the *tobit* and Heckman's *two-step* (selection) regression technique. Finally, the differences in both incidence and extent of CDM adoption across countries and over time as specified in Eq. (3) are estimated, employing the random effects (*RE* hereafter) *tobit* regression.

For countries that have not adopted CDM, the value of the dependent variable in Eq. (2) is set to zero. Because of this censoring, ordinary least squares estimates (OLS) based on this censored sample are likely to be biased. In order to take account of this censoring of the dependent variable, the *tobit* regression technique is employed instead of the OLS regression. The *tobit* model estimates both the incidence (probability) and extent (level) of CDM adoption. While the *tobit* regression assumes that the same probability mechanism determines the incidence and extent of CDM adoption, the *Heckman* model allows for the possibility that the incidence and extent are determined by a different mechanism which may not be independent.

In order to estimate the model specified in Eq. (3), the *RE tobit* estimation technique is applied for two reasons. First, the *RE* estimator is more efficient than the fixed effect estimator. Second, the *tobit* estimator takes account of the censoring on the dependent variable. However, the *RE* estimator is consistent under the stringent assumption that the country effect η_i is uncorrelated with the vector of explanatory variables X_{it}. While the *FE* estimator (i.e., with fixed country effects) does not require this strict assumption, the country dummies absorb a lot of variation in the data, making the estimator relatively inefficient. Caselli and Coleman (2001) provide a compromise solution to this efficiency–consistency trade off. They employ the *RE* estimator with regional dummies and claim that the estimator is more efficient than the *FE* estimator and is consistent if the part of the country effect that is orthogonal to the region effect is also orthogonal to the remaining elements of X_{it}. Following Caselli and Coleman (2001), a full set of dummy variables for the various world regions as classified by the World Bank is included in X_{it}. This technique assumes that the regional dummies capture the nonrandom part of the country effect and treats the residual country effect as random (i.e., η_i and X_{it} are assumed to be uncorrelated).

The vector X_{it} is treated as exogenous for y_{it}, because the reverse causation is extremely unlikely. For example, even for countries like Brazil, China, and India, where a majority of the CDM projects are located, the extent of CDM activity is not large enough to have an impact on GDP or energy use. It is important to acknowledge that many of the CDM projects have power generation capacity which may influence the availability of renewable energy. However, the stock of renewable energy is yet to be altered (even if possible), as most of the projects are still not in operation.

Upon checking the correlation coefficients between each pair of the explanatory variables, it is found that many of the explanatory variables initially included in X_{it} are highly correlated with one another. Also, many of the variables considered for explaining CDM adoption disparity are not found to be significantly correlated with the dependent variables. Therefore, only the analytically and statistically relevant (but not highly correlated) ones from each category of the explanatory variables are used in the final regression specifications. The revised X_{it} for developing countries includes the log of sequestration potential, the log of nonrenewable energy resources, log of per capita real GDP, log of emissions per unit of GDP, agricultural value added as a percentage of GDP, manufacturing value added as a percentage of GDP, total imports as a percentage of GDP, net inflow of

FDI as a percentage of GDP, the impact vulnerability index, years of experience in AIJ, and the cost of business start-up procedures as a percentage of GNI per capita.[5]

The revised X_{it} for the investor (Annex B) countries includes the log of emissions abatement target, the log of average net present cost per tCO_2e emissions abatement, the log of per capita real GDP; value of total imports as a percentage of GDP, manufacturing value added as a percentage of GDP; total imports as a percentage of GDP, the source vulnerability index, and years of experience in AIJ. Per capita real GDP emissions of the Annex B countries are found to be highly positively correlated with per capita energy use and emissions, and negatively correlated with emissions per dollar of GDP (i.e., emissions intensity). Total imports as a percentage of GDP is very highly positively correlated with total trade and net outflows of FDI (both as percentages of GDP).

RESULTS

Growth of CDM in the World and in Individual Countries

The CDM portfolio has grown rapidly since its inception in 2003. As of December 31, 2010, 6,977 CDM projects have been sent to UNFCCC for validation (CDM/JI Pipeline Analysis and Database, UNEP Risoe Center, January 2011).[6] Only 2,703 of these projects have been registered, while 221 projects are in the process of registration, 2,836 projects are in the process of validation, 180 projects were rejected by the executive board, validation of 986 projects were terminated or termed negative by the Designated Operational Entity (DOE), and 51 were withdrawn (CDM/JI Pipeline Analysis and Database, UNEP Risoe Center, January 2011). The 5,760 CDM projects (excluding the rejected, validation terminated, and withdrawn projects) in the pipeline are expected to generate 782.98 million CERs (i.e., reducing approximately 782.98 million tons of CO_2 equivalent

---

[5]The economic indicators are annual averages over 2001–2008. Two-year lagged values are considered.

[6]During the first eight months of 2011, an additional 1,159 projects have been submitted for validation. This paper examines cross-country adoption of CDM using the projects in the pipeline through December 2010.

Table 6.1: An overview of the CDM pipeline, 2003–2010.

Year	No. of projects		Annual CERs (MtCO₂e)		Investments (Mill US $))	
	Flow	Stock	Flow	Stock	Flow	Stock
2003	5	5	5.53	5.53	927.1	927.1
2004	54	59	4.80	10.33	3,898.3	4,825.3
2005	444	503	92.49	102.82	34,774.2	39,599.6
2006	817	1,320	121.05	223.87	82,168.5	1,21,768.1
2007	1,535	2,855	203.71	427.58	1,27,883.8	2,49,651.9
2008	1,537	4,392	164.40	591.99	1,08,235.3	3,57,887.2
2009	1,209	5,601	139.36	731.35	1,29,759.9	4,87,647.0
2010	1,325	6,926	164.97	896.32	1,07,347.8	5,94,994.8

Note: Year represents the year of 30-day public comment period under validation.
Source: CDM Pipeline Database, UNEP Risoe (2011).

greenhouse gases) in each year during the first commitment period of the Kyoto Protocol, and 2.79 billion CERs by the end of the first commitment period (CDM/JI Pipeline Analysis and Database, UNEP Risoe Center, January 2011).[7]

For the purpose of examining the adoption of CDM, this chapter uses all projects in the pipeline except those withdrawn by the submitters since we are interested in what motivates country participation in the program. Table 6.1 shows a summary statistics of the selected CDM projects submitted for validation in each year during 2003–2010.[8] The expected CERs from these projects and estimated (net present value of) capital investments in those projects are also reported in Table 6.1. It is evident from the table that CDM activities, measured in terms of number of projects, expected CERs, and investments, have increased over time, at an upward rate until 2007, while the rate declined thereafter as the window for delivering CERs into the 2008–2012 accounting period began to close and the market for CERs approached saturation. The horizontal S-shaped growth of CDM activity is also evident from Fig. 6.1, which depicts the cumulative number of projects and the expected CERs from the projects in the pipeline.

---

[7]Available estimates of CO₂ emission (WRI, 2011) suggest world total annual emissions of 30.0 and 37.8 billion tons of CO₂ equivalent in 1990 and 2005, respectively.
[8]The starting year of the 30-day public comment period is taken as the start of the project cycle.

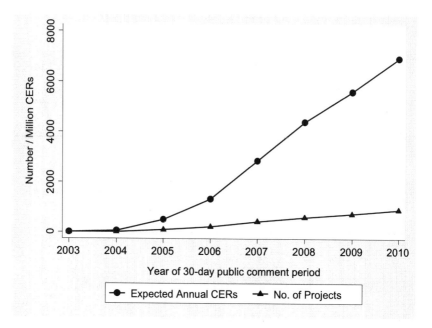

Fig. 6.1: Cumulative number of CDM projects and expected CERs.

While the global CDM growth is impressive, the extent and growth of CDM activity varies widely across the host as well as investor countries. Based on the CDM pipeline dataset for 2003–2010, the projects are located in only half of the host countries. On the other hand, only half of the investor countries have committed to invest in 4,035 CDM projects.[9] Note that 126 of the projects involve credit buyers from two or more investor countries.[10]

---

[9]The US is yet to ratify the Kyoto Protocol while Russia and Ukraine have emissions less than their Assigned Allowance Units (AAUs). Excluding Russia, Ukraine, and the US, there are only 36 potential investor countries.

[10]Although we refer to Annex B countries as "buyers," the participants are often national firms that organize the purchases of credits on behalf of climates in other Annex B countries, including Annex B governments. Although we stick with convention, it is best to think of "buyers" as the set of national institutions under which CDM investments are organized and purchased CERs are distributed. Projects for which credit buyers are not specified are considered to be unilateral. While foreign direct investments are not allowed in CDM in China, many projects have listed credit buyers.

Table 6.2: Developing and industrialized countries' involvement in CDM activity during 2003–2010.

Year	No. of Countries		CDM projects		Annual CERs (MtCO$_2$e)		Annual Elec. (MWh)	
	Total	New	Total	Range	Total	Range	Total	Range
Developing Countries								
2003	5	5	5	1–1	5.53	0.02–3.4	23	0–23
2004	15	11	54	1–17	4.80	0.0005–2.9	2,458	0–958
2005	37	22	444	1–190	92.49	0.006–37.3	21,200	0–6,069
2006	40	15	817	1–283	121.05	0.003–63.3	90,100	0–46,400
2007	52	13	1,535	1–724	203.71	0.006–135.5	195,000	0–134,000
2008	57	10	1,537	1–652	164.40	0.004–88.9	261,000	0–117,000
2009	55	4	1,209	1–500	139.36	0.002–67.8	162,000	0–88,400
2010	63	5	1,325	1–578	164.88	0.002–80.4	309,000	0–161,000
Annex B Countries								
2003	4	4	10	1–4	5.51	0.85–1.8	0	0
2004	8	4	52	1–15	4.15	0.04–1.7	2,118	0–640
2005	15	7	345	1–149	81.23	0.09–24.0	15,000	0–5,331
2006	13	0	428	3–190	81.97	0.22–33.4	40,400	0–19,300
2007	19	4	982	1–348	160.46	0.02–64.8	150,000	0–66,400
2008	19	2	952	2–300	106.31	0.19–41.6	126,000	66–68,700
2009	19	0	668	1–241	85.17	0.02–35.0	109,000	3–41,300
2010	18	0	774	2–337	92.22	0.08–44.2	97,300	31–42,500

Note: Year represents the year of 30-day public comment period under validation.
Source: CDM Pipeline Database, UNEP Risoe (2011).

Table 6.2 depicts the overall scenario of CDM adoption by the host and investor countries during 2003–2010. In 2003, CDM activities started with four bi- or multi-lateral projects initiated by four investor countries in four host countries, and one unilateral project initiated by one host country. Since then, the numbers of participating host and investor countries, number of CDM projects, and expected CERs from those projects have rapidly increased over time. In particular, the number of CDM projects and expected CERs grew at an increasing rate up until 2007. The rate of CDM growth declined during 2008–2009, but increased again in 2010. Table 6.2 also shows the ranges (minimum–maximum) of CDM projects and associated expected CERs. The number of CDM projects and the expected CERs widely varies across countries and years. The largest number of CDM projects (724) and largest CDM project (135.5 million CERs) hosted by a developing country (China) are observed in the year 2007. The largest number of CDM projects (348) and largest CDM project (64.8 million CERs) invested by an Annex B country (the UK) are also observed in the year 2007. Many of the projects are in electric power generation sector. Table 6.2 also reports the expected total electricity generation by the projects adopted in each year, as well as the ranges of electricity output by a single project in each year.

A summary statistics of the dependent variable included in the empirical models is presented in Table 6.3 for both host and investor countries.

The adoption of CDM in selected host and investor countries is depicted in Figs. 6.2–6.4. Figure 6.2 presents the cumulative number of projects that are hosted in selected developing countries during 2003–2010. Figure 6.3 shows the cumulative expected CERs from the projects that are hosted in selected developing countries. Brazil, China, and India appear to be the major host countries for CDM projects. More than 72% of the projects (5,032 of 6,924) submitted for validation during 2003–2010 are located in these countries, which account for more than 75% of the total CERs (675.3 of 896.3 million) expected to be generated every year. Brazil and India are among the countries which adopted CDM projects first in 2003 (other countries are Chile, Guatemala, and South Korea). China appears to be a relatively late adopter of CDM (with no projects in 2003 and only two projects in 2004), but immediately exceeded Brazil and India both in terms of number of projects and expected CERs. As of December 2010, 2,674 (38.6% of the total) CDM projects are located in China, which are expected to generate 473.2 million (more than 52%) of the total CERs per year. With 1,883 (27.2% of the total) projects generating 163.5 million (18.3% of the total) CERs per year, India is the second largest adopter of CDM among the host countries. In terms of annual CER generation, the average size of the projects in China is much larger than the projects in India. While Brazil is the third largest CDM host country, it accounts for only 6.9% of the CDM projects and 4.3% of the expected CERs per year. The other 82 host countries account for only 27.3% of the CDM projects and 24.7% of the expected CERs per year.

In terms of the number of CDM projects and expected CERs per year, the United Kingdom, Japan, Netherlands, and Switzerland are the four largest investor (credit buyer) countries, respectively (Fig. 6.3). As of December 2010, credit buyers from the United Kingdom are involved in 1,583 of the CDM projects (37.6% of bi- or multi-lateral), and are expected to acquire 245.9 million CERs (39.9%) per year. Credit

Table 6.3: Summary statistics of selected explanatory variables.

	Obs.	Mean	Std. Dev.	Min.	Max.
Host Countries					
Sequestration potential (mt oil eqv.)	145	10,002.8	33,689.0	-24.4	261,798.3
Nonrenewable energy (mt oil eqv.)	152	3,197.2	9,947.8	0	62,220.0
Per capita real GDP (US $)	150	4,027.7	7,647.9	0.01	58,010.5
Agricultural value added (% GDP)	141	0.18	0.14	0	0.66
Manufacturing Value added (% GDP)	141	0.13	0.07	0.008	0.42
Value of Imports (% GDP)	145	0.50	0.26	0.003	1.91
Net FDI inflow (% GDP)	142	0.05	0.05	-0.05	0.26
Total volume of trade (% GDP)	145	92.32	51.39	0.57	406.46
Business start-up cost (% pc GNI)	136	0.93	1.42	0.01	11.33
AIJ Experience (years)	156	2	4	0	13
Source vulnerability index (1–100)	152	57.29	13.25	10.44	97.59
Impact vulnerability index (1–100)	152	51.42	20.17	1.00	91.28
Investor Countries					
Kyoto mitigation target (MtCO$_2$e)	32	24,439.7	48,532.3	0.0	184,604.3
Carbon emissions (MtCO$_2$e)	32	186,380.0	277,356.6	2,268.3	1,246,034.0
Abatement cost ($/tCO$_2$e)	32	63.19	58.95	0	192.89
Per capita real GDP (US $)	32	24,754.0	15,871.1	3,138.0	67,335.5
Value of Imports (% GDP)	32	0.50	0.23	0.13	1.31
Total volume of trade (% GDP)	32	100.64	49.79	26.96	288.44
AIJ Experience (years)	32	7	6	0	15
Source vulnerability index (1–100)	32	56.76	10.57	33.05	78.18
Impact vulnerability index (1–100)	32	27.41	13.12	1.00	50.38

Source: World Development Indicator, World Bank (2011), Buys *et al.* (2007), and Larson and Breustedt (2007).

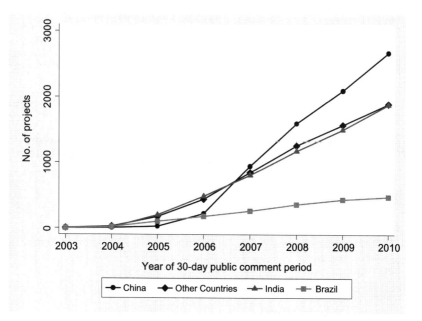

Fig. 6.2: Cumulative number of CDM projects in selected host countries.

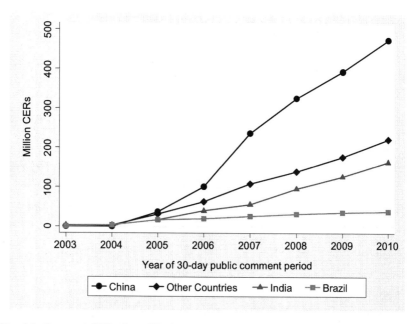

Fig. 6.3: Expected CERs from CDM projects in selected host countries.

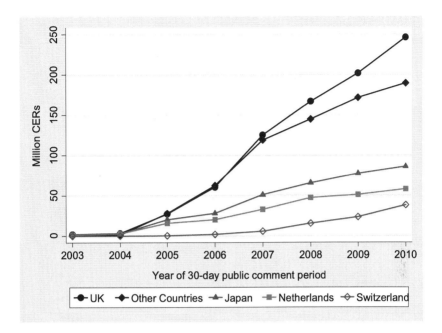

Fig. 6.4: Expected CERs from CDM projects by selected investor countries.

buyers from Japan, the second largest investor country, are involved in 546 of the bi- or multi-lateral projects (13.0%) and are expected to acquire 85.9 million CERs (13.9%) per year. Credit buyers from the Netherlands and Switzerland are involved in another 20% of the bi- or multi-lateral projects and are expected to acquire 15.5% of CERs of the total CERs to be generated per year. Other 17 participating Annex B countries are involved in 29.1% of the bi- or multi-lateral projects and are expected to acquire 30.7% of the CERs per year.

As can be seen from Figs. 6.3 and 6.4, CDM adoption by the host and investor countries has been increasing over time, at an upward rate until 2007.[11] The incidence and extent of CDM adoption, however, vary widely among the participating host and investor countries.

Since the specified empirical models are different for the host and investor countries, separate regressions are run for these two groups of

---

[11]While CDM adoption is depicted in terms of the cumulative expected CERs in Figs. 6.2 and 6.3, similar trends are observed when CDM adoption is represented in terms of cumulative number of projects and capital investments.

countries. The regression results for the host and investor countries are presented in the following two sub-sections, respectively.

CDM Adoption by the Host Countries

The *probit, tobit,* and *Heckman two-step* (selection) regression results for the set of developing countries are reported in Table 6.4. The same explanatory variables are used in each of these models. In addition, a set of regional dummy variables is also used in these models.[12] Both estimated coefficients and corresponding truncated (conditional) elasticities of the continuous variables and semielasticities of the dummy variables are reported in Table 6.4.

The *probit* regression results suggest that sequestration potential, the level of per capita real GDP, agricultural and manufacturing value added, net FDI inflow, the cost of business start-up procedures, and impact vulnerability are significant for the developing countries' decision to participate in the CDM. The estimated coefficients of these variables, except for the impact vulnerability index, also have the predicted signs, thus validating the associated hypotheses. The coefficient for the regional dummy variable for South Asia is positive and significant. However, all other regional dummies and the intercept term do not appear to be significant in the *probit* regression. The same set of continuous variables is also found to be significant in the *tobit* regression and they have the same signs as in the *probit* regression (Table 6.4). In addition, the AIJ experience of the developing countries appears to be positive and significant. None of the regional dummies or the intercept term is significant in the *tobit* regression. The coefficient estimates for emissions intensity and total imports as percentage of GDP do not appear to be significant in the *probit* and *tobit* models.

The *Heckman* model is run imposing an exclusion restriction. In particular, the agricultural value added as percentage of GDP is included in the selection equation but excluded from the outcome equation because, in the model without exclusion restriction, the variable appears to be significant in the selection part but not significant in the outcome part. The estimation results for the selection part of the *Heckman* model is the same

---

[12]Countries are categorized into seven World Bank regions: East Asia and the Pacific, Europe and Central Asia, Latin America and the Caribbean, Middle East and North Africa, North America, South Asia, and Sub-Saharan Africa.

Table 6.4: CDM adoption by host countries — results of *probit*, *tobit* and *Heckman* selection models.

	Probit		Tobit		Heckman	
	Coeff.	Elasticity	Coeff.	Elasticity	Coeff.	Elasticity
Continuous Variables						
Log Sequestration	0.15***	0.08	0.46***	0.26	0.15*	0.15
Potential	(0.05)		(0.15)		(0.08)	
Log nonrenewable	−0.03	−0.02	0.06	0.03	0.22***	0.22
energy	(0.06)		(0.17)		(0.07)	
Log per capita	−0.12*	−0.07	−0.28*	−0.16	−0.1	−0.1
real GDP	(0.07)		(0.16)		(0.07)	
Log of carbon intensity	0.03	0.02	0.37	0.21	0.32	0.32
(kg CO_2/\$GDP)	(0.26)		(0.73)		(0.32)	
Agricultural value	5.36***	0.55	13.25***	1.4		
added (% GDP)	(1.67)		(4.44)			
Manufacturing value	9.55***	0.65	25.27***	1.78	7.67**	0.96
added (% GDP)	(3.40)		(7.58)		(3.32)	
Value of total imports	0.01	0.002	−0.84	−0.22	−0.72	−0.34
(% GDP)	(1.05)		(3.01)		(1.23)	
Net FDI inflow	9.10**	0.25	20.47*	0.58	4.51	0.23
(% of GDP)	(3.76)		(10.79)		(5.14)	
Cost of business	−0.77***	−0.41	−2.09***	−1.15	−0.48*	−0.47
start-up (% pc GNI)	(0.24)		(0.65)		(0.29)	
AIJ experience (years)	0.06	0.06	0.20*	0.22	0.10**	0.2
	(0.04)		(0.11)		(0.04)	
Impact vulnerability	−0.02**	−0.62	−0.08***	−2.38	−0.05	−2.58
index (1–100)	(0.01)		(0.03)		(0.01)	
Regional dummy variables						
East Asia and Pacific	0.42	0.23	0.74	0.06	0.74	0.11
	(0.51)		(1.44)		(0.61)	
Europe and	−0.57	−0.31	−1.68	−0.1	−1.08	−0.12
Central Asia	(0.70)		(2.01)		(0.83)	
Latin Amer.	0.29	0.16	1.2	0.15	0.35	0.08
and the Caribbean	(0.43)		(1.22)		(0.48)	
Middle East &	0.74	0.40	0.5	0.03	−1.71***	−0.18
North Africa	(0.60)		(1.57)		(0.62)	
South Asia	1.03**	0.56	2.22	0.07	0.97	0.06
	(0.52)		(1.73)		(0.72)	
Constant	−0.53		1.5		6.98***	
	(1.12)		(2.71)		(0.98)	
Inverse of Mill's ratio					1.23*	
					(0.70)	

(*Continued*)

Clean Development Mechanism

Table 6.4: (*Continued*)

| | Probit | | Tobit | | Heckman | |
	Coeff.	Elasticity	Coeff.	Elasticity	Coeff.	Elasticity
Observation	122		122		122	
Censored	47		47		47	
Wald/LR χ^2	60.27		81.83		99.1	
Prob $> \chi^2$	0.0001		0.0001		0.0001	

Note: In the *probit* model, the dependent variable is a dummy variable indicating whether a country is engaged in CDM activity. The dependent variable in the *tobit* and *Heckman* selection models is the log of expected CERs from all the CDM projects in a host country. The continuous explanatory variables are averages over the period of 2001–08. Other continuous explanatory variables are fixed over time. The regional dummy for Sub-Saharan Africa was dropped as the benchmark, while the dummy for North America was dropped due to prefect collinearity. Statistical significance of the coefficients are denoted by *(10.0%), **(5.0%), and ***(1.0%).

as the *probit* results, while the last two columns in Table 6.4 present the results for the outcome part. The estimated coefficient for the inverse of the Mill's ratio (i.e., the nonselection hazard) appears to be different from zero. This provides an evidence of selection. In contrast to the *tobit* results, the coefficient estimates of per capita real GDP, net inflow of FDI, and impact vulnerability do not appear to be significant, while the coefficient of nonrenewable energy resource become positive and significant in the *Heckman* outcome equation. Moreover, the coefficient of the regional dummy for oil reach (Middle East and North African countries) appears to be negative and significant. Moreover, and the intercept term becomes positive and significant.

While the *probit*, *tobit*, and *Heckman* models capture variation in CDM adoption across countries, the *RE tobit* model captures variation over time also. The log of cumulative expected CERs in each year during 2003–2010 is regressed on the same set of continuous explanatory variables along with regional and year dummies.[13] Table 6.5 presents the coefficient estimates and corresponding truncated (conditional) elasticities from three alternative specifications of the model: with the regional dummies only, with the year dummies only, and with both the regional and year dummies. The coefficients of the same set of continuous explanatory variables appear to

---

[13] Two-year lagged values of the economic indicators are used for the period of 2003–2010.

Table 6.5: CDM adoption by host countries — results of random effects *tobit* regressions.

	I		II		III	
	Coeff.	Elasticity	Coeff.	Elasticity	Coeff.	Elasticity
Continuous Variables						
Log Sequestration	0.64***	0.19	0.60***	0.18	1.49***	0.43
Potential	(0.16)		(0.15)		(0.33)	
Log nonrenewable	0.01	0.002	−0.003	−0.001	−0.24	−0.07
energy	(0.17)		(0.17)		(0.35)	
Log per capita	−0.40*	−0.12	−0.44**	−0.13	0.03	0.01
real GDP	(0.21)		(0.22)		(0.40)	
Log of carbon intensity	−0.47	−0.14	−0.37	−0.11	−3.10***	−0.9
(kg CO_2/$GDP)	(0.62)		(0.60)		(1.10)	
Agricultural value	−4.33	−0.24	−3.94	−0.22	−45.12***	−2.37
added (% GDP)	(3.84)		(3.68)		(8.44)	
Manufacturing value	12.51**	0.49	15.20***	0.59	−17.03**	−0.63
added (% GDP)	(5.12)		(4.97)		(9.01)	
Value of total imports	1.49	0.21	1.54	0.22	14.86***	2.03
(% GDP)	(1.26)		(1.26)		(2.60)	
Net FDI inflow	−0.03	−0.05	−0.04	−0.06	−0.05	−0.08
(% of GDP)	(0.03)		(0.03)		(0.05)	
Cost of business	−0.01***	−0.28	−0.01**	−0.34	−0.003	−0.07
start-up (% pc GNI)	(0.01)		(0.01)		(0.01)	
AIJ experience (years)	0.34***	0.21	0.41***	0.25	0.58**	0.34
	(0.12)		(0.12)		(0.25)	
Impact vulnerability	−0.10***	−1.69	−0.09***	−1.54	−0.22***	−3.49
index (1–100)	(0.03)		(0.03)		(0.06)	
Regional Dummies						
East Asia and Pacific	2.91**	1.01			5.41*	1.76
	(1.53)				(3.13)	
Europe and Central	1.22	0.39			4.83	1.57
Asia	(2.05)				(4.23)	
Latin America	1.08	0.34			−3.55	−0.97
and the Caribbean	(1.36)				(2.86)	
Middle East &	−1.30	−0.37			−5.79	−1.46
North Africa	(1.78)				(3.74)	
South Asia	3.54*	1.32			7.06*	2.49
	(1.97)				(4.18)	
Time Dummies						
Year 2004	2.33***	0.79	2.32***	0.78		
	(0.60)		(0.60)			
Year 2005	5.78***	2.34	5.78***	2.3		
	(0.57)		(0.57)			

(*Continued*)

Table 6.5: (*Continued*)

	I		II		III	
	Coeff.	Elasticity	Coeff.	Elasticity	Coeff.	Elasticity
Year 2006	7.43***	3.28	7.43***	3.22		
	(0.57)		(0.57)			
Year 2007	9.05***	4.33	9.07***	4.25		
	(0.57)		(0.57)			
Year 2008	9.82***	4.89	9.86***	4.82		
	(0.57)		(0.58)			
Year 2009	10.47***	5.39	10.52***	5.32		
	(0.58)		(0.58)			
Year 2010	10.85***	5.70	10.92***	5.63		
	(0.59)		(0.59)			
Constant	−5.32*		−4.78*		3.4	
	(3.07)		(2.73)		(5.58)	
Observation	904		904		904	
Censored	543		543		543	
Groups	124		124		124	
Wald/LR χ^2	850.61		841.89		90.39	
Prob $> \chi^2$	0.0001		0.0001		0.0001	

Note: The dependent variable in each specification is the log of expected CERs from all the CDM projects in a host country. The continuous explanatory variables such as per capita real GDP, agricultural and manufacturing value added, foreign direct investments, and value of imports are 2-year lagged values. Other continuous explanatory variables are fixed over time. The regional dummy for Sub-Saharan Africa was dropped as the benchmark, while the dummy for North America was dropped due to prefect collinearity. Statistical significance of the coefficients are denoted by *(10.0%), **(5.0%), and ***(1.0%).

be significant with the same signs in both the full model and the model with time dummies only. In contrast to the *tobit* results reported in Table 6.4, the coefficients of agricultural value added and net FDI inflows are not found to be significant in the *RE tobit* models with time dummies, while the coefficient of regional dummies for the East Asian and Pacific and South Asian countries appear to be positive and significant and the intercept terms are negative and significant. However, the coefficients for all of the time dummies are positive and significant in both the full model and the model with time dummies only. The value of the coefficients consistently increases over the years, at an increasing rate up until year 2005 but at a decreasing rate thereafter. Thus, the level of CDM adoption by developing countries increases over time but the rate declines as the first commitment period of the Kyoto Protocol approaches.

The *RE tobit* results for the model with the regional dummies only give somewhat different results as compared to the *RE tobit* models with time dummies or the *tobit* results reported in Table 6.4. In contrast to those models, the coefficients of both the agricultural and manufacturing value added appear to be significant with negative signs, while imports share of GDP is positive and significant. Moreover, the cost of business start-up procedures is not found to be significant in the *RE tobit* model without the time dummies.

We further examine the determinants of CDM adoption in terms of the number of projects in each host country. Employing count data models, the number of CDM projects in each country is regressed on the same set of explanatory variables that are used in the *probit, tobit,* and *Heckman* models. Table 6.6 presents the coefficient estimates and corresponding elasticities from *Poisson, negative binomial (NB),* and *zero-inflated negative binomial (ZINB) regressions*. The estimate of the overdispersion parameter, α, in the NB regression is positive and highly significant (the likelihood ratio chi-squared statistic is 3086.12 with a p-value smaller than 0.0001). Also, the log (pseudo) likelihood of the *NB* regression is substantially higher than that of the *Poisson* regression. The Vuong likelihood ratio test statistic of the *ZINB* regression is 1.02, with a one-sided p-value of 0.15, suggesting that the zero-inflated variant is not essential. Although the log-likelihood and coefficient estimates of the NB and *ZINB* models are found to be similar, the coefficients are not directly comparable as the two models have different conditional means.

Based on the NB regression results in Table 6.6, the number of CDM projects in host countries increases with sequestration potential, nonrenewable energy resources, manufacturing share of GDP, and AIJ experience, but decreases with per capita real GDP, cost of business start-up procedures, and impact vulnerability. The regional dummies for the East Asian and Pacific, Latin American and the Caribbean, and South Asian countries are significant and positive.

One robust finding from the regression results of the *probit, tobit,* and *Heckman, NB,* and *RE tobit* models is that the incidence and extent of CDM adoption by the developing countries significantly vary with sequestration potential, cost of business start-up procedures, AIJ experience, impact vulnerability, per capita real income, and manufacturing share of GDP. In particular, all of these models indicate that the developing countries' decision

Table 6.6: CDM adoption by host countries — results of *Poisson, negative binomial,* and *zero-inflated negative binomial* regressions.

	Poisson		Negative binomial (NB)		Zero-inflated NB	
	Coeff.	Elasticity	Coeff.	Elasticity	Coeff.	Elasticity
Continuous Variables						
Log sequestration	0.26***	0.26	0.18***	0.18	0.18***	0.18
potential	(0.07)		(0.06)		(0.06)	
Log nonrenewable	0.22	0.22	0.15***	0.15	0.15***	0.15
energy	(0.14)		(0.06)		(0.06)	
Log per capita	0.43	0.43	−0.10*	−0.10	30.07	30.07
real GDP	(0.46)		(0.06)		(52.83)	
Log of carbon intensity	0.14	0.14	−0.22	−0.22	−0.18	−0.18
(kg CO_2/\$GDP)	(0.64)		(0.28)		(0.29)	
Agricultural value	4.38	0.83	3.19	0.6	2.97	0.56
added (% GDP)	(4.28)		(2.07)		(2.02)	
Manufacturing value	2.30	0.29	12.54***	1.58	11.65***	1.46
added (% GDP)	(3.54)		(3.13)		(3.28)	
Value of total imports	−1.48	−0.69	−1.10	−0.52	−1.18	−0.55
(% GDP)	(1.03)		(1.09)		(1.10)	
Net FDI inflow	12.04*	0.6	3.92	0.2	3.26	0.16
(% of GDP)	−(6.99)		(4.72)		(4.88)	
Cost of business	−0.46	−0.45	−0.65***	−0.64	−0.34**	−0.33
start-up (% pc GNI)	(0.45)		(0.25)		(0.17)	
AIJ experience	0.08*	0.16	0.09**	0.18	0.10**	0.19
(years)	(0.05)		(0.04)		(0.04)	
Impact vulnerability	0.01	0.36	−0.03**	−1.47	−0.04***	−1.96
index (1–100)	(0.02)		(0.01)		(0.01)	
Regional dummy variables						
East Asia and Pacific	2.22***	2.22	1.29**	1.29	1.49***	1.49
	(0.64)		(0.56)		(0.57)	
Europe and Central	1.50	1.50	0.46	0.46	0.49	0.49
Asia	(0.97)		(0.76)		(0.77)	
Latin America	1.61***	1.61	0.94*	0.94	0.92*	0.92
and the Caribbean	(0.56)		(0.49)		(0.49)	
Middle East &	−1.03	−1.03	−0.66	−0.66	−0.7	−0.7
North Africa	(0.63)		(0.66)		(0.67)	
South Asia	2.94***	2.94	2.03***	2.03	2.14***	2.14
	(0.53)		(0.77)		(0.77)	
Constant	−5.77		0.38		0.17	
	(3.94)		(1.03)		(1.00)	

(Continued)

Table 6.6: (*Continued*)

	Poisson		Negative binomial (NB)		Zero-inflated NB	
	Coeff.	Elasticity	Coeff.	Elasticity	Coeff.	Elasticity
Alpha			1.70***		1.68***	
			(0.29)		(0.28)	
Number of Observations	122		122		122	
Zero Observation	47		47		47	
Wald/LR χ^2	1173.05		148.73		149.37	
Vuong Z-stat					1.02(Pr $> z = 0.15$)	

Note: In each of the models, the dependent variable is the cumulative number of CDM projects located in each country. The continuous explanatory variables are averages over the period of 2001–2008. Other continuous explanatory variables are fixed over time. The regional dummy for Sub-Saharan Africa was dropped as the benchmark, while the dummy for North America was dropped due to prefect collinearity. Statistical significance of the coefficients are denoted by *(10.0%), **(5.0%), and ***(1.0%).

to engage in CDM activity as well as the extent of CDM activity increases with higher sequestration potential, AIJ experience, and manufacturing GDP, but decreases with the costs of setting-up business procedures, vulnerability to the impacts of climate change, and per capita income. While these results confirm our primary predictions, the influences of per capita income, manufacturing GDP, and impact vulnerability on CDM adoption by host countries require further explanation. The result that the likelihood of engaging in CDM activity and the extent of adoption is lower for the countries with relatively higher income may be because higher-income countries have less incentive to attract CDM projects, while Annex B countries are less willing to invest in CDM projects where input costs are higher. The manufacturing share of GDP reflects the intensities of energy (electricity) use and emissions, while most of the developing countries strive to meet the national demand for energy (electricity). Thus, countries with a higher manufacturing GDP would be willing to attract energy-efficient and renewable-resource–based power projects. The result that CDM adoption is lower for the countries ranked higher in the impact vulnerability index is contrary to the predictions of Buys *et al.* (2007).

Another robust finding from the *RE tobit* model is that the rate of CDM adoption increases over time, initially at an increasing rate but eventually at a decreasing rate as the first commitment period nears completion.

The results from the count data models further indicate that the number of CDM projects also increases with the level of nonrenewable energy resources, which is also consistent with the results from the *Heckman* model. While the *probit* and *tobit* results suggest that the decision to engage in CDM and the extent of CDM activity significantly increases with FDI inflow (as a percentage of GDP), the *Heckman* and *RE tobit* models do not confirm these inferences. The *probit* and *tobit* results also suggest that CDM adoption significantly increases with the agricultural share of GDP, but *RE tobit* results (as well as *NB* results) do not support that finding. The influence of nonrenewable energy resources is found to be positive only in the *Heckman* and count data models.

CDM Adoption by the Investor (Annex B) Countries

The *probit, negative binomial, tobit,* and RE *tobit* regression results for the set of developed (Annex B) countries are reported in Table 6.7. The same set of explanatory variables is used in each of these models except that the log of the average net present cost per tCO$_2$e emissions abatement is not included in the *probit* regression because nonzero observations of per unit costs perfectly predict the dependent variable. Regional dummy variables are not included in any of the models because of collinearity. However, year dummies are used in the RE *tobit* model. Both estimated coefficients and corresponding conditional elasticities of the continuous variables and semielasticities of the dummy variables are reported in Table 6.7.

The *probit* regression results suggest that, apart from the average cost of abatement, which perfectly predicts the data, the decision to invest in CDM significantly increases with the levels of emissions reduction target, per capita real GDP, and AIJ experience. Results from the negative *binomial, tobit,* and RE *tobit* regressions consistently show that the incidence and extent of CDM adoption by the investor countries increases with the emissions reduction target, average cost of mitigation, and per capita real GDP, but decreases with the import share of GDP. The coefficient of the AIJ experience does not appear to be significant in any of these models. The coefficients of the dummy variables for each year during 2005–2010 are positive and significant. Dropping the insignificant variables one at a time does not make any of the others significant.

Table 6.7: CDM adoption by investor countries — results of *probit*, *negative binomial*, *tobit*, and *RE tobit* regressions.

	Probit		NGB		Tobit		Panel tobit	
	Coeff.	Elasticity	Coeff.	Elasticity	Coeff.	Elasticity	Coeff.	Elasticity
Continuous Variables								
Log Kyoto target	0.22*	0.05	0.09	0.09	0.16	0.16	0.12*	0.08
Log cost of abatement			1.38***	1.38	2.01***	2	1.54***	1.00
Log per capita real GDP	2.59***	0.57	2.18***	2.18	1.56**	1.55	2.44***	1.58
Value of imports (% GDP)	0.23	0.03	−3.76***	−1.89	−2.81*	−1.41	−2.59**	−0.84
Source vulnerability index	−0.05	−0.61	−0.1	−5.55	−0.03	−1.47	−0.03	−1.00
AIJ experience	0.22**	0.32	0.03	0.19	0.04	0.28	0.08	0.32
Time dummies								
Year 2004							−0.07	−0.04
Year 2005							2.18***	1.67
Year 2006							2.72***	2.16
Year 2007							3.45***	2.82
Year 2008							3.57***	2.93
Year 2009							3.73***	3.08
Year 2010							3.76***	3.11
Constant	−24.48***		−17.29***		−14.57**		−26.19***	

(*Continued*)

Table 6.7: (Continued)

	Probit		NGB		Tobit		Panel tobit	
	Coeff.	Elasticity	Coeff.	Elasticity	Coeff.	Elasticity	Coeff.	Elasticity
Alpha (Dispersion parameter)			1.13					
Obs. (Groups)	32		32		32		256 (32)	
Censored	11		11		11		132	
Wald/LR χ^2	35.29		54.63		81.26		673.08	
Prob $> \chi^2$	0.0001		0.0001		0.0001		0.0001	

Note: In the *probit* model, the dependent variable is a dummy variable indicating whether a country is involved in CDM activity. In the *negative binomial model* the dependent variable is the cumulative number of projects of each investor countries. In the *tobit* and *RE tobit* models, the dependent variable is the log of cumulative expected CERs for each country. The continuous explanatory variables in the *RE tobit* model are 2-year lagged values, while averages over the period of 2001–2008 in other models. Statistical significance of the coefficients are denoted by *(10.0%), **(5.0%), and ***(1.0%).

In order to further investigate the influence of Kyoto obligation, the above models are run replacing the variable representing emissions reduction target with a dummy variable indicating whether the target is positive. Interestingly, the coefficient of the dummy variable indicating whether the Kyoto protocol inflicts a positive emissions reduction target is not found to be significant in any of the models, leaving the level of significance and sign of the other coefficient estimates the same. While this result appears to be counterintuitive, this is quite reasonable, given the Kyoto's third flexibility mechanism — the carbon market. Out of the 32 investor countries considered in the models, 5 countries without a positive emission reduction target are involved in 496 CDM projects and 4 countries with positive Kyoto targets do not have any CDM project.

An intriguing result is that the incidence and extent of CDM adoption is higher for the Annex B countries with higher average cost per tCO_2e. Note that one of the purposes of the mechanism is to provide investor countries with a lower-cost mitigation opportunity. In the absence of available estimates for mitigation costs in investor countries, the average costs of mitigation through the CDM may be considered as the opportunity costs (i.e., the average costs of mitigation at home). Thus, this result can be interpreted as that the incidence and extent of CDM adoption is higher for the investor countries with higher domestic mitigation costs.

While the probability of incidence of CDM adoption is higher for the investor countries with some experience in AIJ, the level of adoption does not vary with the extent of the AIJ experience. Of the 21 investor countries with CDM projects, 9 do not have prior experience in AIJ. On the other hand, eight countries with AIJ experience are yet to adopt CDM.

Except for the year 2004, the RE *tobit* estimates of the coefficients of the year dummies are positive and highly significant. The magnitude of the coefficients consistently increases over the years, at an increasing rate up until year 2007 but at a decreasing rate thereafter. Thus, the level of CDM adoption by the Annex B countries increases over time but the rate declines as the first commitment period of the Kyoto Protocol approaches. This result is consistent with the analytical prediction.

CONCLUSIONS AND POLICY IMPLICATIONS

This chapter empirically examines the determinants of differences in cross-country CDM adoption over time. Various empirical specifications of the logistic model for CDM adoption by developing and developed economies are estimated by regressing alternative measures of CDM adoption on analytically and statistically relevant sets of explanatory variables. Appropriate econometric models such as binary choice, censored data, censored panel data, and count data models are employed to estimate the empirical models.

The main findings of this study are as follows. First, the rate of CDM adoption by both developing and industrialized countries increases over time, initially at an increasing rate but eventually at a decreasing rate as the first commitment period nears the completion. Thus, CDM adoption by individual countries follows a logistic pattern. Second, the developing countries' decision to engage in CDM activity as well as the level of CDM adoption increases with sequestration potential, AIJ experience, and manufacturing share of GDP, but decreases with the costs of business start-up procedures (measured in terms of percentage of GNI per capita), vulnerability to the impacts of climate change, and real GDP per capita. Third, the incidence and extent of CDM adoption are higher for the industrialized countries with higher emissions reduction target, domestic mitigation costs, and income per capita. Fourth, the Kyoto Protocol's third flexibility mechanism, the carbon market, allows for optimal allocation of emissions abatement given the restriction.

An important aspect of the CDM mechanism — the development component — is still debated among scholars (Olsen, 2007). One argument is that the CDM is yet to demonstrate its contribution toward the development objective. An important result of this study that the incidence, extent, and rate of CDM adoption are higher for the developing countries with relatively lower per capita income that indicates at least a partial fulfillment of the development objective of the mechanism.

A large share of sequestration potentials of developing countries accounts for available renewable energy resources. Our result is thus consistent with the finding of Winkelman and Moore (2010) that countries with growing markets for electricity are more likely to be CDM hosts. The manufacturing share of GDP of the developing countries is highly positively correlated with the level of carbon emissions. Thus the result that the level of engagement in CDM is higher for relatively more industrialized developing countries also implies that the extent of CDM is higher for the countries with higher level of emissions. However, our results do not confirm the finding of Winkelman and Moore (2010) that economies with higher carbon intensity (carbon emissions per unit of GDP) had greater CER production. The result that the level of engagement in CDM activities is lower for the countries that are more vulnerable to climate change impacts is consistent with the finding of Dinar *et al.* (2011) in the case of cooperation in CDM between host and investor countries.

While it is frequently suggested that institutional strength is a prerequisite of better performance, the indicator of the quality of governance in developing countries does not appear to be a significant determinant of CDM adoption (see the results in Annex 6.1 tables). This result is also consistent with the finding of Dinar *et al.* (2011).

Our results show that the net FDI inflow (as a percentage of GDP) does not explain variation in the level of CDM adoption across developing countries (see the *Heckman* and *RE tobit* regression results). One possibility is that countries better able to attract foreign direct investments for power generation or other types of projects that might receive financing under the CDM, are willing to forgo mitigation incomes in favor of a more streamlined and certain investment project. It is worth keeping in mind that these investments may have a similar development impact, since CDM financing is often additional and designed to change the way electricity or other outputs are produced, rather than changing what is produced.

What do all of the above results mean for policy? First, the finding that the cost of business start-up procedure is a major impediment toward CDM adoption implies that developing economies aiming to attract FDI through CDM need to design and implement policies to reduce the costs of initiating and implementing projects under the CDM. While a more facilitating environment for doing business is often prescribed for faster economic growth, in order to extract maximum benefits from the CDM, developing countries need to substantially reduce particular direct and indirect costs of initiating and implementing the projects. Second, the finding that countries more at risk from climate change are not themselves more likely to host CDM projects shows that awareness alone does not significantly motivate investment flows, suggesting that close attention must be paid to the full set of investment costs.

REFERENCES

Acemoglu, KD (2001). Directed technical change. NBER Working Paper 8287. National Bureau of Economic Research.

Barro, RJ and X Sala-i-Martin (1997). Technological diffusion, convergence, and growth. *Journal of Economic Growth*, **2**, 1–27.

Bass, FM (1969). A new product growth model for consumer durables. *Management Science*, **15**, 215–217.

Basu, S and DN Weil (1998). Appropriate technology and growth. *Quarterly Journal of Economics*, **113**, 1025–1054.

Bewley, R and DG Fiebig (1988). A flexible logistic growth model with application in telecommunications. *International Journal of Forecasting*, 4, 177–192.

Brezis, ES, PR Krugman and D Tsiddon (1993). Leapfrogging in international competition: A theory of cycles in national technological leadership. *American Economic Review*, **83**, 1211–1219.

Buys, P, U Deichmann, C Meisner, T That and D Wheeler (2007). Country stakes in climate change negotiations: Two dimensions of vulnerability. World Bank Policy Research Working Paper No. 4300. Washington, D.C.

Caselli, F and WJ Coleman II (2001). Cross-country technology diffusion: The case of computers. *American Economic Review*, **91**(2), 328–335.

Climate Solutions (2007). Available at: www.climatesolutions.ca. Accessed 7 December 2012.

Coe, DT and E Helpman (1995). International R&D spillovers. *European Economic Review*, **39**, 859–887.

Coleman, KS (1964). *Introduction to Mathematical Sociology*. London: Collier Macmillan.

Comin, D and D Beunza (2003). Power in the medieval manor. New York University Mimeo.

Davies, S (1979). *The Diffusion of Innovations*. Cambridge: Cambridge University Press.

Dinar, A, SM Rahman, DF Larson and P Ambrosi (2011). Local actions, global impacts: International cooperation and the CDM. *Global Environmental Politics*, **11**(4), 108–133.

Dinar, A and D Yaron (1992). Adoption and abandonment of irrigation technologies. *Agricultural Economics*, **6**, 315–332.

Dinar, A, SM Rahman, DF Larson and P Ambrosi (2011). Act locally affect globally: International cooperation in carbon abatement projects. *Global Environmental Politics*, **11**(4), 10–132.

Dixon, R (1980). Hybrid corn revisited. *Econometrica*, **48**, 1451–1461.

Doessel, DP and SM Strong (1991). A neglected problem in the analysis of the diffusion process. *Applied Economics*, **23**, 1335–1340.

Eeckhout, J and B Jovanovic (2002). Knowledge spillovers and inequality. *American Economic Review*, **92**, 1290–1307.

Feder, G and DL Umali (1993). The adoption of agricultural innovations: A review. *Technological Forecasting and Social Change*, **43**, 215–239.

Fleck, R and A Hansen (2003). The origins of democracy: A model with application to ancient Greece. Department of Agricultural Economics, Montana State University Working Paper, Boseman, Montana.

Gore, AP and UA Lavaraj (1987). Innovation diffusion in a heterogeneous population. *Technological Forecasting and Social Change*, **32**, 163–168.

Gregg, JV, CH Hassell and JT Richardson (1964). *Mathematical Trend Curves: An Aid to Forecasting*. Edinburgh: Oliver and Boyd.

Gilchrist, S and J Williams (2001). Transition dynamics in vintage capital models: Explaining the postwar catch-up of Germany and Japan. *Finance and Economics Discussion Series*, 2001-7. Federal Reserve Board of Governors.

Griliches, Z (1957). Hybrid corn: An exploration in the economics of technological change. *Econometrica*, **25**, 501–522.

Griliches, Z (1980). Hybrid corn revisited: A reply. *Econometrica*, **48**, 1451–1461.

Grossman, GM and E Helpman (1991). *Innovation and Growth in the Global Economy*. Cambridge, MA: MIT Press.

Helpman, E and M Trajtenberg (1998). Diffusion of general purpose technologies. In E Helpman (ed.), *General Purpose Technologies and Economic Growth*, pp. 86–119. Cambridge: MIT Press.

Hobijn, B (2001). Is equipment price deflation a statistical artifact? FRBNY Staff Report 139. New York: Federal Reserve Bank of New York.

Holmes, TJ and JA Schmitz Jr (2001). A gain from trade: From unproductive to productive entrepeneurship. *Journal of Monetary Economics*, **47**, 417–446.

Johansen, L (1959). Substitution versus fixed production coefficients in the theory of economic growth: A synthesis. *Econometrica*, **27**, 157–176.

Jotzo, F and A Michaelowa (2002). Estimating the CDM market under the Marrakech accords. *Climate Policy*, **2**(1), 179–196.

Jovanovic, B (1998). Vintage capital and inequality. *Review of Economic Dynamics*, **1**, 497–530.

Jovanovic, B and Y Nyarko (1996). Learning by doing and the choice of technology. *Econometrica*, **64**, 1299–1310.

Kaufmann, D, A Kraay and M Mastruzzi (2007). Governance matters VI: Aggregate and individual governance indicators 1996–2006. World Bank Policy Research Working Paper No. 4280. Washington, D.C.

Knudson, MK (1991). Incorporating technological change in diffusion models. *American Journal of Agricultural Economics*, **73**, 724–733.

Laitner, J and D Stolyarov (2002). Technological change and the stock market. University of Michigan, Ann Arbor, Mimeo.

Larson, DF, P Ambrosi, A Dinar, SM Rahman and R Entler (2008). A review of carbon market policies and research. *International Review of Environmental and Resource Economics*, **2**(3), 177–236.

Larson, DF and G Breustedt (2009). Will markets direct investments under the Kyoto protocol? *Environmental and Resource Economics*, **43**(3), 433–456.

Larson, DF, A Dinar and JA Frisbie (2011). Agriculture and the clean development mechanism. World Bank Policy Research Working Paper 5261.

Lekvall, P and C Wahlbin (1973). A study of some assumptions underlying innovation diffusion function. *Swedish Journal of Economics*, **75**, 362–377.

Lizzeri, A and N Persico (2003). Why did the elites extend the suffrage? Democracy and the scope of government, with an application to Britain's age of reform, Mimeo, New York, New York University.

Mahajan, V and MEF Schoeman (1977). Generalized model for the time pattern of the diffusion process. *IEEE Transactions of Engineering Management*, **24**, 12–18.

Mansfield, E (1961). Technical change and the rate of imitation. *Econometrica*, **29**, 741–765.

Metcalfe, JS (1981). Impulse and diffusion in the study of technical change. *Futures*, **13**, 347–359.

Michalakelis, C, D Varoutas and T Sphicopoulos (2008). Diffusion models of mobile telephony in Greece. *Telecommunications Policy*, **32**(3/4), 234–245.

Olsen, KH (2007). The clean development mechanism's contribution to sustainable development: A review of the literature. *Climatic Change*, **84**, 59–73.

Payne, J, J Fernandez-Cornejo and S Daberkow (2006). Factors affecting the likelihood of corn rootworm Bt seed adoption. *AgBioForum*, **6**(1/2), 79–86.

Rahman, SM, A Dinar and DF Larson (2010). Diffusion of Kyoto's clean development mechanism. *Technological Forecasting and Social Change*, **77**, 1391–1400.

Rogers, EM (2003). *Diffusion of Innovations*. 5th ed. New York, NY: Free Press.

Solow, R (1960). Investment and technical progress. In K Arrow (ed.), *Mathematical Methods in the Social Sciences*. Palo Alto, CA, US: Stanford University Press.

Snell, BC (1974). American ground transport: A proposal for restructuring the automobile, truck, bus & rail industries. US Government Report. US Congress/Senate Judiciary Committee, February 26.

Teklewold, H, L Dadi, A Yami and N Dana (2006). Determinants of adoption of poultry technology: A double-hurdle approach. *Livestock Research for Rural Development*, **18**(3), No. 40.

United Nations Environment Programme (UNEP) Risoe Center (2007). CDM/JI Pipeline Analysis and Dataset. Available at: http://cdmpipeline.org. Available at 8 December 2007.

Winkelman, AG and MR Moore (2010). Explaining the differential distribution of clean development mechanism projects across host countries. *Energy Policy*, **39**, 1132–1143.

World Bank (2007). World Development Indicators 2007. Available at: http://publications.worldbank.org/WDI. Accessed 8 December 2012.

World Bank (2010). World Development Indicators (WDI) 2010. Washington, DC: World Bank.

WRI (World Resources Institute) (2011). Climate Analysis Indicators Tool (CAIT) Version 8.0. Washington, DC: World Resources Institute.

ANNEX 6.1: Methodology for the Data Collection on the Capital Cost Data From Clean Development Mechanism Project Activity.[14]

CDM project capital cost data is not a reporting criterion but is sometimes used in the demonstration of additionality for the project. As such, the way in which this information is presented is not normalized and some interpretation is required.

Of those PDDs that contain capital cost information, it is often reported as "capital costs" or "fixed costs" for the project, and as a single number either in host country currency units or USD. From what is reported, capital cost in the CDM PDDs generally includes procurement of any plant and/or machinery dedicated to the realization of the CDM project construction and civil works engineering consultation (non-ongoing).

In some cases, the following were included in the capital costs: Costs incurred for the validation, registration, and verification of the project as a CDM project, contingency, and margin money for working capital interest during construction licenses.

Unfortunately, it was not possible to disaggregate the costs as only one (all inclusive) number was reported. In some cases, project participants reported all costs, including variable costs in a table. For these cases, capital cost had to be reconstituted into a single number in order to record it into the dataset.[15]

Methods in Obtaining Capital Cost Data

As stated earlier, information on project costs is sometimes used in the demonstration of "additionality" of the CDM project. Participants submitting a project to the CDM have to prove the additionality of the project they submit in Section B.5 of the PDD.

---

[14]We thank Stephen Seres for helping with this Annex.

[15]Most PDDs provided a single capital cost value which generally included construction, equipment, and engineering costs. Where detailed tables were included, only the values for construction, equipment, and engineering costs were summed to produce a single value for the dataset with hopes at maintaining comparability.

In each of the PDDs, this section was thoroughly reviewed to determine if capital cost data was included. In addition, the entire PDD was searched using keywords such as USD, $, investment, cost, capital, and currency acronym for the host country (e.g., for projects in China, keywords included CNY, RMB, yuan).

All cost data was recorded in the spreadsheet in the currency units used in the PDD. All cost data were converted into USD using the spot exchange rate on November 20, 2007. The exchange rates used were included in the dataset.

Perspective in Capital Cost Data

It may be important to note two facts with regard to the capital cost data from CDM project activity. First, it should not be assumed that the CDM projects have been implemented yet and so capital cost outlays may not have occurred. The CDM project data represents all projects that have been put forth for validation and registration. This may, and often does, occur prior to commitments on capital purchases have been made. However, it is largely expected that these projects will be implemented.

Second, it should not be assumed that the reported capital expenditures on CDM projects are solely attributable to the CDM. In many cases, capital expenditures would have taken place in its absence. For instance, wind farm and hydro projects are implemented to increase the host country's power generation capacity. In the absence of the CDM, it is likely that capital expenditures would have taken place regardless, in order to increase the host country's power generation capacity, albeit with a different technology and less of a capital outlay. However, for certain project types, where there is no revenue stream other than CDM credits, i.e., landfill gas and animal waste flaring projects, it would be fair to assume that the capital cost expenditures are solely attributable to the CDM.

Table 6.1A: CDM adoption by host countries — results of *probit*, *tobit* and *Heckman* selection models.

	Probit		Tobit		Heckman	
	Coeff.	Elasticity	Coeff.	Elasticity	Coeff.	Elasticity
Continuous Variables						
Log sequestration	0.08	0.02	0.21	0.90	0.05	0.05
potential	(0.07)		(0.15)		(0.07)	
Log nonrenewable	−0.04	−0.01	0.11	0.27	0.27***	0.27
energy	(0.08)		(0.15)		(0.06)	
Log per capita	−0.12*	−0.04	−0.26*	−1.15	−0.06	−0.06
real GDP	(0.06)		(0.14)		(0.06)	
Log of carbon intensity	−0.42	−0.13	−0.49	−0.01	0.31	0.31
(kg CO_2/\$GDP)	(0.37)		(0.72)		(0.31)	
Agricultural value	7.53***	0.41	11.99**	1.61		
added (% GDP)	(2.46)		(4.57)			
Manufacturing value	9.13**	0.38	19.14***	1.94	4.27	0.6
added (% GDP)	(3.86)		(7.05)		(2.83)	
Value of total imports	0.39	0.05	−1.19	−0.38	−1.79	−0.79
(% GDP)	(1.73)		(2.97)		(1.16)	
Net FDI inflow	22.1***	0.29	35.26***	1.08	3.28	0.14
(% of GDP)	(6.86)		(11.42)		(5.76)	
Cost of business	−1.25***	−0.39	−2.3***	−1.67	0.11*	−0.3
start-up (% pc GNI)	(0.42)		(0.63)		(0.06)	
Governance indicator	−0.07	0.06	−0.08	0.17	−0.06	−0.07
	(0.07)		(0.14)		(0.33)	
AIJ experience	0.08	0.05	0.17	0.24	0.07*	0.14
(years)	(0.08)		(0.11)		(0.04)	
Impact vulnerability	0.002	0.04	−0.01	−0.33	−0.02*	−1.11
index (1–100)	(0.01)		(0.03)		(0.01)	

(*Continued*)

Table 6.1A: (Continued)

	Probit		Tobit		Heckman	
	Coeff.	Elasticity	Coeff.	Elasticity	Coeff.	Elasticity
Regional dummy variables						
East Asia and Pacific	1.78**	0.54	2.43	0.22	0.91	0.11
	(0.74)		(1.50)		(0.64)	
Europe and Central	−0.28	0.08	−0.58	−0.06	−0.3	−0.04
Asia	(0.74)		(1.92)		(0.79)	
Latin America	1.36***	0.41	2.37**	0.38	0.31	0.07
and the Caribbean	(0.53)		(1.17)		(0.49)	
Middle East &	1.91**	0.58	1.52	0.14	−1.83***	−0.23
North Africa	(0.86)		(1.45)		(0.59)	
South Asia			2.36	0.09	0.16	0.01
			(1.72)		(0.72)	
Constant	−2.32**		−0.39		7.42***	
	(1.11)		(2.47)		(1.02)	
Inverse of Mill's					0.08	
ratio					(0.69)	
Number of Observations	91		96		96	
Censored	25		25		25	
Wald/LR χ^2	60.27		81.83		99.1	
Prob > χ^2	0.0001		0.0001		0.0001	

Note: In the *probit* model, the dependent variable is a dummy variable indicating whether a country is engaged in CDM activity. The dependent variable in the *tobit* and *Heckman* selection models is the log of expected CERs from all the CDM projects in a host country. The continuous explanatory variables are averages over the period of 2001–2008. Other continuous explanatory variables are fixed over time. The regional dummy for Sub-Saharan Africa was dropped as the benchmark, while the dummy for North America was dropped due to prefect collinearity. Statistical significance of the coefficients are denoted by *(10.0%), **(5.0%), and ***(1.0%).

Table 6.2A: CDM adoption by host countries — results of Random Effects *tobit* regressions.

	I		II		III	
	Coeff.	Elasticity	Coeff.	Elasticity	Coeff.	Elasticity
Continuous Variables						
Log sequestration	0.26	0.10	0.29*	0.11	0.44	0.15
potential	(0.18)		(0.18)		(0.34)	
Log nonrenewable	0.03	0.01	0.02	0.01	−0.24	−0.09
energy	(0.16)		(0.17)		(0.32)	
Log per capita	−0.27	−0.10	−0.32*	−0.12	0.02	0.01
real GDP	(0.18)		(0.19)		(0.35)	
Log of carbon intensity	−0.82	−0.32	−0.60	−0.23	−4.04***	−1.41
(kg CO_2/\$GDP)	(0.63)		(0.62)		(1.10)	
Agricultural value	−5.19	−0.36	−5.71	−0.40	−52.17***	−3.26
added (% GDP)	(4.25)		(4.17)		(8.16)	
Manufacturing value	9.06***	0.51	12.63***	0.7	−18.79**	−0.94
added (% GDP)	(5.03)		(4.88)		(8.64)	
Value of total imports	1.48	0.26	1.55	0.27	15.81***	2.44
(% GDP)	(1.26)		(1.27)		(2.60)	
Net FDI inflow	−0.03	−0.05	−0.03	−0.06	−0.09*	−0.13
(% of GDP)	(0.03)		(0.03)		(0.05)	
Cost of business	−0.01**	−0.30	−0.01***	−0.39	−0.01*	−0.42
start-up (% pc GNI)	(0.00)		(0.00)		(0.01)	
Governance indicator	−0.17	0.17	−0.16	0.16	−1.26***	1.12
	(0.15)		(0.16)		(0.31)	
AIJ experience	0.32***	0.26	0.39***	0.31	0.59**	0.42
(years)	(0.13)		(0.13)		(0.25)	
Impact vulnerability	−0.02	−0.42	−0.01	−0.27	−0.03	−0.59
index (1–100)	(0.04)		(0.04)		(0.07)	
Regional Dummies						
East Asia and Pacific	4.18**	2.03			8.29***	3.63
	(1.65)				(3.19)	
Europe and Central	1.48	0.62			2.43	0.91
Asia	(2.03)				(3.87)	
Latin America	2.3*	0.99			−0.08	−0.03
and the Caribbean	(1.38)				(2.67)	
Middle East &	−0.07	−0.03			−1.65	−0.55
North Africa	(1.76)				(3.37)	
South Asia	4.33**	2.20			8.67**	4.01
	(2.07)				(4.05)	

(*Continued*)

Table 6.2A: (*Continued*)

	I		II		III	
	Coeff.	Elasticity	Coeff.	Elasticity	Coeff.	Elasticity
Time Dummies						
Year 2004	2.32***	1.03	2.31***	1.00		
	(0.59)		(0.59)			
Year 2005	5.75***	3.01	5.74***	2.92		
	(0.56)		(0.56)			
Year 2006	7.44***	4.22	7.43***	4.09		
	(0.56)		(0.56)			
Year 2007	8.96***	5.41	8.97***	5.25		
	(0.56)		(0.56)			
Year 2008	9.68***	6.02	9.70***	5.86		
	(0.56)		(0.57)			
Year 2009	10.22***	6.50	10.25***	6.34		
	(0.57)		(0.57)			
Year 2010	10.58***	6.83	10.63***	6.67		
	(0.58)		(0.58)			
Constant	−7.83***		−6.86***		−0.29	
	(2.90)		(2.48)		(5.36)	
Number of Observations	711		711		711	
Censored	365		365		365	
Groups	98		98		98	
Wald/LR χ^2	830.25		821.23		96.67	
Prob $> \chi^2$	0.0001		0.0001		0.0001	

Note: The dependent variable in each specification is the log of the expected CERs from all the CDM projects in a host country. The continuous explanatory variables such as per capita real GDP, agricultural and manufacturing value added, foreign direct investments, and value of imports are 2-year lagged values. Other continuous explanatory variables are fixed over time. The regional dummy for Sub-Saharan Africa was dropped as the benchmark, while the dummy for North America was dropped due to prefect collinearity. Statistical significance of the coefficients are denoted by *(10.0%), **(5.0%), and ***(1.0%).

Table 6.3A: CDM adoption by host countries — results of *Poisson, negative binomial,* and *zero-inflated negative binomial* regressions.

	Poisson		Negative binomial (NB)		Zero-inflated NB	
	Coeff.	Elasticity	Coeff.	Elasticity	Coeff.	Elasticity
Continuous Variables						
Log sequestration	0.19**	0.19	0.08	0.08	0.09	0.09
potential	(0.08)	(0.08)	(0.06)	(0.06)	(0.06)	(0.06)
Log nonrenewable	0.29***	0.29	0.17***	0.17	0.18***	0.18
energy	(0.09)	(0.09)	(0.05)	(0.05)	(0.05)	(0.05)
Log per capita	0.03	0.03	−0.14***	−0.14	31.34	31.34
real GDP	(0.41)	(0.41)	(0.05)	(0.05)	(56.30)	
Log of carbon intensity	−0.04	−0.04	−0.49*	−0.49	−0.44	−0.44
(kg CO_2/\$GDP)	(0.43)	(0.43)	(0.30)	(0.30)	(0.30)	(0.30)
Agricultural value	7.49*	1.39	4.84**	0.9	4.76**	0.88
added (% GDP)	(4.55)	(0.84)	(2.27)	(0.42)	(2.28)	(2.28)
Manufacturing value	2.42	0.34	9.79***	1.36	8.37**	1.17
added (% GDP)	(3.70)	(0.52)	(3.07)	(0.43)	(3.30)	(3.30)
Value of total imports	−3.66***	−1.61	−1.65	−0.72	−1.69	−0.74
(% GDP)	(1.11)	(0.48)	(1.08)	(0.47)	(1.10)	(1.10)
Net FDI inflow	16.76**	0.71	9.26*	0.39	7.03	0.3
(% of GDP)	(7.89)	(0.33)	(5.15)	(0.22)	(5.49)	(5.49)
Cost of business	0.26***	−0.73	0.05	−0.14	0.05	−0.13
start-up (% pc GNI)	(0.07)	(0.19)	(0.06)	(0.16)	(0.06)	(0.06)
Governance indicator	−0.36	−0.36	−0.91***	−0.91	−0.39**	−0.39
	(0.30)	(0.30)	(0.28)	(0.28)	(0.18)	(0.18)
AIJ experience	0.05	0.1	0.09**	0.18	0.10**	0.2
(years)	(0.03)	(0.07)	(0.04)	(0.09)	(0.04)	(0.04)
Impact vulnerability	0.02	0.79	−0.004	−0.19	−0.02	−0.87
index (1–100)	(0.02)	(1.12)	(0.01)	(0.62)	(0.01)	(0.01)
Regional dummy variables						
East Asia and Pacific	2.78***	2.78	1.94***	1.94	2.29***	2.29
	(0.67)	(0.67)	(0.61)	(0.61)	(0.65)	(0.65)
Europe and Central	1.66*	1.66	0.63	0.63	0.83	0.83
Asia	(0.95)	(0.95)	(0.81)	(0.81)	(0.81)	(0.81)
Latin America	1.77***	1.77	1.22***	1.22	1.30***	1.3
and the Caribbean	(0.61)	(0.61)	(0.47)	(0.47)	(0.47)	(0.47)
Middle East &	−0.61	−0.61	−0.39	−0.39	−0.35	−0.35
North Africa	(0.52)	(0.52)	(0.60)	(0.60)	(0.61)	(0.61)
South Asia	2.26***	2.26	2.28***	2.28	2.49***	2.49
	(0.62)	(0.62)	(0.79)	(0.79)	(0.79)	(0.79)

(Continued)

Clean Development Mechanism

Table 6.3A: (*Continued*)

	Poisson		Negative binomial (NB)		Zero-inflated NB	
	Coeff.	Elasticity	Coeff.	Elasticity	Coeff.	Elasticity
Constant	−2.63		0.25		−0.16	
	(4.11)		(1.03)		(1.02)	
Alpha			1.37***		1.38***	
			(0.24)		(0.24)	
Number of Observations	96		96		96	
Zero Observation	25		25		25	
Wald/LR χ^2	1055.03		132.58		130.7	
Vuong Z-stat					1.02 (Pr > z = 0.15)	

Note: In each of the models, the dependent variable is the cumulative number of CDM projects located in each country. The continuous explanatory variables are averages over the period of 2001–2008. Other continuous explanatory variables are fixed over time. The regional dummy for Sub-Saharan Africa was dropped as the benchmark, while the dummy for North America was dropped due to prefect collinearity. Statistical significance of the coefficients are denoted by *(10.0%), **(5.0%), and ***(1.0%).

7. CLEAN DEVELOPMENT MECHANISM AS A COOPERATION MECHANISM[*]

With Contribution by Philippe Ambrosi

The Clean Development Mechanism (CDM)[1] has come a long way since its launch in Marrakech in 2001. As of December 31, 2009, 5,687 CDM projects have been submitted to the CDM Board for validation (UNFCCC, 2010). It is expected that by 2012, the transition year when the Kyoto Protocol terminates and a new protocol is reckoned to be in place, the CDM Board would issue Certified Emission Reductions (CERs) equivalent to 800–1,150 million tons of CO_2, approximately 42% of which would be abated through the CDM projects with partnerships between developed and developing countries (UNDP, 2006: p. 11).[2] (The reader is referred to the Epilogue section in Chapter 1, where the results of the COP 15 are discussed). This would be an impressive achievement, and it is believed and expected that the interest in CDM projects by governments and private sector entrepreneurs would extend beyond 2012.

While the future of the CDM crucially depends on political decisions, it is also affected by the performance of the carbon market and by the fulfillment of the basic CDM objectives: greenhouse gas emission reductions that can be credited to the developed-investor country from projects implemented locally that support sustainable development in the developing-host country. Thus, CDM projects provide *a priori* incentives for cooperation between host and investor countries.

Despite skepticism regarding CDM's ability to contribute toward its development objective (Olsen, 2007: p. 84; Sirohi, 2007: p. 105; Da Cunha

---

[*]This chapter is based on Dinar *et al.* (2011). Permission from the journal *Global Environmental Politics* is acknowledged.

[1]The Kyoto Protocol, where more explanation on the CDM are provided, can be accessed at: http://unfccc.int/resource/docs/convkp/kpeng.html.

[2]The remaining projects are presented to the Board "unilaterally" by the host country and do not necessarily involve foreign investors.

et al., 2007; Sutter and Parreno, 2007: p. 75), the number of CDM projects submitted to the CDM Board has grown at an increased rate during the first 7 years of the program (5 projects in 2003; 55 in 2004; 450 in 2005; 832 in 2006; 1,568 in 2007; 1,557 in 2008; and 1,220 in 2009). What are the attributes that make CDM attractive to both host and investor countries? From the perspective of the host countries, investment in CDM projects can be seen as a means of development assistance, with all derived benefits to them. Thus, certain development attributes may play important roles in explaining the levels of investment in CDM projects. Moreover, with the expectation that the demand for CERs would further increase beyond 2012, it would make sense to examine the factors that determine the location and extent of investment in CDM projects by investor countries.

With a development objective, CDM trends can be explained using several supply-side variables, such as export promotion, political hegemony, donor budget allocations, and donor internal politics, which are mainly political economy variables (Michaelowa and Michaelowa, 2007). But, CDM trends can also be explained using demand-side considerations, where the developing countries formulate policies to investor country investments in CDM projects (Brechet and Lussis, 2006).

The literature summarizing the various carbon investment mechanisms such as Activities Implemented Jointly (AIJ), Joint Implementation (JI), and CDM is quite extensive. Larson and Breustedt (2009) provide a detailed history and background work related to the pilot program of AIJ between 1992 and 2001. Dolšak and Dunn (2006) examine bilateral host–investor cooperation via the AIJ mechanism. The AIJ mechanism was in effect for a limited period and attracted much fewer countries and projects. However, it was used as a laboratory for both participating countries and the UNFCCC secretariat for the transition to the CDM. For a review of the history, status, and prospects of the CDM, see Lecocq and Ambrosi (2007). Larson *et al.* (2008) review carbon market policies and their recent development. The literature cited in these studies allows comprehension of the relationship between global environmental agreement on climate and its actual operation and relationship to the rest of the economy in terms of promoting low-carbon growth.

In this chapter, we identify factors that affect cooperation in carbon abatement projects between the governments of investor countries and host countries. We examine bilateral and multilateral CDM projects that were submitted to UNFCCC between 2003 and 2009 in order to provide useful assessment of policy interventions for possible enhancement and extension of the CDM mechanism beyond 2012. We are interested in understanding the grouping of countries in the CDM market, namely what explains cooperation in CDM between certain dyads of countries and noncooperation between other dyads, and why certain countries are heavily involved while others are not. We use different measures of cooperation levels, including the number of joint CDM projects, the amount of CO_2 abated through CDM projects,[3] and the level of investments in CDM projects. We examine characteristics of potential and actual investor–host country dyads, building on previous economic, political, and institutional work.

CONCEPTUAL FRAMEWORK

We look at CDM joint investment projects between two countries as a cooperative investment decision that is affected by both domestic factors and economic and political interactions between these countries. For this reason, variables related to mitigation opportunities and business environments are likely to affect investment decisions. At the same time, CDM projects require the issuance of an approval letter by the host country, which implies an additional level of cooperation. Consequently, we utilize theories on international cooperation from international relations and international economics literature to explain this additional aspect of CDM cooperation.

In general, the determinants of cooperation relate to the bilateral characteristics of the pairing (e.g., trade), or unilateral characteristics of the investor and the host (e.g., characteristics of their respective energy sectors). With this in mind, cooperation between a given dyad of countries i and h can be written as:

$$C_{ih} = C(D_{ih}, \underline{I}_i, \underline{H}_h, \underline{I}_i \times \underline{H}_h) \tag{1}$$

where C is the level of cooperation, D represents the bilateral characteristics of a given host–investor pair, and $\underline{I}$ and $\underline{H}$ are vectors of variables strictly attributable to investor and host country i and h, respectively. We expect some interaction effects between i and h because certain variables in host countries are linked to considerations by investor countries.

---

[3]Investor country's ultimate interest is in project CER credits, while host country's interest is in the project investment funds in their countries and the likely multiplier effect.

CDM is expected to evolve into a form of Foreign Direct Investment (FDI) with opportunities for collaboration for project developers in investor countries to interact with host-country investors (UNEP/GRID-Arendal, 2000). In order to analyze the level of engagement in CDM projects by investor and host countries, we apply the theory used for explaining FDI flows and stocks. Dunning (1993, 1996), Nunnenkamp (2002), and Siegel *et al.* (2010) provide a review of theories used to support the empirical literature, linking variables in host countries and considerations by investor countries. While we include a wide list of variables based on previous relevant work in this section, we will restrict the set of variables we use in the empirical estimation of the level of cooperation to only variables that apply to both host and investor countries to provide a systematic comparison of the factors affecting CDM cooperation and their relative impact.

Several factors enhance investor- and host-country interests in CDM projects. According to Dunning, the interest of firms in investor countries to consider foreign investments is affected by tax policy in the investor country (Dunning, 1996); transaction costs in the investor and host countries[4]; and the size and status of the market for the particular product/technology.[5] In the case of the CDM market, one should also take account of the opportunity cost of meeting the Kyoto CO_2 reduction quota in the investor country. This depends on the country economy structure and growth trajectory, the energy dependency of the economy, the level of CO_2 emission of the economy, and the clean energy resources it possesses (Velasco, 2007; UNEP/GRID-Arendal, 2000).

Vulnerability to climate change and natural disasters as an incentive for needed related actions has been well documented in the literature (Tsur and Zemel, 2008). Countries that face harsher environmental conditions would be early adopters of technologies, and would implement policies and look for partners to sign treaties to ease their scarcity situation (Dinar, 2009).

But cooperation in the CDM market not only depends on country-specific variables. Higher levels of joint investment indicate higher degrees of cooperation, and no investment suggests no cooperation. Therefore, it is conceivable that international relations theories are likely to play some role alongside the profit maximization motives of the parties as in any international cooperation such as trade and FDI. We follow the literature

---

[4]The ease of doing business variable aggregates all of these considerations.

[5]For discussion on additional variables, see Michaelowa and Michaelowa (2007).

on trade and FDI in the international conflict and cooperation literature (Polacheck, Seiglie, and Xiang, 2007).

Foreign Direct Investment, Foreign Aid, and International Trade

Like other forms of FDI, many CDM projects are irreversible, with an economic value that depends upon a stream of future benefits. In turn, these benefits are subject to a variety of risks tied to contract enforcement and counter-party risk and, in the extreme case, expropriation. Consequently, CDM investors are motivated by opportunities to meet emission reduction goals at a lower cost. In a similar way, developing countries often promote policies that attract FDI since the investments are expected to speed growth by building up capital and by facilitating knowledge spillovers. For CDM projects, there is a corresponding expectation that the projects will contribute to the host country's development objective and promote technology transfer, leading to multiplier effects from clean energy technologies.

There is a large general literature on the determinants of FDI and the consequences of this form of investment for growth and knowledge transfer (Blonigen, 2005; De Mello, 1997; Smeets, 2008). Of special interest for our study is a subset of the studies by economists and political scientists that emphasizes how the strength of bilateral relationships affects FDI. Strong relationships are expected to lower transaction costs related to asymmetric information, reduce search costs, and also reduce many types of risks, especially political risks. Culture is often seen as an underlying determinant of strong bilateral ties.[6] However, trade or security agreements between countries can also be seen as political institutions that reduce risks and transaction costs in a more formal way (Busse and Hefeker, 2007; Büthe and Milner, 2008; Biglaiser and DeRouen, 2007). In the specific case of carbon projects, Larson and Breustedt (2009) and Dolsak and Dunn (2006) find that the strength of bilateral ties influenced early investment under national pilot programs that preceded the CDM.

In a similar vein, aid donor–recipient relationships are also affected by the set of incentives facing the countries and existing governance (e.g., rent-seeking and corruption) structures (Paul, 2006; Svensson, 2000). A similar finding is suggested by Linebarger (2009), where a higher level

---

[6]Kogut and Singh (1988), Choi (1999), Shenkar (2001), and Siegel *et al.* (2010) address the link between culture and investment.

of democratization of the host country leads to a higher level of foreign aid injections. However, while democracy is significant, greater importance is attributed by the donor countries to prior aid commitment, prior colonial ties, peace/war relationship in the recipient country, and its economic performance.

Several empirical studies argue that the extent of trade between countries provides an appropriate measure of their overall relations. Trade is a measure for both openness of a country to the global economy and the interaction between countries. The international relations literature's assessment of the link between trade, conflict, and cooperation has been quite mixed. On one hand, there has been the general claim that increased trade between countries reduces incidents of militarized conflict between them and promotes peace (Russett and Oneal, 2001). The fear of losing the gains from trade deters conflict. Along the same lines, it has been argued that nations with cooperative political relations will engage in more trade, while conflictive nations are expected to trade less (Pollins, 1989). On the other hand, there has been the conjecture that high international trade, interdependence, and conflict are positively related (Waltz, 1979). Intensive interactions increase frictions among the countries and may therefore lead to conflict.[7]

International trade also acts as a contract-enforcing mechanism. Stein argues that trade increases the likelihood of certain disputes between countries but provides the parties with an opportunity to resolve them at a lower level of international conflict (Stein, 2003). In essence, the coercive potential of trade reduces conflict, the occurrence of political crisis, and the need for militarized actions.

The above examination of the literature leads us to suppose that the level of relations among countries, measured by the extent of trade among them, is an appropriate measure for assessing the likelihood of cooperation (Neumayer, 2002). It is suggested therefore that the likelihood of a CDM project is relatively higher in the case of better or stronger relations among countries.

Such relations also include a history of colonial ties and membership in organizations that allow the states achieving common objectives, such as International Governmental Organizations (IGOs). Colonial ties may be important in explaining CDM partnership because many former colonies

---

[7]Barbieri (2002: p. 121) finds that the higher the interdependence and trade between countries the higher the likelihood of militarized conflict.

still maintain strong ties with their former colonizers (Dolšak and Dunn, 2006). IGOs may reduce the transaction cost of establishing and executing a CDM project (Mitchell and Hensel, 2007).

Enabling Environment: Governance, Regulations, and Business Climate

When considering international cooperation in general, and international investment in projects in particular, domestic institutions may play a major role in either facilitating or inhibiting the success of the cooperation project in question. Dinar, Dinar, and Kurukulasuriya (2011) suggest that political, legal, and economic institutions, constituting an enabling environment, often sustain the functioning of the state both domestically and internationally. It reflects not only the state's interest in the project but also its ability to enter into, and honor, an investment agreement, which may require financial investments (Congleton, 1992: pp. 412–413). The political stability and enabling institutions of a given state are, therefore, a principal mode to judge the viability of its domestic institutions, its general inclination to negotiate a project agreement, and its capacity to support the project.

Politically unstable countries have less institutional capacity to carry a project, and more politically stable countries may, in turn, have little interest in cooperative ventures with such nations. Similarly, investments are not secure and property rights poorly defined in unstable countries characterized by political turmoil (Deacon, 1994). Being part of an agreement requires both competence (also in terms of appropriate investment climate and supporting regulation) and stability inherent in a particular polity, which will in turn be able to honor the signed project agreement (Young, 1989: p. 365).

HYPOTHESES

We selected a particular set of variables for inclusion in the regression analysis. These variables were selected because, at least theoretically, each can explain both investor and host countries' likelihood to cooperate. From the above discussion and based on previous work on FDI and AIJ determinants that resemble behavioral patterns similar to those of CDM (Agarwal, 1980; Nonnemberg, Bragaand, and de Mendonca, 2005; Nunnenkamp, 2002; Larson and Breustedi, 2007), it is reasonable to hypothesize that, while all other variables are held constant, the CDM level of cooperation between the host and investor countries will increase (decrease) with higher (lower) levels of energy use (or economic development), and thus emission intensities, of its economy. We hypothesize that, for an investor country, the level of cooperation will decrease (increase), and for a host country, it will increase (decrease) with the increased availability of renewable energy resources in that country; and the more (less) vulnerable to climate change the economies are, the higher (lower) will the cooperation be.

Additional variables included in the empirical models are trade, business environment, political constraints, contiguity relationships, IGO membership, and governance. Based on our conceptual framework, we expect that the level of cooperation between host and investor countries with regard to the CDM will increase (decrease) as trade widens (shrinks); will decrease (increase) as transaction cost of doing business (notice that the higher the value of Ease of Doing Business [EDB] the higher the transaction cost) decreases (lowers); will decrease (increase) as level of political constraints increases (decreases); will increase (decrease) as length of the contiguity relationship grows (reduces); will increase (decrease) as the number of joint IGO membership increases (decreases); will increase (decrease) as governance level in the country increases (decreases); and will increase (decrease) as climate change vulnerability level in the country increases (decreases).

DATA DESCRIPTION, VARIABLE CONSTRUCTION, AND EMPIRICAL SPECIFICATION

Data used in this study are derived from several different sources. A dataset consisting of all CDM projects that have been sent to the UNFCCC CDM Board for validation up until December 31, 2009, is obtained from the CDM/JI Pipeline Analysis and Database of the United Nations Environment Programme (UNEP) (Risoe Center, 2010). During this period, 5,687 CDM projects were sent to UNFCCC for validation. The dataset provides detailed information about each individual CDM project. Information includes project name, type, and current status; host country; expected emission reduction ($ktCO_2$ per year and total CO_2 reduction up until 2012 and 2030); credit buyers; potential energy outputs, etc. The projects in the CDM pipeline are at various stages of the project cycle. Of the 5,687 projects, 4,053 are at validation stage, 1,066 have already been registered, 46 were rejected, 18 were withdrawn, and the rest are in various stages of evaluation. The dataset includes 2,354 (41%) unilateral projects, located mainly in India, China, and Brazil, and 3,182 (56%) bilateral projects. The rest (131) are multilateral projects, with three to seven investor countries (Rahman *et al.*, 2011, Table A, Supplemental Materials).

We measure the cooperation level using three variables, namely, *Number of Projects*, *Total CO_2 Abatement* in million tones of Certified Emissions Reductions of CO_2 equivalent, and *Volume of Investment* in million constant US dollars. When direct information on project costs is missing (only 2,804 projects have direct capital investment cost data[8]), we categorized projects by type (nine types: subsectors) and size (two sizes: small and large) and calculated an average investment cost value for each type-size. We used the average investment cost to extrapolate to projects for which we did not have investment cost data.

For our analysis, we drop 18 projects that entered the CDM project cycle but were subsequently withdrawn. Unilateral projects do not entail cooperation as such and, accordingly, are not included in our analysis. However, they do represent an alternative to cooperative investment and likely affect bilateral investment outcomes. Consequently, we take into account the capacity to arrange domestic project financing into our empirical models. For the multilateral projects, project activities are equally divided and attributed to all plausible dyads. For example, for a CDM project with $N > 2$ investor countries, N separate dyads are formed with the same host. The amount of carbon abatement and capital costs are then equally divided and attributed to n investor countries in the dyads. For the project count variable, we do not distinguish between bilateral and multilateral cooperation. We keep the projects that were subsequently rejected by the CDM board because they indicate a propensity to cooperate, which is the subject of this chapter.

As discussed in the context of Eq. (1), we use both pairwise and country characteristics as determinants in our statistical models. For the pairwise measures, we use the level of bilateral trade among the countries (*Trade*); a measure of the colonial ties between the countries (*Contiguity Length*); and a measure of the number of International Governmental Organizations (IGOs) both are members of (*Num of Joint IGO Membership*). We also

---

[8]See Appendix 1 in Dinar *et al.* (2008). Dataset was prepared by Seres (2007).

include several additional country characteristics for both the hosts and investors: the economic development of the countries measured in terms of energy use (*Average Annual Energy Use*), the energy sources status (*Renewable Energy Stock*), climate vulnerabilities of the countries (*Impact Vulnerability*), governance level of the countries (*Governance*), and ease of doing business in the countries (*Ease of Doing Business*).

Data for major development indicators such as annual GDP, energy use, and the volume of CO_2 emissions for all countries of the world during 1960–2003 are obtained from the World Development Indicators (World Bank, 2007).[9] In addition, country-level estimates of total energy available from nonrenewable sources (e.g., coal, oil, gas, oil shale, and bitumen) and annual energy available from renewable (e.g., solar, onshore and offshore wind, hydro, geothermal, and biofuels) sources are obtained from Buys *et al.* (2007).

Energy resources of each country are constructed by adding up potential nonrenewable and renewable energy resources. Two separate variables are constructed to reflect the intensity of energy use in each country: *Average Annual Energy Use* and *Annual per Capita Energy Use.*

Buys *et al.* also provide measures for countries' vulnerability to climate change and emissions reduction mandates. They first construct individual indices for alternative sources of vulnerability and then calculate composite index values by categorizing the sources of vulnerability into two major groups: impact and source vulnerabilities. Impact vulnerability refers to the country's ability to sustain climate change impacts such as weather damage and sea level rise. The quantitative score (scale of 1 to 100) of the *Impact Vulnerability* for the host and investor countries of the CDM projects from Buys *et al.* is used in our empirical analysis (Buys *et al.*, 2007).

Estimates of six dimensions of governance (Voice and Accountability, Political Stability and Absence of Violence, Government Effectiveness, Regulatory Quality, Rule of Law, and Control of Corruption) of the host and investor countries are obtained from Kaufmann, Kraay, and Mastruzzi (2007) from 212 countries during the period of 1996–2006. Combining the six governance measures of Kaufmann, Kraay, and Mastruzzi, a *Governance* variable is constructed using a Principal Component Analysis (PCA) that reflects overall governance level of the host and investor countries of each of the CDM projects (Rahman *et al.* 2011, Appendix, Supplemental Materials).

---

[9]Data on CO_2 per dollar of 2000 PPP GDP were not available prior to 1975.

We used the EDB indicators as a proxy to the transaction costs associated with the CDM projects implementation. EDB indicators, which compare business regulations and protection of property rights across 178 countries and over time, are obtained from World Bank (2008). The EDB index ranks economies from 1 to 178 by measuring regulations affecting 10 stages of a business's life: starting a business, dealing with licenses, employing workers, registering property, getting credit, protecting investors, paying taxes, trading across borders, enforcing contracts, and closing a business. EDB reflects the ranking of simple average of country percentile rankings on each of the 10 topics, with a higher rank indicating a less favorable business atmosphere.[10] The rankings remained almost the same over the years 2003–2007. However, a simple average of the rankings over the years is used to calculate the overall EDB in each country.

In order to take account of the political feasibility for government policy change, we use the political constraints index for each individual country constructed by Henisz (2002). The political constraint index (III) ranges from 0 to 1, with a larger value indicating that the political environment of a country is less favorable for government policy change. Thus, a country with a higher political constraints index faces a higher level of difficulty in CDM cooperation.

Three different measures are used to represent the strength of bilateral ties within each dyad: colonial/dependency contiguity relationship, joint membership in international governmental organizations, and bilateral trade. The length of colonial/dependency contiguity data is obtained from Correlates of War 2 Project.[11] Version 3.0 of the Correlates of War Colonial/Dependency Contiguity data identifies all contiguity relationships between states in the international system from 1816 to 2002 through their colonies or dependencies. That is, if two dependencies of two states are contiguous, or if one state is contiguous to a dependency of another, the data set reports a contiguity relationship between the two main states (The classification system for contiguous dyads can be found in the website reported in footnote 11). For the purpose of this study, we consider the longest contiguity length (in years) for each dyad. The longer the length of the contiguity relationship, the higher is the likelihood for the extent of CDM cooperation.

---

[10] The choice of aggregation method has little influence on the ranking. More complex aggregation methods such as principal components and unobserved components yield nearly identical rankings (Djankov, Montalvo, and Reynal-Querol, 2006).

[11] Available at: http://correlatesofwar.org.

The number of international governmental organizations (IGOs) both countries in each dyad are members of are obtained from the IGO dataset constructed by Pevehouse, Nordstrom, and Warnke (2004). The IGO data sets contain information about intergovernmental organizations (international organizations that have at least three nation-states as their members), identifying all state members of the IGOs during 1815–2000.[12] For each dyad, joint memberships in each IGO are derived from individual country membership. A larger number of joint IGO memberships for a dyad indicates a higher possibility of CDM cooperation.

Data on annual bilateral trade between all countries in the world are obtained from International Monetary Fund (IMF, 2007), for the period 1960–2003. Using the sum of the volumes of bilateral trade and GDP (in current US$) of the host and investor countries, the trade variable, *Trade*, is constructed following Dinar, Dinar, and Kurukulasuriya (2011). The trade variable expresses total trade (the sum of the volume of bilateral imports and exports) between the host and investor countries as a fraction of the sum of the countries' GDPs and is referred to as trade importance.[13] For a group of $N \geq 2$ countries *Trade* is calculated as follows:

$$Trade^{\{1,\dots,N\}} = \frac{\sum_{t=1}^{T}\left\{\sum_{j=1}^{N}(IMP_{jkt} + EXP_{jkt})\right\}}{\sum_{t=1}^{T}\sum_{j=1}^{N}(GDP_{jkt})},$$

$$\forall k \in N; \ j \in N; \ k \neq j \qquad (2)$$

where IMP and EXP are import and export, respectively, and t is year.

ESTIMATION PROCEDURES

As described earlier, the level of CDM cooperation between the host and investor countries is represented by three alternative measures: the number of CDM projects, amount of CO_2 abatement, and volume of capital investments. When the level of cooperation (the dependent variable) is measured by the *Number of CDM Projects*, we employ a zero-modified count model,

---

[12]The IGO data are collected at 5-year intervals from 1815–1965, and annually thereafter.
[13]For multiple investor countries, *Trade* expresses trade as the sum of total volume of exports and imports between the host country and each investor country as a fraction of the sum of GDP of each of the country involved in the CDM project.

which can be interpreted as a generalization of the standard Poisson regression model (Long, 1997).

Dependent variables representing *Total CO_2 Abatement*, and *Volume of Investment* have observations at 0, corresponding to dyads that do not cooperate in the CDM activity. The OLS estimates based on such a censored sample are likely to be biased. Since values of explanatory variables are also available for the countries not participating in the CDM activity, a *tobit* model seems appropriate, which determines both the probability of participating in the CDM activity and the levels of emissions abatement and investments when these are positive.

Note that the dependent variables used in the regressions are highly correlated (Supplemental Materials, Rahman *et al.* (2011), Table B). While the high correlation between the number of CDM projects, amount of CO_2 abatement, and volume of capital investments may suggest that we select one of them for presentation, the interpretation of the results for each dependent variable could shed light on different policy implications and thus, we keep all three.

DESCRIPTIVE STATISTICS RESULTS

We provide a descriptive statistics of project-level variables for 5,669 projects in Table C (Supplemental Materials, Rahman *et al.*, 2011, Table B). We describe descriptive statistics of country-level variables for both 175 host countries (including island countries) and 36 investor countries (Australia and US are excluded. See footnote 11). We present the descriptive statistics separately for the host and investor countries in Tables D and E, respectively (Supplemental Materials, Rahman *et al.*, 2011). Finally, we provide descriptive statistics of main variables for the dyad-level variables.

Dyad-level Descriptive Statistics

With 34 investor countries (excluding Australia and the US) and 175 host countries, there are 5,950 plausible host–investor pairs.[14] Only 305

---

[14]Australia and the US are excluded from the dataset because Australia did not ratify Kyoto until 2005 and the US is yet to ratify Kyoto (as of 2009). Few host countries are also omitted from the dataset because they are very small and country-level data are not available for those. [Our descriptive statistics in Table C (Supplemental Materials, Rahman *et al.*, 2011) includes Australia.]

Table 7.1: Descriptive statistics results for dyad-level variables in the analysis.

Variable	Obs	Mean	Std. Dev.	Min	Max
Number of CDM Projects	2,771	1.246	16.40	0	686
Total CO_2 Abatement	2,771	3,480.22	61,002.8	0	2,794,367
Total Volume of Investment	2,771	46,173.02	820,721.8	0	38,000,000
Trade	2,771	0.038	0.102	0	2.40
hst_Average Annual Energy Use	2,771	33.03	95.20	0.885	790.79
inv_Average Annual Energy Use	2,771	82.97	129.83	1.69	640.80
hst_Ease of Doing Business	2,771	98.90	42.00	1	178
inv_Ease of Doing Business	2,771	37.46	33.26	2	139
hst_Governance	2,771	−2.39	4.45	−12.45	11.34
inv_Governance	2,771	7.91	4.74	−4.11	13.48
hst_Renewable Energy Stock	2,771	135.40	277.61	0	1545.40
inv_Renewable Energy Stock	2,771	113.97	353.60	0.1	1937
hst_Impact Vulnerability	2,771	46.45	16.88	1	80.72
inv_Impact Vulnerability	2,771	27.51	12.53	1	50.38
hst_Political Constraint	2,771	0.130	0.126	0	0.529
inv_Political Constraint	2,771	0.323	0.151	0.014	0.534
Contiguity Length	2,771	0.880	10.120	0	176
Number of Joint IGO Mem.	2,771	13.93	11.25	0	45.97

Note: Interaction terms are not shown. See Annexe Table 7.1.A for units of measurement.

of the host–investor pairs have CDM project activity, while 57 host countries have unilateral projects. Dyads without any CDM projects can be regarded as the noncooperation dyads. Because we use three different left-hand side variables, the missing values problem results in different sample size for each dependent variable and making it harder to compare the results. Therefore, we use only 2,771 dyad-level observations, the descriptive statistics of which is presented in Table 7.1. Average *Total CO_2 Abatement* is approximately 3,480 kilotons per dyad, ranging between 0 and 2,794,367 kilotons. The average *Volume of Investment* by each dyad is $46.17 million, and mean *Trade* ratios are 0.038. Mean values for *Impact Vulnerability* suggest that, on average, host countries are much more vulnerable (46.44) than investor countries (27.51). Mean values for *Political Constraint* suggest that, on average, host countries are much less politically constrained (0.13) than investor countries (0.32). Mean value of *Contiguity Length* is 0.88 and mean *Number of Joint IGO Membership* is 13.93. (The independent variables are presented for host and investor countries separately.) The interaction variables (host × investor) are not presented.

Several results are worth mentioning. First, we note main differences in the different variables between host and investor countries in the dyads. Investor countries have higher *Average Annual Energy Use*, better ranking of *Ease of Doing Business*, better *Governance*, higher *Political Constraints*, and lower *Impact Vulnerability*. However, host countries have higher endowments of *Renewable Energy Stock* than do investor countries. As hypothesized earlier, we expect this difference to attract investor countries to host countries.

Results for the Cooperation Estimates

All variables incorporate values for the two countries in the dyad that are engaged in the CDM activity. For all variables except *Trade, Contiguity Length, and Number of Joint IGO Membership*, we use values for host, investor, and the interaction between the host and investor countries. For *Trade, Contiguity Length, and Number of Joint IGO Membership*, values are calculated based on the two countries' data as explained earlier.

We present results for a set of 2,771 country dyads that have all needed data in all regression specifications. We also report (Rahman *et al.*, 2011, Table F, Supplemental Materials) the results of regressions that include *Average Annual GDP* rather than *Average Annual Energy Use* as an independent variable. While we selected *Average Annual Energy Use* in the reported results in the main text because most CDM projects are associated with energy use, still these two variables are highly correlated (0.743 and 0.588 for host and investor countries, respectively). Regressions with *Average Annual GDP* have a larger number of observations (3,411) compared with 2,711 observations in regressions with *Average Annual Energy Use*, due to missing values. The fact that the results, using these two independent variables, are similar suggests that our estimation is highly robust.

Table 7.2 presents the results for the estimates of *Number of CDM Projects*. Coefficient estimates behave as expected. Higher economic development levels measured as *Average Annual Energy Use* by both host and investor countries are significant and positive; *Ease of Doing Business* behaves also as expected with a negative and significant sign assigned to the host country and an insignificant coefficient assigned to the investor country. *Governance* of the host country is not significant and that of the investor

Table 7.2: Results from zero-inflated negative binomial model for number of CDM projects per host–investor pair.

Variables	Coefficient estimates		Marginal effects
	Estimates	Standard errors	
Intercept	−10.0365***	1.3368	
Hst_Avg. Annual Energy Use	0.0036***	0.0009	0.0026
Inv_Avg. Annual Energy Use	0.0094***	0.0011	0.0018
Hst_Inv_Avg. Annual Energy Use	0.0003	0.0059	0.00003
Hst_Ease of Doing Business	−0.0115***	0.0036	0.2931
Inv_Ease of Doing Business	0.0012	0.0127	0.7767
Hst_Inv_Ease of Doing Business	0.0825	0.1143	0.0079
Hst_Governance	0.0365	0.0925	−0.0042
Inv_Governance	0.5091***	0.0633	0.0508***
Hst_Inv_Governance	−0.0102	0.0087	−0.0010
Hst_Renewable Energy Stock	0.0008**	0.0004	−0.0104
Inv_Renewable Energy Stock	−0.0009**	0.0004	−0.0126
Hst_Inv_Renewable Energy Stock	−0.0010	0.0008	−0.0001
Hst_Impact Vulnerability	0.0668***	0.0157	−0.0198*
Inv_Impact Vulnerability	0.0805***	0.0250	−0.0365**
Hst_Inv_Impact Vulnerability	−0.0101**	0.0045	−0.0010**
Trade	0.0550***	0.0135	0.0052***
Hst_Political Constraints	0.0440	0.7578	−0.0042
Inv_Political Constraints	−3.1538***	0.8204	−0.3000***
Contiguity Length	0.0132***	0.0044	0.0013***
Num of Joint IGO Mem.	0.0143*	0.0074	0.0014*

Dependent Variable	No. of CDM projects for host-investor pairs
Predicted No. of Events	0.095
No. of Observations	2,771
No. of Nonzero Observations	281
Log Likelihood	−1220.664
LR χ^2 (20)	694.10
Probability $> \chi^2$	0.0001

Note: ***,**, and * indicate 1%, 5%, and 10% significance levels, respectively.

country is positive and significant as expected. The *Renewable Energy Stock* of the host country has a positive and significant coefficient and that of the investor country has a negative and significant one, as expected. *Impact Vulnerability* is positive and significant for both host and investor country. The *Trade* variable has a positive and significant coefficient. *Political Constraints* of the investor country is negative and significant, but insignificant for the host country. Coefficient estimates of *Contiguity Length* and

Number of Joint IGO Membership are positive and significant. Most inter-action terms are insignificant, except for the *Impact Vulnerability* which is negative and significant.

The conditional mean of the *Number of Projects* as estimated by the zero-inflated negative binomial models is 0.10. The last column of Table 7.2 presents the marginal effects of the covariates on the conditional mean. Marginal effect of *Ease of Doing Business* has the highest impact. A one-unit change in *Ease of Doing Business* in host and investor countries increases the expected number of CDM projects by approximately 0.29 and 0.78, respectively. Also, a one-unit change in the *Political Constraints* in the investor countries reduces the expected number of CDM projects by 0.30. All other independent variables are much less effective.

We tested in the case of the Zero-Inflated Negative Binomial count model whether the capacity to host unilateral projects affects the number of partnership projects using a negative binomial count model. Using a test proposed by Vuong (1989), we first test the negative binomial model against two less general alternatives — a standard Poisson regression and a zero-inflated Poisson model. In both cases, the negative binomial model performs better. We next test to see if including the number of unilateral projects in the host country reduces the number of bilateral projects. The associated parameter is negative and statistically significant, indicated that it does.[15]

Table 7.3 presents results for the *tobit* estimates of *Total CO_2 Abatement* model. Coefficients behave in a similar way as those in Table 7.2. The estimated coefficients of the *Average Annual Energy Use* by the host and investor countries are significant and positive, with a positive and significant interaction term. *Ease of Doing Business* behaves also as expected with a negative and significant sign assigned to the host country and an insignificant coefficient assigned to the investor country. *Governance* of the host country is not significant and that of the investor country is positive and significant as expected. *Renewable Energy Stock* of the host country has a positive and significant coefficient and that of the investor country has a negative but insignificant one. *Impact Vulnerability* is positive and significant for both host and investor countries. The coefficient of *Trade* variable is positive and significant. *Political Constraints* of both the host

---

[15]The Vuong test statistics comparing first the zero-inflated model to the Poisson and then the negative binomial to the zero-inflated model were 5.17 and 6.33, respectively. Both were significant at the 1% level. The associated parameter on the unilateral project variable was −0.64 and was also significant at the 1% level.

Table 7.3: Extent of CDM — results from *tobit* model for estimated CERs generation by each host–investor pair.

Variables	Coefficient estimates		Marginal effects	
	Estimates	Std. errors	Pr(CER > 0) = 0.026	E[CER|CER > 0] = 1,595.46
Intercept	−772,729.20***	101,250.00		
Hst_Avg. Annual Energy Use	262.78***	70.37	0.07***	4,726.40***
Inv_Avg. Annual Energy Use	537.45***	79.58	0.03***	1,932.73***
Hst_Inv_Avg. Ann. Energy Use	2,213.20***	388.08	0.001***	58.08***
Hst_Ease of Doing Business	−641.72**	290.65	0.06	4,088.52
Inv_Ease of Doing Business	−7.06	1,053.21	0.16	10,837.88
Hst_Inv_Ease of Doing Business	4,175.29	9,477.92	0.002	109.58
Hst_Governance	−1,092.28	7,500.91	−0.0001	−5.01
Inv_Governance	30,301.19***	4,682.70	0.008	788.08***
Hst_Inv_Governance	113.83	673.07	0.0001	2.99
Hst_Renewable Energy Stock	74.89***	25.95	−0.012***	−822.51***
Inv_Renewable Energy Stock	−49.69	31.47	−0.01***	−980.88***
Hst_Inv_Ren. Energy Stock	−275.66***	69.53	−0.0001***	−7.23***
Hst_Impact Vulnerability	2,694.40**	1,150.20	−0.002	−161.63
Inv_Impact Vulnerability	4,108.13**	1,763.62	−0.004	−284.37
Hst_Inv_Impact Vulnerability	−321.73	330.40	−0.0001	−8.44
Trade	1,092.82*	637.89	0.0005*	31.30*
Hst_Political Constraints	46,781.67	539,995.3	0.018	1,227.75
Inv_Political Constraints	−28,673.48	65,320.22	−0.011	−752.52
Contiguity Length	705.17**	345.71	0.0003**	18.51**
Num of Joint IGO Mem.	861.47	546.52	0.0003	22.61

(*Continued*)

Table 7.3: (*Continued*)

Variables	Coefficient estimates		Marginal effects	
	Estimates	Std. errors	Pr(CER > 0) = 0.026	E[CER|CER > 0] = 1,595.46
Dependent Variable	CERs generation by host–investor pairs (1,000 CERs)			
No. of Observations	2,771			
No. of Nonzero Observations	281			
Log Likelihood	−4,080.41			
LR χ^2 (20)	574.30			
Probability > χ^2	0.0001			
Pseudo R-squared	0.066			

Note: CERs refers to certified emission reduction credits. ***, **, and * indicate 1%, 5%, and 10% significance levels, respectively.

and investor countries appear not to be significant. Estimated coefficient of *Contiguity Length* is positive and significant while the coefficient of *Number of Joint IGO Membership* is not significant. Coefficient estimates of most interaction terms appear not to be significant except for the *Average Annual Energy Use*, which is positive, and *Renewable Energy Stock*, which is negative.

The last two columns of Table 7.3 present the marginal effects on censored probability and left-censored mean of dyad-level CERs, respectively. The estimated censored probability and left-censored mean are 0.026 and 1,595.56, respectively. While the probability of a dyad to have CDM projects appear to be very small given the sample, the average annual energy use by the host (developing) and investor (developed) countries have significantly large and positive effects on both the censored probability and mean CERs (Table 7.3). Available renewable energy stock of the host and investor countries have significant negative marginal effects on the probability and mean, while contiguity length has a significant positive effect. Marginal effects of other covariates of the model are not found to be significant.

Table 7.4 presents results for the estimates of the *Volume of Investment* model. Coefficients behave in a similar way as those in Tables 7.2 and 7.3. Estimates of the coefficients of *Average Annual Energy Use* by the host and investor countries are significant and positive. *Ease of Doing Business* behaves also as expected with a negative and significant sign assigned to the host country and an insignificant coefficient assigned to the investor

Table 7.4: Extent of CDM — results from *tobit* model for the volume of capital investments in CDM projects by each host–investor pair.

Variables	Coefficient estimates		Marginal effects	
	Estimates	Std. errors	Pr(CAP > 0) = 0.026	E[CAP|CAP > 0] = 21,387.50
Intercept	−10,600,000***	1,382,412		
Hst_Avg. Annual Energy Use	3,556.77***	958.67	0.07***	62,951.5***
Inv_Avg. Annual Energy Use	7,381.99***	1,083.13	0.03***	25,215.4***
Hst_Inv_Avg. Ann. Energy Use	29,236.63***	5,311.94	0.001***	757.6***
Hst_Ease of Doing Business	−8,617.74**	3,959.74	0.06	53,257.9
Inv_Ease of Doing Business	571.35	14,374.21	0.15	141,203.9
Hst_Inv_Ease of Doing Business	55,090.22	129,241.60	0.002	1,427.5
Hst_Governance	−11,809.84	102,895.00	−0.0001	−54.1
Inv_Governance	42,0431.60***	64,041.52	0.008	1,0818.0***
Hst_Inv_Governance	1,227.52	9226.33	0.0001	31.8
Hst_Renewable Energy Stock	1,008.28***	353.78	−0.012***	−11,389.1***
Inv_Renewable Energy Stock	−712.90*	432.51	−0.015***	−13,581.1***
Hst_Inv_Ren. Energy Stock	−3,865.54***	959.79	−0.0001***	−100.2***
Hst_Impact Vulnerability	38,999.38**	15,677.48	−0.003	−2,474.3
Inv_Impact Vulnerability	56,433.40**	24,080.30	−0.005	−4,394.1
Hst_Inv_Impact Vulnerability	−4,887.47	4,501.21	−0.0001	−126.6
Trade	1,4191.49	9,006.64	0.0004	367.7
Hst_Political Constraints	664,370.20	735,073.40	0.012	17,215.0
Inv_Political Constraints	−558,727.0	888,076.10	−0.016	−14,477.6
Contiguity Length	9,547.37**	4,702.95	0.0003**	247.4**
Num of Joint IGO Mem.	11,849.84	7,443.66	0.0003	307.1

(Continued)

Table 7.4: (*Continued*)

Variables	Coefficient estimates		Marginal effects	
	Estimates	Std. errors	Pr(CAP > 0) = 0.026	E[CAP|CAP > 0] = 21, 387.50
Dependent Variable	Capital investments by host–investor pairs (1,000 US$)			
No. of Observations	2,771			
No. of Nonzero Observations	281			
Log Likelihood	−4, 814.08			
LR χ^2 (20)	566.05			
Probability > χ^2	0.0001			
Pseudo R-squared	0.06			

Note: CAP refers to the volume of capital investments. ***, **, and * indicate 1%, 5%, and 10% significance levels, respectively.

country. *Governance* of the host country is not significant and that of the investor country is positive and significant as expected. The *Renewable Energy Stock* of the host country has a positive and significant coefficient and that of the investor country has a positive and significant at the 10% significance level. *Impact Vulnerability* is positive and significant for both host and investor countries. Coefficient estimates of bilateral *Trade*, *Political Constraints*, and the *Number of Joint IGO Membership* appear not to be significant. The estimated coefficient of *Contiguity Length* is positive and significant. Coefficient estimates of investor–host interaction terms appear not to be significant, except for the *Average Annual Energy Use*, which is positive and *Renewable Energy Stock* which is negative. As reported in the last two columns of Table 7.4, the covariates have similar marginal effects on censored probability and left-censored mean of dyad-level investments as on CERs. We conducted another robustness test by excluding the observations of China, India, and Brazil that are characterized by many unilateral projects. We found that the results of this analysis are similar to those presented in Tables 7.2–7.4. The results of the subset without China, India, and Brazil are presented in Table G (Supplemental Materials, Rahman *et al.*, 2011).

Corresponding elasticities at the sample mean as presented in Table 7.5 clearly depict the impact of country and dyad characteristics on the level of CDM cooperation between host and investor countries. It is worth noting that while the elasticities are not directly comparable — for example, the

Table 7.5: Estimated elasticities at the mean.

Variables	Estimated elasticities		
	ZINB: Projects $E[NUM] = 0.095$	*Tobit*: CERs $E[CER|CER > 0]$ $= 1,595.46$	*Tobit*: Investments $E[CAP|CAP > 0]$ $= 21,387.50$
Hst_Avg. Annual Energy Use	0.90	99.92***	97.23***
Inv_Avg. Annual Energy Use	1.59	100.51***	97.83***
Hst_Inv_Avg. Ann. Energy Use	0.001	0.10***	0.10***
Hst_Ease of Doing Business	304.67	253.46	246.29
Inv_Ease of Doing Business	305.85	254.50	247.35
Hst_Inv_Ease of Doing Business	0.31	0.25	0.25
Hst_Governance	0.11	0.01	0.01
Inv_Governance	4.22***	33.91***	4.01***
Hst_Inv_Governance	0.19	−0.04	−0.03
Hst_Renewable Energy Stock	−14.87	−69.81***	−72.10***
Inv_Renewable Energy Stock	−15.07	−70.07***	−72.37***
Hst_Inv_Ren. Energy Stock	− 0.01	−0.07***	−0.08***
Hst_Impact Vulnerability	−9.66*	−4.71	−5.37
Inv_Impact Vulnerability	−10.55**	−4.90	−5.65
Hst_Inv_Impact Vulnerability	−1.28**	−0.68	−0.76
Trade	0.21***	0.07*	0.07
Hst_Political Constraints	−0.01	0.10	0.10
Inv_Political Constraints	−1.02***	−0.15	−0.22
Contiguity Length	0.01***	0.01**	0.01**
Num of Joint IGO Mem.	0.20*	0.20	0.20

Note: ZINB refers to zero-inflated negative binomial model, NUM refers to number of projects per dyad, CERs refers to certified emission reduction credits, and CAP refers to the volume of capital investments. ***, **, and * indicate 1%, 5%, and 10% significance levels, respectively.

count model elasticities relate to the percentage change in the number of projects, while the *tobit* elasticities refer to changes in investments on expected CERs — the marginal effects across the three models are remarkably similar. For all the independent variables, the calculated elasticities are very similar. In particular, results indicate that energy use by the host and investor countries and governance of the investor countries have significantly large and positive impact on CDM cooperation, while available renewable energy stock of the host and investor countries have negative impact on cooperation. Bilateral trade and contiguity relationship have significantly positive but small impacts. For the variables with significant coefficient estimates, estimated elasticities from the count model are also similar those from the *tobit* models. In addition, elasticities from the count model indicate that impact vulnerability of the countries have significantly large impact on CDM cooperation.

CONCLUSIONS AND POLICY IMPLICATIONS

Our analysis of CDM cooperation used three types of variables that indicate the extent of joint involvement of host and investor countries in carbon abatement projects. Following the two objectives of the CDM mechanism, our dependent variables that measure CER generation and volume of capital investment suggest that indeed, the two objectives are comparable and explain a great deal of host–investor cooperation. Both greenhouse gas emission reductions that can be credited to the investor country (measured by the CER generation by the CDM projects) and the investment in CDM projects that support sustainable development in the host country provide *a priori* incentives for cooperation between the host and investor countries.

We found that countries with strong trade relations, also implying other types of international relation ties, are more likely to cooperate in CDM activities. Therefore, the general conclusion is that any type of active relations among the countries in host-investor dyads would lead to higher likelihood of cooperation in CDM projects.

Similarly, colonial ties and previous contiguity length are a major factor explaining CDM cooperation. While it is quite reasonable to accept such results, conclusions could be far reaching. Colonial ties may not only refer to dependency but also to better cultural exchanges that allow countries to feel more comfortable working together. It also could be that infrastructure and existing institutions are more familiar and make cooperation more comfortable. In turn, this is expected to reduce transaction costs among countries with shared cultural heritages.

The level of development of the country, measured as average annual energy use, is an important factor in promoting cooperation. While coefficients of the investor country are always two to three times higher than those of the host country, still coefficients of both host and investor are highly significant.

Another variable that has similar impact in other studies of international cooperation is the level of governance in the countries. It is frequently suggested that governance matters and that institutional strength is a prerequisite for better performance, both domestic and international. A similar interpretation can be attributed to the variable measuring the ease of doing business. Our results suggest that the situation in the investor country doesn't matter. What matters is the level of ease of doing business in the host country, which attracts domestic and international investors. It is quite straightforward but needs empirical proof. Studies on FDI demand and supply identify ease of doing business in the investor (source) country to be negatively correlated with FDI supply.

All other variables measure natural endowment of a country and thus may be less affected by policy interventions. Our policy discussion would therefore, be focused only on the suggestion that international development institutions focus mainly on the strengthening of multilateral interactions between countries and on domestic structural changes and reforms of economies, so that they are better prepared not only to adapt to climate change but also to cooperate in the CDM market and take advantage of the CDM dividend — development — that results from CDM joint investment.

One issue that has been raised in carbon finance discussions is the complications of the CDM project clearance process, which becomes a barrier to CDM project development. Simplifying the CDM project clearance cycle is an important policy option. *EDB* goes hand in hand with *Governance*, although they are not necessarily correlated. Improved governance in the host and investor countries means higher political stability and trust between the countries for business. Finally, trade, or other long-term economic activities that connect the countries, is an important promoter for CDM cooperation.

This study shows that three factors, namely better business environment, higher level of governance, and stronger international trade relation, have positive impacts, increasing the future viability of the CDM. Thus, there are scopes for both state-level and international-level policy interventions in these three factors, which governments and international development institutions have already identified as important directions for their future commitment. The analysis in this chapter provides further empirical rationale for these declared commitments.

REFERENCES

Agarwal, JP (1980). Determinants of foreign direct investment: A survey. *Weltwirtschaftliches Archiv*, **116**, 737–773.

Barbieri, K (2002). *The Liberal Illusion: Does Trade Promote Peace?* Ann Arbor, MI: The University of Michigan Press.

Biglaiser, G and K DeRouen (2007). Following the flag: Troop deployment and U.S. foreign direct investment. *International Studies Quarterly*, **51**(4), 835–854.

Brechet, T and B Lussis (2006). The contribution of the clean development mechanism to national climate policies. *Journal of Policy Modeling*, **28**, 981–994.

Blonigen, BA (2006). A review of the empirical literature on FDI determinants. *Atlantic Economic Journal*, **33**(4), 383–403.

Busse, M and C Hefeker (2007). Political risk, institutions and foreign direct investment. *European Journal of Political Economy*, **23**(2), 397–415.

Büthe, T and HV Milner (2008). The politics of foreign direct investment into developing countries: Increasing FDI through international trade agreements? *American Journal of Political Science*, **52**(4), 741–762.

Buys, P, U Deichmann, C Meisner, TT That and D Wheele (2007). Country stakes in climate change negotiations: Two dimensions of vulnerability. World Bank Policy Research Working Paper No. 4300. Washington, DC.

Choi, CJ (1999). Global competitiveness and national attractiveness. *International Studies of Management and Organization*, **29**(1), 3–13.

Congleton, R (1992). Political institutions and pollution control. *Review of Economics and Statistics*, **74**, 412–421.

Correlates of War 2 Project (2010). Colonial/Dependency Contiguity Data, 1816-2002. Version 3.0. Available at: http://correlatesofwar.org (accessed on 6 October 2010).

Da Cunha, KB, A Walter and F Rei (2007). CDM implementation in Brazil's rural and isolated regions: The Amazon case. *Climatic Change*, **84**, 111–129.

De Mello, LR (1997). Foreign direct investment in developing countries: A selective survey. *The Journal of Development Studies*, **34**(1), 1–34.

Dinar, A, SM Rahman, DF Larson and F Ambrosi (2008). Factors affecting levels of international cooperation in carbon abatement projects. Policy Research Working Paper 4786. Development Economics Group, World Bank.

Dinar, S, A Dinar and P Kurukulasuriya (2011). Scarcity and cooperation along international rivers: An empirical assessment of bilateral treaties. *International Studies Quarterly*, **55**, 809–833.

Dinar, S (2009). Scarcity and cooperation along international rivers. *Global Environmental Politics*, **9**(1), 109–135.

Dolšak, N and M Dunn (2006). Investments in global warming mitigation: The case of activities implemented jointly. *Policy Sciences*, **39**, 233–248.

Dunning, JH (1993). *Multinational Enterprise and the Global Economy*. Wokinghan: Addison-Wesley.

Dunning, JH (1996). The role of FDI in a globalizing economy. In CJ Green and TL Brewer (eds.), *Investment Issues in Asia and the Pacific Rim*, pp. 43–64. New York, NY: Oceania.

Henisz, WJ (2002). The institutional environment for infrastructure investment. *Industrial and Corporate Change*, **11**(2), 355–389.

International Monetary Fund (2007). Direction of Trade Data. Available at: http://www.imfstatistics.org/dot/ (accessed on 20 October 2010).

Kaufmann, D, A Kraay and M Mastruzzi (2007). Governance matters VI: Aggregate and individual governance indicators 1996–2006. Policy Research Working Paper 4280. Development Economics Group, World Bank.

Kogut, B and H Singh (1988). The effect of national culture on the choice of entry mode. *Journal of International Business Studies*, **19**(3), 411–432.

Larson, DF and G Breusted (2009). Will markets direct investments under the Kyoto protocol? Lessons from the activities implemented jointly pilots. *Environmental and Resource Economics*, **43**(3), 433–456.

Larson, FD, P Ambrosi, A Dinar, SM Rahman and R Entler (2008). A review of carbon market policies and research. *International Review of Environmental and Resource Economics*, **2**(3), 177–236.

Lecocq, F and P Ambrosi (2007). The clean development mechanism: History, status, and prospects. *Review of Environmental Economics and Policy*, **1**(1), 134–151.

Linebarger, C (2009). Foreign aid and democracy: A quantitative analysis of the determinants of development assistance. Unpublished Paper Presented at the Annual Meeting of the International Studies Association, New York City, NY. Available at: http://citation.allacademic.com/meta/p_mla_apa_research_citation/3/1/1/3/1/pages311310/p311310-1.php. Accessed 8 December 2012.

Michaelowa, A and K Michaelowa (2007). Climate or development: Is ODA diverted from its original purpose? *Climatic Change*, **84**, 5–21.

Mitchell, SM and PR Hensel (2007). International institutions and compliance with agreements. *American Journal of Political Science*, **51**(4), 721–737.

Neumayer, E (2002). Does trade openness promote multilateral environmental cooperation? *World Economy*, **25**, 815–832.

Nonnemberg, M, B Mario, and JC de Mendonça (2005). The Determinants of foreign direct investment in developing countries. *Estudos Econômicos, São Paulo*, **35**(4), 631–655.

Nunnenkamp, P (2002). Determinants of FDI in developing countries: Has globalization changed the rules of the game? Kiel Working Paper 1122, Kiel Institute for World Economics.

Olsen, KH (2007). The clean development mechanism's contribution to sustainable development: A review of the literature. *Climatic Change*, **84**, 59–73.

Paul, E (2006). A survey of the theoretical economic literature on foreign aid. *Asian-Pacific Economic Literature*, **20**(1), 1–17.

Pevehouse, JC, T Nordstrom and K Warnke (2004). The COW-2 international organizations dataset version 2.0. *Conflict Management and Peace Science*, **21**(2), 101–119.

Polacheck, SW, C Seiglie and J Xiang (2007). Globalization and international conflict: Can FDI decrease conflict? Unpublished Paper Presented at the Allied Social Science Association Winter Meeting, Chicago, IL.

Pollins, B (1989). Conflict, cooperation, and commerce: The effect of international political interactions on bilateral trade flows. *American Journal of Political Science*, **33**, 737–761.

Rahman, SM, A Dinar and DF Larson (2010). Diffusion of Kyoto's clean development mechanism. *Technological Forecasting & Social Change* **77**, 1391–1400.

Russett, B and J Oneal (2001). *Triangulating Peace: Democracy, Interdependence, and International Organizations*. New York, NY: W.W. Norton & Company. Russett and Oneal.

Seres, S (2007). Data Processing of capital cost in CDM Projects. Available at: Climatesolutions.ca. Accessed 8 December 2012.

Shenkar, O (2001). Cultural distance revisited: Towards a more rigorous conceptualization and measurement of cultural differences. *Journal of International Business Studies*, **32**(3), 519–535.

Siegel, JI, AN Licht and Schwartz, Shalom H (2010). Egalitarianism, Cultural Distance, and FDI: A New Approach. Available at: http://papers.ssrn.com/sol3/papers.cfm?abstract_id=957306 (accessed on 20 October 2010).

Sirohi, S (2007). CDM: Is it a win-win strategy for rural poverty alleviation in India? *Climatic Change*, 84, 91–110.

Smeets, R (2008). Collecting the pieces of the FDI knowledge spillovers puzzle. The *World Bank Research Observer*, **23**(2), 107–138.

Sutter, C and JC Parreno (2007). Does the current clean energy development mechanism (CDM) deliver its sustainable development claim? An analysis of officially registered CDM projects. *Climatic Change*, **84**, 75–90.

Svensson, J (2000). Foreign aid and rent seeking. *Journal of International Economics*, **51**, 437–461.

Tsur, Y and A Zemel (2008). Regulating environmental threats. *Environmental and Resource Economics*, **39**, 297–310.

UNDP United Nations Development Program (2006). *An Assessment of Progress with Establishing the Clean Development Mechanism*. New York, NY: UNDP.

UNFCCC (2010). Clean Development Mechanism (CDM). Available at: http://cdm.unfccc.int/index.html (accessed on 3 March 2010).

United Nations Environment Programme (UNEP) Risoe Center (2007). CDM/JI Pipeline Analysis and Database. Available at: http://cdmpipeline.org (accessed on 6 November 2008).

United Nations Environmental Program UNEP/GRID-Arendal (2000). Methodological and Technological issues in Technology Transfer. Available at: http://www.grida.no/climate/ipcc/tectran/index.htm (accessed on 29 July 2007).

Velasco, AP (2007). Variables Underpinning Technology Transfers Through the CDM. *Joint Implementation Quarterly*, **13**(3), 5–6.

Vuong, QH (1989). Likelihood ratio tests for model selection and non-nested hypotheses. *Econometrica*, **57**(2), 307–333.

Vrolijk, C (2000). Quantifying the Kyoto commitments. *Review of European Community and International Environmental Law*, **9**, 285–295.

Waltz, K (1979). *Theory of International Politics*. New York, NY: McGraw-Hill.

WDI (World Development Indicators) and The World Bank (2007). Available at http://publications.worldbank.org/WDI (accessed on 6 October 2010).

World Bank (2007). World Development Indicators 2007. Washington, DC: World Bank.

Young, O (1989). The politics of international regime formation: Managing natural resources and the environment. *International Organization*, **43**(3), 349–375.

ANNEXE 7.1

Table 7.1A: Definition of variables used in the regression analyses.

Variable	Description	Unit of measurement
Ease of Doing Business	Ease of doing business, a relative ranking of the countries reflecting the state of business regulation	Smaller value indicates less favorable business environment
CDM Incidence	A dichotomous variable with 0 if there are no, and 1 if there are any number of CDM dyad projects.	0 or 1
Avr. Annual Energy Use	Average annual energy use over the period 1960–2003	Thousand trillion tons of oil equivalent
Governance	Indicator reflecting the overall governance level, a principal component product of six governance indicators	Smaller value indicates poorer level of governance
Impact Vulnerability	Impact vulnerability index (reflecting country vulnerability in terms of various impacts of climate change)	Scale of 1 to 100 (1 = lowest, 100 = highest)
Number of Projects	Number of CDM projects	
Renewable Energy	Renewable energy resources (annual) available per capita	Thousand trillion tons of oil equivalent
Total CO_2 Abatement	Total amount of CO_2 abatement (CERs) until 2012	Kiloton of oil equivalent
Annual CO_2 Abatement	Annual amount of CO_2 abatement (CERs) until 2012.	Kiloton of oil equivalent
Trade	Total trade (the sum of the volume of bilateral imports and exports) between the host and investor countries as a fraction of the sum of the countries' GDPs	Share
Volume of Investment	Volume of investment in CDM projects: _TOT reflecting total investment and _YR reflecting annual investment	Thousand US\$ (constant 2000)
*hst_**	Variable related to the host country	*represents the variables described above
*inv_**	Variable related to the investor country	*represents the variables described above
*hst_*inv_**	An interaction term	*represents the variables described above

8. WHY SO FEW AGRICULTURAL PROJECTS IN THE CLEAN DEVELOPMENT MECHANISM?*

With Contribution by J. Aapris Frisbie

One of the objectives of the CDM is to enhance development in host countries, while allowing for cost-effective mitigation. Agriculture is the most sensitive sector to climate change and is said to contribute 5% of the global national GDP on average (CIA, 2011), use about one-third of the world's land (FAO, 2006), and act as the source of livelihood for three-quarters of the rural poor in the developing world (Smith *et al.*, 2007).

On the other hand, according to the Intergovernmental Panel on Climate Change (IPCC), agriculture accounted for an estimated 5.1 to 6.1 $GtCO_2e$ in 2005, or roughly 12% of global anthropogenic emissions of greenhouse gases. At the same time, there is a consensus that agriculture's net contribution to global warming could be greatly reduced, since the sector also provides ample mitigation opportunities — enough to remove or sequester up to 1.6 $GtCO_2e$ annually at relatively low carbon prices. Most opportunities identified to date involve the use of agricultural biomass to generate power or involve changes in how agricultural lands are used (Smith *et al.*, 2007). Especially important for mitigation are efforts to restore carbon pools in soil on degraded land. This closely links mitigation in agriculture with development, since most agricultural land-use opportunities are in developing countries where agriculture is an important source of income for the poor. Moreover, projects that sequester carbon in soils also help to reverse declining soil fertility, a root cause of stagnant agricultural productivity in Africa. Further, summarizing the debate in the UNFCCC

---

*Permission to use material from Chapter 13 (The Present and Future Role for Agricultural Projects under the Clean Development Mechanism) (Larson, Dinar, and Frisbie) in the *Handbook on Climate Change and Agriculture* (Dinar and Mendelsohn, 2011) was granted by Edward Edgar.

meeting in Durban, and in a report prepared for that meeting, Gilbert (2011: p. 279) cites that agriculture is the "single largest contributor to greenhouse-gas pollution on the planet." The report estimated that farming footprints (including forest deforestation for farming) amounts to 49 giga-tonnes of CO_2e per year. These numbers are expected to double (unless agricultural production becomes more efficient) by 2050 as demand for food will grow.

Is the vulnerability of the agricultural sector on one hand and its potential on the other hand reflected in the CDM portfolio? In this chapter, we examine the types of agricultural projects currently financed under the CDM. We find that most projects have to do with agriculture as a source of bio-energy, and that few projects tap the mitigation potential associated with changing how agricultural lands are used. We explore why this is so. We look at the aspects of agricultural land-use projects that make them complex and costly to implement under current CDM rules. We also examine the origins of the current CDM institutions and look at the feasibility of changing CDM rules to provide greater scope for agricultural projects. We review a set of new instruments arising from decisions taken by parties to the UNFCCC in Copenhagen and Cancun and explore new mechanisms outside of the CDM that could be used to integrate mitigation, development, and sustainable resource management goals.

POTENTIAL SOURCES OF MITIGATION IN AGRICULTURE

In 2007, the IPCC reviewed projections across a range of modeling efforts to assess potential sources of mitigation by sector (Barker _et al._, 2007). Table 8.1 summarizes the report's assessment of mitigation opportunities at US$20 per tCO_2e.[1] Recalling that the CDM is meant to target low-cost abatement opportunities in developing countries, the assessment suggests that the opportunities are greatest in the building, industry, and agricultural sectors. Moreover, the report concludes that most energy-saving efforts in the building sector would be profitable without additional carbon

---

[1] The Kyoto Protocol covers six gases: carbon dioxide (CO_2), methane (CH_4), nitrous oxide (N_2O), hydrofluorocarbons (HFCs), perfluorocarbons (PFCs), and sulphur hexafluoride (SF_6). By convention, aggregate emission and mitigation amounts are expressed in terms of CO_2e, the amount of CO_2 needed to have the same global warming potential.

Table 8.1: Estimated potential for GHG mitigation
in 2030 by sector at or below $20/tCO$_2$e.

	Total	Developing countries
Agriculture	1.60	1.10
Forestry	1.25	1.05
Energy	1.90	0.80
Buildings	5.50	2.85
Transport	1.75	0.13
Other	1.50	0.97
Total	13.50	6.90

Note: Potential given in Gt CO$_2$e per year. Mitigation from burning agricultural residue is attributed to sector in which the fuel-use takes place. The IPCC estimates that mitigation opportunities for this class of project at 1.26 Gt CO$_2$e per year. *Source*: Barker *et al.* (2007) and Smith *et al.* (2007).

payments and are therefore ineligible for CDM crediting.[2] Consequently, modeling results imply that agricultural projects should feature prominently in the CDM.

As the more detailed chapter of the IPCC on agriculture makes clear, the consensus estimate of 1.6 GtCO$_2$e in mitigation potential is based on models in which the sector is narrowly defined, focusing on on-farm activities primarily involving crops and livestock and the handling of animal wastes (Smith *et al.*, 2007). The authors note that, as a consequence, additional opportunities linked to the use of organic agricultural waste products, such as baggasse or rice husks, as a renewable fuel are not counted toward agriculture, but are attributed to sectors in which the fuel-switching takes place. Top-down studies referenced in the report suggest that this class of opportunities for mitigation is nearly as large as agriculture's on-farm potential, with mitigation estimates ranging from 0.7 to 1.26 gtCO$_2$e per year by 2030 at costs of US$20 or below.

As Smith *et al.* (2008) emphasize, measuring the mitigation potential for agricultural land-use is complex because a single activity can initiate

---

[2]In the CDM parlance, these projects lack "economic additionality," that is, under a business-as-usual scenario, firms would find investing in this type of energy saving profitable and do not face hurdles that would prevent them from doing so.

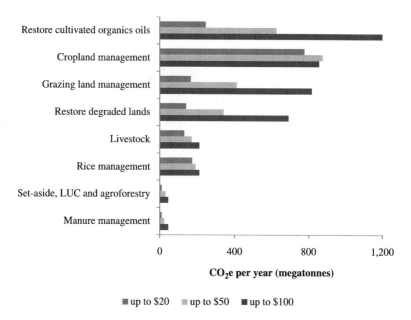

Fig. 8.1: Potential for mitigation in agriculture at selected prices.

Note: The totals exclude bioenergy and improved energy efficiency.

Source: Smith *et al.* (2007).

a chain of emission outcomes among a portfolio of greenhouse gases that also depend on local soils and local climate conditions. As an example, the authors cite evidence presented in Paustian *et al.* (2004) showing that composting manure can suppress methane emissions while simultaneously accelerating emissions of another greenhouse gas, nitrous oxide. Similarly, soil restoration can encourage carbon uptake in plants and soils, while stimulating the release of carbon through the decomposition of organic matter.

After accounting for interrelated effects, the authors provide a further breakdown of the mitigation potential for a set of agricultural activities under a range of carbon prices, shown in Fig. 8.1. Keeping in mind that mitigation activities linked to agricultural biomass are excluded, the reported literature suggests that most mitigation opportunities are related to soil and land management practices that generate net sequestration gains. At low carbon prices (less than US$20), cropland management practices are key sources of mitigation, along with other land management practices, including the restoration of organic soils and degraded lands and improved management of grazing.

In the case of cropland management, improved agronomy is important, for example, converting crop production from traditional to improved higher-yielding varieties. So is the use of chemical fertilizers, which can provide net emission benefits when soils are poor. This is true even though carbon is released in the production and transport of chemical fertilizers and nitrous oxide is generated when nitrogen fertilizers are used. Other productivity-enhancing activities identified in the report include the use of ground cover between perennial tree crops and the adoption of crop-rotation schemes involving nitrogen-fixing legumes. Better water management and application of organic matter to cropland are also identified as activities that both enhance agricultural productivity and contribute to the restoration of organic soils on degraded lands. Important but smaller mitigation opportunities are tied to efforts designed to reduce methane emissions from wetland rice, livestock, and manure.

AGRICULTURAL AND LAND-USE PROJECTS UNDER THE CDM

We next turn our attention to the set of agricultural projects approved or awaiting approval by the CDM Board. The purpose is to both describe the flow of investments to agriculture under the CDM and gauge the degree to which the mechanism has been able to tap potential mitigation opportunities identified in the IPCC report. The first step in that process is settling on a definition, since the classification systems used by the IPCC in their mitigation reports and by the United Nations Environment Programme Risoe Center on Energy, Climate, and Sustainable Development (Risoe) to report on CDM projects are not harmonized. Indeed, Risoe classifies only two projects as agricultural.[3] Projects related to land use, the primary focus of the IPCC chapter on agriculture, are included under afforestation/reforestation projects, which we refer to as land-use forestry projects.[4] Other projects related to agriculture — for example, systems to manage manure or projects that use agricultural waste products to generate

---

[3]Both projects, only one of which remained active in 2010, reduced pump-well emissions by installing more efficiency drip irrigation systems.

[4]In UNFCCC parlance, the class of mitigation projects that sequester carbon in soils and forests are known as land use, land-use change, and forestry (LULUCF) projects, since the net mitigation comes from changing how land is used.

energy — fall into other aggregate categories in the Risoe classification system, such as biomass energy or methane avoidance, which include non-agricultural projects as well. Consequently, for our purposes, we follow the lead of the United Nations' Food and Agriculture Organization (FAO) and define an agricultural project as a project that uses agricultural residuals, outputs or agricultural processes to directly or indirectly reduce greenhouse gas emissions (FAO, 2010). This definition is broad enough to include projects that sequester carbon in soils. Like the IPCC, we do not classify biofuel projects as agricultural, but we do include projects in which residual agricultural organic matter is used to produce energy. We include projects that reduce methane emissions from composting agricultural waste products, but do not include waste water projects, even though some waste water is likely associated with processing agricultural products.

There are multiple stages in the CDM project cycle, and projects can leave the project cycle at several points. For the purpose of this chapter, we focus on 5,824 projects that were active as of December 1, 2010. The number of projects and their projected cumulative and average mitigation impacts by project type are given in Table 8.2. By our definition, about 17% of the projects are classified as agricultural and land-use forestry projects; a category that includes mixed-use agro-forestry projects and other projects that restore agricultural land comprise another 1%. In combination, this is a significant share when compared to other categories, and only the hydro-power and alternative energy categories contain more projects. Based on Risoe's analysis of project documents, the identified agricultural projects are expected to reduce business-as-usual emissions by nearly $220\,mtCO_2e$ by 2012 and $582\,mtCO_2e$ by 2020. In addition, land-use forestry projects are expected to account for another $17\,mtCO_2e$ and $69\,mtCO_2e$, respectively, for the two periods. Even so, as the last two columns of the table indicate, agriculture projects and, to a lesser degree, land-use projects, tend to be smaller scaled than other types of projects, so the share of the mitigation impact shares are smaller than the project count shares.

The task of comparing the potential for mitigation identified by the IPCC and the expected level of mitigation from projects in the CDM pipeline requires a series of assumptions and extrapolation. For one, the modeling efforts behind the IPCC estimates envisage annual flows by 2030 under a set of certain prices and established markets. In contrast, the CDM market has been built from scratch and investments have been made under uncertainty. Moreover, project offset prices have stayed below US$20 per ton since 2008, hovering mostly between US$10 and US$13 per ton. It is

Table 8.2: CDM projects by type and expected mitigation impact by 2012 and 2020.

Project type	Projects		Mitigation impact by 2012		Mitigation impact by 2020		Average project impact $(ktCO_2e)$	
	Number	Share	$ktCO_2e$	Share	$ktCO_2e$	Share	2012	2020
Agriculture	964	0.17	219,507	0.08	582,081	0.07	228	604
Land-use forestry	58	0.01	16,638	0.01	69,109	0.01	287	1,192
Non-agriculture								
Hydro	1,558	0.27	482,160	0.17	1,894,491	0.22	309	1,216
Alternative energy	1,221	0.21	326,170	0.11	1,154,888	0.13	267	946
Energy Efficiency	837	0.14	332,619	0.12	1,139,571	0.13	397	1,361
Methane avoidance	340	0.06	191,296	0.07	596,638	0.07	563	1,755
Landfill gas	326	0.06	204,097	0.07	537,122	0.06	626	1,648
Assorted gases	145	0.02	340,797	0.12	904,581	0.10	2,350	6,238
Biomass energy	141	0.02	36,958	0.01	101,004	0.01	262	716
Fossil fuel switch	133	0.02	191,523	0.07	585,274	0.07	1,440	4,401
Cement	44	0.01	35,444	0.01	76,590	0.01	806	1,741
Transport	34	0.01	10,157	0.00	39,160	0.00	299	1,152
HFCs	23	0.00	476,541	0.17	1,100,353	0.13	20,719	47,841
Total	5,824	1.00	2,863,906	1.00	8,780,862	1.00	492	1,508

Note: The non-agriculture categories are based on Risoe's classification system, net of those projects considered agricultural by the authors.

also worth pointing out that the CDM was never expected to finance the full set of mitigation opportunities in developing countries and that the CDM is in fact on tract to exceed expectations (Rahman, Dinar, and Larson, 2010.) Still, the comparisons, though inexact, are indicative, since they give a sense of how effectively the CDM has tapped opportunities across sectors.

With this in mind, converting the total cumulative stock of offsets expected from the pipeline for the period 2008 to 2020 works out to an annual flow of about 675 mtCO$_2$e. Since the start of the CDM, the pace of projects entering the pipeline has increased and there are good reasons to expect this to continue if uncertainty over crediting after 2012 can be resolved. Still, the projected impact of pipeline projects represents less than 10% of the potential 2030 flow of 6,900 mtCO2e of low-cost mitigation opportunities in developing countries identified by the IPCC.

Drawing a similar comparison about the gap between mitigation potential and the expected output from implemented projects is more difficult for agriculture. Part of this is conceptual and has to do with the already discussed differences between the modeling evaluations of what types of mitigation processes are agricultural and the classification system we use to categorize projects under the CDM. However, setting this aside, there is a practical problem in that the agricultural bio-energy estimates from the IPCC report do not identify the potential from developing countries separately. In general, the IPCC estimates that roughly 42% of the mitigation opportunities in energy are in developing countries and, by that rubric, about 302.4 mtCO$_2$e of the agriculture-biomass potential should be in developing countries. Combining this with the potential from agriculture gives an estimate of about 1,629 mtCO$_2$e. Generously combining the mitigation estimates for all 1,022 projects associated with land-use and agriculture provides a flow of just over 50 mtCO$_2$e, a bit more than 3% of the IPCC total. Because we have included all reforestation and afforestation projects in the CDM total (regardless of whether they relate to the restoration of agricultural land), and because we have been generous in estimating the share of agricultural biomass potential attributed to developing countries, this already small share is most likely inflated.

A well-documented, if not anticipated, feature of the CDM is that a large portion of the projects are located in a handful of countries. The same holds true of agricultural projects. As shown in Table 8.3, China, India, Brazil, Mexico, and Malaysia account for 78% of all the CDM projects in our analysis, regardless of project type. Although there are minor differences in the ranking, the same five countries account for about 79% of agriculture projects. Relatively few projects are located in Africa. However, this is not the case for forestry projects. Even though this category accounts for few projects, the projects are more broadly distributed across hosting countries with a significant share of the projects in Africa.

Baseline Methodologies for Agricultural and Land-use Forestry Projects

Because the developing countries that host CDM projects do not limit overall emissions, project mitigation affects are measured against a business-as-usual counterfactual. In UNFCCC parlance, the way of assessing the net mitigation consequences of a particular project is known as a CDM methodology. The methodologies are detailed and specific to particular

Table 8.3: Host countries ranked by the number of CDM projects hosted.

Rank	All projects			Agricultural projects			Land-use forestry projects		
	Host	Number	Cumulative share	Host	Number	Cumulative share	Host	Number	Cumulative share
1	China	2,316	0.398	India	326	0.338	India	9	0.155
2	India	1,549	0.664	Brazil	137	0.480	Kenya	8	0.293
3	Brazil	365	0.726	China	119	0.604	Uganda	6	0.397
4	Mexico	176	0.757	Mexico	104	0.712	Colombia	6	0.500
5	Malaysia	136	0.780	Malaysia	77	0.791	China	4	0.569
6	Vietnam	129	0.802	Philippines	53	0.846	Chile	3	0.621
7	Thailand	126	0.824	Indonesia	33	0.881	Congo DR	2	0.655
8	Indonesia	114	0.843	Thailand	27	0.909	Bolivia	2	0.690
9	South Korea	85	0.858	Chile	8	0.917	Moldova	2	0.724
10	Chile	77	0.871	Honduras	7	0.924	Brazil	2	0.759
11	Philippines	76	0.884	Sri Lanka	5	0.929	Ethiopia	1	0.776
12	Colombia	68	0.896	Ecuador	5	0.935	Ghana	1	0.793
13	Peru	40	0.903	Israel	5	0.940	Madagascar	1	0.810
14	South Africa	39	0.909	Colombia	5	0.945	Albania	1	0.828
15	Argentina	38	0.916	Nepal	4	0.949	Lao PDR	1	0.845
16	Israel	33	0.922	Cyprus	4	0.953	Paraguay	1	0.862
17	Honduras	31	0.927	Vietnam	4	0.957	Tanzania	1	0.879
18	Pakistan	25	0.931	Uruguay	3	0.961	Nicaragua	1	0.897
19	Ecuador	23	0.935	Morocco	3	0.964	Costa Rica	1	0.914
20	Sri Lanka	21	0.939	Kenya	3	0.967	Uruguay	1	0.931

Source: Risoe (2010) and authors' calculations.
Note: The full list of host countries is given in Annex Table 8.1A.

processes. For example, specific methodologies lay out procedures for measuring the impact of updating municipal heating systems or incinerating hydrofluorocarbons. New projects can use methodologies that have already been approved when appropriate; however, projects that introduce new methods or modify existing ones must have those methods approved by an expert committee before it can considered by the CDM Board.

The methodologies used for the 1,022 projects studied here are listed in Table 8.4.[5] The projects rely on 33 approved methodologies, but the 10 most frequently used methodologies account for 80% of the projects. Often, more than one methodology is used in a given project. For example, a project might move organic material that would normally be left to decompose in a contained area, capture methane released during decomposition, and use it to generate electricity. When requesting credit from the CDM Board, project sponsors may use one methodology to account for the conversion of methane to less harmful carbon dioxide as the methane is burned, and another to calculate the benefits of displacing electricity produced with fossil fuels with electricity from a renewable resource.[6]

The fixed costs of bringing a project to the CDM Board and the ongoing monitoring costs can be high, so to encourage small-scale projects, the CDM Board distinguishes between small-scale and large-scale project methodologies. As can be seen in Table 8.4, agricultural and forestry projects contain a mix of small- and large-scale projects. Because of this, the methodologies that are most used are not strictly the same as those methodologies associated with high levels of expected mitigation.

Once approved, methodologies enter the public domain and can be used by subsequent project developers. For this reason, methodologies tend to follow a life cycle in which the use of the methodology increases as developers look for low-cost opportunities to replicate the methodology and then declines as replicable opportunities are more fully exploited (Table 8.5).

The methodologies exactly define the specific activities allowed under the CDM. Table 8.4 suggests that there are 33 actions associated with agriculture and forestry. However, a close look at the most widely used

---

[5] As the set of methodologies grows, similar methodologies are harmonized in a "consolidated" methodology. In our classification, we use the most recent methodology designation; that is, we group each consolidated method with their respective antecedents.

[6] Consequently, the sum of methods used exceeds the number of projects.

Table 8.4: Methodologies used for agriculture and land-use forestry projects.

Methodology	Number of projects	Mitigation (ktCO$_2$e) 2012	Mitigation (ktCO$_2$e) 2020	Project scale	Mitigation action
AMS-I.D.	252	37,615	95,220	Small scale	Displacement of electricity produced by more GHG-intensive means
ACM6	191	71,139	206,925	Large scale	Renewable energy
AMS-III.D.	191	15,661	42,668	Small scale	GHG destruction
AMS-I.C.	187	27,259	77,867	Small scale	Displacement of more GHG-intensive thermal energy or heat
AMS-III.F.	48	4,757	14,635	Small scale	GHG destruction
ACM2	42	18,850	53,332	Large scale	Renewable energy
AMS-III.E.	28	12,790	32,279	Small scale	GHG emission avoidance
ACM3	26	11,120	28,032	Large scale	Fuel Switch and renewable energy
AR-AMS1	23	773	6,213	Small scale	GHG removal by sinks
AMS-III.R.	18	2,226	9,314	Small scale	GHG destruction and fuel switching
AMS-III.H.	15	1,464	5,630	Small scale	GHG destruction
AM36	12	5,295	19,332	Large scale	Renewable energy
AM39	11	7,666	17,707	Large scale	GHG emission avoidance
ACM10	9	3,629	13,862	Large scale	GHG destruction
ACM18	8	2,450	13,381	Large scale	Renewable energy
AM25	7	1,389	4,994	Large scale	GHG emission avoidance, renewable energy
AMS-I.A.	7	650	1,885	Small scale	Displacement of more GHG-intensive service
AMS-I.E.	7	865	3,260	Small scale	Displacement of non-renewable biomass by renewable sources
AR-AM4	7	3,701	12,985	Large scale	GHG removal by sinks
AR-AM5	7	6,436	28,183	Large scale	GHG removal by sinks
AR-ACM2	4	1,154	3,183	Large scale	GHG removal by sinks

(*Continued*)

Table 8.4: (*Continued*)

Methodology	Number of projects	Mitigation (ktCO₂e)		Project scale	Mitigation action
		2012	2020		
AR-AM3	4	632	1,591	Large scale	GHG removal by sinks
AM73	3	870	3,323	Large scale	GHG destruction
AMS-III.G.	3	684	1,801	Small scale	GHG destruction
AMS-II.D.	2	47	183	Small scale	Energy efficiency
AR-AM2	2	1,077	3,314	Large scale	GHG removal by sinks
AM57	1	325	976	Large scale	GHG emission avoidance
AMS-II.F.	1	18	100	Small scale	Energy efficiency in agriculture
AMS-III.Q.	1	46	168	Small scale	Energy efficiency
AMS-III.Z.	1	134	413	Small scale	Energy efficiency, renewable energy, fuel switch
AR-AM10	1		3,444	Large scale	GHG removal by sinks.
AR-AM9	1	236	657	Large scale	GHG removal by sinks
AR-AMS3	1	24	55	Small scale	GHG removal by sinks

Note: Because some projects employ more than one methodology, the number of methodology appearances exceeds the number of analyzed projects.
Source: Risoe (2010) and authors' calculations.

methodologies, suggests that the methods are variations around a smaller set of core actions.

AMS-I.D is methodology used to calculate the mitigation effects of displacing fossil fuels to generate electricity that enters a power grid from small-scale projects. ACM6 is a related consolidated methodology for larger scale projects in which fossil fuels used to generate electricity and heat under the business-as-usual baseline are replaced by biomass residuals — for example, risk husks or the residual from crushed sugar cane. The methodology takes into account methane avoided by burning the residue rather than allowing it to decay. AMS-III.D is a methodology to account for recovering and burning methane in small-scale animal manure management systems. AMS.I.C is also a methodology based on burning biomass; however, it also can be applied to small projects that improve the efficiency of existing biomass projects — for example, the installation of equipment that improves the efficiency of thermal power components of a sugarcane

Table 8.5: Number of projects using selected methodologies by project-start year.

Methodology	2004	2005	2006	2007	2008	2009	2010	Total
ACM10	5	40	7	5	1	0	2	60
ACM2	0	6	8	4	14	7	3	42
ACM3	0	7	1	5	5	2	6	26
ACM6	3	35	51	22	54	34	21	220
AM36	0	1	0	1	3	5	2	12
AM39	0	0	0	8	1	2	0	11
AMS-I.C.	0	12	18	24	50	32	51	187
AMS-I.D.	2	47	63	51	31	29	29	252
AMS-III.D.	0	14	84	29	28	24	12	191
AMS-III.E.	0	2	12	4	4	2	4	28
AMS-III.F.	0	0	5	17	14	7	5	48
AMS-III.H.	0	0	0	0	5	2	8	15
AMS-III.R.	0	0	0	1	2	1	14	18
AR-AMS1	0	0	0	2	10	9	2	23
Other	0	2	5	9	20	7	26	69

Note: Because some projects employ more than one methodology, the number of methodology appearances exceeds the number of analyzed projects.
Source: Risoe (2010) and authors' calculations.

crushing facility. AMS-III.F is another small-scale methodology based on the avoidance of methane emissions. In this case, methane emissions are avoided by composting organic material normally left in the open to decay, or by capturing biogas that is flared and potentially used to produce electricity. The methodology is often implemented at palm oil processing plants. ACM2 is a large-scale consolidated baseline methodology for grid-connected electricity generation from renewable sources. In the case of the projects studied here, it is most often used in connection with ACM6. AMS-III.E is another methodology based on the avoidance of methane produced from decay, mostly through controlled burning or through gasification. ACM3 is a large-scale consolidated methodology based on the use of alternative fuels in the production of cement. In a few cases, the alternative fuel is based on agricultural residues, which is how the methodology came to be included in our study. Allowing for some double counting of projects that use multiple methods, these eight methodologies account for roughly 86% of the projects and about 78% of expected mitigation impact from the projects that we include in our study.

Among the remaining methodologies, five are significant for agricultural land use. The most used land-use methodology in our sample is AR-AMS1, a simplified baseline and monitoring methodology for planting trees on grasslands or cropland while maintaining most pre-project activities. This is significant, since some land-use methodologies prohibit continued grazing on lands covered by the project. AR-ACM2 is a related large-scale methodology, where pre-existing farming activities are continued after project implementation. AR-AM4 is a methodology based on planting trees and shrubs on degraded land that is used for agricultural purposes. AR-AM5 is a related methodology for commercial agricultural purposes. Land-use methodologies account for about 4% of the study sample and about 8% of expected mitigation.

Table 8.6 uses information from the methodologies to reclassify projects by a core set of activities. From the table, it is clear that more than 80% of the projects and expected mitigation impact is associated with either using left-over agricultural matter (primarily rice husks, baggasse, and oil palm husks), or the management of manure in a way that captures methane and converts it to less harmful carbon dioxide and frequently energy as well. Afforestation, reforestation, and composting projects account for most of the remaining projects. The remaining two projects are based on energy efficiency gains.[7]

Table 8.6: CDM projects expected mitigation impact by core set of activities.

	Number of projects	Expected mitigation ($ktCO_2e$)	
		2012	2020
Agricultural residues	615	153,768	428,634
Manure	288	52,837	119,486
Composting	60	12,883	33,861
Land use	57	16,614	69,054
Irrigation	1	18	100
Mangroves	1	24	55
Total	1,022	236,145	651,189

Source: Risoe (2010) and authors' calculations

---

[7]The irrigation project, set in India, saves fuel by using more intensive farming methods; the mangrove project, set in Cameroon, improves the efficiency of wood-burning stoves used in smokehouses, thereby reducing wood consumption.

Table 8.7: Volume and value of project-based transactions, 2008–2009.

	2008		2009	
	Volume MtCO$_2$e	Value US$ Million	Volume MtCO$_2$e	Value US$ Million
CDM	404	6,511	211	2,678
Joint implementation	25	367	26	354
Voluntary market	57	419	46	338
Total	486	7,297	283	3,370

Source: State and Trends of the Carbon Market 2010, World Bank.

PROJECT MARKETS OUTSIDE THE CDM

Not all projects designed to mitigate greenhouse gas emissions from agriculture operate under the UN Framework. Voluntary markets offer an alternative way of financing agricultural land-use projects. Overall, these markets are small relative to regulated markets, including the CDM (Table 8.7). However, they are significant and collectively finance a greater volume of offsets than Joint Implementation (JI).[8] Most voluntary market transactions originate in the US, which is not a party to the Kyoto Protocol.[9] Projects traded in voluntary markets are not subject to the same types of review and public disclosure that characterize the CDM market; however, the application of third-party standards is common. In their annual review of voluntary markets, Hamilton *et al.* (2010) estimated that over 90% of voluntary transactions in 2008 and 2009 adhered to third-party standards, but also counted 18 competing standards active in voluntary markets.

In some cases, the types of projects financed by voluntary markets are similar to classes of projects eligible for financing under the CDM. For example, in 2009, landfill and wind projects accounted for 39% of the offsets financed by voluntary markets (Hamilton *et al.*, 2010). Still, investors have been attracted to the voluntary market as a way to invest in land-use projects that are difficult to finance or have been excluded from financing under the CDM.

---

[8]Joint Implementation is a second project-based mechanisms established by the Kyoto Protocol for projects based in countries that have pledged reductions.

[9]Hamilton *et al.* (2010) estimates that 56% of voluntary project transactions took place in the US.

Table 8.8: Land-use based offsets traded on voluntary OTC markets.

Project type	Volume (ktCO$_2$e)		Share of voluntary market (%)	
	2008	2009	2008	2009
Afforestation/Reforestation	4,091	4,253	8.00	10.00
Avoided Deforestation	730	2,846	1.00	7.00
Forest Management	431	1,349	1.00	3.00
Agricultural Soil	267	1,250	0.50	3.00
Agro-Forestry		625		1.00
Other Land-based projects	130	109	0.03	0.03
Total	5,649	10,432	10.53	24.03

Source: Hamilton *et al.* (2010).

An estimate of land-based credits financed through voluntary markets is reported in Table 8.8. Though the combined volumes of land-based projects in 2008 and 2009 were small, the projects collectively represented a significant share of the voluntary market. Nevertheless, among these, the portion of credits arising from agricultural land-use projects remained quite small, constituting 1% of the voluntary market in 2009 and less than 4% in 2008.

HURDLES TO INCLUDING AGRICULTURAL PROJECTS IN THE CDM

In the previous section, we described the gap between the available mitigation opportunities in agricultural land-use projects and capital flows from the CDM and from voluntary markets. In this section, we examine specific design features of the CDM that work against land-use projects in general and discuss the origins of these features. We then explore how the practical concerns that gave rise to this structure also work to limit funding from markets outside of the Kyoto mechanisms.

Purposely, the CDM is designed to facilitate capital flows to developing countries to tap low-cost mitigation opportunities and to promote sustainable development in countries that have not themselves pledged emission reductions. But this basic design tenet of the mechanism has vocal critics, and support for the mechanism, even among some signatories of the Kyoto Protocol, has been equivocal. One consequence is a set of varied national policies and a complex set of international implementation rules that try to remediate concerns about the environmental efficacy of the CDM and its impact on development. Additionally, and separate from the underlying questions that motivated their genesis, the mechanism's implementation rules give the CDM a particular institutional structure that has practical consequences, influencing the type of mitigation efforts feasible in developing countries within the UNFCCC. For the most part, this structure works against the development of projects related to how land is used and this, in turn, works to preclude the types of projects that would target the largest sources of low-cost mitigation opportunities within agricultural sectors. More generally, it also explains why the country and sector composition of the projects that now constitute the CDM project cycle pipeline differ from estimates of the sector-distribution of low-cost mitigation opportunities discussed earlier.

Objections to the CDM and their Influence on Its Design

The Clean Development Mechanism (CDM), dubbed the "Kyoto surprise," emerged late in the negotiations of the Kyoto Protocol and has been called the least loved of Kyoto's contentious flexibility mechanisms (Werksman, 1998). The mechanism was intended to address two divergent sets of interests: a desire by developed countries to access low-cost mitigation opportunities in developing countries, and a need by developing countries for a new channel for development assistance (Grubb *et al.*, 1999; Lecocq and Ambrosi, 2007). Moreover, for the mechanism to work, the difficult problem of finding a way to create environmentally sound credits in countries without pledged limits had to be solved.

Although the CDM was outlined in broad strokes in the 1997 Kyoto Protocol, the practical design of the mechanism was worked out in a protracted set of negotiations, which were not fully concluded until 2003. The rules that emerged partly reflected the early divergent views that had made negotiation over the mechanism so difficult. But they also reflected the difficult and technical challenges of designing and verifying project-based mitigation efforts when only one of the parties faces emission limits.[10]

---

[10]The mechanics of project-based mitigation had been explored prior to Kyoto in a series of national pilot programs known collectively as Activities Implemented Jointly, with mixed results. See Larson and Breustedt (2009) and references therein.

Lecocq and Ambrosi (2007) identify four key areas of conflict that still shape the CDM: (i) tensions over the use of flexibility mechanisms in general; (ii) disagreement over the procedures for creating new credits under the CDM; (iii) tension over how to accommodate the twin objectives of mitigation and development under the CDM; and (iv) controversy over the consequences and permanency of forestry and other land-use projects.[11]

Flexibility Mechanisms

In the lead-up to the Kyoto Protocol, flexibility mechanisms were strongly opposed by several NGOs and some European negotiators, largely on normative grounds. For these groups, developed countries that contributed most to the accumulative of greenhouse gases over time were morally bound to redress the problem by acting within their own borders. Other groups went further, arguing that CDM would be exploitive and erode the authority of developing country governments.[12]

In some cases, opposition to the flexibility mechanism may have been tactical. Negotiators had reached agreement on emission allocations before discussions on the flexibility mechanisms were complete. Consequently, groups already concerned that the aggregate supply of allowances had been set too high, may have chosen to focus on limiting how allowances could be used or new allowances created rather than revisiting the allocation decision.

The value of using CDM offsets and other tradable permits to reduce the cost of mitigation was questioned on positive grounds as well, as some modeling work suggested that low carbon prices would reduce incentives for new innovative technologies and result in long-run welfare losses.[13] The

---

[11]Briefly, the Kyoto Protocol, an international agreement linked to the United Nations Framework Convention on Climate Change, allows the developed and transition countries that have pledged to limit their greenhouse gas emissions (Annex B countries) during the first commitment period (2008–2012) to meet their targets through domestic measures or by acquiring three types of tradable offsets that represent reductions taken abroad. One type of tradable "Kyoto units," Assigned Amount Units, is created when an Annex B country aggregate emissions fall below pledged levels. The other two types, Emission Reduction Units and Certified Emission Reduction credits (CERs) credits are project based and stem from investments in Annex B and non-Annex B countries (countries that have signed the Kyoto Protocol but have not pledged emission limits), respectively.

[12]Harvey and Bush (1997) provide an early discussion of normative issues.

[13]Conceptual and numerical models suggest that this construct holds under special circumstances. Arguments related to the long-term benefits, via induced innovation, of restricting emission trading are discussed in Matschoss and Welsch (2006) and Weber and Neuhoff (2010). See Larson *et al.* (2008) for a review.

basic logic of the argument is that investments made when carbon prices are high are more likely to be associated with innovative technologies that generate positive externalities that, in turn, improve the productivity of other firms. Said differently, advocates maintained that innovation increases as the shadow-price of capital devoted to mitigation increases — at least for a relevant set of carbon prices — and over time, the benefits of improving the productivity of the mitigation function exceed the initially high costs of abatement.

In Kyoto, negotiators divided into separate camps and a coalition led by the EU and Swiss delegations pushed to place quantitative limits on the use of tradable credits. Language emerged in the final draft of the Protocol, stating that the flexibility mechanisms would be "supplemental" to domestic actions, but, with the exception of forestry credits, quantitative restrictions were never imposed in subsequent rounds of rule making (Platjouw, 2009).[14] Nevertheless, national governments have leeway on how the flexibility mechanisms can be used within their borders, and several countries have imposed quantitative restrictions.

In the case of the European Emission Trading Scheme (EU-ETS), the aggregate use of Kyoto units is limited to 13.36% of the 2008–2012 emission allocations; however, national rules vary. For example, Estonia forbids the use of Kyoto units, while Lithuania, Norway, and Spain place a cap at 20% (Larson *et al.*, 2008).[15] Moreover, in addition to general restrictions on CDM offsets, CERs originating from land-use projects are completely excluded from the EU-ETS, which has additional implications for pricing and finance, a topic that we return to later.

Creating New Credits

There was also great skepticism about project-based mitigation (Lecocq and Ambrosi, 2007). A core concern had to do with the idea of using a hypothetical business-as-usual counterfactual scenario to determine the number of credits earned by a particular project. Elements of the counterfactual cannot be observed and the full implications of the project are to a degree speculative, opening the evaluation process to strategic manipulation.

---

[14]See in particular Articles 6, 12, and 17 of the Kyoto Protocol.

[15]Operating since 2005, the EU-ETS mandates an overall limit or cap on carbon emissions that originate from large industrial facilities and electric power generating plants and allows the trading of emission permits under the cap. The program affects firms in the EU's 27 member states, plus Iceland, Liechtenstein, and Norway.

Conceptually, firms that face binding constraints under cap-and-trade or in the form of a carbon tax will undertake mitigation efforts to the degree that the costs are matched by the added revenue associated with additional emissions. Importantly, the firms make their own judgment about the efficacy of capital invested in mitigation. Outside of the cap, a different set of incentives are in place. Firms that fail to take mitigation efforts are not penalized but can be induced to mitigate if it is profitable to do so. Indeed, this is the underlying essence of the CDM, since many low-cost mitigation opportunities are located in countries where greenhouse gas emissions are not regulated.

In this case, a judgment external to the firm must be made about how an investment affects emissions, and this leads to potential problems of information asymmetry. This is because firms both inside and outside of the cap stand to benefit from an exaggerated evaluation of an investment's impact since they can share a larger number of credits. A related difficulty is that new investments often affect emissions and production costs jointly. In this case, the private benefits from the investment (for example, from energy efficiency gains) must be subtracted from the cost of the investment used in the mitigation calculations. This becomes especially complex for projects where host firms face restricted access to capital, since the cost of capital enters into the calculation of economic additionality.[16]

A final difficulty has to do with indirect "leakages," i.e., when a portion of the mitigation gains from a project is lost via general equilibrium effects. This can occur when actions taken by firms in the aggregate influence the set of relevant input and output prices, inducing a change in the behavior of others. As a consequence, a set of unexaggerated mitigation claims can be overvalued in the aggregate when the business-as-usual baseline analysis is performed on a firm-by-firm basis. Burniaux and Martins (2000), Barker *et al.* (2007), and Larson *et al.* (2008) provide reviews of the literature.

Because of the incentives for firms to exaggerate their mitigation claims and the technical challenges of fully accounting for the secondary effects of project investments, negotiators decided that environmental additionality would be tested on a project-by-project basis, rather than at a program level, as some negotiators had proposed. Moreover, the review would be undertaken under the guidance of an independent Executive Board. This

---

[16]These questions have to do with economic additionality, the situation where the mitigation benefits exceed the private benefits of the investment. In so-called win-win projects, this is not the case.

resulted in the current rules whereby the creation of credits requires both an initial approval of the baseline (counter-factual) methodology and monitoring methodology by the Executive Board, and a final certification of ex-post evidence that the mitigation had occurred.

The development objective and bilateral approval

As negotiations proceeded, there were several calls for a mechanism that would provide developing countries with a stream of revenue that could be used to promote mitigation activities. Most notable was the 1997 "Brazilian proposal," which envisioned penalties for countries that exceeded their pledged emission targets to be paid into a clean development fund to support mitigation efforts in non–Annex-I countries (Matsuo, 2003). As the negotiations progressed, the idea of a central fund managed under the UNFCCC gave way to the notion that individual projects would likely benefit developing countries by improving access to capital and by fostering technology transfer. Consequently, it was left to host countries to determine on a case-by-case basis whether an individual project contributed to the host country's development objectives.[17]

The decision resulted in a series of implementation protocols. For a project to go forward, project developers must obtain a letter of approval from the host country government stating that the proposed CDM project activity contributes to sustainable development. Project developers must seek approval from the investor country as well, although it is only the host country that makes a determination of the project's developmental impact. To make this practical, each country designates a responsible agency (known as the designated national authority) to formally certify the project's contribution.

Not all designated authorities are equally efficient, so country-specific differences in transaction costs emerge. Moreover, not all host countries were equally prompt in establishing a designated authority. Both factors have likely influenced the skewed geographic distribution of projects discussed earlier.

Although the potential for the CDM to promote technology transfers motivated the mechanism's late inclusion in the Kyoto Protocol, no formal

---

[17]Though separate from the CDM, special funds such provisions of the Global Environment Facility and the Clean Technology Fund have been established to assist mitigation efforts in developing countries.

mandate merged. Still, some project organizers claim to promote transfers in the documents they present to the Executive Board. Based on an examination of 854 early projects, Haites, Duan, and Seres (2006) found that 81% of projects related to agriculture claim technology transfer. By way of comparison, only 41% of wind-energy projects and 15% of hydro projects in their sample claimed to have transferred technology.

Land Management Projects

Rule-making for sinks and land-use projects proved especially difficult. While most rules for the CDM were in place following conferences in Bonn and Marrakech in 2001, it was not until a final set of rule-making in 2003 that the full set of guidelines for Land Use, Land-Use Change, and Forestry (LULUCF) projects emerged (Lecocq and Abrosi, 2007). The rules that did eventually emerge were cautious and restrictive and placed strict limits on the creation of land-use credits and special restrictions that distinguished land-use credits from the credits produced in other sectors.[18]

As discussed, land-use projects are technically complex since changes made to capture greenhouse gases can initially release carbon into the atmosphere. A full accounting of the type required for most CDM projects involves measuring the net change in carbon stocks for particular sites as well as any related increases in emissions off-site, taking into account above-on-and-below-ground biomass and soil organic carbon. The projects are also long-lived and subject to reversibility because of human activity such as logging or natural events such as forest fires or disease. Consequently, many negotiators held deep reservations about whether the projects would deliver sound and permanent environmental benefits. Added to this was a concern that CDM-market economics would favor projects based on fast-growing industrial plantations, crowding out projects that are community-based and that promote biodiversity (Hunt, 2008; Boyd, 2009).

In particular, current rules permit afforestation and reforestation projects but exclude projects designed to slow deforestation.[19] Moreover, rules limit the total amount of land-use CERs that can be used to meet

---

[18]The fact that rules for LULUCF projects came late penalized this class of projects as well, since it left less time for the project to generate offsets by 2012, the close of the first commitment period.

[19]Reforestation is the restoration of depleted forests, while afforestation is the conversion of other lands to forestlands.

Kyoto obligations during the first commitment period to 5% of their base-year emissions; Bernoux *et al.* (2002) estimate that this limits the market for CDM land-use credits to 11 $MtCO_2e$ for the first commitment period.

To address reversibility, a new set of credits were created with a special set of rules. To start, net removals from the project are certified every five years. Project developers can choose between two types of CERs: long-term CERs (lCERs), which expire at the end of the project's crediting periods, or temporary CERs (tCERs) that expire at the end of the next commitment period. (For example, tCERs issued during the first commitment period would expire at the end of the second commitment period.) If the project performs as planned, new tCERs are issued to replace expiring ones until the end of the project's crediting period. However, Annex B countries that use tCERs during the first commitment period have to replace them during the next commitment period with so-called permanent credits (for example AAUs or CERs from non-LULUCF projects). The same restriction does not apply to the use of lCERs; however, if the accumulated stocks of stored carbon from a projects for which lCERs have been issued declines during the five-year certifications, Annex B countries must replace a proportional share of the lCERs that they used. If a project fails to submit a certification report, all lCERs issued to the project must be replaced.

Consequences for Pricing and Profitability

Built to redress weaknesses related to business-as-usual counterfactuals, features of the CDM project cycle also influence a set of transaction costs that vary among types of projects. Because of this, the overall cost of operating a project under the CDM can be high even when abatement costs are low. This is the case for agricultural land-use projects, where the design of the CDM, the complex biochemistry of soil carbon sequestration, and the frequent need to coordinate the activities of many land-users combine to inflate transactions costs. Moreover, many transaction costs are fixed, and this works against small-scale projects in general, and smallholder and community-based projects in particular (Michaelowa *et al.*, 2003; Skutsch, 2005).

Drawing on Dudek and Wiener (1996) and Cacho, Marshall, and Milne (2005), Cacho and Lipper (2007) provide a topology of transaction costs for soil sequestration projects based on five categories: (i) search and negotiation; (ii) board approval; (iii) project management; (iv) monitoring, and (v) enforcement and insurance. Using this framework, the authors draw on published project reports for smallholder reforestation and afforestation projects to calculate project transaction costs by category. They find disparate results with wide differences among projects across all categories. They report search and negotiation costs ranging from US$22,000 to $160,000; and approval costs from $12,000 to $120,000. Differences in monitoring costs were remarkable, ranging from $5,000 to $270,000.[20]

As discussed, the formal rules associated with implementing the CDM also work to limit demand. For example, limits on how CERs can be used under the EU ETS prevent full arbitrage between the markets and, consequently, CDM credits trade at a discount to their European counter-parts.[21] The restriction spills into formal markets for price discovery and risk management as well; for example, CERs originating from land-use projects are excluded from the European Climate Exchange. Rules that exclude projects from the CDM also shift some projects to voluntary markets where credits trade at a steep discount to credits traded under the European Union ETS (EU ETS) or the CDM. For example while all carbon prices fell dramatically in 2008 as global economic conditions worsened, spot prices for CDM offsets still remained above US$15 tCO_2e for most of 2009. By comparison, the World Bank (2010) estimates that the price for voluntary credits averaged less than US$5 per ton.

In addition, market sentiment disfavoring land-use projects appears to extend beyond the effects of the formal rules. Outside of the CDM, this is revealed in the voluntary markets where offsets from land-use projects sell at a discount to other types of mitigation projects. In their review, Hamilton *et al.* (2010) noted that all of the over-the-counter agricultural soil credits they tracked originated on the Chicago Climate Exchange and, in line with that market, traded for an average price of US$1.20 per ton; forest carbon offsets sold for just under US$3 per ton, and afforestation and reforestation credits sold for just over US$4 per ton, on average.

Evidence of revealed preferences for particular types of projects can be found within formal CDM markets as well, even though all types of tradable Kyoto offset units are notionally equivalent for the purpose of meeting treaty obligations. For example, State and Trends of the Carbon Market (World Bank, 2010) reports that owners of the most desirable renewable

---

[20] The authors found that enforcement and insurance costs were largely unreported.
[21] For example, the EUA-CER price spread ranged between 2–3 Euros during the first 9 months of 2010. (Tendances Carbone, 2010).

energy projects often by pass exchange platforms where no distinction made among CERs by origin in order to retain premiums of roughly 5 Euros per CER. A similar price differentiation occurs via the private branding of CDM projects, as land-use projects are frequently ineligible for some well-known third-party certification programs, including Gold Standard certification (Gold Standard Foundation, 2010.)

Taken together, the restrictions land-use projects face during the CDM cycle, the formal restrictions placed on their use by governments, their disfavor among buyers, and higher transaction costs all work against the economic viability of land-use projects.

ANCILLARY BENEFITS AND SUSTAINABLE RURAL DEVELOPMENT

For many, the limited scope for agricultural land-use projects under the CDM represents a missed opportunity to finance sustainable development. This argument rests on two foundations. The first has to do with the sector composition of current investment flows, already discussed in an earlier section. The notion here is that while the benefits of slowing climate change are especially important to the rural poor, the current composition of projects favor the energy sectors and manufacturing and consequently have little impact on this generation of the rural poor.[22] The second set of arguments, explored in the next section, has to do with the fundamental role played by soil carbon for agriculture and soil fertility management.

Soil Carbon Sequestration and Productivity

Especially in Africa, soil carbon sequestration is closely tied to agricultural productivity and consequently food security and reduced poverty. Vågen, Lal, and Singh (2005) note that soils are degraded on more than 3.5 million km^2 of land in Sub-Saharan Africa and this accounts for roughly 20%–25% of land area. Of this, estimates suggest that 1.1 million km^2 is severely degraded. To make matters worse, Henao and Baanate (2006), reported in Morris *et al.* (2007), estimate that 85% of African farmland suffers soil nutrient losses at a rate of 30 kg per year or greater.[23]

---

[22]See, for example, Sirohi (2007), who looks at the composition of CDM investments in India.
[23]Smaling *et al.* (1993) report even higher levels in Western Kenya.

Especially in remote places, high transport and transaction costs push up the farm-gate price of chemical fertilizers and this encourages farming practices that further degrade the land and discourages the adoption of higher yielding grain varieties.[24] Marshalling payments for the adoption of farming practices that reverse this downward cycle is seen as a strategic way of promoting sustainable agricultural practices (Antle and Diagana, 2003).

Numeric studies suggest that the ancillary productivity benefits of adopting carbon sequestering farming practices that come via higher yields are the dominant source of welfare gains for farmers working degraded soils. This comes about because of a confluence of factors, primarily the price of carbon credits, the price of agricultural output, the sequestration capacity of the soils, and monitoring costs. Using indicative numbers, Graff-Zivin and Lipper (2008) estimated that carbon-market related returns associated with switching from traditional to carbon-sequestering conservation methods ranged from US$0.90 to US$15 per hectare, amounts that are unlikely to motivate changes in farming practices. To emphasize their point, the authors reference a study set in Senegal (FAO, 2004) that estimated the returns from marketable soil carbon credits amounted to less than 4% of household income. In contrast, productivity benefits are often large. This is illustrated in Table 8.9. The table is constructed from a study by Tennigkeit *et al.* (2009) that looks at a stylized carbon sequestration problem for African maize on degraded soils under four farming practices. In all cases, the returns from improved yields exceed the gains from carbon credit sales.

Still, the juxtaposition of large ancillary benefits from adopting soil-sequestering farming methods and the widespread use of farming practices that degrade soils is part of a large puzzle of why farmers in developing countries fail to adopt more profitable and sustainable technologies (Larson and Plessmann, 2009). Hurdles to technology adoption include farmers' limited knowledge about the practices, in combination with poor access to extension services. Limited access to credit can constrain technology adoption as well, since productive practices often require the up-front purchases of more costly seeds and fertilizers that poor farmers are unable to self-finance. Moreover, adopting new technologies can be risky since the higher up-front costs can magnify potential economic losses due to bad weather or poor

---

[24]See Zerfu and Larson (2010) and references therein.

Table 8.9: Carbon soil sequestration and net revenue gain under alternative farming practices.

	No external inputs	Improved seeds	Improved seeds and fertilizer	Agroforestry
Carbon sequestration rate (tCO$_2$e)	0.5	1.0	1.5	4.0
Values ($/ha)				
Annual carbon payments	$1.15	$4.90	$8.65	$27.40
Annual revenues from yield improvements	$34	$225	$450	$225
Total additional revenues	$35	$230	$459	$252
Seed costs	$0	$29	$29	$23
Fertilizer costs	$0	$0	$60	$0
Additional labor costs	$45	$68	$90	$75
Total additional costs	$45	$68	$150	$75
Net revenues	−$10	$162	$309	$177

Note: Carbon is prices at $4.90 per ton CO$_2$e, maize at $0.15/kg.
Source: Tennigkeit *et al.* (2009).

output prices. Consequently, farmers may choose not to adopt improved technologies when formal and informal insurance markets are weak and they are unable to self-insure.

Many of the same hurdles apply to the decision to take up soil carbon sequestering technologies and often additional hurdles as well. Particularly in the case of conservation agriculture, changes in soil management practices lead to a change in the soil ecosystem; indeed, this is the underlying objective. However, during a transition stage in which the soil system move from one equilibrium to another, vulnerabilities associated with weeds or soil-borne pests or pathogens shift, leading to greater uncertainty about yields (Hobbs, 2007; Graff-Zivin and Lipper, 2008). Consequently, the adoption of land-management practices that can improve yields brings the same type of uncertainties that are associated with adopting new seed varieties or other innovative practices.

The limited empirical literature on the adoption of soil fertility management technologies is consistent with the general literature on smallholder technology adoption. In a study based on a survey of smallholder farmers in western Kenya, Marenya and Barrett (2007) report that resource constraints prevent farmers from adequately investing in soil fertility, even when their livelihoods depended crucially on agriculture. Moreover, many farmers in the study who tried using modern management techniques later dropped the practice. Dropout rates were particularly high for agro-forestry soil management techniques. A study by Odendo, Obare, and Salasya (2009), which also uses data from Kenya, also found a negative relationship between resource constraints and investments in soils.

Problems that lead to land degradation in the first place often stand in the way of improved practices as well. Chief among these are tragedy-of-the-commons problems, where unfettered access results in the over-use of land resources through over-grazing or shifting agriculture. The related problem of weak property and tenure rights also discourage sustained investments in soil fertility. In both instances, farmers are not confident that they will be able to claim future productivity gains from current efforts. Potentially, both types of problems can be resolved in a project setting, but compensating for the absence of working formal or informal land institutions adds to the cost of the project and can introduce a high level of risk from coordination failures.[25]

It is also worth mentioning that carbon sequestration can be an ancillary benefit of activities focused on other objectives. This is especially true of group of actions designed to promote agricultural productivity in a sustainable way. For example, the development of farming approaches that conserve soil moisture or soil nutrients can generate costs savings for farmers and deliver sequestration as well. Developing new high-yielding seeds that promote intensification can lead also to positive "leakages" when, in the aggregate, they reduce the conversion of forests to farmland. Moreover, though a sharp distinction is made between mitigation and adaptation under the UNFCCC framework, the distinctions become especially blurred in the case of land use. To continue the example above, the development of soil management technologies that conserve soil moisture and water resources also increase resilience to climate change. This implies an important role for government-supported agricultural research that has resource management and sustainability objectives in mind. A recent World Bank (2010) points to Brazil's efforts in low-fertility Cerrados areas as an example of sponsored research that jointly promotes productivity, adaptation, and mitigation.

---

[25]A counter-example is given in Minten *et al.* (2010), where good extension and well-defined property rights resulted in the adoption of new composting methods by smallholder farmers that improved productivity and soil fertility.

Carbon Sequestration and Other Environmental Services

Though the link between soil carbon sequestration and soil fertility is emphasized, agriculture is associated with a wide range of externalities. As detailed by Lichtenberg (2002), agriculture is also a major contributor to environmental pollution through pesticides, fertilizers, animal wastes, and sediment releases. While simultaneously affecting the environment, agriculture also depends on the environment. Agricultural productivity is enhanced by services provided by the natural environment, such as pollination, water supply, and pest control. Agriculture may reciprocate by contributing to the stability or productivity of the natural environment, such providing support for bird or insect populations.

Daily (1997), cited in Heal and Small (2002: p. 1347) lists the various ecosystem services, most, if not all, of which can be also be attributed to agriculture. Some services are better measured than others and most of them are also interconnected.[26] These ecosystem services can be divided into four somehow different types (MEA, 2005): (i) provisioning services, mainly associated with production of food, fiber, fresh water, and hydropower; (ii) regulating services, mainly associated with affecting environmental conditions that include flow regulation, recharge groundwater basins, water quality regulation, climate regulation, air quality, and carbon sequestration; (iii) cultural services, mainly associated with recreation and ecotourism, aesthetic values, spiritual renewal, and religious and cultural values; and (iv) supporting services, mainly associated with soil formation and fertility, photosynthesis, nutrient cycling, and water cycling.

In some instances, positive externalities associated with farming practices can be used to earn a premium for an associated product — for example, coffee grown in a way that encourages biodiversity. Even so, there can be large disparities between what consumers are willing to pay and the

---

[26]The list includes control of the vast majority of potential agricultural pests; cycling and movement of nutrients; detoxification and decomposition of wastes; dispersal of seeds; generation and preservation of soils and renewal of their fertility; maintenance of biodiversity; mitigation of droughts and floods; moderation of weather extremes and their impacts; pollination of crops and natural vegetation; protection from the sun's harmful ultraviolet rays; protection of coastal shores from erosion by waves; provision of aesthetic beauty and intellectual stimulation that lift the human spirit; purification of air and water; and stabilization of the climate.

notional values of the associated environmental service or the cost of providing it.[27] Efforts have been made to market carbon in a similar way and some third-party certifications focus on processes that safeguard the environmental integrity of the project credits. However, early evidence suggests that labels or certifications are of secondary importance for project credit pricing (Conte and Kotchen, 2009).

As Antle and Capalbo (2002) point out, many important phenomena in agriculture involve the behavior of complex systems whose behavior is affected by the interactions of two or more subsystems. In turn, because ecosystem services are interweaved, policies that address only one particular service or a subset of services may lead to distortive outcomes. Said in a different way, because agriculture is a complex and interactive system, creating an incentive mechanism that pays for only one stream of natural resource services may lead to perverse and unexpected outcomes when the payments affect other services adversely. In the particular context of carbon sequestration, the modification of management practices changes the overall economic profitability of their business as well as the level of externality impact on the natural system (Antle and Capalbo, 2001; Pfaff *et al.* 2000). In some instances, the positive aspects of improving soil carbon complement other environmental services such as the provision of water resources. However, this is not guaranteed.

A generalization of the idea of paying for greenhouse gas mitigation is the idea of paying farmers or communities directly for undertaking a range of activities that safeguard environmental resources. For example, payments for environmental services (PES) have been used for protecting municipal water supplies in Colombia, Mexico, Ecuador and El Salvador (Pagiola, Arcenas, and Platais, 2004). And in the case of Costa Rica, PES programs have been used to encourage carbon sequestration while simultaneously protecting watersheds, biodiversity, and scenic beauty (Wunder, Engel, and Pagiola, 2008).[28] The approach is attractive since conservation outcomes are rewarded directly. Moreover, it also provides a mechanism for harnessing revenue from dispersed beneficiaries to pay for local activities that generate positive externalities, which is itself an underlying motive for the CDM.

A case study of how carbon income incentives affect projects with multiple objectives is given by Nelson and de Jong (2003) and Löbrand,

---

[27] See, for example, the discussion in Moon *et al.* (2002).

[28] See also a comparative analysis pf PES systems by Wunder, Engel, and Pagiola (2008) and a review of PES efforts in Brazil's Amazonia by Hall (2008).

Rindefjäll and Nordqvist (2009); both papers discuss Scolel Té, a land-use agro-forestry sequestration project in Chiapas, Mexico, established under an US-sponsored pilot project and part of the UNFCCC's Activities Implemented Jointly (AIJ) program.[29] The pilot featured a mix of community development and environmental objectives organized around a local trust fund (Fondo Bilclimatico), established in 1997 to broker carbon contracts between farmers and the voluntary carbon market. Under the AIJ, carbon credits were not eligible for credit against future greenhouse gas reduction commitments, but long-lived programs were eligible for conversion under the CDM once it was established. An effort was made in 2002 to assess the project's eligibility for conversion. Although the project currently remains outside of the CDM, Löbrand, Rindefjäll, and Nordqvist (2009) argue that efforts to make the project viable under the CDM have resulted in a shift in emphasis away from the social and environmental objectives toward the provisioning of carbon sequestration.

As discussed, one of the hurdles with carbon sequestration projects has to do with the cost of coordinating actions among a large number of project participants. And one characteristic of PES systems is that they provide a shared mechanism for delivering payments for services. Shared organizational structures can be put to other uses as well. An example is Niger's Community Action plan, designed to organize local government to deliver services that promote development. In this case, the program promotes social protection and the build-up of local infrastructure, in addition to pilot soil conservation and afforestation projects (World Bank, 2010).

PATHS FORWARD

To summarize, there are substantive mitigation opportunities associated with agriculture, and the CDM has proven successful in funneling private capital into certain types of agricultural mitigation projects, primarily projects that convert organic waste products to energy and projects that limit methane emissions. However, large opportunities for mitigation remain related to land use that the CDM in its current form has not tapped. In this section, we look at how the CDM can be improved to partially

---

[29]The AIJ program was a voluntary predecessor of the CDM, established as an umbrella framework for national voluntary mitigation pilot projects. See Larson and Breustedt (2009).

redress current restraints. Even so, because the CDM is not intended to fund ancillary benefits separate from mitigation, it is likely that land-use projects will remain underfunded. We then discuss supplemental or alternative mechanisms, within or outside of the UNFCCC framework.

Modifying the CDM

As discussed, uncertainties about the permanence of agricultural land-use sequestration have resulted in restrictions on how agricultural credits are created and how they are valued in the marketplace. In addition, project characteristics add to the cost of implementing land-use projects, even when underlying abatement costs are low. Still, there are several ways that the current implementation rules can be changed so that they might benefit from the substantial investment flows that the CDM has been able to harness for other sectors.

Perhaps the most promising area has to do with reducing the cost of evaluating and monitoring soil sequestration outcomes. To start, it is worth pointing out that all parties to the UNFCCC have, individually, already settled on or will soon settle on a methodology for calculating the amount of greenhouse gas sequestered by soils or released through changes in land use. This is because all parties to the Convention are expected to declare national greenhouse gas inventories. Moreover, Annex I countries are asked to submit annual inventory reports and have done so since 1996. The reports have economic significance, since the factor in determining the extent to which countries have met their treaty obligations.

Lokupitiya and Paustian (2006) describe the reporting process and review the methods. They conclude that methodologies used currently to account for soil carbon inventories in developing countries are weak, but they attribute this primarily to weak measurement networks and the consequent lack of location-specific activity data, problems that can be remedied through fundamental investments. Ringius (2002) and González-Estrada et al. (2008) report on the benefits and hurdles associated with soil sequestration projects in the context of Sub-Saharan Africa; Soto-Pinto et al. (2010) describe field measurements for mixed land use in Chiapas, Mexico.

Finding reliable ways to calculate the impact of land-use practices on soil carbon sequestration that take into account local agro-climatic differences are also important for developing efficient policies. For example, in a study based in the US, Antle et al. (2003) show that mitigation contracts based on per-ton sequestration incentives are five times more efficient than contracts that pay farmers to adopt soil conservation practices on a per hectare basis.

All of this points to a need for site-specific measures of how agricultural land-use practices affect net greenhouse gas emissions. It also indicates the possibility that methodologies currently employed in developed countries to assess their compliance with pledged emission reductions can be used to quantify the net benefits of agricultural land-use projects in developing countries. To be practical, this would in turn require adjustments in the types of baseline methodologies accepted by the CDM Board. Approaches put forth recently include a household multiple-criteria approach and related bench-marking techniques. A related idea is to allow trading of offsets within sectors. This has appeal, since a land-use offset created under the CDM would be matched with a land-use emission from a regulated market using a common methodology.

A second, somewhat technical point is that there is some scope under current CDM rules for addressing some of the investment hurdles associated with land-use projects. One recognized tool for establishing baselines uses what the CDM Board terms "barrier analysis" (UNEP Risoe, 2005). This step allows the project organizers to identify non-financial barriers that would prevent apparently economically viable investments from taking place outside of the CDM. This class of constraints can include risks associated with the technology, limits to credit, and barriers that result from prevailing practices. First-of-kind projects often benefit from barrier analysis as do projects that are traditionally difficult to finance. Still, barrier analysis tends to be used to address the special circumstances of an individual projects and may not be well suited to broad application as an integral part of frequently used methodologies.

Supplemental and Additional Mechanisms for Investing in Land-use Mitigation Projects

As discussed earlier, the PES systems can be organized to reward multiple objectives, such as the preservation of biodiversity or the safeguarding of water supplies, and several examples of comprehensive systems are given in an earlier section. In this sense, a land-use CDM project can be viewed as a kind of PES system that pays for carbon sequestration, a particular type of environmental service. However, the funding of CDM projects is organized differently, since the Kyoto Protocol creates incentives for private payments. In general, the same is not true for the ancillary services provided by land-use projects, and their financing is left to governments, international organizations, and voluntary organizations. These sources are likely constrained, so land-use projects will be underfunded even if the private sector adequately funds sequestration. Fortunately, there are old and new mechanisms that could be harnessed to better fund agricultural land-use projects.

The first has to do with innovations in carbon funds. While it is difficult to find examples of mechanisms that leverage carbon revenue streams to finance the full set of benefits from land use projects, several funds pursue multiple objectives linked to conservation and the promotion of sustainable agriculture and development. Examples include the BioCarbon Fund, the Community Development Carbon Fund, both managed by the World Bank, and the World Wildlife Fund's conservation-carbon-finance projects.

In addition, multi-donor financing mechanisms have been established in recent years that can be used to supplement land-use mitigation activities. The largest and oldest is the Global Environmental Facility (GEF), a grant-making institution established in 1991 as a pilot project within the World Bank. The institution is now the financing instrument for the UNFCCC, as well as several other environmental conventions. Though the GEF climate program is diffused across capacity building and adaptation programs, there is scope for mitigation activities and, in the case of agriculture, there is overlap with land management efforts designed to slow desertification that are also managed by the GEF.

In 2008, two climate investment funds were established under the auspices of UNFCCC. The Clean Technology Fund is designed to speed up the transfer and deployment of low-carbon technologies in order to slow greenhouse gas emissions. The programs are designed and implemented by countries with assistance from the Regional Development Banks and the World Bank Group. Fourteen country and regional plans were endorsed through 2010, funding US$4.4 billion in programs. Potentially, the fund could be tapped to address land-use mitigation efforts, although that has not yet occurred (World Bank, 2010).

The second fund, the Strategic Climate Fund, funds programs in three areas relevant for agriculture. The first is the Forest Investment Program (FIP), which is intended to support developing countries efforts to stem deforestation and forest degradation. The program is also meant to build-up experience in anticipation of REDD (reduced emissions from deforestation and degradation). The program funds efforts to encourage alternatives to extensive agricultural practices that can drive deforestation. A second pilot program for climate resilience (PPCR) is meant to integrate adaptation efforts into development planning and implementation. However, the program has relevance to out discussion, because some adaptation activities also lead to mitigation outcomes. For example, the Niger program discussed earlier is partially financed by the PPCR (World Bank, 2010). The third window, Scaling up Renewable Energy (SREP), promotes renewable energy projects, including biomass energy pilots in rural areas.

Another potential source of financing is more recent. In the area of mitigation, COPs in Copenhagen and Cancun have focused on voluntary steps that developing countries can take to slow emissions or improve sinks, and on new vehicles to finance those mitigation efforts. As part of that process, developing countries have been asked to submit a list of policies, programs and projects designed to mitigate domestic emissions, which are known as Nationally Appropriate Mitigation Actions (NAMAs). By the close of 2010, 44 countries had signaled their intention to undertake domestic mitigation in some form. In the context of NAMAs, agriculture is a natural area of focus for many of the countries because of the links between land-management, soil fertility, and rural development. For example, in its NAMA, the Government of Ethiopia proposes projects that would add compost to agricultural lands and implement agroforestry projects to improve rural livelihoods and sequester carbon in soils.

A related Green Climate Fund was introduced in Copenhagen and approved in Cancun that might provide direct funding to developing country governments for adaptation and mitigation efforts under NAMAs. Another idea, introduced by the Government of New Zealand, would be to finance NAMAs using tradable credits similar to CERs (Macey, 2009).

CONCLUSIONS

Agricultural activities are an important and ubiquitous part of the on-going build-up of atmospheric greenhouse gases, and they are also an abundant source of low-cost mitigation opportunities in developing countries. Currently, the CDM is the only formal channel by which countries that have pledged to reduce greenhouse gas emissions can invest in credit-earning mitigation projects in developing countries. The CDM has proved successful at mobilizing capital for mitigation projects and is on-track to exceed initial expectations. Still, the sectoral and geographic distribution of projects has been narrow. Moreover, to the degree that model predictions of mitigation potential are a fair gauge, the CDM has not tapped deeply into the reserve of mitigation opportunities.

Within the agricultural sector, the CDM has been an effective conduit for mitigation projects that use residual agricultural organic matter as an alternative fuel source and projects that manage methane from composting and from manure. However, land-use projects that are designed to sequester carbon in soils face special hurdles under current rules. This is significant, since changing how land is used is an inexpensive way to slow the buildup of atmospheric carbon stocks, and because managing soil carbon stocks is important for agricultural productivity, especially in Africa where soils are badly degraded.

At the same time, addressing land-use in a project context is difficult. The projects need to deal with the permanency of the mitigation they achieve in the short run and account for the cascading consequences of altering dynamic soil systems. Moreover, the degradation of lands often arises because of incomplete property rights and common use. As a consequence, reversing this type of degradation faces coordination hurdles, as effective management requires the participation of many stakeholders. What's more, local conditions factor significantly in soil systems, so that the set of parameters used to establish net emission outcomes vary from place to place, making it difficult to replicate successful projects. All of this adds to steeper monitoring, measurement, and implementation costs, making agricultural land-use projects less attractive to investors. Consequently, agricultural land-use projects, and especially soil carbon sequestration projects, are scarce, even in markets outside of the Kyoto Protocol where they face fewer restrictions.

Even so, the consequences of land-use changes are measured as part of the inventory-taking that parties to the UNFCCC are obligated to report. In addition, land-use changes affect carbon markets because they are part of the accounting that determines the demand of developed countries for CDM offsets. As a result, considerable effort has been put into measurement methodologies and these methods could be adapted for agricultural projects under the CDM. To the extent that parties to the UNFCCC are confident in the accuracy of the methodologies and soil information networks are built-up, this opens the door for including agricultural land-use projects under the CDM.

Still, this method may leave investments in soils underfunded. This is because there are largely positive externalities associated with land-use projects. Well thought-out and appropriately funded projects can generate ancillary benefits by protecting habitats and watersheds and by contributing to food security and poverty reduction. Paying for the carbon component alone seldom provides the resources to generate all ancillary benefits. This leaves a role for communities and governments interested in sustainable agricultural development, biodiversity, and other aspects of natural resource stewardship to fund the remaining investment gap.

REFERENCES

Antle, JM and B Diagana (2003). Creating incentives for the adoption of sustainable agricultural practices in developing countries: The role of soil carbon sequestration. *American Journal of Agricultural Economics*, **85**(5), 1178–1184.

Antle, JM and S Capalbo (2002). Agriculture as a managed ecosystem: Policy implications. *Journal of Agricultural and Resource Economics*, **27**(1), 1–15.

Antle, JM, S Capalbo, S Mooney, E Elliott and K Paustian (2003). Spatial heterogeneity, contract design, and the efficiency of carbon sequestration policies for agriculture. *Journal of Environmental Economics and Management*, **46**(2), 231–250.

Barker, T, I Bashmakov, A Alharthi, M Amann, L Cifuentes, J Drexhage, M Duan, O Edenhofer, B Flannery, M Grubb, M Hoogwijk, FI Ibitoye, CJ Jepma, WA Pizer, K Yamaji (2007). Mitigation from a cross-sectoral perspective. In B Metz, OR Davidson, PR Bosch, R Dave and LA Meyer (eds.), *Climate Change 2007: Mitigation. Contribution of Working Group III to the Fourth Assessment Report of the Intergovernmental Panel on Climated Change*. Cambridge and New York: Cambridge University Press.

Bernoux Martial, Vincent Eschenbrenner, Carlos C. Cerri, Jerry M. Melillo, and C Feller (2002). LULUCF-based CDM: Too much ado for a small carbon market. *Climate Policy*, **2**(4), 379–385.

Boyd, E (2009). Governing the clean development mechanism: Global rhetoric versus local realities in carbon sequestration projects. *Environment and Planning A*, **41**(10), 2380–2395.

Burniaux, J-M and JO Martins (2000). Carbon emission leakages: A general equilibrium view. OECD Economics Department Working Papers 242. Paris: Organization for Economic Co-operation and Development.

Cacho, OJ, GR Marshall and M Milne (2005). Transaction and abatement costs of carbon-sink projects in developing countries. *Environment and Development Economics*, **10**(5), 1–18.

Cacho, OJ and L Lipper (2007). Abatement and transaction costs of carbon-sink projects involving smallholders. Fondazione Eni Enrico Mattei Working Paper 32. Milano: Fondazione Eni Enrio Mattei.

CDM Climate Research (2010). Tendances Carbone 51 (October). Arcueil, France.

Conte, MN and MJ Kotchen (2009). Explaining the price of voluntary carbon offsets. NBER Working Paper 15294. Cambridge, MA: National Bureau of Economic Research.

Corbera, E, K Brown and WN Adger (2007). The equity and legitimacy of markets for ecosystem services. *Development and Change*, **38**(4), 587–613.

Daily, GC (ed.) (1997). *Nature's Services: Societal Dependence on Natural Ecosystems*. Washington, DC: Island Press.

Dinar, A, SM Rahman, DF Larson and P Ambrosi. Forthcoming. Act Locally-Affect Globally: International Cooperation in Carbon Abatement Projects. *Global Environmental Politics*.

Dudek, DJ and JB Wienar (1996). Joint implementation, transaction costs, and climate change. Paris: OECD.

FAO (2004). Carbon Sequestration in Dryland Soils. World Soil Resources Report No 102. Rome: Food and Agricultural Organization.

FAO (Food and Agriculture Organization of the United Nations) (2006). FAOSTAT. Available at: http://faostat.fao.org/portals/_Faostat/documents/pdf/world.pdf (accessed on 22 July 2012).

FAO (2010). Global Survey of Agricultural Mitigation Projects. Rome: Food and Agricultural Organization. Also available at: http://www.fao.org/docrep/012/al388e/al388e00.pdf (accessed on 27 October 2010).

Gilbert, N (2011). Summit urged to clean up farming. *Nature*, **479**, 279.

Gold Standard Foundation (2010). The Gold Standard Premium Quality Carbon Credits Requirements. Available at: www.cdmgoldstandard.org. Accessed 8 December 2012.

González-Estrada, E, LC Rodriguez, VK Walen, JB Naab, J Koo, JW Jones, M Herrero and PK Thornton (2008). Carbon sequestration and farm income in West Africa: Identifying best management practices for smallholder agricultural systems in Northern Ghana. *Ecological Economics*, 67(3), 492–502.

Graff-Zivin, J and L Lipper (2008). Poverty, risk, and the supply of soil carbon sequestration. *Environment and Development Economics*, **13**(3), 353–373.

Grubb, M, C Vrolijk and D Grack (1999). *The Kyoto Protocol: A Guide and Assessment*. London: Earthscan/ James and James.

Haites, E, M Duan and S Seres (2006). Technology transfer by CDM projects. *Climate Policy*, **6**(3), 327–344.

Hamilton, K, M Sjardin, M Peters-Stanley and T Marcello (2010). Building bridges: State of the voluntary carbon markets 2010. Ecosystem Marketplace and Bloomberg New Energy Finance. New York and Washington.

Harvey, LDD and E Bush (1997). Joint implementation: An effective strategy for combating global warming? *Environment*, **39**(8), 14–20, 36–44.

Heal, GM and AA Small (2002). Agriculture and ecosystem services. In B Gardner and G Rausser (eds.), *Handbook of Agricultural Economics. Volume 2A. Agriculture and its External Linkages.* Handbooks in Economics, Vol. 18. Amsterdam; London and New York: Elsevier Science, North-Holland.

Henao, J and C Baanante (2006). Agricultural production and soil nutrient mining in Africa: Implications for resource conservation and policy development. IFDC, Muscle Shoals, AL.

Hobbs, PR (2007). Conservation agriculture: What is it and why is it important for future sustainable food production? *Journal of Agricultural Science,* **145**(2), 127–137.

Hunt, C (2008). Economy and ecology of emerging markets and credits for bio-sequestered carbon on private land in tropical Australia. *Ecological Economics,* **66**(2/3), 309–318.

Larson, DF and F Plessmann (2009). Do farmers choose to be inefficient? Evidence from Bicol. *Journal of Development Economics,* **90**(1), 24–32.

Larson, DF, P Ambrosi, A Dinar, SM Rahman and R Entler (2008). A review of carbon market policies and research. *International Review of Environmental and Resource Economics,* **2**(3), 177–236.

Lecocq, F and P Ambrosi (2007). The clean development mechanism: History, status, and prospects. *Review of Environmental Economics and Policy,* **1**(1), 134–151.

Lichtenberg, E (2002). Agriculture and the environment. In BL Gardner and GC Rausser (eds.), *Handbook of Agricultural Economics,* Vol. 2, pp. 1249–1313. Amsterdam: North-Holland.

Lokupitiya, E and K Paustian (2006). Agricultural soil greenhouse gas emissions: A review of national inventory methods. *Journal of Environmental Quality,* **35**, 1413–1427.

Löbrand, E, T Rindefjäll and J Nordqvist (2009). Closing the legitimacy gap in global environmental governance? Lessons from the emerging CDM market. *Global Environmental Politics,* **9**(2), 74–100.

Macey, A (2009). Climate change: Governance challenges for Copenhagen. *Global Governance: A Review of Multilateralism and International Organizations,* **15**(4), 443–449.

Marenya, PP and CB Barrett (2007). Household-level determinants of adoption of improved natural resources management practices among smallholder farmers in western Kenya. *Food Policy,* **32**(4), 515–536.

Matschoss, P and H Welsch (2006). International emissions trading and induced carbon-saving technological change: Effects of restricting the trade in carbon rights. *Environmental and Resource Economics,* **33**(2), 169–198.

Matsuo, N (2003). CDM in the Kyoto negotiations: How CDM has worked as a bridge between developed and developing worlds? *Journal Mitigation and Adaptation Strategies for Global Change,* **8**(3), 1381–2386.

Michaelowa, A, M Stronzik, F Eckermann and A Hunt (2003). Transaction costs of the Kyoto mechanisms. *Climate Policy*, **3**(3), 261–278.

Millenium Ecosystem Assessment (MEA) (2005). Millenium Assessment Reports. Washington DC: Island Press.

Minten, B, P Meral, L Randrianarison and J Swinnen (2010). Trade liberalization, rural poverty and the environment: Two studies of agricultural exports in Madagascar. In J Cook, O Cylke, DF Larson, J Nash and P Stedman-Edwards (eds.), *Vulnerable Places, Vulnerable People: Trade Liberalization, Rural Poverty and the Environment*. Cheltenham, UK, Northhampton, MA: Edward Elagar.

Moon, W, WJ Florkowski, B Brückner and I Schonhof (2002). Willingness to pay for environmental practices: Implications for eco-labeling. *Land Economics*, **78**(1), 88–102.

Morris, M, VA Kelly, RJ Kopicki and D Byerlee (2007). *Fertilizer Use in African Agriculture: Lessons Learned and Good Practice Guidelines*. Washington, DC: World Bank.

Nelson, KC and BHJ de Jong (2003). Making global initiatives local realities: Carbon mitigation projects in Chiapas, Mexico. *Global Environmental Change*, **13**(1), 19–30.

Odendo, M, G Obare and B Salasya (2009). Factors responsible for differences in uptake of integrated soil fertility management practices amongst smallholders in western Kenya. *African Journal of Agricultural Research*, **4**(11), 1303–1311.

Pagiola, S, A Arcenas and G Platais (2004). Can payments for environmental services help reduce poverty? An exploration of the issues and the evidence to date from Latin America. *World Development*, **33**(2), 237–253.

Paustian, K, BA Babcock, J Hatfield, R Lal, BA McCarl, S McLaughlin, A Mosier, C Rice, GP Robertson, NJ Rosenberg, C Rosenzweig, WH Schlesinger and D Zilberman (2004). Agricultural mitigation of greenhouse gases: Science and policy options. CAST (Council on Agricultural Science and Technology) Report, R141 2004, ISBN 1-887383-26-3.

Pfaff, ASP, S Kerr, RF Hughes, S Liu, GA Sanchez-Azofeifa, D Schimel, J Tosi and V Watson (2000). The Kyoto protocol and payments for tropical forest: An interdisciplinary method for estimating carbon-offset supply and increasing the feasibility of a carbon market under the CDM. *Ecological Economics*, **35**(2), 203–221.

Platjouw, FM (2009). Reducing greenhouse gas emissions at home or abroad? The implications of Kyoto's supplementarity requirement for the present and future climate change regime. *Review of European Community and International Environmental Law*, **18**(3), 244–256.

Rahman, SM, A Dinar and DF Larson (2010). Diffusion of Kyoto's clean development mechanism. *Technological Forecasting and Social Change*, **77**(8), 1391–1400.

Ringius, L (2002). Soil carbon sequestration and the CDM: Opportunities and challenges for Africa. *Climatic Change*, **54**(4), 471–495.

Sirohi, S (2007). CDM: Is it a win–win strategy for rural poverty alleviation in India? *Climatic Change*, **84**(1), 91–110.

Skutsch, MM (2005). Reducing carbon transaction costs in community-based forest management. *Climate Policy*, **5**(4), 433–443.

Smaling EMA, JJ Stoorvogel and PN Windmeijer (1993). Calculating soil nutrient balances in Africa at different scales nutrient cycling in agroecosystems, **35**(3), 237–250.

Smith, P, D Martino, Z Cai, D Gwary, H Janzen, P Kumar, B McCarl, S Ogle, F O'Mara, C Rice, B Scholes and O Sirotenko (2007). Agriculture. In B Metz, OR Davidson, PR Bosch, R Dave and LA Meyer (eds.), *Climate Change 2007. Mitigation. Contribution of Working Group III to the Fourth Assessment Report of the Intergovernmental Panel on Climate Change*. United Kingdom and New York, NY, USA: Cambridge University Press, Cambridge.

Smith, P, D Martino, Z Cai, D Gwary, H Janzen, P Kumar, B McCarl, S Ogle, F O'Mara, C Rice, B Scholes, O Sirotenko, M Howden, T McAllister, G Pan, V Romanenkov, U Schneider, S Towprayoon, M Wattenbach and J Smith (2008). Greenhouse gas mitigation in agriculture. *Philosophical Transactions of the Royal Society B: Biological Sciences*, **363**, 789–813.

Soto-Pinto, L, M Anzueto, J Mendoza, GJ Ferrer and B de Jong (2010). Carbon sequestration through agroforestry in indigenous communities of Chipas, Mexico. *Agroforest Systems*, **78**(1), 39–51.

Tennigkeit, T, F Kahrl, J Wölcke and K Newcombe (2009). Agricultural carbon sequestration in Sub-Saharan Africa: Economics and institutions. Washington, DC: World Bank.

United Nations Risoe Center (2005). *Baseline Methodologies for Clean Development Mechanism Projects: A Guidebook*. Roskilde, Denmark: UNEP Risoe Centre on Energy, Climate and Sustainable Development.

US-CIA (2011). CIA World Factbook. Available at: http://cia.gov/library/publications/the-world-factbook/goes/xx.html (accessed on 22 July 2012).

US-EPA (2002). Projected greenhouse gas emissions. *US Climate Action Report 2002*, Chap. 5, pp. 70–80. Washington: DC: Environmental Protection Agency.

Vågen, T-G, R Lal and BR Singh (2005). Soil carbon sequestration in Sub-Saharan Africa: A review. *Land Degradation and Development*, **16**(1), 53–71.

Weber ,TA and K Neuhoff (2010). Carbon markets and technological innovation. *Journal of Environmental Economics and Management*, **60**(2), 115–132.

Werksman, J (1998). The clean development mechanism: Unwrapping the Kyoto surprise. *Review of European Community & International Environmental Law*, **7**, 147–158.

World Bank (2010). *State and Trend of Carbon Markets 2010*. Washington, DC: World Bank.

World Bank (2010). The Hague conference on agriculture, food security and climate change, opportunities and challenges for a converging agenda: Country examples. Washington, DC: World Bank.

Wunder, S, S Engel and S Pagiola (2008). Taking stock: A comparative analysis of payments for environmental services programs in developed and developing countries. *Ecological Economics*, **65**(4), 834–852.

Zerfu, D and DF Larson (2010). Incomplete markets and fertilizer use: Evidence from Ethiopia. World Bank Policy Research Working Paper 5325. Washington, DC: World Bank.

ANNEXE

Table 8.1A: Number of CDM projects hosted by country and share of total.

Host country	Number of projects			Share of global total		
	All Sectors	Agriculture	Forest	All Sectors	Agriculture	Forest
China	2,316	119	4	0.398	0.123	0.069
India	1,549	326	9	0.266	0.338	0.155
Brazil	365	137	2	0.063	0.142	0.034
Mexico	176	104	0	0.030	0.108	0.000
Malaysia	136	77	0	0.023	0.080	0.000
Vietnam	129	4	1	0.022	0.004	0.017
Thailand	126	27	0	0.022	0.028	0.000
Indonesia	114	33	1	0.020	0.034	0.017
South Korea	85	0	0	0.015	0.000	0.000
Chile	77	8	3	0.013	0.008	0.052
Philippines	76	53	0	0.013	0.055	0.000
Colombia	68	5	6	0.012	0.005	0.103
Peru	40	2	1	0.007	0.002	0.017
South Africa	39	2	0	0.007	0.002	0.000
Argentina	38	3	1	0.007	0.003	0.017
Israel	33	5	0	0.006	0.005	0.000
Honduras	31	7	0	0.005	0.007	0.000
Pakistan	25	3	0	0.004	0.003	0.000
Ecuador	23	5	0	0.004	0.005	0.000
Sri Lanka	21	5	0	0.004	0.005	0.000
Guatemala	19	1	0	0.003	0.001	0.000
Panama	19	1	0	0.003	0.001	0.000
Kenya	18	3	8	0.003	0.003	0.138
Egypt	16	0	0	0.003	0.000	0.000

(*Continued*)

Table 8.1A: (*Continued*)

Host country	Number of projects			Share of global total		
	All Sectors	Agriculture	Forest	All Sectors	Agriculture	Forest
Morocco	16	3	0	0.003	0.003	0.000
Uzbekistan	15	0	0	0.003	0.000	0.000
Uganda	13	1	6	0.002	0.001	0.103
Uruguay	13	3	1	0.002	0.003	0.017
Armenia	12	1	0	0.002	0.001	0.000
Nigeria	10	0	0	0.002	0.000	0.000
Costa Rica	10	2	1	0.002	0.002	0.017
Dominican Republic	10	2	0	0.002	0.002	0.000
Cyprus	10	4	0	0.002	0.004	0.000
Moldova	9	0	2	0.002	0.000	0.034
Iran	9	0	0	0.002	0.000	0.000
United Arab Emirates	9	1	0	0.002	0.001	0.000
Nicaragua	8	1	1	0.001	0.001	0.017
Georgia	7	0	0	0.001	0.000	0.000
Cambodia	7	2	0	0.001	0.002	0.000
Tanzania	6	0	1	0.001	0.000	0.017
Azerbaijan	6	0	0	0.001	0.000	0.000
Papua New Guinea	6	0	0	0.001	0.000	0.000
Bolivia	6	1	2	0.001	0.001	0.034
El Salvador	6	2	0	0.001	0.002	0.000
Nepal	6	4	0	0.001	0.004	0.000
Congo DR	5	0	2	0.001	0.000	0.034
Jordan	5	0	0	0.001	0.000	0.000
Singapore	5	2	0	0.001	0.002	0.000
Paraguay	4	0	1	0.001	0.000	0.017
Bangladesh	4	0	0	0.001	0.000	0.000
Cameroon	4	0	0	0.001	0.000	0.000
Mongolia	4	0	0	0.001	0.000	0.000
Rwanda	4	0	0	0.001	0.000	0.000
Syria	4	0	0	0.001	0.000	0.000
Tunisia	4	0	0	0.001	0.000	0.000
Lao PDR	4	1	1	0.001	0.001	0.017
Albania	3	0	1	0.001	0.000	0.017
Bhutan	3	0	0	0.001	0.000	0.000
Cuba	3	0	0	0.001	0.000	0.000

(*Continued*)

Table 8.1A: (*Continued*)

Host country	Number of projects			Share of global total		
	All Sectors	Agriculture	Forest	All Sectors	Agriculture	Forest
Côte d'Ivoire	3	0	0	0.001	0.000	0.000
Macedonia	3	0	0	0.001	0.000	0.000
Senegal	3	2	0	0.001	0.002	0.000
Madagascar	2	0	1	0.000	0.000	0.017
Fiji	2	0	0	0.000	0.000	0.000
Mauritius	2	0	0	0.000	0.000	0.000
Qatar	2	0	0	0.000	0.000	0.000
Sudan	2	0	0	0.000	0.000	0.000
Ethiopia	1	0	1	0.000	0.000	0.017
Ghana	1	0	1	0.000	0.000	0.017
Bahamas	1	0	0	0.000	0.000	0.000
Cape Verde	1	0	0	0.000	0.000	0.000
Jamaica	1	0	0	0.000	0.000	0.000
Lebanon	1	0	0	0.000	0.000	0.000
Lesotho	1	0	0	0.000	0.000	0.000
Liberia	1	0	0	0.000	0.000	0.000
Mali	1	0	0	0.000	0.000	0.000
Malta	1	0	0	0.000	0.000	0.000
Saudi Arabia	1	0	0	0.000	0.000	0.000
Serbia	1	0	0	0.000	0.000	0.000
Yemen	1	0	0	0.000	0.000	0.000
Zambia	1	0	0	0.000	0.000	0.000
Guyana	1	1	0	0.000	0.001	0.000

Source: Risoe (2010) and authors' calculations.

9. CONCLUSION

The Clean Development Mechanism (CDM) was created to sequester or reduce greenhouse gas emissions, but in a particular way. Because the task was large relative to the resources of governments, both the JI and the CDM, in conjunction with allowance trading, were designed to motivate private capital flows to drive down the cost of meeting emission reduction targets pledged under the Kyoto Protocol. Of the two, the CDM was to induce investments among the poorest countries, and as a result, CDM investments were also meant to spur development, especially by speeding the transfer of new technologies.

As discussed in Chapter 1, the genesis of the CDM is linked with the notion that all countries are not equally responsible for the historical accumulation of greenhouse gases in the atmosphere, and that many low-cost mitigation opportunities resided in low-income countries. Still, while these points were generally accepted by negotiators of the Kyoto Protocol, there was less agreement about whether the mitigation efforts could or should be hosted in developing countries. And, as discussed in Chapter 2, when the CDM did emerge during eleventh-hour negotiations, it was met with surprise and suspicion. Moreover, despite the number of countries and private firms that participate in the mechanism and the scale of public and private resources raised by program incentives, distrust among some stakeholders is an enduring feature of the CDM. For many reasons, the CDM is likely the least loved of the flexibility mechanisms.

In this concluding chapter, we first review key findings from the chapters and then return to the arguments and evidence to assess how well the mechanism has performed relative to what it was meant to do. To the extent possible, we try to avoid normative evaluations and focus on the tasks to which the CDM was assigned.

AIJ AS A MODEL

Analyses of national AIJ pilot programs describe approval processes that allowed general national policy objectives to influence project investment outcomes. The findings are consistent with this characterization and suggest more specifically that AIJ investments were partly determined by the same factors that determined bilateral aid projects. Quantitative evidence supporting this conclusion is robust and holds up under a series of alternative specifications. Another key finding regarding AIJ is that the cost-reducing benefits of the project-based components of Kyoto's flexibility mechanisms may be less than what empirical studies predict. This is because the numeric models that provide the best guidance on how alternative policies might affect the implementation costs do not take into account either regulatory or private bilateral transaction costs that were important during the AIJ pilots and that may be important currently. From a methodological point of view, the results suggest that taking bilateral relationships into account might allow numeric models to better predict cost savings and the geographic distribution of project investment under the Kyoto Protocol investment mechanisms.

The findings suggest also that national investor-country policy goals did not exclusively drive the AIJ investment process, leaving room for host countries to influence outcomes by implementing specific policies. By implication, countries that implement policies that generally support investment and build specific institutions needed to facilitate Kyoto-related markets will likely see greater investment flows under the Protocol's Joint Implementation (JI) and CDM.

ABATEMENT COSTS VIA CDM

Several conclusions apply to the nature and structure of the cost of abatement: CDM projects were found to be characterized with constant to increasing returns to scale, except in China. Longer-duration projects also translated into higher costs, although costs did not increase proportionately. Costs of mitigation through HFCs, PFCs, and N_2O reduction; fossil fuel switch; and methane avoidance projects are much lower than those of afforestation and reforestation, transportation, demand- and supply-side energy efficiency, and renewable-resource–based projects. Mitigation costs are lower for the later projects in the pipeline, exhibiting the learning process. The cost of mitigation through CDM projects in Latin and North American developing countries are lower relative to Asian developing countries. Finally, results indicate that the largest CDM host country, China, has a comparative advantage in smaller-scale but longer-duration CDM projects relative to the second and third largest hosts, India and Brazil, respectively. Projects that are first certified for seven years have the potential for renewal while this is not the case for longer-duration projects. While the CDM projects in China are characterized by diseconomies of scale and economies of time, the average size of the projects in this country has decreased over time, with the average duration remaining the same. Increased number of relatively longer-duration (10-year as opposed to 7-year) projects in China in recent years may reflect a shifting view of the value and prospects for project renewal post-2012. In contrast, a majority of the projects in India have a longer duration (10 years), perhaps reflecting a relative degree of risk tolerance of the investors in these two countries. Note that about 90% of the projects in China are multilateral (with foreign investors) while more than 82% of the projects in India are unilateral (with domestic investors only).

The average and marginal costs of abatement are substantially higher for the CDM projects that start receiving emission reduction credits after the first commitment period. This reflects the uncertainty of the Kyoto provisions beyond the first commitment period. While non-decreasing costs of abatement over time implies a tougher prospect for the CDM in future commitment periods, we are still observing a rapid growth in the number of projects and the volume of investment in CDM projects suggesting the contrary — that this provision of the Kyoto Protocol is still highly attractive for the host and investor countries, relative to other options. Further, despite higher average and marginal costs of abatement than that of the Latin and North American developing countries, about two-thirds of the projects in the pipeline are located in Asian developing countries.

Looking beyond 2012, there is a need to better understand components other than cost which drive CDM investment. An underlying principle of most studies about the consequences of Kyoto's flexibility mechanisms is that investors will seek out low-cost abatement opportunities to lower the cost of meeting the mitigation objectives of the Protocol. Finding differences in abatement costs among CDM projects is consistent with other studies showing large productivity differences in firms and farms. However, theory supported by empirical evidence suggests that such differences fade among firms engaging in trade.

Finally, it is worth considering whether additional incentives are needed to take advantage of projects that generate significant co-benefits. Our results suggest that, all things equal, transport projects and land-use sequestration projects in forestry or agriculture are expensive when compared to projects in other sectors. In general, these projects are also associated with significant co-benefits not directly related to climate change. Consequently, policies motivated by carbon prices alone will lead to an under-investment in these projects since only the carbon-abatement components of the projects generate revenue.

DIFFUSION OF THE CDM

The CDM is the only formal way developed countries can access mitigation opportunities in developing countries to meet their commitments under the Kyoto Protocol. Concerns have been raised on whether the constraints stemming from the design of the CDM will drive up the cost of meeting Kyoto's environmental goals.

Rates of adoption suggest that participation in the CDM was consistent with the diffusion patterns associated with new technologies. And halfway through the first crediting period, the CDM was on track to deliver an average annual flow of roughly 700 million tCO_2e in reductions and sequestrations by 2012, exceeding the most optimistic early model predictions by roughly 30%.

From a policy perspective, the results suggest that the CDM has been, in one sense, extremely successful in achieving significant levels of mitigation by motivating private capital flows. However, the skewed sector composition of CDM projects also suggests that the CDM alone may not be up to the task of fully exploiting known and economically viable opportunities for mitigation. This suggests great scope for finding additional ways of investing in the mitigation potential of developing countries.

ADOPTION DETERMINANTS

The main findings regarding adoption of CDM suggest that the rate of CDM adoption by both developing and industrialized countries increases over time in an increasing and then decreasing way as we get closer to the completion of the first commitment period. In addition, we found major differences in the set of variables affecting adoption in host and investor countries. An important finding is that the incidence, extent, and rate of CDM adoption are higher for the developing countries with relatively lower per capita income, which indicates at least a partial fulfillment of the development objective of the mechanism.

The result that the level of engagement in CDM is higher for relatively more industrialized developing countries also implies that the extent of CDM is higher for the countries with higher level of emissions. However, our results do not confirm the finding in recent work that economies with higher carbon intensity (carbon emissions per unit of GDP) had greater CER production. The result that the level of engagement in CDM activities is lower for the countries that are more vulnerable to climate change impacts is consistent with the finding in Chapter 7, which analyzes the case of cooperation in CDM between host and investor countries.

CDM AS A COOPERATION MECHANISM

Several conclusions regarding enhancement of CDM cooperation apply. The general conclusion is that any type of active relations among the countries in host–investor dyads would lead to higher likelihood of cooperation in CDM projects. Similarly, colonial ties and previous contiguity length are a major factor explaining CDM cooperation. While it is quite reasonable to accept such results, conclusions could be far reaching. Colonial ties may reflect better cultural exchanges that allow firms to feel to work together more efficiently. It also could be that infrastructure and existing institutions are more familiar and make cooperation more comfortable. In turn, this is expected to reduce transaction costs among countries with shared cultural heritages.

The level of development of the country is an important factor in promoting cooperation. Another variable that has similar impact in other studies of international cooperation is the level of governance in the countries. It is frequently suggested that governance matters and institutional strength is a prerequisite for better performance, both domestic and international. A similar interpretation can be attributed to the variable measuring the ease of doing business. Our results suggest that the situation in the investor country does not matter. What matters is the level of ease of doing business in the host country, which attracts domestic and international investors. It is quite straightforward but needed empirical proof. Studies on FDI demand and supply identify ease of doing business in the investor (source) country to be negatively correlated with FDI supply. All other variables measure natural endowment of a country and thus, may be less affected by policy interventions.

The policy discussion would therefore, be focused only on the suggestion that international development institutions focus mainly on the strengthening of multilateral interactions between countries and on domestic structural changes and reforms of economies, so that they are better prepared not only to adapt to climate change but also to cooperate in the CDM market and take advantage of the CDM dividend — development — that results from CDM joint investment. The analysis shows that three factors, namely better business environment, higher level of governance, and stronger international trade relation, have positive impacts, increasing the future viability of the CDM. Thus, there is scope for both state-level and international-level policy interventions in these three factors, which governments and international development institutions have already identified as important directions for their future commitment.

WHY SO FEW AGRICULTURAL PROJECTS?

Recent estimates by the IPCC suggest that a significant portion of the mitigation opportunities in developing countries are in agriculture, forestry, and improving building efficiency. But so far, project investments under the CDM leave these broad areas of potential untouched. So, how could the CDM address this void? Since the oversight of agricultural investments is generic, it could be that CDM shall be adjusted.

Uncertainties about the permanence of agricultural land-use sequestration have resulted in restrictions on how agricultural credits are created and how they are valued in the marketplace. In addition, project characteristics add to the cost of implementing land-use projects, even when underlying abatement costs are low. Still, there are several ways that the current implementation rules can be changed so that they might benefit from the substantial investment flows that the CDM has been able to harness for other sectors. Perhaps the most promising area has to do with reducing the cost of evaluating and monitoring soil sequestration outcomes. Finding reliable ways to calculate the impact of land-use practices on soil carbon sequestration that take into account local agro-climatic differences are also important for developing efficient policies.

The need for site-specific measures of how agricultural land-use practices affect net greenhouse gas emissions indicates the possibility that methodologies currently employed in developed countries to assess their compliance with pledged emission reductions can be used to quantify the net benefits of agricultural land-use projects in developing countries. Approaches put forth recently include a household multiple-criteria approach and related bench-marking techniques. A related idea is to allow trading of offsets within sectors. This has appeal, since a land-use offset created under the CDM would be matched with a land-use emission from a regulated market using a common methodology.

A second, somewhat technical point is that there is some scope under current CDM rules for addressing some of the investment hurdles associated with land-use projects. One recognized tool for establishing baselines uses what the CDM Board terms "barrier analysis." This class of constraints can include risks associated with the technology, limits to credit, and barriers that result from prevailing practices. First-of-kind projects often benefit from barrier analysis as do projects that are traditionally difficult to finance. Still, barrier analysis tends to be used to address the special circumstances of an individual projects and may not be well suited to broad application as an integral part of frequently used methodologies.

THE DEBATE ON CDM PERFORMANCE COMPARED TO ITS ORIGINAL OBJECTIVES

Many have criticized the CDM for not meeting its dual goals. While we do not intend to confront the various arguments used in the literature, the results of the analysis in this book can help taking side in the debate.

The Mitigation Impact of the CDM

As discussed in earlier chapters, the twin project-based components were novel instruments when introduced as components of the Kyoto Protocol's flexibility mechanisms. Caps and tradable allowances were features of earlier programs to manage natural resources and limit atmospheric emissions but these were closed systems that included a specific set of firms that would profit by innovating or investing in reducing their own emission and thereby freeing for sale a fixed number of allowances. In the case of JI and CDM, allowances could be created as well. Under the open systems, reductions were not measured against history, but relative to a constructed counter-factual. This in turn introduced an additional type of moral hazard since both producers and buyers of project credits faced incentives to exaggerate mitigation claims, thereby potentially eroding the environmental benefits of the Protocol. In the case of JI, the allowances still circulated within an otherwise closed set of countries that had collectively pledged to limit their greenhouse gas emissions; however, the CDM opened the allowance system to countries and firms that did not face domestic limits.

Notionally, the projects already in the CDM project cycle will generate significant levels of mitigation. As of August 2012, Risoe (2012) listed over 8,800 projects that were expected to generate 1,234 million tons of reductions and sequestrations annually. This is roughly equivalent to Japan's emissions in 2008, the world's fifth largest emitter of greenhouse gases at that time. The pipeline is expected to generate cumulative totals of 2,613 MT by the end of 2012 and 11,887 MT by the end of 2020. As discussed in Chapter 5, this exceeds the projections of most analysts when the CDM was launched.

Still, there are three types of uncertainties surrounding these projections. The first is has to do with potential problems as the projects reach the certification stage of the project cycle. Methodological and measurement problems might arise that were not recognized in ex ante reviews presented to the CDM Board. In late 2012, only 19% of the projects had issued CERs, although the projects themselves were relatively large and generated nearly 974,000 CERs, about 37% of the 2012 expected levels. Certification lags mitigation, and there is the possibility that many or most of the projects that have not issued CERs have generated mitigation benefits. Nonetheless, the late delivery of CERs by so many projects raises doubts about their ultimate ability to meet projections.

A second uncertainty has to do with levels of performance even when there are not technical issues related to baseline performance indicators. Many of the projects are linked to the demand for co-produced outputs. As discussed in Chapter 4, a large number of investments increased the power generation capacity of firms, and the mitigation impact of the projects is directly linked to whether or not the increased capacity is utilized. Similarly, as discussed in Chapter 8, projects are linked to agricultural or forestry by-products and rely ultimately on the demand for those products. Slow economic activity since 2008 has likely affected project performance as well.

And finally, there is the fundamental concern about weaknesses in the project cycle's environmental safeguards, which would imply that simply counting CERs overstates the mechanism's environmental impact. Though the projects and their direct consequences are given close scrutiny, some types of projects may generate second-order effects (leakages) that partially offset environmental gains suggested by the baseline analysis against which CERs are issued. Their aggregate effect is hard to know with certainty. This is especially true for induced behaviors since firms have direct interests in protecting streams of income linked to specific baselines that are themselves tied to environmentally harmful activities, especially those related to the destruction of highly potent greenhouse gases. Cap-and-trade systems can be used to potentially detach "pollution rights" from production in a way that is difficult under the current structure of the Kyoto Protocol. Not all types of projects elicit the same level of concern about leakages, so even subjective evaluations of the environmental performance of the CDM are tied to the first two performance concerns. For example, over 42% of the CERs issued by August 2012 are from a handful of controversial HFC destruction projects, even though CERs from this type of project is expected to ultimately account for about 9% by 2020.

So did the CDM succeed in its existential purpose of mitigating climate change? On balance it seems likely. Many of the projects are long lived — about 31% will generate CERs for 10 years or more — and will continue to generate benefits beyond the first accounting period. In addition, the life of the underlying investments, for example, a run-of-river hydro plant, can exceed the CDM project life and may continue to displace greenhouse gas emissions beyond the time the project is eligible for crediting. Leakages and perverse incentives detract from the CDM's environmental benefits, although it is hard to judge their significance. And it is doubtless that rule changes could be incorporated to improve the environmental performance of the CDM by limiting the worse examples of perverse incentives.

From a policy perspective, practical choices among the alternative instruments are limited by political realities, and the performance of each instrument is also shaped by the same forces, albeit in possibly different ways. Chapters 2 and 8 illustrate this in the case of the CDM. Consequently, the environmental performance of the CDM should be compared to the performance of alternative instruments, for example carbon taxes or cap-and-trade systems, which have their own weaknesses when applied.

Stimulate Capital Flows

As discussed in Chapter 2, researchers and stakeholders soon established that increased government expenditures would not by themselves substantially slow greenhouse gas emissions. This in turn motivated early negotiators of the Kyoto Protocol to introduce trading systems that would price greenhouse gas emissions and provide incentives for private investments. The decision was also taken to include CDM projects and credits.

In this area, the CDM has performed well in absolute terms. Keeping in mind that annual FDI flows to developing countries were about US$354 billion in 2009 (MIGA, 2010),[1] US$ 210 billion between 2004 and the first eight months of 2012 for projects in which the investment levels were known (Risoe, 2012). Still, the flow of investments by country has been remarkably skewed. Among tracked projects, about 82% of capital went to Asia, with most going to China and India. The poorest countries attracted less than 2% of the investments.

Did the CDM Tap the Lowest Cost Abatement Opportunities?

As discussed in Chapter 2, an important objective of the IPCC reports was to indicate low-cost mitigation opportunities by industry as well as by geographic location. In general, the sectors and countries indicated as low-cost sources were not those which attracted the most projects. As discussed in Chapter 8, soil carbon sequestration related to land and forestry practices were identified as potentially important areas for investment, but these sectors were limited due to baseline and measurement challenges and associated restrictions that emerged as implementing rules were written. This likely limited some investments in Latin America and Eastern Europe, where the opportunities for soil restoration and forestry projects are significant.

Even after taking these restrictions into account, analysis presented in Chapter 4 suggests that the direct investment costs of generating CERs did not seem to drive investments in terms of technology or host. The finding is consistent with the inferred presence of significant transaction costs. Chapter 7 finds that the pairing of host- and investor-country can be explained in part by cultural and economic ties that are likely to reduce unobservable transaction costs as well. Chapter 3 suggests this was also the case under the voluntary AIJ programs that preceded the CDM.

As Chapter 2 explains, implementation rules associated with the CDM project cycle and national programs also introduced their own sets of

---

[1] World Bank, MIGA (2011).

transaction costs, and an unanswered question is whether the mismatch between the set of activities the IPCC reports signal as low-cost and the projects which received financing under the CDM are driven primarily by CDM rules. A related question is whether rules could be modified that would reduce transaction costs without further eroding the environmental integrity of the investment.

As discussed in Chapter 8, rule modifications can be made that might lower transaction costs and spur investment in the particular case of land-use projects, but alternative instruments — including host-country–based mitigation plans — might have advantages. This may well be the case for other sectors and hosts less well served by the CDM.

Technology Transfer

A key objective of the CDM was to promote technology transfer. Among Parties to the UNFCCC, there was a view that the rates of transfer were low and additional programs intended to promote technology transfer were introduced subsequent to the Kyoto Protocol and third-party have established guidelines based in part on judgments about types of technologies employed (Chapter 2).

To a degree, any implemented CDM project employs an advanced technology in the sense that the production or sequestration method differs from baseline business-as-usual practices. It is also unclear how technology preferences are reconciled with other potentially important positive externalities (co-benefits) such as improved soil productivity or better health. However, within the broader climate change community, technologies like renewable energy appear to be favored. Moreover, there is price evidence from both voluntary and Kyoto-credit markets that would seem to bear this out (Larson, Dinar, and Frisbie, 2011).

Turning to the types of technologies most prevalent under the CDM, wind power projects and hydro projects (mostly employing run-of-the-river techniques) are both featured prominently, comprising 28% and 26% of the projects by number, respectively (Risoe, 2012).

Promote Development

As Chapter 1 points out, promoting development is an explicit objective of the CDM; however, while the process for establishing and certifying mitigation benefits are carefully defined, it is left to host countries to evaluate whether or not a given project contributes to development goals. This is an important and appropriate rule, since it allows host countries to decide on a case-by-case basis whether a project is in their best interests, but it leaves much room for differences of opinion based on objective measures. It is beyond the scope of this volume to provide a definitive answer; however, it is possible to reframe some of the previous conclusions in terms of a key development objective: whether or not the poor benefited directly or indirectly.

A large number of studies suggest that the cost of climate change adaptation will fall most heavily on the poor (Dinar *et al.*, 2008; Mendelsohn and Dinar, 2009), so they are likely to benefit most by the real mitigation benefits that the CDM generates. The links between mitigation, climate change, and the distribution of adaptation costs are difficult to quantify; on balance it seems likely that the CDM generated tangible benefits. Conceptually, these are benefits that would have been generated elsewhere, since the credits are created to be used by industrial countries to meet pledged reductions. But some countries are likely to miss their targets at the end of the first accountant period, so in practice it is likely that, absent the CDM, the total net emissions would have been higher. Moreover, as mentioned earlier, the projects themselves may generate mitigation benefits beyond their crediting life, yielding greater cumulative effects.

Another potential channel for development is the significant investment flow under the CDM. In general, foreign direct investments are expected to relieve capital constraints and spur grow, which can benefit the poor. CDM investments are different, in that they are meant to influence the way goods and services are produced without, in theory, influencing what is produced. Usually this is done by financing a switch in the energy component of production — for example, producing electricity using agricultural residuals rather than diesel fuel. Consequently, CDM investments are less likely. In some instances, the fuel switch can generate significant co-benefits by reducing air pollution and improving health. And land-use projects can generate additional benefits in the form of improved watersheds and by sustaining soil productivity.

Each CDM project is an example of how things can be done in a way that reduces net greenhouse gas emissions, a special type of knowledge transfer. Some countries that did not pledge reductions under Kyoto have done so and others may decide to more actively pursue mitigation efforts. This is driven in part by an expanding European Union, but there are financial incentives for countries to devise and implement national mitigation plans. Should this occur, the body of knowledge built up under the CDM and the AIJ program before it will prove invaluable.

FINAL REMARKS

The CDM was "Kyoto's Surprise" and it still surprises many both in its unexpected success and difficulties. We were surprised in some of the results that indicate performance of CDM over and above the planned delivery of CERs, the cost of abatement via CDM, and the high level of cooperation in CDM projects.

There are also some disappointments, including the less satisfactory achievement of the development goal in the CDM charter, despite the significant delivery of direct public and private investment. There are likely significant direct knowledge building benefits and indirect benefits and co-benefits associated with many of the projects. Unlike the global mitigation effects, these benefits are local. Consequently, the uneven geographical distribution of the projects means that these benefits are concentrated in relatively few countries.

The Kyoto Protocol is an institution designed to address several fundamental aspects of climate change, namely the notion of common but differentiated responsibilities across states, a guiding principle for treaty negotiators; a need to leverage private investment capital, and the observation that many of the cost effective and efficient opportunities for mitigating climate change reside in poorer countries. These starting points have shaped the CDM, and whether they are relevant for future agreements will dictate the future relevancy of the CDM as well.

REFERENCES

Dinar, A, R Hassan, R Mendelsohn, J Benhin *et al.* (2008). *Climate Change and Agriculture in Africa: Impact Assessment and Adaptation Strategies.* London: EarthScan.

Larson, DF, A Dinar and JA Frisbie (2011). The present and future role for agricultural projects under the clean development mechanism. In *Handbook on Climate Change and Agriculture.* A Dinar and R Mendelsohn (eds.). Cheltenham: Edward Elgar Publishers.

Mendelsohn, R and A Dinar (2009). *Climate Change and Agriculture: An Economic Analysis of Global Impacts, Adaptation, and Distributional Effects.* Cheltenham: Edward Elgar.

MIGA (Multilateral Investment Guarantee Agency, World Bank Group) (2010). *World Investment and Political Risk.* Washington, DC: The World Bank.

Risoe (2012). UNEP Risoe Center Website Updated on 1 August 2012. Available at: http://www.cdmpipeline.org/ (accessed on 18 August 2012).

World Bank, Multilateral Investment Guarantee Agency (2011). World Investment and Political Risk 2010. Washington, DC: World Bank (MIGA).

INDEX